SPECIAL ADVERTISING SECTION

Risk and reward.

BP's long-running insurance cover dispute was one of the biggest cases before the Commercial Court in recent years.

Join us and make your own headlines.

Get the full story on our training programme and vacation schemes by requesting a brochure from

Kerry Jarred on 020 7374 8000 or graduate.recruitment@herbertsmith.com or visit our website at

www.herbertsmith.com

Herbert Smith

Herbert Smith in association with Gleiss Lutz and Stibbe

The media's watching Vault! Here's a sampling of our coverage.

"Lawyers looking for the scoop on the nation's biggest law firms now have a place to go."
– **The Wall Street Journal**

"With reviews and profiles of firms that one associate calls 'spot on', [Vault's] guide has become a key reference for those who want to know what it takes to get hired by a law firm and what to expect once they get there."
– **New York Law Journal**

"The best place on the Web to prepare for a job search."
– **Fortune**

"Vault is indispensable for locating insider information."
– **Metropolitan Corporate Counsel**

"[Vault tells] prospective joiners what they really want to know about the culture, the interview process, the salaries and the job prospects."
- **Financial Times**

"Thanks to Vault, the truth about work is just a tap of your keyboard away."
- **The Telegraph**

Elisabeth, associate

RUTHLESS.

IF THE CLIENT NEEDS HER TO BE.

As you'd expect from one of the world's biggest and most successful law firms, delivering the right results for our clients is our first priority. But that doesn't mean it's heads down and everyone for themselves.

We believe in creating a friendly, supportive culture where everyone learns from each other. So, while a ruthless streak occasionally comes in useful, you'll find a sense of humour is every bit as important.

To find out more about our graduate opportunities go to:

www.freshfields.com/graduates

 FRESHFIELDS BRUCKHAUS DERINGER

VAULT GUIDE TO THE TOP 50 LONDON LAW FIRMS

© 2006 Vault Inc.

Thank You.

To our Associates.
For your dedication which continues to be a source of
recognition and respect for our Firm worldwide.

Chicago   London   Los Angeles   Munich   New York   San Francisco   Washington, D.C.

KIRKLAND & ELLIS INTERNATIONAL LLP

www.kirkland.com

VAULT GUIDE TO THE
TOP 50 LONDON LAW FIRMS

BRIAN DALTON
AND THE STAFF OF VAULT

© 2006 Vault Inc.

Copyright © 2006 by Vault Inc. All rights reserved.

All information in this book is subject to change without notice. Vault makes no claims as to the accuracy and reliability of the information contained within and disclaims all warranties. No part of this book may be reproduced or transmitted in any form or by any means, electronic or mechanical, for any purpose, without the express written permission of Vault Inc.

Vault, the Vault logo, and "the most trusted name in career information™" are trademarks of Vault Inc.

For information about permission to reproduce selections from this book, contact Vault Inc., 150 W. 22nd St., 5th Floor, New York, NY 10011, (212) 366-4212.

Library of Congress CIP Data is available.

ISBN-13: 978-1-58131-446-5

ISBN-10: 1-58131-446-9

Printed in the United States of America

ACKNOWLEDGEMENTS

Thank you to all the Vault sales, graphics, editorial and IT staff for writing, selling, designing and programming the guide.

Special thanks to Claire Smith of Claire Legal, Vera Djordjevich, Laurie Pasiuk and Kristina Tsamis.

The book is dedicated to all the solicitors who took time out of their busy schedules to complete our survey.

Associate with us.
Linklaters

Linklaters advises the world's leading companies, financial institutions and governments on their most challenging transactions and assignments. With offices in major business and financial centers, we deliver an outstanding service to our clients anywhere in the world.

Amsterdam	Bratislava	Dubai	Luxembourg	New York	Shanghai
Antwerp	Brussels	Frankfurt	Madrid	Paris	Singapore
Bangkok	Bucharest	Hong Kong	Milan	Prague	Stockholm
Beijing	Budapest	Lisbon	Moscow	Rome	Tokyo
Berlin	Cologne	London	Munich	São Paulo	Warsaw

www.linklaters.com

Table of Contents

INTRODUCTION 1

A Guide to this Guide 1
State of the Law 3
The Vault Prestige Rankings 11
The Vault Quality of Life Rankings 19

LAW FIRM PROFILES 27

Addleshaw Goddard LLP 28
Allen & Overy LLP 32
Ashurst 40
Baker & McKenzie 48
Barlow Lyde & Gilbert 55
Beachcroft LLP 63
Berwin Leighton Paisner LLP 67
Bird & Bird 71
Cadwalader, Wickersham & Taft LLP 75
Charles Russell LLP 80
Cleary Gottlieb Steen & Hamilton LLP 84
Clifford Chance LLP 91
Clyde & Co 98
CMS Cameron McKenna LLP 102
Covington & Burling LLP 106
Davis Polk & Wardwell 113
Debevoise & Plimpton LLP 119
Dechert LLP 126
Denton Wilde Sapte 132
Dewey Ballantine LLP 136
DLA Piper Rudnick Gray Cary 144

LATHAM & WATKINS

One Firm ... A World of Opportunities

From the global capabilities of our 22 offices worldwide to the abundant and challenging opportunities that our new associates enjoy, Latham & Watkins is the perfect place for your career to soar. We are proud of our spirit of teamwork, community involvement, strong associate training and career development programme and our commitment to deliver the highest standards of client service.

Together with our dedication to diversity and equal opportunity, you'll find that at Latham & Watkins the sky really is the limit for your career. Find out more on campus or visit us online at www.lw.com.

❝ Among the best American law firms working in the Old Smoke, there is no denying that Latham & Watkins has become one of the City's major players."
 – *Vault Guide to Top London Law Firms 2007*

BEST IN SOLICITOR / PARTNER RELATIONS
Ranked #1 out of more than 75 law firms

BEST IN SOLICITOR SATISFACTION
Ranked #1 out of more than 75 law firms

BEST IN COMPENSATION
Ranked #1 out of more than 75 law firms

BEST IN INFORMAL TRAINING
Ranked #3 out of more than 75 law firms

BEST IN PRO BONO
Ranked #5 out of more than 75 law firms

BEST IN DIVERSITY FOR WOMEN
Ranked #4 out of more than 75 law firms

Brussels	London	New Jersey	Paris	Silicon Valley
Chicago	Los Angeles	New York	San Diego	Singapore
Frankfurt	Milan	Northern Virginia	San Francisco	Tokyo
Hamburg	Moscow	Orange County	Shanghai	Washington, D.C.
Hong Kong	Munich			

Latham & Watkins operates as a limited liability partnership worldwide with an affiliate in the United Kingdom and Italy, where the practice is conducted through an affiliated multinational partnership.

Eversheds LLP	152
Farrer & Co	157
Field Fisher Waterhouse LLP	161
Freshfields Bruckhaus Deringer	165
Fried, Frank, Harris, Shriver & Jacobson LLP	172
Gibson, Dunn & Crutcher LLP	176
Hammonds	182
Herbert Smith LLP	186
Holman Fenwick & Willan	191
Ince & Co	195
Irwin Mitchell	200
Jones Day	207
Kilpatrick Stockton LLP	214
Kirkland & Ellis LLP	218
Kirkpatrick & Lockhart Nicholson Graham LLP	226
Latham & Watkins LLP	234
Lawrence Graham LLP	242
LeBoeuf, Lamb, Greene & MacRae LLP	248
Linklaters	255
Lovells	264
Macfarlanes	272
Mayer, Brown, Rowe & Maw LLP	276
McDermott Will & Emery LLP	281
McGrigors	285
Milbank, Tweed, Hadley & McCloy LLP	291
Nabarro Nathanson	295
Norton Rose	299
Olswang	304
Orrick, Herrington & Sutcliffe LLP	309
Osborne Clarke	313
Penningtons Solicitors LLP	317
Pinsent Masons	322

We've built our firm on the sharing of knowledge and experience in an informal and friendly atmosphere. Whatever legal problems you come across – in your training or subsequently – you'll find someone who's already an expert, and is ready and willing to share the relevant knowledge with you.

Unrestrictive practice.

SLAUGHTER AND MAY

LEARN MORE about graduate traineeships and vacation placements at one of the world's most respected law firms by contacting:

Charlotte Houghton, Slaughter and May, One Bunhill Row, London EC1Y 8YY. Telephone 020 7600 1200.

www.slaughterandmay.com

Reed Smith LLP 328

Reynolds Porter Chamberlain LLP 335

Richards Butler LLP 339

Shearman & Sterling LLP 343

Sidley Austin LLP 348

Simmons & Simmons 352

Simpson Thacher & Bartlett LLP 356

SJ Berwin LLP 363

Skadden, Arps, Slate, Meagher & Flom LLP and Affiliates 367

Slaughter and May 374

Speechly Bircham 381

Stephenson Harwood 385

Sullivan & Cromwell LLP 390

Taylor Wessing 397

Travers Smith 401

Trowers & Hamlins 409

Watson, Farley & Williams LLP 413

Weil, Gotshal & Manges LLP 417

White & Case LLP 424

Wilmer Cutler Pickering Hale and Dorr LLP 433

Withers LLP 437

Wragge & Co LLP 445

ABOUT THE AUTHOR   450

Teach First's graduate programme is a unique opportunity to be different and to make a difference. It's an innovative combination of teaching with management skills training and leadership development, plus unparalleled internship, networking and coaching opportunities.

Whatever you aim to do with your career, Teach First.

I taught first

www.teachfirst.org.uk

Teach First
LEARNING TO LEAD

Introduction

A Guide to this Guide

If you're wondering how our entries are organized, read on. Here's a handy guide to the information you'll find packed into each entry of this book.

The Buzz

When it comes to other law firms, our respondents certainly like to dish. We asked them to tell us their opinions and observations about firms other than their own. We've collected a sampling of these comments in "The Buzz."

When selecting The Buzz, we included quotes representative of the common outsider's perceptions of the firms, even if (in our opinion) the quotes did not accurately describe the firm. In the interest of fairness, we chose four Buzz comments for each firm—two in which the solicitor had good things to say about the firm and two that were more negative. Please keep in mind when reading The Buzz that it's often more fun for outsiders to trash than praise a competing law firm. Nonetheless, we have found The Buzz to be another valuable means of gauging a firm's reputation.

Firm facts

Other Locations: A listing of the firm's offices besides London, with the headquarters bolded. You may see firms with no bolded location. This means that these are self-proclaimed decentralized firms without an official headquarters.

Practice Areas : Practice areas that employ a significant portion of the firm's lawyers as reported by the firms.

Base Salary: The firm's base salary in London. Pay is for 2006 except where noted.

Notable Perks: A listing of perks and benefits outside the norm.

Pluses and Minuses: Good points and bad points about working at the firm, as gleaned from solicitor surveys. Pluses and minuses are the perceptions of insiders and are not based on statistics.

Graduate Recruitment Contact: The person that the firm identifies as the primary contact to receive resumes or to answer questions about the recruitment process.

More than one contact is sometimes given. In some instances, we refer the reader to the firm web site.

The Stats

No. of lawyers: The total number of lawyers at the firm in all offices as of Spring 2006. Sometimes the number is an estimate.

No. of lawyers in London: The total number of lawyers at the firm's London office(s) as of Spring 2006. Sometimes the number is an estimate.

No. of offices: The firm's total number of offices worldwide.

Trainee intake: The number of law students given full-time training contracts by the firm.

Percentage of trainees retained: The percentage of trainees offered permanent positions with the firms at the conclusion of the training contract.

Chairman, Managing Partner, Senior Partner, etc.: The name and title of the leader of the firm. Sometimes more than one name is provided.

Ranking Recap

A summary of all categories in which the firm ranked particularly well, including departmental, quality of life and diversity rankings.

The Profiles

The law firm profiles are divided into three sections: The Scoop, Getting Hired and Our Survey Says.

The Scoop: The firm's history, clients, recent deals, recent firm developments and other points of interest.

Getting Hired: The qualifications the firm looks for in trainee solicitors, tips on getting hired and other notable aspects of the hiring process.

Our Survey Says: Actual quotes from surveys of current solicitors of the firm on various topics related to law firm life, including the firm's assignment system, feedback, partnership prospects, levels of responsibility, training program, culture, hours, pay, and much more. Some profiles also contain brief "firm responses" to solicitor criticism or clarification of points of confusion expressed in the profile. Vault editors sometimes modified associate quotes to correct grammar or spelling.

State of the Law

All change in London

The City of London's legal market is arguably the most competitive in the world. Ten years ago, there were only a handful of top law firms populating the City. However, with London's ever-increasing significance as a global crossroads, things have changed quite a bit over the past decade.

The key moment came in the mid-1990s, when British law was modified to allow American lawyers to go into partnership with English lawyers. Since then, American firms have been flooding in and show no signs of slowing down. While a few English law firms might harbour ambitions to open offices in New York, their expansionist proclivities pale in comparison to the Americans', as the number of American firms doing business in London now tops 100. The top 50 of these, according to London law magazine *Legal Business*, now employ more than 3,000 lawyers in the capital alone—2,200 of them English qualified. It's no secret that the aggressive American firms have a comparative advantage: a lot of money to throw around.

The Americans can afford to pay more because they are, by and large, more profitable businesses. A part of the reason for American firms' relative success is that they haven't made the extensive overseas investment that many top English law firms have. A larger reason lies in the U.S. litigation culture and its mind-boggling revenues. Of course U.K. firms do litigation, but it's a smaller part of their business, typically constituting 10-20 per cent within the Magic Circle. This would be highly unusual for a major American firm, as it is standard for half of a U.S. firm's lawyers to work solely on the contentious side of the business. Of added significance is that litigation is not only profitable, but counter-cyclical; when capital markets and M&A were quiet at the start of this century, American law firms saw no dip in revenue while U.K. firms suffered. Even when businesses aren't merging, absorbing and raiding one another, companies love to sue—which means a steady flow of cash to the firms representing them.

Last year was a banner one for U.S. firms doing business in London. According to *The Lawyer*, virtually every American law firm saw solid to stellar performance in

2005. Debevoise & Plimpton, for example, posted an unprecedented 67.5 per cent increase in revenue coming out of the London office (accounting for 10 per cent of Debevoise's total revenue in 2005). LeBoeuf Lamb Greene & MacRae reported similarly impressive earnings, marking 2005 with a 43 per cent rise in U.K. revenue. Meanwhile, Shearman & Sterling's U.K. partners took home, on average, £950,000—not a great leap over 2004's figures, as *The Lawyer* reports, but still 20 per cent higher than the global average for profits per equity partner (PEP). Dechert partners also had some cause for celebration, as 2005 saw the firm's U.K. revenue climb by 15 per cent and U.K. PEP leap nearly 30 per cent to £846,500. White-shoe Wall Street firm Simpson Thacher boasted a 30 per cent rise in U.K. revenue. Impressive numbers like that (with equally impressive profits per equity partner) will surely demand the attention of both English lawyers and their employers—English firms.

When it comes to the war for talent in the London market, U.S. firms take a different approach to partner compensation, which has attracted some of the England's top advocates. As a rule, Americans pay partners according to how much work they generate (aka the "eat what you kill" rule). The largest U.K. firms, on the other hand, pay partners according to seniority. This means that the highest-billing at English firms (rarely the most senior, rarer yet the highest-paid) would be better off parlaying their professional zealotry into higher earnings at a U.S. firm.

There are other factors luring English attorneys to American firms, of course. As *The Lawyer* reported in March 2006, the recent defection of two high-level Linklaters private equity partners to Chicago-based Kirkland & Ellis seemed linked to tension between Linklaters' private equity team and its banking group. Kirkland, operating through a headhunter (who reportedly blabbed about the move months in advance), capitalized on Linklaters' internal strife, taking Graham White and Raymond McKeeve—along with a portable book of clients including CVC and TDR Capital. The move demonstrates that American firms—which, being comparatively new to the market, are freer to try new things—may be more willing to accommodate disgruntled attorneys' professional whims than traditional U.K. firms.

All of this means that for a talented lawyer entering London's legal market, U.S. firms offer a viable—and rather lucrative—alternative as a place to begin a career. However, you would be gravely mistaken to think you can make a killing working at an American firm without putting in American hours. As a result of the whizbang billable ethos, all of the law firms in London (American and English alike) now expect their associates to earn their keep, and then some.

A little M&A

The second half of 2005 and early 2006 have seen the first signs of serious mergers and acquisition (M&A) activity reappearing in Europe since the downturn that began in 2001. When M&A and capital markets went quiet following the dotcom crash and the 11 September attacks, English law firms, like so many businesses around the world, found things difficult. After a decade of unprecedented expansion both in their London offices and their international networks, firms suddenly found that they had a lot of lawyers with very little to do. That's an expensive overhead, and through a combination of redundancies and aggressive performance reviews, the numbers of fee-earners were driven down to more manageable levels.

The six so-called Magic Circle law firms in London are, in order of turnover, Clifford Chance, Linklaters, Freshfields Bruckhaus Deringer, Allen & Overy, Slaughter and May, and Herbert Smith. These are the firms widely recognised as dominating the corporate work and advising on the highest value litigation and capital markets transactions. All six have had to focus on raising their profitability levels in the wake of the economic downturn, not least to keep their partners happy in the face of tempting offers from the Yanks. The result has been a paradigm shift: like their U.S. counterparts, there is an increasing focus on the dreaded billable hour. Lawyers are expected not only to log the hours, but to be on call for clients day and night. Annual targets of 2,000 billable hours are not unusual as the days of long lunches and carrying less productive colleagues have become a thing of the past.

Return of the good old days

Law firms in London, wherever headquartered, are cautiously optimistic that the market is only going to improve. M&A seems to be coming back, with big deals like Spanish telecoms group Telefónica bidding a grand £17.7 billion for English mobile company O2. The merger, if and when executed, would break records as the largest takeover of a U.K. company since 2000. There are also rumours of a multibillion quid bid from another Spanish company for U.K. airports operator BAA. Meanwhile, U.K. gas group BOC has been the subject of a $14.9 billion bid from Germany's Linde. More recently, ports and ferries group P&O had been at the heart of a bid battle between rivals in Dubai and Singapore. In 2005, however, DP World (the same Dubai Ports involved in the recent American uproar over ports control), agreed to a £3.92 billion takeover of P&O.

The other big corporate work for law firms is in capital markets, which has been a dismal state of affairs since 2000. With the world's two largest capital markets in

New York and London, it's readily apparent why law firms are so keen to establish themselves in both markets. But a confluence of ill-fated events—the aforementioned dotcom bust and terrorist attacks, and widespread corporate chicanery à la Enron caused many investors' cash and confidence levels to drop. Since Enron's collapse, the American Securities and Exchange Commission introduced tough compliance and reporting rules for public companies in an attempt to avoid similar blow-ups from happening again. The measures have been a mixed blessing: increased corporate confidence but more red tape. The so-called Sarbanes-Oxley Act in particular makes it a lot more expensive to sell shares in the U.S., and has thus benefited London by ushering businesses to a more forgiving market. As testament to that fact, the number of flotations in London has just returned to something approaching 2000 levels, with 421 IPOs (initial public offerings) in 2005, compared to 486 in 2000. There were only 97 in the year 2002, but with many Russian, Israeli and Eastern European companies now choosing to list in London rather than New York, the U.K. exchange is again as busy as ever.

Also active on the corporate side is private equity work, with a huge number of private equity houses now investing in ever-larger European businesses. Private equity firms take money from institutional investors and then buy established companies with a view to improving their performance. They then either sell them or take them public in hopes of delivering huge returns to the institutional investors. Since it began as a niche practice during the 1980s, this business has developed enormously, with a number of large American private equity firms opening European operations and buying businesses here. Late 2005 saw the record-breaking $12 billion bid for Danish telecoms group TDC, the largest acquisition by these buy-out groups ever seen on this side of the Atlantic.

Practice makes perfect

For all the sizeable English law firms, the return of corporate work is the most important development for their practices since 2000, as it is the mainstay of their revenue and profit generation. Other departments, like real estate, banking and litigation, are less cyclical and often less remunerative than the big M&A and capital markets work. That said, business is now booming across the board for most firms. The property and projects teams are kept busy through a combination of building work for the Olympics (coming to London in 2012—sorry Paris), and the arrival of a new U.K. law that introduces property investment vehicles to England for the first time. These so-called Real Estate Investment Trusts, or REITS, are immensely popular in the U.S. and continental Europe.

The litigation market is also busy, with the U.K. emerging as a major centre for international arbitrations, and the increasing prospect of U.S.-style class actions coming to Europe. Cases like the Railtrack litigation, where a group of shareholders came together to sue the U.K. government over its handling of the company's demise, are seen as the forerunners of group actions this side of the pond.

But while the Magic Circle firms may be returning to form, they now view their competition in Europe as the U.S. firms that have built significant presences here—firms like Latham & Watkins, White & Case, Shearman & Sterling and Skadden. Historically, a second tier of major U.K. firms would have challenged the Magic Circle for big deals, but those practices—Norton Rose, Lovells, Simmons & Simmons, Denton Wilde Sapte and Ashurst—are finding it ever harder to compete.

It is that second tier of U.K. law firms that has been hardest hit by the arrival of American law firms. They have lost some of their best-performing partners and, in many cases, have been unable to compete like their Magic Circle colleagues. This group of firms is also squeezed from below by the national U.K. law firms, which can compete by offering more competitive billing rates to clients, and are frequently more entrepreneurial and aggressive in addition to being tightly managed. The likes of DLA—which merged in 2005 to form DLA Piper Rudnick Gray Cary, the third largest law firm in the world—Eversheds, Addleshaw Goddard and Pinsent Masons, now give the London firms a run for their money.

National goes international

DLA is an interesting case in point. The firm began in Sheffield, and as recently as five years ago was regarded as a regional law firm with ambitions to make its mark on London. That is precisely what DLA achieved—the firm's business model is based on hiring a few high quality partners, paying them a lot of money, and getting the work done by more junior people often operating out of less costly regional business centres.

Such leveraging, as it is called, may concentrate the power in the hands of the few, but it satisfies the clients, who get a cheaper and more commercial service. DLA's combination with two U.S. law firms in 2005 takes the model one step further. While it may not compete with firms like Clifford Chance and Skadden Arps for M&A work, it will pick up global mandates from clients looking to use one firm worldwide for all sectors.

But size isn't everything, and the firms at the polar opposite from DLA have done well by staying small and focusing on filling a niche. This group in London includes

Macfarlanes, SJ Berwin and Travers Smith, three corporate firms that continue to attract some of the biggest domestic work around, and Berwin Leighton Paisner, which is arguably the top law firm in the U.K. for real estate work and has now added a strong corporate and finance business on the back of that brand.

These firms do not have the costly international networks of their larger rivals, but instead work in collaboration with independent firms in other jurisdictions when they must. This strategy, dubbed a "best friends" model and demonstrated on a larger scale by the strategy of Slaughter and May (the only Magic Circle law firm without an overseas network), is attractive to certain clients. Macfarlanes, for example, last year advised its longstanding French client Pernod Ricard on a £7.6 billion takeover of U.K. rival Allied Domecq.

Merger market

For U.K. firms looking to expand across the Atlantic, a merger maybe the smartest move. Freshfields Bruckhaus Deringer announced at the start of 2006 that it is hoping to merge with an American law firm in the next five years. New York is the only significant financial market where the firm has yet to establish a sizeable presence, and the firm says that the only way to do so is to combine with a U.S. law firm. Freshfields, along with Clifford Chance, Linklaters and Allen & Overy, is one of a so-called Global Quartet of U.K. law firms. Clifford Chance merged in 2000 with New York firm Rogers & Wells—a merger that was beset by difficulties and is only now settling down after a series of departures. Allen & Overy and Linklaters have both decided to build their New York offices by hiring lawyers from U.S. firms, despite the fact that they can rarely offer them more money than they are earning elsewhere—a hard sell at best.

To date, the transatlantic mergers of law firms have usually involved at least one second-tier law firm, with the deal by DLA being the first true merger of equals, albeit outside the Magic Circle and Wall Street domain. Chicago firm Mayer Brown & Platt took over City corporate boutique Rowe & Maw in 2002, and in 2003 Cleveland's Jones Day took over another small City firm, Gouldens.

While there is still no shortage of American law firms looking to break into the European market by acquiring an existing, established practice, most firms prefer to take over smaller ones and impose their own corporate culture. The top U.S. law firms are both much more profitable, and smaller, than the top English firms. Skadden Arps is amongst the largest, with 1,600 lawyers, compared to 3,300 lawyers at the U.K.'s largest firm Clifford Chance. The average Skadden partner earns $1.7 million, while at Clifford Chance the average is $1.2 million.

If Freshfields succeeds in convincing a top-tier New York firm that it wants to be taken over by a larger, less profitable, European suitor, it will undoubtedly lead to a raft of similar deals, as clients reconsider their options.

Consolidation, transformation

For now, the most likely law firm mergers are likely to be domestic or pan-European. These are easier to achieve, and there are many firms outside the Magic Circle who feel they simply need more resources to compete with their larger rivals.

If that isn't enough to make the London legal market a darn interesting place to be for the next few years, consider that the government is planning some pretty serious reforms of the rules governing law firms. In 2005, Parliament asked Sir David Clementi, a former chairman of the Prudential, to review the market for legal services and he made some serious recommendations which look set to totally transform the way law is practiced in the U.K.

Chief amongst Clementi's suggestions: a change to the current law which allows only lawyers to be partners and owners of law firms. That means that big businesses, including retailers like Tesco, might buy a law firm so that they could offer their customers legal services, in addition to the host of insurance and financial services products they currently sell. It also means accounting firms might team up with legal firms to offer a one-stop shop advisory service to clients, or law firms could make their finance directors partners. The permutations are limitless. Even more fundamental, is the prospect that law firms might one day float on the Stock Exchange, and thus raise cash from external shareholders to make investments. The government is still deciding precisely what form the new rules will take, but there's no doubt that big changes are on the way.

In demand

The London legal market is buzzing again, and young lawyers are once more in high demand. In 2000, a global salary war originated in Silicon Valley, when law firms hiked wages to prevent associates from fleeing to dotcoms offering big perks and even bigger bonuses. The fever spread to New York, where attorneys were leaving for the investment banks, and then to London.

When the market went quiet, associates were worried about losing their jobs, rather than inadequate salaries. Now that firms are busy, they are once again short of staff. The battle to hire the best lawyers, and the brightest graduates entering the profession, has arguably never been tougher, as this time around there are not just U.K. law firms but sizeable U.K. offices of American law firms looking to hire the best people.

Salaries are rising again, but wage is not the only factor driving job seekers' decisions. Firms now look to attract people by showing that they take things like diversity initiatives, corporate social responsibility, and flexible working policies, seriously—things that were traditionally neglected at the expense of profit drives.

The pressure to keep profits up means the chances of making partnership in any law firm are now scarcer than ever. Law firms operate an up-or-out policy—you join a track to the partnership, and each year you are appraised to see whether you are still in line for the prize. Fewer and fewer make it now, but for those who do, the lucre is filthy.

The American law firms in London offer a whole new set of options for young lawyers. They pay more, no doubt, and whilst they still have a reputation for longer hours, it's now fair to say that all serious law firms in London bow down to the almighty billable hour. Smaller offices—most U.S. firms still have less than 100 lawyers in the U.K.—mean more responsibility earlier on, but they can also mean a shortage of resources and partner time for tutoring. The training schemes may be less developed, but the work is just as good. English law firms are another matter entirely, and have a huge battle on their hands: to attract the best lawyers, to retain their market share in their home market, and to win on the incredibly competitive global legal stage.

THE VAULT
PRESTIGE
RANKINGS

Ranking Methodology

For the 2006 Vault Solicitor survey, we selected a list of top London law firms to include. These firms were selected because of their prominence in the legal industry and their interest to law students. This year, nearly 1,000 solicitors responded to our survey.

The Vault survey was distributed through the firms on Vault's list. In some cases, Vault contacted practicing solicitors directly. Survey respondents were asked to do several things. They were asked to rate each law firm on the survey on a scale of 1 to 10 based on prestige, with 10 being the most prestigious. Solicitors were unable to rate their own firm. They were asked only to rate firms with which they were familiar.

Vault collected the survey results and averaged the score for each firm. The firms were then ranked, with the highest score being No. 1.

We also asked survey respondents to give their perceptions of law firms other than their own. A selection of those comments is featured on each firm profile as The Buzz.

Remember that Vault's Top 50 London Law Firms are chosen by practicing solicitors at top firms. Vault does not choose or influence the rankings. The rankings measure perceived prestige and not revenues, size or lifestyle.

The Vault 50 • 2007

[The 50 most prestigious London law firms]

RANK	FIRM	SCORE
1	Slaughter and May	8.447
2	Freshfields Bruckhaus Deringer	8.220
3	Allen & Overy LLP	7.994
4	Linklaters	7.982
5	Clifford Chance LLP	7.632
6	Skadden Arps Slate Meagher & Flom LLP and Affiliates	7.615
7	Herbert Smith LLP	7.166
8	Sullivan & Cromwell LLP	6.969
9	Macfarlanes	6.904
10	Shearman & Sterling LLP	6.883
11	Lovells	6.824
12	Ashurst	6.749
13	White & Case LLP	6.648
14	Cleary Gottlieb Steen & Hamilton LLP	6.628
15	Latham & Watkins LLP	6.419
16	Weil, Gotshal & Manges LLP	6.408
17	Simpson Thacher & Bartlett LLP	6.365
18	Davis Polk & Wardell	6.148
19	Baker & McKenzie	6.117
20	Sidley Austin LLP	6.103
21	Mayer, Brown, Rowe & Maw LLP	6.000
22	Debevoise & Plimpton LLP	5.933
23	Simmons & Simmons	5.930
24	Norton Rose	5.903
25	SJ Berwin LLP	5.779

The Vault Prestige Rankings

RANK	FIRM	SCORE
26	Olswang	5.772
27	Travers Smith	5.738
28	CMS Cameron McKenna LLP	5.737
29	Jones Day	5.698
30	Milbank, Tweed, Hadley & McCloy	5.686
31	DLA Piper Rudnick Gray Cary	5.672
32	Cadwalader, Wickersham & Taft LLP	5.569
33	McDermott Will & Emery LLP	5.504
34	Fried, Frank, Harris, Shriver & Jacobson LLP	5.371
35	Berwin Leighton Paisner LLP	5.286
36	Bird & Bird	5.219
37	Kirkland & Ellis LLP	5.177
38	Gibson, Dunn & Crutcher LLP	5.083
39	Dewey Ballantine LLP	5.076
40	Clyde & Co	5.056
41	Nabarro Nathanson	5.046
42	Denton Wilde Sapte	5.036
43	Taylor Wessing	5.025
44	Eversheds LLP	5.010
45	Wragge & Co LLP	4.984
46	Richards Butler LLP	4.932
47	Wilmer Cutler Pickering Hale & Dorr	4.874
48	Dechert LLP	4.791
49	Farrer & Co	4.761
50	Addleshaw Goddard LLP	4.667

Practice Area Ranking Methodology

Vault also asked solicitors to rank the best firms in several practice areas. These areas are corporate, tax, property, intellectual property, mergers and acquisitions, litigation and capital markets. Solicitors were allowed to vote for up to three firms as the best in each area.

The following charts indicate the rankings in each practice area, along with the total percentage of votes cast in favour of each firm. (As long as at least one solicitor voted for more than one firm, no firm could get 100 per cent of the votes; if every solicitor had voted for the same three firms, for example, the maximum score would be 33.3 per cent.)

Corporate

RANK	FIRM	% VOTE
1	Slaughter and May	24.58
2	Freshfields Bruckhaus Deringer	23.96
3	Linklaters	18.28
4	Clifford Chance LLP	8.91
5	Allen & Overy LLP	5.99
6	Ashurst	3.38
7	Skadden Arps Slate Meagher & Flom LLP & Affiliates	2.30
8	Macfarlanes	2.00
9	Herbert Smith LLP	1.23
10 (tie)	Shearman & Sterling LLP	0.92
10 (tie)	Travers Smith	0.92

Litigation

RANK	FIRM	% VOTE
1	Herbert Smith LLP	28.57
2	Freshfields Bruckhaus Deringer	12.62
3	Lovells	8.97
4	Clifford Chance LLP	8.64
5	Allen & Overy LLP	4.65
6 (tie)	Linklaters	3.99
6 (tie)	Clyde & Co	3.99
8	Barlow Lyde & Gilbert	3.32
9	Reynolds Porter Chamberlain LLP	2.66
10	Slaughter and May	2.33

Property

RANK	FIRM	% VOTE
1	Berwin Leighton Paisner LLP	27.85
2	Nabarro Nathanson	11.39
3	Clifford Chance LLP	7.59
4 (tie)	Lovells	6.33
4 (tie)	Linklaters	6.33

Tax

RANK	FIRM	% VOTE
1	Freshfields Bruckhaus Deringer	25.00
2	Slaughter and May	21.67
3	Linklaters	13.33
4	Macfarlanes	8.33
5	Ashurst	6.67

Intellectual Property

RANK	FIRM	SCORE
1	Bird & Bird	31.25
2	Taylor Wessing	18.75
3	Olswang	12.50
4 (tie)	Field Fisher Waterhouse LLP	6.25
4 (tie)	Simmons & Simmons	6.25
4 (tie)	Wragge & Co.	6.25

Capital Markets

RANK	FIRM	% VOTE
1	Clifford Chance LLP	24.04
2	Allen & Overy LLP	22.45
3	Linklaters	19.95
4	Freshfields Bruckhaus Deringer	12.02
5 (tie)	Sidley Austin LLP	2.27
5 (tie)	Slaughter and May	2.27

Mergers & Acquisitions

RANK	FIRM	% VOTE
1	Slaughter and May	24.73
2	Freshfields Bruckhaus Deringer	23.08
3	Linklaters	19.78
4	Clifford Chance LLP	9.62
5	Allen & Overy LLP	4.67

THE VAULT
QUALITY OF LIFE RANKINGS

Quality of Life Ranking Methodology

In addition to ranking other firms in terms of prestige, survey respondents were asked to rate their own firms in a variety of categories. On a scale of 1 to 10, with 10 being the highest and 1 the lowest, respondents evaluated their firms in the following "quality of life" areas:

- Overall satisfaction
- Compensation
- Hours
- Formal training
- Informal training/mentoring
- Partner/solicitor relations
- Firm culture
- Offices
- Pro bono
- Diversity with respect to women
- Diversity with respect to minorities
- Diversity with respect to gays and lesbians

Ranking the firms

A firm's score in each category is simply the average of these rankings. In compiling our quality of life rankings, we only ranked firms from whose solicitors we received sufficient responses for that particular question.

Satisfaction (Average score: 7.49)

On a scale of 1 to 10, where 1 means unsatisfactory and 10 means entirely fulfilling, overall, you find working at your firm:

RANK	FIRM	SCORE
1	Latham & Watkins LLP	8.15
2	LeBoeuf, Lamb, Greene & McRae LLP	8.06
3	Clifford Chance LLP	8.04
4	Linklaters	7.97
5	Jones Day	7.88
6	Travers Smith	7.81
7	Ashurst	7.80
8 (tie)	Slaughter and May	7.79
8 (tie)	Withers LLP	7.79
10 (tie)	Baker & McKenzie	7.62
10 (tie)	Barlow Lyde & Gilbert	7.62

Solicitor/Partner Relations (Average score: 7.67)

On a scale of 1 to 10, where 1 means poorly and 10 means with great respect, partners usually treat solicitors at your firm:

RANK	FIRM	SCORE
1	Latham & Watkins LLP	8.94
2	Baker & McKenzie	8.62
3	Jones Day	8.50
4	Linklaters	8.23
5	Clifford Chance LLP	8.14
6	Ashurst	8.10
7	Travers Smith	8.00
8	Withers LLP	7.90
9 (tie)	Covington & Burling LLP	7.87
9 (tie)	Barlow Lyde & Gilbert	7.87

Compensation (Average score: 6.72)

On a scale of 1 to 10, where 1 means too low and 10 means superior, you feel your compensation is:

RANK	FIRM	SCORE
1	Latham & Watkins LLP	9.10
2	LeBoeuf, Lamb, Greene & McRae LLP	8.71
3	Withers LLP	7.76
4	White & Case LLP	7.62
5	Covington & Burling LLP	7.50
6	Skadden Arps Slate Meagher & Flom LLP and Affiliates	7.33
7	Cadwalader, Wickersham & Taft LLP	7.22
8	Travers Smith	7.12
9	Allen & Overy	6.76
10	Baker & McKenzie	6.75

Hours (Average score: 6.20)

On a scale of 1 to 10, where 1 means not at all satisfied and 10 means very satisfied, please rank your satisfaction with the number of hours you spend in the office:

RANK	FIRM	SCORE
1	Reed Smith LLP	7.81
2 (tie)	Jones Day	7.50
2 (tie)	Withers LLP	7.50
4	Barlow Lyde & Gilbert	7.16
5	Baker & McKenzie	7.12
6	LeBoeuf, Lamb, Greene & McRae LLP	7.00
7	Travers Smith	6.85
8	Slaughter and May	6.41
9	Cadwalader, Wickersham & Taft LLP	6.20
10	Latham & Watkins LLP	6.10

Formal Training (Average score: 7.66)

On a scale of 1 to 10, where 1 means minimal and 10 means extensive, the level and utility of your firm's formal training program is:

RANK	FIRM	SCORE
1	Slaughter and May	8.90
2	Allen & Overy LLP	8.74
3	Clifford Chance LLP	8.71
4	Linklaters	8.65
5	Ashurst	8.30
6	Withers LLP	8.23
7	Lovells	8.00
8	Freshfields Bruckhaus Deringer	7.95
9	Barlow Lyde & Gilbert	7.86
10	Baker & McKenzie	7.75

Informal Training and Mentoring (Average score: 6.78)

On a scale of 1 to 10, where 1 means minimal and 10 means extensive, the level and utility of informal training and mentoring you are receiving from partners is:

RANK	FIRM	SCORE
1	Travers Smith	7.84
2	Ashurst	7.70
3	Latham & Watkins LLP	7.55
4	Withers LLP	7.47
5	Linklaters	7.42
6 (tie)	Clifford Chance LLP	7.28
6 (tie)	Jones Day	7.28
8	Baker & McKenzie	7.00
9	Allen & Overy LLP	6.88
10	Lovells	6.80

Diversity With Respect to Women (Average score: 7.27)

On a scale of 1 to 10, where 1 means needs a lot of improvement and 10 means very welcoming, how receptive and effective is your firm in terms of diversity for women in hiring, promotion, and mentoring?

RANK	FIRM	SCORE
1	Covington & Burling LLP	9.33
2	Withers LLP	9.09
3	Baker & McKenzie	8.50
4	Latham & Watkins LLP	8.18
5	Clifford Chance LLP	7.88
6	Linklaters	7.68
7	Reed Smith LLP	7.55
8	Allen & Overy LLP	7.27
9	DLA Piper Rudnick Gray Cary	7.23
10	Freshfields Bruckhaus Deringer	7.15

Diversity With Respect to Minorities
(Average score: 7.26)

On a scale of 1 to 10, where 1 means needs a lot of improvement and 10 means very welcoming, how receptive and effective is your firm in terms of diversity for minorities in hiring, promotion, and mentoring?

RANK	FIRM	SCORE
1	Lawrence Graham LLP	9.16
2	LeBoeuf, Lamb, Greene & McRae LLP	9.12
3	Covington & Burling LLP	8.83
4	Clifford Chance LLP	8.61
5	Cadwalader, Wickersham & Taft LLP	8.12
6	Latham & Watkins LLP	8.00
7	Reed Smith LLP	7.66
8	Allen & Overy LLP	7.56
9	Linklaters	7.44
10	DLA Piper Rudnick Gray Cary	7.30

Diversity With Respect to Gays and Lesbians
(Average score: 7.56)

On a scale of 1 to 10, where 1 means needs a lot of improvement and 10 means very welcoming, how receptive and effective is your firm in terms of diversity for gays and lesbians in hiring, promotion, and mentoring?

RANK	FIRM	SCORE
1	Withers LLP	9.42
2	Latham & Watkins LLP	9.00
3	Baker & McKenzie	8.66
4	Cadwalader, Wickersham & Taft LLP	8.14
5	Clifford Chance LLP	8.09
6	Linklaters	7.94
7	Reed Smith LLP	7.80
8	Allen & Overy LLP	7.52
9	DLA Piper Rudnick Gray Cary	7.33
10	Slaughter and May	7.28

Pro Bono (Average score: 7.18)

On a scale of 1 to 10, where 1 means not at all committed and 10 means strongly committed, how committed is your firm to pro bono work?

RANK	FIRM	SCORE
1	Covington & Burling LLP	9.12
2	Clifford Chance LLP	8.75
3	DLA Piper Rudnick Gray Cary	8.66
4	Cadwalader, Wickersham & Taft LLP	8.44
5	Latham & Watkins LLP	8.33
6	Allen & Overy LLP	8.18
7	Linklaters	8.00
8	Lovells	7.59
9	Freshfields Bruckhaus Deringer	7.45
10	Reed Smith LLP	7.26

Selectivity (Average score: 7.88)

On a scale of 1 to 10, where 1 means easy and 10 means extremely competitive, getting hired at your firm is:

RANK	FIRM	SCORE
1	Linklaters	8.88
2	Ashurst	8.62
3	Baker & McKenzie	8.57
4	Covington & Burling LLP	8.50
5	Slaughter and May	8.42
6	Latham & Watkins LLP	8.27
7	Travers Smith	8.26
8	Freshfields Bruckhaus Deringer	8.20
9	Cleary Gottlieb Steen & Hamilton LLP	8.16
10	Allen & Overy LLP	8.07

Office Space (Average score: 7.67)

On a scale of 1 to 10, where 1 means uncomfortable and 10 means posh and luxurious, in terms of space, comfort and decor, the offices you work in are:

RANK	FIRM	SCORE
1	Clifford Chance LLP	9.38
2	Jones Day	9.37
3	Skadden Arps Slate Meagher & Flom LLP and Affiliates	8.72
4	Covington & Burling LLP	8.50
5	Slaughter and May	8.38
6	White & Case LLP	8.37
7	Withers LLP	8.19
8	Linklaters	8.02
9	Lovells	7.87
10	Latham & Watkins LLP	7.79

LAW FIRM
PROFILES

Addleshaw Goddard LLP

150 Aldersgate Street
London EC1A 4EJ
Phone: +44 (0)20 7606 8855
www.addleshawgoddard.com

OTHER LOCATIONS

London (2 additional)
Leeds
Manchester

THE STATS

No. of lawyers: 575
No. of offices: 5
Senior partner: Paul Lee

BASE SALARY

Trainee: £29,000 (London)
Newly Qualified: £50,000 (London)

GRADUATE RECRUITMENT CONTACT

Simran Foote
E-mail: grad@addleshawgoddard.com

MAJOR DEPARTMENTS & PRACTICES

Advertising & Marketing • Asset Finance & Leasing • Aviation Finance • Charities • Commercial Agreements • Commercial Tax • Competition (EU & UK), including Dawn Raids • Construction • Construction Litigation • Corporate Finance • Corporate Real Estate • Corporate Restructuring & Insolvency • Corporate Services • Credit Cards • Data Protection & Information • Debt Transfers & Securitisation • Defamation & Media Litigation • Derivatives • Dispute Resolution & Litigation • Domain Name Recovery • E-commerce • Education Sector Finance • Employment • Family • Film Finance & Production • Financial Regulation • Financial Services • Freedom of Information • General Banking • Human Rights • Information Technology • Insurance & Reinsurance • Media & Internet • Mergers & Acquisitions • Music • Outsourcing • Partnership • Pensions • Pensions Trustee Service • PFI/Projects • Power of Attorney • Private Equity • Project Finance • Protection of Rights & Reputation Online • Public Law & Judicial Review • Regulatory • Retail • Share Incentives & Employee Tax • Social Housing Finance • Sport • State Aid • Telecommunications • Television Broadcast & Production • Theatre • Treasury/Capital Markets • Trusts, Estates & Tax • Wealth Planning • Wills

THE BUZZ
WHAT EMPLOYEES AT OTHER FIRMS ARE SAYING

- "Inconsistent"
- "Outstanding"

THE SCOOP

Addleshaw Goddard was formed in 2003 through the merger of Addleshaw Booth & Co—a firm that grew up in the regions of Leeds and Manchester—and the City of London firm Theodore Goddard. The combination ranked 16th in the U.K. by fee income in 2004, with a turnover of £125 million across the three English locations. One of the major drivers behind the merger was simply size: both firms felt they needed to be larger in order to thrive in the evermore competitive legal marketplace.

Strategic objective

Two years in, and so far the market reaction to the merger has been good: Addleshaw Goddard is seen as a hot place to be. The firm won Management Team of the Year at *The Lawyer* Awards 2004, and *Legal Week*'s U.K. Law Firm of the Year award the same year.

When the two firms combined, Addleshaw Goddard was restructured into five main business divisions and these continue to provide the focus for the firm. They are finance and projects; commercial; corporate; property; and litigation and employment. Within the divisions the firm has some niche sector strengths, particularly in sport, media and entertainment, and private client.

Hello! vs. *OK!*

In all, Addleshaws now acts for 80 of the FTSE 350 companies, and ranks seventh in the U.K. by Hemscott for its representation of FTSE 100 organisations, with a list of clients that includes 3i, Associated British Foods, BT, British Airways, Diageo and United Utilities. The firm also acts for over 160 financial institutions and more than 100 public sector bodies, so its work is nothing if not diverse.

But aside from the good diet of corporate work, there is no doubt that Addleshaws picks up more than its fair share of high-profile "sexy" clients. The firm acted for Hollywood megastars Catherine Zeta Jones and Michael Douglas, and the magazine *OK!*, in their long-running dispute with *Hello! Magazine* about the publication of the couple's wedding photos. On the sporting side, the firm represents the U.K.'s Football League on broadcasting deals, and is in fact one of the leading law firms for football-related work. Other clients include the FA Premier League, Football DataCo, The Football Association, and a raft of clubs and sponsors.

Work aside

The firm's reputation for sports advice has extended off the pitch as well - its name was blasted across the world when it lined up as one of the key sponsors of the Commonwealth Games when they were held in Manchester in 2002. The firm was appointed legal adviser to the organising committee of the Games, and advised on broadcasting rights, sponsorship and merchandising contracts, and infringement issues.

That was just one example of the firm's commitment to community involvement. The firm is one year into a three-year project to raise £100,000 for the Prince's Trust, a charity run by HRH The Prince of Wales to help young people. Also, for over 30 years the firm has been providing volunteers for the Springfield Legal Advice Centre in London, helping out on everything from employment to debt disputes. One of the firm's biggest pro bono achievements, though, must undoubtedly be its work giving free legal representation to the parents of autistic children who are challenging decisions regarding provision for their children's educational needs. The firm is conducting the advocacy before the Special Educational Needs Tribunal pro bono.

Public property

What sets Addleshaw Goddard apart from a lot of its City competitors is a deep investment in real estate and project finance work. The property practice accounts for around 13 per cent of the firm's total turnover—projects are an even bigger proportion—and the London team has been one of the real winners from the merger, seeing revenue jump nearly 20 per cent. That's down to the firm leveraging off its regional links, says Addleshaw Goddard. The strategy is to win high-end, City type real estate work, and service a large amount of it out of the regions where the cost is lower. It seems to be working. In 2005 the firm advised the hotel group Travelodge on a massive sale-and-leaseback transaction, while other major loyal clients on the property side include Standard Life, Anglo-Irish, Scottish Widows, J Sainsbury and Admiral Taverns.

Top-tier beer

Legal work doesn't come much more top tier, or international, than when Addleshaws advised Diageo, the world's premium drinks business, on a 2004 joint venture in South Africa with Heineken and Namibia Breweries. The firm then went on to represent the group combining their businesses in Ghana.

On the projects side, Addleshaw's national practice is a leader for PFI work, where private finance is invested in public projects. The firm is advising Partnerships for Schools and the government's Department for Education and Skills on the set-up of a £2.2 billion Building Schools for the Future programme. It also acts for the public sector in Northern Ireland on its new schools programme, and for the Department of Health in its £2.3 billion programme of outsourcing clinical activity to the private sector.

Allen & Overy LLP

One New Change
London EC4M 9QQ
Phone: +44 (0)20 7330 3000
www.allenovery.com

OTHER LOCATIONS

Amsterdam • Antwerp • Bangkok • Beijing • Bratislava • Brussels • Budapest • Dubai • Frankfurt • Hamburg • Hong Kong • London • Luxembourg • Madrid • Milan • Moscow • New York City • Paris • Prague • Rome • Shanghai • Singapore • Tokyo • Turin • Warsaw

THE STATS

No. of lawyers: 2,466
No. of lawyers in London: 1,173
No. of offices: 25
Trainee positions: 120 (2005)
Trainees retained: 83% (2005)
Managing partner: David Morley

MAJOR DEPARTMENTS & PRACTICES

Alternative Dispute Resolution • Antitrust • Asset Finance • Aviation • Banking & Finance • Banking & Finance Litigation • Central & Eastern Europe • Charity & Not-For-Profit • Chartered Corporations • China • Communications • Competition • Construction • Corporate • Corporate Trustee • Debt Capital Markets • Derivatives • Dutch Desk • E-commerce • Employment • Energy & Utilities • Environment • Environmental Litigation • Equity Capital Markets • Estate Planning & Trusts • EU Law • Financial Institutions • Financial Services Regulatory • Foreign direct investments • Franchising • German Desk • Global Loans • Health & Safety • Immigration • Incentives • India • Infrastructure • Inquiries & Investigations • Insurance • Intellectual Property • International Capital Markets • International Commercial Arbitration • Investment Funds • Islamic Finance • Joint Ventures • Korea Group • Latin America • Leveraged Finance • Litigation & Dispute Resolution • Media • Mergers & Acquisitions • Middle East • Mining & Metals • Nordic Desk • Notarial Services • Outsourcing • Partnerships • Pensions • PFI/PPP • Pharmaceutical & Bioscience • Planning, Projects & the Environment • Private Equity • Privatisation • Product Liability • Professional Negligence • Projects & Project Finance • Public & Administrative Law • Public Procurement • Public Takeovers • Rail • Real Estate • Real Estate Finance • Real Estate Securitisation • Restructuring • Satellite • Securitisations • Shipping • Sport • Structured Finance • Taiwan • Tax • Technology • Telecoms Finance • Trusts for Commercial Use • Trusts, Asset Tracing & Fraud • US Law • Vision • Water • Workplace Representation & Consultation

THE BUZZ
WHAT EMPLOYEES AT OTHER FIRMS ARE SAYING

- "Best Magic Circle firm to work for"
- "Problems with associate retention"

PLUSES

- Prestigious reputation and cutting-edge deals
- Supportive and friendly culture

MINUSES

- High billable hours pressure
- Inflexible working arrangements

NOTABLE PERKS

- Free gym and language lessons
- In-house doctor

BASE SALARY

Trainee: £31,000
Newly Qualified: £55,000

GRADUATE RECRUITMENT CONTACT

E-mail: graduate.recruitment@allenovery.com

THE SCOOP

Allen & Overy made its name back in 1936 when, as a six-year-old firm, it advised King Edward VIII in the abdication crisis that rocked the British monarchy. Some 20 years later the firm acted on the first hostile takeover, the so-called Aluminium Wars. But the Allen & Overy that we know today really staked its claim on a City brand in 1963, when it drafted and developed the first ever Eurobond, on behalf of Italian state-owned company Autostrade. Ever since, A&O has been at the forefront of crafting sophisticated new financing techniques and can claim a place among the top financing law firms in the world. With a client list that reads like a directory of the world's top financial institutions, A&O has banking running through every vein of its now vast empire.

Seeing the globe

If there is one type of client that demands its law firm to have offices across the globe, it is the international investment bank. As the likes of Citigroup, Barclays and Deutsche Bank have expanded, so A&O has followed, first into Dubai and Brussels in 1978, then on into New York in 1985, and most recently Shanghai in 2002. A&O now covers 25 locations across the globe. In the course of the 1990s, A&O grew from 1,000 to 2,500 lawyers as it expanded beyond the U.K.

The hub of the firm remains well and truly in London though, where 198 the firm's 420-plus partners reside, and where A&O was the first major law firm to establish a second office. The London practice is split between the City headquarters and a sizeable 220-lawyer outpost in Canary Wharf to the East, home to so many financial institutions.

In Autumn 2006, A&O will move into sparkling new purpose-built offices in Spitalfields, close to Liverpool Street station in the City. According to recent reports, there have been complaints by some Canary Wharf-based lawyers that they feel isolated from the heart of the firm. In response, the firm maintains that if it can manage offices across the world, it should be able to manage having two bases in its hometown.

More than money

There is much more to A&O's practice than banking: the firm's global restructuring business is a real leader, not least because of its strength in dispute resolution, and the M&A team gives the highly successful banking group a run for its money year-on-year.

A&O spent 2003 advising the enormous telecoms and IT group Marconi on its turnaround, a piece of work that involved more than 900 lawyers across the firm and ultimately netted some £31 million in fees. In 2004 the firm did the same for Western Europe's largest coal-fired power station Drax Holdings, where a successful rescue called on 150 lawyers and billed some £10 million.

On the litigation side, A&O is defending six of the 15 former Equitable Life directors who are being sued by Ernst & Young for misfeasance in public office, a ground breaking case playing out in the High Court for much of 2005, and testing how much directors can be blamed for company problems. In M&A, the corporate team advised controversial U.S. tycoon Malcolm Glazer in his successful £800 million buyout of Manchester United Football Club. For its efforts, the firm snagged the Corporate Team of the Year 2005 at the *Legal Business* Awards 2006. The firm also elected a new corporate head this spring when Alan Paul replaced Mark Wippell in May 2006. As the newly titled client development partner, Paul told *The Lawyer* that his priority will be to expand the firm's private equity practice.

Leading the way

In 2004, Allen & Overy became the first of the U.K.'s Magic Circle law firms to convert to limited liability partnership status, which apart from meaning it now has LLP after its name, also means the partners are less exposed if things go wrong, and the firm has to publish its accounts for all to see. It was the first major English law firm to do that in May 2005, revealing some healthy profits to be shared out between the partners. But the partnership doesn't bank the lot—the firm has a staff bonus pool that is divided between all employees. That pool amounted to some £19 million in 2005, giving each member of staff an annual bonus payment worth six weeks' salary. What's more, the firm's accounts revealed a healthy contribution to the community and pro bono projects. In total, lawyers recorded 50,000 hours of pro bono work, roughly equivalent to £12 million in fee income. As well as giving free legal advice, the firm's people act as trustees for local charities, help in primary school numeracy and literacy projects, and mentor secondary school pupils.

The Beijing office expanded this spring when Thomas Jones, former China practice head at Freshfields Bruckhaus Deringer, defected to A&O in May.

Expanding horizons

Though one of the most international of the U.K.'s leading law firms, A&O still has ambitions to grow further, and when it announced its results it set out plans to expand in both China and North America. The firm is actually the largest employer of U.S.-qualified lawyers outside of the United States, with a U.S. law group of 230 lawyers sitting not just in America, but also in London, Beijing, Frankfurt, Hong Kong, Milan, Moscow, Paris, Rome, Singapore and Tokyo. The idea is to be able to offer both English and American legal advice to a client wherever they are, though the firm has also devoted some serious resources to building up New York, hiring high-profile M&A star Daniel Cunningham from Cravath, Swaine & Moore in 2001, reportedly the only partner ever to leave that storied firm for a rival.

In China, Allen & Overy now has three offices, in Beijing, Shanghai and Hong Kong, and with over 100 lawyers it has one of the largest practices there. The Beijing office expanded this spring when Thomas Jones, former China practice head at Freshfields Bruckhaus Deringer, defected to A&O in May. From Hong Kong, a team recently advised on the landmark U.S.$1.25 billion financing of the Nam Theun 2 hydropower project in Laos, the largest Laotian hydro project ever financed and a major boost to the Laotian economy. The firm won Asia Law Firm of the Year at the Chambers Awards in 2004, and European Law Firm of the Year at the IFLR Awards the same year. In fact, Allen & Overy has racked up quite a run of gongs of late, including *Legal Business* Financial Institutions Team of the Year 2005, Hungarian Law Firm of the Year 2005 (IFLR) and Czech Law Firm of the Year (IFLR).

GETTING HIRED

High standards getting higher

Allen & Overy's solicitors call the hiring process "tough", "practical", and oddly enjoyable. "I thought the interview was very fair, a general chat about my CV followed by a short business case-study exercise," says one young litigator. "This did not require any legal knowledge, but did test one's ability to absorb a lot of information in a short time and then talk intelligently with a partner about whether one would advise the client to invest in the business opportunity that was the subject of the case study." Another young litigator from London adds, "The interview takes the form of a personal interview and a case study. I was surprised how much I enjoyed the interview process, considering that interviews are usually dreadful things. The personal interview can give you an opportunity to talk about almost anything, not simply your qualifications and achievements."

Standards are high and getting higher at A&O, the solicitors report. In addition to degree ranking, the firm also looks for a number of particular traits, specifically "intelligent, proactive candidates with strong academic background and the drive to turn knowledge into practical results", says one first-year. A&O wants solicitors that are "keen to learn and to share that knowledge with colleagues."

OUR SURVEY SAYS

Relatively satisfied

Allen & Overy's solicitors report that they are relatively satisfied with their jobs and their firm. "I get a lot of responsibility, client contact and a varied workload, which combines to make it a satisfying place to work," reports one junior trusts and estates specialist. A property law lawyer says that the firm offers "interesting work" on "a variety of transactions," which provides "a good range of experience." However, a second-year solicitor adds, "While the work itself is generally interesting, long hours can put a dent in the enjoyment of it." A senior solicitor worries about his chances of promotion. He works on "great deals" with "generally good people," he says, "but advance prospects are becoming more and more limited and unclear." And another midlevel solicitor complains about the work, reporting "insufficient mental stimulation, lack of incentive to excel, and extremely document-intensive" assignments.

Relaxed and friendly, social and professional

Insiders describe the firm as "relaxed," "friendly," "sociable", and "professional." "It is very social, more so with other lawyers who were in the same intake as me, but I see a lot of the people I work with outside the firm," says a first-year solicitor. A second-year says that there is a "professional attitude to work and client relationships, whilst a friendly and supportive atmosphere among the majority of associates and partners alike." A corporate finance specialist adds, "The firm makes an effort to encourage a social culture. However, work pressure and hours often mean that, understandably, people are reluctant to spend their spare time at work-related social functions." However, a senior corporate finance expert complains that while the firm may be "relaxed and friendly," that "due to the pressures of work there is not that much socialising."

Solicitous partners

A&O solicitors give their firm high scores for solicitor/partner relationships. "It's very good as a whole," reports a young corporate solicitor. "We are kept well informed of firmwide policies and decisions." An employment solicitor says, "Most partners are approachable and part of the team. Some are less approachable but that is probably true of any law firm." However, a corporate finance solicitor adds, "It is mixed. In my department the partners treat us very well. In other departments I've worked in, including the overseas offices, solicitors are treated very badly." Other solicitors complain about the institutional treatment of solicitors by the firm. "We are kept informed by the partnership more or less regularly, but I don't think we participate in many firmwide decisions," says a junior banking solicitor. Or, as a junior trusts and estates solicitor puts it, "Whilst we aren't always involved in global firmwide decisions, we are kept updated."

Superb formal training ...

One of the banes of young solicitors everywhere is a general lack of formal training. Not so at Allen & Overy, however, where solicitors give the firm's training program uncommonly high marks. As one corporate solicitor puts it, "There is as much training as you can fit in around your work." Or, as a banking specialist (quite similarly) puts it, "The training on offer is very good if you have time to go on it." A junior employment solicitor adds that the firm places "a great emphasis on training and increasing your skills base." And a first-year solicitor sums up the program in two words: "Fantastic training."

... and superb informal training, as well

The firm's solicitors also give A&O high scores for its mentoring and informal training. "As above, a formal mentoring scheme is in place, which I have found very constructive," reports a source. "Most partners are always willing to respond to any queries, if possible." Another junior labour solicitor advises, "Supervision varies depending on partners' workload, but is generally good." However, a midlevel property specialist believes that there is "relatively little informal training from partners." Instead, he reports, associates tend to rely on other associates and "of counsels" in the firm. "There are a number of very senior associates and consultants, all of whom have been partners here or in other firms, who are very approachable and provide plenty of good quality advice," we are told.

Compensation is a bonus

Allen & Overy's solicitors have very few, if any, complaints about their compensation. "A&O's salary is very good and I don't have any complaints about it. I also particularly like our across-the-board bonus scheme, because I feel that this contributes to maintaining within the firm a friendly atmosphere, which may be altered if a merits-based bonus scheme were introduced," advises a junior banking solicitor. "I work hard and it has taken a number of years to qualify so I feel my salary is justified," opines one trust and estates solicitor. "We have a very good bonus system and good other benefits," adds another first-year solicitor. The one gripe comes from an insider who says that perhaps the solicitors should makes a little less money. "I would rather be paid less and have a better work/life balance," he fantasizes.

Long hours, even for a major firm

Indeed, the one area that receives across-the-board criticism is the firm's billable hours requirements. "My department is absolutely obsessed with billable hours targets and busy-ness," reports a fourth-year. "You really need to be billing between 130 and 160 per cent of target otherwise you'll get more work." One corporate solicitor reports, "Work hours are long but that is what everyone should expect if they work in this firm. Of course it's not ideal, but the nature of working in the city and the demands of clients means that sometimes long hours must be worked, although this can have a demoralising effect if long hours persist over long periods of time." Another (rather polite) first year adds, "I frequently have 55-hour weeks, which is not very satisfactory." However, another insider suggests the problem is with the field, not with the firm. "I would say that across the city the hours associates are expected to work are too high and ultimately unsustainable."

Ashurst

Broadwalk House
5 Appold Street
London EC2A 2HA
Phone: +44 (0)20 7638 1111
www.ashurst.com

OTHER LOCATIONS

Brussels
Frankfurt
Madrid
Milan
Munich
New Delhi
New York
Paris
Singapore
Tokyo

THE STATS

No. of lawyers: 720
No. of lawyers in London:
No. of offices: 11
Managing partner: Simon Bromwich

THE BUZZ
WHAT EMPLOYEES AT OTHER FIRMS ARE SAYING

- "Run a tight ship"
- "Punching above their size"

MAJOR DEPARTMENTS & PRACTICES

Arbitration • Banking & Finance Litigation • Commercial • Commercial Contracts • Commercial Litigation • Communications • Contentious & Non-contentious Construction • Corporate • Corporate Tax • E-commerce Tax Issues • Employee Benefits & Incentives • Employment • Energy • Energy, Transport & Infrastructure Litigation • Energy, Transport & Infrastructure Tax Issues • Enterprise Zone Tax Issues • Environmental & Health & Safety • EU & Competition • EU & Competition Litigation • Financial Regulatory Litigation • Financial Institutions • Healthcare • Information Technology • Inland Revenue Investigation/Tax Litigation • Insolvency Litigation • Intellectual Property • International Arbitration • International Finance • International Finance Tax Issues • International Tax Advice • Investment Fund Tax Issues • Investment Funds • IP & IT Litigation • Leveraged Finance • Litigation • M&A/Corporate Finance • Outsourcing • Pensions • PFI/PPP • Planning & Public Sector • Private Equity & Buy-Outs • Product Liability & Environmental Litigation • Project Finance • Public International Law • Real Estate • Real Estate Finance • Real Estate Litigation • Real Estate Tax • Restructuring & Insolvency • Securities & Structured Finance • Sport • Stamp Duty Land Tax/Stamp Duty • Tax • Telecommunications • Transport • US Securities/M&A • VAT & Excise Duties • World Trade

PLUSES

- Assistant involvement in client development
- High-quality deals

MINUSES

- Some complaints about base pay
- Low prospects for partnership

NOTABLE PERKS

- Gym membership
- In-house doctor, dentist, optician and massage therapists

BASE SALARY

Trainee: £30,000
Newly Qualified: £55,000

GRADUATE RECRUITMENT CONTACT

Stephen Trowbridge
Apply online at:
www.cvmailuk.com/ashurst/begin.cfm

THE SCOOP

When Ashurst Morris Crisp re-branded as plain and simple Ashurst in 2004, it marked the transformation of one of the oldest legal brands in London. The firm was founded in 1822 by the leading radical William Ashurst, who was later joined by liquidation specialist John Morris and company formation and flotation expert Sir Frank Crisp. They shaped a firm that is still renowned today for advising corporates and financial institutions, and has the questionable claim to fame of having trained the eminent Messrs Slaughter and May.

Bright stars

With the demise of the lengthy moniker, Ashurst has also tried hard to ditch what it thought was a stuffy image, with a high profile ad campaign that has seen its name in primary colours emblazoned across billboards, publications, and even London taxis. Ashurst lawyers now carry business cards in a variety of colours, which they distribute according to the perceived mood of the recipient on the day. Beneath the quirky exterior though, Ashurst is a serious City law firm just trying to make its way in competition with some of the much larger players. Regarded as a real alternative to the Magic Circle on M&A, the firm's corporate and financial institution client base now includes the likes of P&O Stena Line, Hitachi, Virgin, Royal Bank of Scotland, BNP Paribas, Centrica, Imperial Tobacco, Deutsche Telekom, Mitsubishi Corporation and Marriott Hotels.

Though not always the first choice for the mega deals, Ashurst typically is in the running. When retail supremo Philip Green launched his audacious bid to buy high street stalwart Marks & Spencer for some £9 billion in 2004, he first picked Freshfields Bruckhaus Deringer as his law firm. When that firm was revealed to have a conflict of interest, it was Ashurst that got the call. It was one of the instructions of the year, and while the deal did not ultimately go ahead, Green remains a dream acquisitive client for the firm.

Private major

Ashurst was one of the few top-tier City law firms to really take an interest in the private equity market when it was but a fledgling industry in the 1980s. Its team was one of the first to advise on major leveraged buyouts, and as the market has matured, so has the firm's practice. Ashurst continues to act for some of Europe's leading buyout shops, advising them on everything from raising their funds, to investing and then selling out. In recent years the firm has acted for Terra Firma Capital Partners on its acquisition of two of the U.K.'s largest cinema chains, Odeon and UCI, and for a consortium led by Cinven buying the Unique and Voyager pub estates for €3.14 billion. The pub deal was one of the biggest private equity transactions ever closed in the U.K. The firm also represented a consortium led by Goldman Sachs in a failed bid to take over airports operator BAA. In June 2006, after months of offers and counteroffers, BAA accepted a rival bid by the Spanish construction group Ferrovial.

The firm's pre-eminence on the private equity side does not mean it is not doing public M&A, quite the contrary. The corporate group acted for Wm Morrison Supermarkets buying Safeway for £3 billion in 2004, and also for Smith & Nephew in its €1.6 billion offer for Centerpulse.

Beyond the deals

In recent years Ashurst's banking and structured finance capabilities have been the focus of lateral hiring, it has devoted some serious effort to becoming one of the go-to firms for finance in the U.K. Signs of success have included advising on some 150 European collateralised debt obligations since 2000—a truly cutting-edge structured finance technique. The finance team also acted for the banks that lent money to fund the purchase of Italy's yellow pages business, Seat Pagine Gialle, by private equity buyers in 2003, in what was at the time the biggest European leveraged buyout of all time. What's more, while M&A, corporate and structured finance are undoubtedly the focus, Ashurst is a full-service firm capable of turning its hand to almost anything a client desires. It acts for The Ritz Hotel and The Ritz Casino on trademark and domain name cases, and also has significant litigation prowess and a specialism in energy, transport and infrastructure.

Global appeal

Unlike some of the larger U.K. law firms, Ashurst has resisted the temptation of overseas merger, despite various dalliances with the idea. The firm has—largely through organic growth—built an international network that spans 10 countries. What appeared to trouble the firm at the start of this decade was its lack of U.S. law capability, and as a result it considered a merger with Latham & Watkins of Los Angeles, and then later New York's Fried, Frank, Harris, Shriver & Jacobson. In the end, neither deal quite matched up to expectations, and instead Ashurst is now fostering "best friends" links with a number of American law firms, and has added its own U.S. law team to its London office. In any case, it seems that Ashurst is doing something right: according to *The Lawyer*, the firm posted an impressive 23 per cent increase in partner profits (PEP) and a seven per cent increase in firm revenue for the 2005-2006 financial year.

The Ashurst way

Ashurst attempts to foster a real interest in its local community through a team of about 40 volunteers who help out at a local primary school on a regular basis, and the firm is also a long-standing supporter of CARE, one of the world's largest nonpolitical, nonsectarian international relief and development organisations. The firm gives CARE pro bono legal advice on everything from commercial contracts and employment matters to contractual disputes with suppliers and conveyancing work. It also regularly plays host to the charity's annual general meeting at its offices. Ashurst has been heavily involved representing Caribbean death row prisoners since 1996, but just to show that even its community efforts are a little quirky, it also gives a lot of pro bono help to Spitalfields City Farm, an urban farm close to the very heart of the City of London. All that good work can make a lawyer thirsty: Ashurst is one of the few City law firms that still has a partners' bar in its office.

GETTING HIRED

What's it take to get hired at Ashurst?

"To get to interview you obviously have to have a good CV and cover letter, which is better than an application form as it is easier for the candidate and in fact tells you more about a person rather than the usual set of questions to which everyone repeats the same answer," reports a first-year litigator. "I think a lot of weight is put on how early the application comes in as this shows that the candidate is both keen and organised. The interview process is a general chat and case study with a junior solicitor, which is a good way to get to know a candidate, less intimidating and you can see their commercial awareness. A second interview straight after is then held with two partners, which is again basically a chat."

A second-year solicitor suggests, "I think that this question can be answered by looking at our firm's recruitment brochure or online." Following that advice, we've excerpted some highlights from Ashurst's web site: "Although technical knowledge and ability to do the job is of course essential, individuals have personalities and this is seen as most important. If you are invited to attend an interview, you will probably meet two partners from your preferred practice area; only in this way can we and you judge whether there is a meeting of minds. If so, we may proceed to a second interview and suggest that you meet your potential colleagues; after all, changing jobs is a big decision and we want you to be sure."

OUR SURVEY SAYS

Happy people, more or less

Most Ashurst solicitors report that they are, more or less, happy with their jobs. "I think that it's almost impossible for anyone to find a job which is 100 per cent wonderful," reports a typical second-year. "That said, I genuinely enjoy coming to work and I am involved in interesting, and often high-profile, matters from which I am gaining a great deal of useful experience." A first-year adds, "I enjoy the work I do, it is certainly challenging, and I get a great deal of responsibility."

Solicitors call the firm "friendly," "collegial," and "social." "One of the best things about this firm is the people", remarks a junior IP specialist. "Obviously everyone is intelligent and professional but, in addition, there are genuinely interesting, approachable, and (much as I dislike the word) nice people here." A first-year adds, "Socialising amongst colleagues is certainly encouraged and there are plenty of opportunities to do so. Like any firm, the politics can be a little tedious, but at the lower end it is easy to avoid."

Nothing short of fantastic

The firm's solicitor/partner relations get high marks. "I am genuinely made to feel part of a team and my views, as well as those of my colleagues, are welcomed by the partners that I had worked with", says a junior solicitor. A litigator adds, "On the whole partners treat the solicitors very well, certainly in the department I am in anyway. They are very friendly and encourage you to take the initiative and plenty of responsibility. We are kept pretty well informed with regard to firm management but are not involved in firmwide decisions."

Ashurst's formal training program is nothing short of fantastic, insiders report. "The training and know-how system at Ashurst is excellent," a second-year solicitor tells us. "I regularly refer to the internal resources available to us and the courses and seminars are wide-ranging across all departments, and very well prepared and presented." A junior litigator adds, "We get lots of internal training, including regular updates. The training is virtually all internal and of a very high standard."

Please, sir, may I have some more?

One area in which the firm could stand to improve is its compensation plan, solicitors say. There's "no banding of individuals according to quality" and "too much reliance on billable hours," according to one midlevel associate. He also suggests that, in order to retain senior associates, "pay needs to dramatically increase." A junior solicitor moans, "I realise we are paid a lot in terms of careers in general, however compared to City salaries, considering we are working City hours, I do not believe we are paid enough, particularly bearing in mind the amount of training we need, the technicality of the work and the fact that there is not the job security there may have been a few years ago." That's not to say that everyone at Ashurst is unhappy with his or her pay. "There will be a firmwide bonus this year in addition to those bonuses calculated on the basis of billable hours," according to a second-year. "Overall, I believe that people are rewarded if they have worked hard. We also receive other benefits, such as private health care and gym membership."

The hours at Ashurst may be rough, but that's the nature of the beast, solicitors say. "This is probably the only area that I find difficult in my job", reports a junior litigator. "The hours are long and more importantly unpredictable, which inevitably interferes with your social life. However, this is the sacrifice you make if you work for a City law firm." Another junior solicitor adds, "Obviously, given that we are a City firm, there are occasions when you have to work long and intense hours. That said, Ashurst does seem to recognise that people have lives and interests outside of work." Or, as a junior corporate attorney puts it, "Corporate law hours, can't really complain, but obviously every one will."

"I genuinely enjoy coming to work and I am involved in interesting, and often high-profile, matters from which I am gaining a great deal of useful experience."

— *Ashurst solicitor*

Baker & McKenzie

...w Bridge Street
London EC4V 6JA
Phone: +44 (0)20 7919 1000
www.bakernet.com

OTHER LOCATIONS

Almaty • Amsterdam • Antwerp • Bahrain • Baku • Bangkok • Barcelona • Beijing • Berlin • Bologna • Bogota • Brasilia • Brussels • Budapest • Buenos Aires • Calgary • Cancun • Cairo • Caracas • Chicago • Chihuahua • Dallas • Düsseldorf • Frankfurt • Geneva • Hanoi • Ho Chi Minh City • Hong Kong • Houston • Jakarta • Kuala Lumpur • Kyiv • Madrid • Manila • Melbourne • Mexico City • Miami • Milan • Monterrey • Moscow • Munich • New York • Palo Alto • Paris • Porto Alegre • Prague • Rio de Janeiro • Riyadh • Rome • San Diego • San Francisco • St Petersburg • Santiago • São Paulo • Singapore • Shanghai • Stockholm • Sydney • Taipei • Tijuana • Tokyo • Toronto • Vienna • Valencia • Warsaw • Washington, DC • Zurich

THE STATS

No. of lawyers: 3,357
No. of lawyers in London: 290
No. of offices: 70
Trainee intake: 30 (2005)
Trainees retained: 78% (2005)
London managing partner: Gary Senior

MAJOR DEPARTMENTS & PRACTICES

Antitrust & Trade • Banking & Finance • Corporate • Dispute Resolution • Employment • Insurance • Intellectual Property • International/Commercial • IT/Communications • Major Project & Project Finance • Pharmaceuticals & Healthcare • Real Estate/Construction/Environment & Tourism • Tax

THE BUZZ
WHAT EMPLOYEES AT OTHER FIRMS ARE SAYING

- "Strong performer"
- "Size isn't everything"

PLUSES
- "Open-door policy"
- "Non-hierarchical"

MINUSES
- Bureaucracy
- No bonuses

NOTABLE PERKS
- Associate Training Programme
- Starbucks in canteen

BASE SALARY
Trainee: £29,000 + £3,000 joining bonus
Newly Qualified: £55,000

GRADUATE RECRUITMENT CONTACT
Suzanne Dare
Graduate Recruitment & Development Manager
E-mail: london.graduate.recruit@baker net.com

THE SCOOP

Once upon a time, a man named Russell Baker, growing up in the American Southwest, decided he wanted to be a lawyer. He travelled in a cattle car to go to college in Chicago, and later secured a law degree. In 1925 he founded the law firm Baker & Simpson with a school friend, specialising in immigration, bankruptcy and criminal law. Fourteen years later, in 1949, he founded what would be the first international law firm, Baker & McKenzie. His partner was John McKenzie, a lawyer he met by chance during his daily transit home from work. Soon after, in 1955, the firm's second office opened in Caracas, Venezuela. Today, that law firm has grown to be the largest in the world, with some 3,357 lawyers spread over 70 offices across the globe.

The most international

Baker & McKenzie, as it is now arguably the most international firm in the world, and would bristle at being called a "U.S. law firm." While its administrative headquarters remains in Chicago, the firm's founding office in London is its largest office by headcount, at 290 lawyers, and is also its most profitable.

In late 2004, John Conroy replaced Christine Lagarde as chairman of the executive committee when she left to join the French government. Conroy, a finance partner based in Chicago, had been head of the North American practice for five years. Some said the firm was going back to its roots, but there is simply no getting away from the fact that, with a European in charge or without, the London office of Baker & McKenzie remains truly central, and crucial, to this global law firm's ambitions.

London line

The U.K. office of Baker & McKenzie has been having a very good run of late. The average amount of profit that each equity partner takes home grew 32 per cent in the most recent financial year, up to £445,000 and putting it well up in the elite of the U.K.'s mid-market. Particularly, the corporate and finance departments both did well, with major clients including BP on the corporate side, and Scandinavian private equity firm EQT on the acquisition finance side. The firm's strong presence in Asia has also been a source of some chunky London work recently, including advice to Shanghai Motor Company on its bid to buy Rover out of administration last year, and ongoing work for Sony.

The office has a broad mix of work covering all the key disciplines you'd expect in a solid domestic law firm. Particular gems in the City practice are intellectual property—both contentious and non-contentious—telecoms, IT, antitrust and trade, outsourcing, employment, pensions, private banking, corporate, banking and finance, and environment.

New partners and a bunch of awards

In June, the office announced that four new partners were to be made up (in the competition, corporate and IP departments) and also received quite a boost when it added a four-partner securitisation team from Norton Rose asserting its place at the top table when it comes to structured finance in the City. The finance group added another lateral partner in March 2006 when Nick Tostivin joined from Linklaters and the private banking department added partner Ashley Crossley from Clifford Chance.

Among the many recent accolades bestowed on Baker & McKenzie are its ranking as Top International Law Firm in London by The Lawyer 100, and Top U.K. Global Law Firm by Legal 500. Additionally, the firm was named a Top 100 Graduate Employer 2005 by the *Times* and Best Trainer—Large City Firm at the LawCareers.Net/Trainee Solicitors' Group Training & Recruitment Awards 2005.

When in England ...

Baker & McKenzie was undoubtedly one of the first law firms to really understand global legal practice, and has been employing lawyers from all kinds of jurisdictions since back in Mr Baker's day. For a young lawyer looking to travel the world and do truly cross-border work, the firm has few peers. Furthermore, having done it for so long, Bakers is well versed in letting its international practices run themselves, so there is no risk of someone flying in from New York and changing the way things are done. Baker & McKenzie London works to London charge-out rates, on London hours, with London holiday entitlements and London attitudes. Not always the case amongst its competitors.

Public spirit

One of the benefits of working for a firm with U.S. roots is their serious commitment to pro bono work. Again, at Bakers this dates right back to the man himself, the founder, who believed vehemently that lawyers had a professional duty to provide free legal services to those unable to access them otherwise. Hence, the firm organises its pro bono efforts into six streams: legal services, partnering with clients, civic presence, employee volunteerism, fellowships and charitable giving. The firm practices all six worldwide. As a result, Bakers has won the Child Advocacy Award from Lawyers for Children America, the Employer of Choice, Community Support and Environment award at the 2004 Australian Law Awards, and the Pro Bono Partner award from corporateprobono.org, to name but a few accolades.

The last decade has seen the firm hit some impressive milestones—after becoming the first law firm with 1,000 lawyers in 1987, it tripled it by 2001. That same year it was the first firm to hit $1 billion in revenue. In 2004, Bakers opened its 69th office, in Chihuahua, Mexico, with a team of lawyers once part of Ernst & Young's legal network. The year before, it integrated its entire legal IT system, and again won awards for this impressive feat. It opened its 70th office in Cancun, Mexico, in January 2006.

GETTING HIRED

High marks for hiring

Baker & McKenzie's solicitors give the firm's hiring program exceedingly high marks. "A surprising range of universities are represented, but the majority come form the top 10 (Oxbridge, Durham, Manchester, Bristol, Warwick, etc.)," reports a third-year solicitor. "I think we concentrate recruitment (in terms of evening presentations, etc.) on these schools." Degree ranking will also be seriously scrutinized, with 2:1 expected, according to insiders. Here's how the firm itself describes its recruitment strategies: "Baker & McKenzie hires lawyers who are smart and academically accomplished, but other qualities are just as important ... To be successful at our firm, a lawyer must be comfortable working in an informal environment and have the initiative and imagination to deal with novel legal issues. The ability to speak a foreign language or an interest in international practice is not a prerequisite for hiring."

OUR SURVEY SAYS

Collegial, collegiate

Baker & McKenzie's solicitors call the firm a fairly satisfying place to work. Among the chief reasons, they say, is the firm's culture. Solicitors call Baker & McKenzie "relaxed", "extremely friendly", "very sociable", "collegial" *and* "collegiate." "The firm is known as one of the most sociable in London," reports a junior labour attorney. "Lawyers here tend to be quite proud of that reputation and do socialise together." A senior corporate finance and capital markets solicitor adds, "The firm has an excellent culture—the right mix of work/life balance where possible, and normal people—no Magic Circle arrogance. Socially there is loads going on and people do socialise together."

Great partners, who act as great mentors

Solicitors give Baker & McKenzie very high marks for both partner/solicitor relations and the firm's formal training program, though they do have a gripe or two. "Partners are generally pleasant, polite and friendly," says one fourth-year. "There is no mechanism for participating in firmwide decisions, but given the size of B&M, that would not be practical in any event." An attorney in the London office's labour department echoes those concerns. "We are certainly informed of firm strategy, but I do not think associates really get a chance to influence it in any meaningful way," he says. "There is more interaction on a departmental basis in my experience, although ultimately direction will be determined by the partners."

Salary? Great! Bonuses? Eh, not so much ...

Don't be misled by the fact that Baker & McKenzie provides a base salary as high as any Magic Circle firm's, solicitors say. The lack of large, dependable bonuses lower the firm's compensation programme from great to merely middling. "Base salaries are certainly up there with the best London City practices (at the top end, higher than top 10 and Magic Circle), based on informal discussions (although it's not actually discussed much in my experience)," says one fourth-year attorney. "We do not have any bonus system, however, which probably moves us more into the 'good' rate for large city practice, rather than top end." A property attorney echoes these sentiments. "We tend not to get given a bonus unless working in a department such as corporate where hours are a lot longer," he reports.

Mixed feelings about the hours

There's no one singular experience at Baker & McKenzie in terms of hours. "It entirely depends on department," reports a midlevel tax attorney. "Corporate and finance have been very busy this last year (as have all departments—I have been significantly busier than the previous two years, due in large part to new legislation in my area). My hours are reasonably consistent—I have never personally done client work on a weekend in five years in total, but there are inevitably the odd late nights on major projects, and some months can be significantly busier than others." Another midlevel solicitor adds, "I record about 2,200 hours a year of which about 1,600 are chargeable. Given the market at present, chargeable hours are likely to increase, but as there is no bonus this will not make much difference to the associates."

Part-time schedules are rare at Baker & McKenzie, though they are at least a possibility. "I do not have experience of part-time working, but the culture is that if your supervising partner is happy for you to work from home, then you can do so, which is great," reports one senior solicitor.

Not all offices are created equal

Baker & McKenzie's office space reflects the eclectic character of some of the firm's partners, solicitors report. "Most people think our offices are quite nice (there is some 'interesting artwork,' too—a headless horse anyone?)," reports a junior solicitor. "There is always going to be somewhere more new and swanky, though." And if you have any say in an office, try to get an external one. The "internal rooms with windows facing onto the atrium do not have enough natural daylight," warns a senior solicitor.

Barlow Lyde & Gilbert

Beaufort House
15 St Botolph Street
London EC3A 7NJ
Phone: +44 (0)20 7247 2277
www.blg.co.uk

OTHER LOCATIONS

Hong Kong
London (1 additional)
Shanghai
Singapore

MAJOR DEPARTMENTS & PRACTICES

Aerospace
Banking
Commercial
Corporate
Employment
Healthcare
Insurance & Reinsurance
Litigation & Dispute Resolution
Manufacturing & Retailing
Professional Practices
Shipping
Transport & Trade
Technology

THE BUZZ
WHAT EMPLOYEES AT OTHER FIRMS ARE SAYING

- "Successful"
- "Still trying to get there"

THE STATS

No. of lawyers: 300
No. of offices: 4
Trainee intake: 18 (2005)
Trainees retained: 85% (2005)
Senior partner: Richard Dedman

PLUSES

- Work/life balance
- Friendly environment and interesting work

MINUSES

- No bonus
- "Poor" maternity policy

NOTABLE PERKS

- Subsidised restaurant and gym membership
- 28 days' holiday
- Pension plan
- Private health care

BASE SALARY

Trainee: £28,000
Newly Qualified: £47,000

GRADUATE RECRUITMENT CONTACT

Caroline Walsh
Head of Graduate Recruitment and Trainee Development
Phone: +44 (0)20 7643 7642
E-mail: grad.recruit@blg.co.uk

THE SCOOP

Barlow Lyde & Gilbert lives and breathes insurance, and has done so since the Victorian Era. Back in 1880, the firm advised Cuthbert Heath when he became a Lloyd's underwriter at the tender age of 21. He set up his own brokerage—CE Heath & Co—and his own insurance company—the Excess Insurance Company—and went on to single-handedly transform the London insurance market.

Inventing insurance

It was Heath, with BLG in tow, who fathered non-marine insurance, inventing forms of insurance for loss of profits, earthquakes, hurricanes, burglary and household comprehensive cover, among others. He famously sent a cable to his San Francisco agent after the earthquake of 1906, saying "Pay all our policyholders in full, irrespective of the terms of their policies"—thereby cementing the reputation of Lloyd's in the United States. For many years BLG remained the exclusive adviser to the Heath syndicate in Lloyd's, and from that developed the specialism that is now its core business. The firm has one of the most highly regarded insurance practices in the City, particularly in contentious insurance work and the reinsurance market. BLG even has a small secondary office in the Lloyd's building.

Sector-specific

Barlow Lyde & Gilbert has built its practice along sector lines, focusing on seven industries beyond insurance and reinsurance, namely professional practices, aerospace, transport and trade, technology, manufacturing and retail, and health care. The strategy has been to advise these clients on their disputes as well as their corporate and commercial activities, though in truth the firm remains best known for its contentious work.

In June 2006, BLG endured a self-inflicted public relations debacle when the firm published a full-page advert in the *Times* listing the names and companies of over 200 in-house lawyers with the tagline: "If you'd like to keep your name out of the legal papers, take note of ours." Whoops. The named in-house counsel, the vast majority of whom were not actually firm clients, were reportedly more than annoyed that their names were used without permission. The loss of at least one major banking client of the firm has been attributed to the incident.

Commercial litigation

The litigation team has acted on some massive cases of late: representing PricewaterhouseCoopers in its dispute with Elton John; advising Ernst & Young in the successful defence of a $2.6 billion claim from Equitable Life; and helping the former chief financial officer of Shell navigate FSA and SEC investigations into the overstatement of oil reserves.

Recognition of BLG's broad commercial litigation expertise is indeed rising: in a rare double, the firm won Dispute Resolution Team of the Year at the *Legal Business* Awards in February and 2006 and Litigation Team of the Year at the *Legal Week* Awards in November 2005.

The firm's head of commercial litigation is a colourful character—Clare Canning is a confirmed leader in her field, running both the Elton John and Equitable cases, whilst working four days a week and simultaneously practising as a trained psychotherapist from her home on Fridays. Proof, if any were needed, that BLG combines top-drawer work with a slightly more flexible approach than some of its larger rivals.

Canning took the helm of the litigation practice in late 2004 with a brief to educate the market that BLG is about more than just insurance litigation. There is clearly more to BLG than just insurance. Of particular note is the firm's outsourcing practice, which has advised on the National Health Service's £7 billion national IT programme to different consortia, and on the outsourcing of Barclays Life's actuarial functions to Watson Wyatt. Also thriving is the firm's practice in financial services regulatory work, representing corporate finance stockbroking houses and key individuals in relation to the FSA investigation into the Split Capital Investment Trust sector, for example.

The firm chose to restructure its corporate department when the market dipped, creating three new departments: commercial and technology, corporate, and employment. This led to three partner departures.

Claims against the competition

In technology, the firm acts for a bumper crop of serious IT providers, including IBM, UBS, the Royal Bank of Scotland Group, Fujitsu, UPS, Munich Re, 3 and the Hutchison Whampoa Group, PwC, Ernst & Young and TUI. The firm advises this dynamic client base on such matters as technology procurement and development, data protection and outsourcing. Perhaps less exciting as organisations but just as demanding work-wise are the firm's professional practice clients. Acting for everything from solicitors and accountants through stockbrokers and construction professionals, BLG is undoubtedly one of the most renowned firms when it comes to professional negligence claims. These cases often deal with some pretty meaty claims against the firm's competitors.

Dedman driving

Barlows has become known as a steady financial performer, regularly ranking well against its peers for profitability. Much of that is thanks to the leadership of Richard Dedman, who took over at the start of 2001 having decided while driving east to west across America on sabbatical that he wanted a new challenge. His first job was to focus on communication within the firm, aiming to increase cross-selling and improve everyone's motivation. The result was a list of four core values that he hopes now describe the firm: ambitious, client-focused, communicative and supportive. Such an approach means BLG is seen as a nice place to work—in 2004 it won the Best Recruiter award for a medium City firm at the LCN/TSG awards, just another gong to add to the stock of insurance-industry silverware.

Dedman runs a tight ship though, and despite the attraction of overseas expansion as a means of competing with its larger rivals, the firm maintains only a Southeast Asia presence outside London. The firm opened in Hong Kong in 1986 and now has 25 lawyers in the region, with a Shanghai post opening in 2000 and a Singapore branch in 2004. These officers advise corporations doing business in China, plus a number of major Hong Kong-listed insurers and a whole range of clients in commercial disputes.

As yet, the firm has found no need for European expansion, where it prefers to work with "best friend" affiliate law firms in other jurisdictions.

GETTING HIRED

Not so magical?

Should you find yourself lacking the "minimum 2:1" and still wish to have a go at a place at Barlows, iron your tie, polish your social skills and for God's sake, get a hobby. The "firm is looking for people with interests outside of law, who are personable and socially adept," a fifth-year tells us. The competition is tough; there are only "16 places per intake" and up to four interviews—described by one solicitor as "fairly relaxed ... despite being partner heavy and intense." A co-worker recalls just two interviews but the additional burden of "a written test." A few insiders are discouraged by the firm's recent spate of Magic Circle recruitments: "At NQ level, it seems a shame that the firm is taken with recruiting anyone from Magic Circle firms (who usually have had little or no litigation experience and have not managed to qualify at their own firm) at the expense of some trainees who have trained here and who have, aside from other issues, gained an enviable 18 months training in litigation."

OUR SURVEY SAYS

Striking a balance

BLG solicitors—NQs in particular—are delighted with a firm environment that is equal portions "supportive" and "challenging", with "top-quality work" and clients as well as a "good team atmosphere." "No complaints whatsoever, very friendly colleagues and high-quality work", a content fifth-year PQE shares, proving happiness stretches up the ranks. Moreover, BLG is reportedly populated by "really pleasant, balanced people."

Working life

In fact, as their peers at other firms bemoan their workloads, BLG folk fondly embrace responsibility with a whiff of pride. "My work varies dramatically as an NQ, from practically managing arbitrations to assisting with the preparation of bundles", a young legal mind brags. "On the whole I feel as though I am gaining good exposure to litigation work." "Lots of client contact" is an additional advantage. The outward joy of involving oneself with "academically challenging and rewarding work" may also stem from BLG's "reasonable" hours—i.e., "no pressure to work late when not necessary", a rare corporate luxury. "One good thing, that I was a little surprised about, is that there appears to be no expectation that fee-earners will remain in the office simply for the sake of it", a pleased Londoner reports. Solicitors with the loftiest ambitions may not find any of this to be great news, however, as all of that sound work could very well lead to an occupational dead end: "The work is very good. The prospects of partnership for any senior associate are not", one seasoned lawyer divulges. Nevertheless the firm reports 11 new partners made up over the last three years.

Drinks and netball

BLG attorneys" rule of thumb is "work hard and play hard"—hardly surprising at a firm where "employees are often hired for character and social savoir-faire as well as being strongly capable lawyers." Though socialising is more prevalent in some practices than others (our condolences to the corporate team) and there are whispers of cliques excluding "outsiders" from events, the firm is broadly thought of as "friendly, collegiate [and] relaxed." Aside from firmwide events that include "all employees"—not just lawyers—there are "drinks, client events and sports teams" to be enjoyed. Some lawyers even find that they're more than just drinking buddies; "I count some of my team members as friends," a seventh-year shares. A younger peer concurs: "I have formed genuine friendships here." On the whole, "BLG has a very professional feel about it," raves a third-year. "… In terms of work, people and the social aspects of the firm, I think BLG does better then many firms in striking a good balance. My friends at other firms all seem to be leaving as soon as they have paid off their student loans!"

There is, of course, the opportunity to opt out of activities if you'd prefer the office be reserved for shuffling papers. "Thankfully, most people also have lives outside the office environment", according to a lawyer with some history at BLG. Agrees another source, "Lawyers do socialise together but there's plenty of scope for a life away from the firm." In fact, the mostly "nonpolitical" disposition of BLG leaves little fear of reprisal for those who'd rather polish the family silver than spend leisure time with workmates. The genial, "highly professional" and "open" office has "little or no politics between the fee earners"; we're told the "pretty political" partners reserve the game-playing for each other.

Who needs money when you have a subsidised canteen?

"Everyone thinks they should be paid more!" exclaims a contact. But at BLG that's not quite the truth; base salary strikes most as just, considering the hours worked. "Fairly good remuneration in all the circumstances. If you want a six-figure salary, find a Magic Circle or U.S. firm and until then, enjoy the sunlight while you can," quips a solicitor. A co-worker finds that benefits adequately balance out any monetary shortcomings: "In addition [to reasonable hours for salary] we receive subsidised gym membership, health insurance and employer contribution to our pension. The canteen is also subsidised." He does acknowledge that "Pay does vary between one department and other departments, even at the newly qualified level," a situation that can breed conflict. "My pay, for the work and hours I am undertaking at present is about what I would expect," explains a lawyer. "I know others, however, earning the same who are involved in cases which run their entire lives and I would say that their pay is too low." Chimes in a colleague, "Only by comparison to larger firms, compensation is too low, surprising given that the law we do is the same (as evidenced by the fact that all our cases are against the bigger firms)." "Can't expect Magic Circle wages if we're not doing Magic Circle hours," concedes a BLG employee. "However, more is expected of associates now than in the past so they should keep a close eye on the salaries of competitors to make sure they're in line with the types of firms we're often up against."

Bonus blues

The compensation issue that draws the greatest ire is the elusive bonus. The dangling carrot of many firms is nonexistent at BLG, offering solicitors "little financial incentive or recognition of hard work," gripes an attorney. The firm's fee earners all seem to agree that "bonuses ... based on the performance of a department would be beneficial and motivate [them]." Much of their annoyance is due to the firm's giving absolutely no extras "for the last four years despite rising profits." A situation, the same contact continues, that is "rather disheartening especially following a good year where the whole firm has worked extremely hard." Some see it more as an inequality among peers than an issue of greed at the top: "No bonuses—can be galling if you're getting exactly the same as people who put in far less hours and never overexert themselves when new work is being shared out."

Learning (or not) from the best

Quality by-the-book training is plentiful, with a "wide programme of good seminars and lectures" that is "comprehensive and tailored." It only strikes a sour note among one of the respondents, who feels—fairly we suspect—that "some of the "soft skills", management consultancy guru style role-play we could do without." Those who prefer a baptism-by-fire approach will find that without a firmwide "mentoring scheme" a good deal depends on the partners with whom one works. "Most are good at imparting knowledge and practice, although fewer take an interest in associates and their careers as individuals", comments a lawyer. As for mentoring, one insider opines "[it] could be better, if that is the sort of guidance you are looking for. There is very little day-to-day feedback, and certainly no career mentoring. You are only likely to hear anything if it is wrong and appraisals tend to be more of an HR exercise than a matter of career development. However, as a lawyer and working in an environment where you need a robust approach and a degree of self-confidence, worrying about a lack of partner validation is unlikely to be constructive."

Good for a drink and a laugh

Despite the tepid assessment of the firm's mentoring efforts, most Barlows insiders report that firm's management often "makes an effort to know the associates" and treat them with "the greatest of respect." As ever, there are a couple partners who are "not so good", but overall they are reportedly "social", "friendly" and "open." "[N]on-partners are rarely belittled or bullied", and superiors are eager to hear opinions and suggestions of minions at quarterly meetings. Despite their efforts, some solicitors do view partners with a degree of wariness and are prone to keep the relationship on a fee-earning, drinks-related level. "On a day-to-day basis partners treat associates with a great amount of respect and this is reflected by the associates", remarks an insider. "However, on the issue of promotion and partnership prospects the level of respect given to associates is a lot lower." In other words, the firm feels there are limits to what the rank-and-file need. As one source tells us, "In recent years there has been a concerted effort to inform staff of the firm's business and aspirations. Its effectiveness is, however, slightly unconvincing and the information we are given often has a Delphic quality. One would be wise to query its value and treat it with a degree of scepticism while staff should remember that they should not expect to be privy to partnership matters."

Beachcroft LLP

100 Fetter Lane
London EC4A 1BN
Phone: +44 (0)20 7242 1011
www.bwlaw.co.uk

OTHER LOCATIONS

Birmingham
Bristol
Brussels
Manchester
London (City)
Leeds
Winchester

THE STATS

No. of lawyers: 563
No. of offices: 8
Trainee intake: 38 (2006)
Trainees retained: 91% (2005)
Senior partner: Simon Hodson

MAJOR DEPARTMENTS & PRACTICES

Affinity Marketing • Banking & Finance • Catastrophic Injury • Commerce • Commercial Litigation • Commercial Tax • Company & Corporate • Construction & Engineering • Construction & Engineering • Corporate Finance • Data Protection & Privacy • Directors & Officers • Education • Employment • Employment Litigation • EU/Competition • Financial Services • Fraud • Health • Health Advice • Healthcare and Clinical Risk • Information Technology • Insolvency • Intellectual Property • Interactive Commerce & New Media • Pensions • Personal Injury • PFI/PPP • Private Clients and Trusts • Product Liability • Professional Advisers • Professional and Financial Risks • Property • Property Litigation • Public Law • Regulatory Counsel • Risk Counsel • Safety, Health & Environment • Sports Law • Technology & Commerce Telecommunications • Warranty & Indemnity

BASE SALARY

Trainee: £29,000
Newly Qualified: £48,000

GRADUATE RECRUITMENT CONTACT

E-mail: bwtrainee@bwlaw.co.uk

THE BUZZ
WHAT EMPLOYEES AT OTHER FIRMS ARE SAYING

- "Classy outfit"'
- "Pedestrian"

THE SCOOP

Back in 1999, three of the U.K.'s leading defendant personal injury law firms combined to form what is now Beachcroft LLP. Beachcroft Stanleys provided the City might—and specialisms in insurance, health care and commercial work—while Wansbroughs Willey Hargrave brought offices in Bristol, Leeds, Birmingham, London, Sheffield and Winchester. Throwing Vaudreys in Manchester into the mix created a 122-partner national law firm, headquartered in London and designed to service the insurance market as the industry itself consolidated nationwide.

Success insured

The first six years have had their bumpy moments, as consolidation of such a weighty practice took time. But this year Simon Hodson, the former head of commercial, was elected as the new senior partner, and Paul Murray, the former head of litigation, became managing partner, signalling a new generation raring to take the firm to the next stage. Though it may not have always been plain sailing, there are clear signs that Beachcroft has emerged from its combination a bigger and more serious force in the U.K. market. In 2004 its profits jumped some 25 per cent—something is clearly working.

And the secret to success? The three firms shared one vision, which was insurance. Beachcroft now makes most of its money in insurance and health care, doing a variety of work for the often massive companies in those sectors.

Rare mix

A healthy mix of commercial and litigation helps give the firm a counter-cyclical hedge—it is rare amongst the English law firms to find one like Beachcrofts, which is split right down the middle between litigation and commercial work. The firm's sector focus is not unique, but Beachcroft does it well: it focuses on financial institutions, company and corporate work, professional advisers, education and health. Financial institutions is still broadly a euphemism for insurance companies, though the firm is now trying hard to extend its reach into broader regulatory work for the banks.

For the last five years, the senior partner of the firm has been Lord Hunt of Wirral, the former conservative cabinet minister who left government in 1995 and returned to the firm as leader. He lives and breathes insurance and has done for 40 years: his decision to stand down this year, after 10 years at the helm, sees him stay on as a partner and focus on the financial services group. Hunt won a lifetime achievement award at the British Insurance Awards this year, and is also now acting as the first independent chairman of the Professional Standards Board of the Chartered Insurance Institute.

Historically the firm's largest client was the Solicitors' Indemnity Fund—the Law Society's own insurer for lawyers. That closed for new business in 2000, but though it appeared to be a dreadful blow to the new firm, it in fact prompted a strategic review that saw Beachcrofts fight back with gusto. Top clients are now a much more diverse list: Allianz Cornhill, Aviva, BAE Systems, Balfour Beatty and Zurich, to name but a few.

Project management

Outside of insurance, the firm's national presence has enabled Beachcrofts to stake its claim on the lucrative projects market, particularly private finance initiatives and public private partnerships. Hence the health care and education focus—both sectors have been huge beneficiaries of private investment into public projects. In all, Beachcrofts has advised on 60 PFI/PPP transactions, with health care projects ranging from discrete health facilities to whole hospital schemes. The firm acted for the Dudley Group of Hospitals NHS Trust on its PFI Scheme, which was, at the time, the largest PFI scheme to adopt the new standard form of contract, and for the Interserve/Kier/HSBC consortium on the Bro Morgannwg NHS Trust PFI Scheme in Wales, which is the largest health PFI Scheme in Wales to date. In education, the work ranges from the development of student accommodation to IT procurement for schools and developing higher education service delivery.

Like so many of its competitors, the drive for Beachcrofts now is to expand its relationships with the big clients it works for in insurance and projects, and start doing corporate and commercial work for them. Allianz Cornhill is a case in point—the firm now acts for it in all practice areas—for others like BAE Systems there is still an opportunity, at the moment it is still largely accident and serious incident claims that land at the firm.

Disputes and deals

While the bumper crop of litigation continues to feed growth at Beachcrofts, it has not been built at the expense of the non-contentious side. The firm continues a drive to balance its practice half and half: thus corporate work has had serious investment. Back in 2003, for instance, Beachcrofts hired corporate finance veteran Peter Jay from Finers Stephens Innocent, where he had been senior partner. Jay has energetically set to work building the firm's AIM practice—floating companies on the junior stock market at quite a rate. He worked on 11 IPOs in his first six months.

At the heart of the corporate strategy are technology and communications companies, so the firm does some fun work. Earlier this year it advised on the merger of independent computer games companies Traveller's Tales and Giant Interactive Entertainment, who combined to launch the LEGO *Star Wars* video game series.

A Chinese gamble

What's more, while the firm has no presence outside the U.K. bar a mini outpost in Brussels, the corporate guys nevertheless picked up work on China's lottery through Jay's efforts. The first non-Chinese company to obtain a legal betting license in China, Betex, hired the firm when it was appointed to manage the State Sports Lottery for the Chinese province of Guizhou. The firm also played host to a delegation of senior officials from the Prosecution Service of China this summer, and other anticorruption agencies of the Chinese government, when they visited on a trip aimed at increasing Anglo-Chinese cooperation in tackling corruption and serious financial crime.

Berwin Leighton Paisner LLP

Adelaide House
London Bridge
London EC4R 9HA
Phone: +44 (0)20 7760 1000
www.blplaw.com

OTHER LOCATIONS

Brussels
London (1 additional)

THE STATS

No. of lawyers: 525
No. of offices: 3
Trainee intake: 40 (2006)
Trainees retained: 82% (2005)
Managing partner: Neville Eisenberg

MAJOR DEPARTMENTS & PRACTICES

Alternative Dispute Resolution • Asset Finance • Banking & Capital Markets • Betting & Gaming • Charities • Commercial Contracts • Consumer Credit & Retail Finance • Contentious Trusts & Probate • Corporate Finance • Corporate Recovery • Data Protection • E-business • Employment, Pensions & Incentives • Energy, Natural Resources & Infrastructure • Engineering, Construction & Procurement • Environment • EU & Competition • Health • Health & Safety • Hotels • Insurance & Reinsurance • Intellectual Property • International Arbitration • Investment Management • IPOs • Leisure • Licensing • Litigation & Commercial Dispute Resolution • Media • Outsourcing • Planning • Private Equity & Venture Capital • Product Liability (Food Law) • Professional Indemnity • Project Finance • Property Finance • Public Private Partnerships (PPP) & Private Finance Initiative (PFI) • Public Sector • Real Estate • Real Estate Disputes • Retail • Shipping Finance • Tax—Corporate Tax • Tax—Trusts & Personal Tax Planning • Technology & Telecoms • Transport

BASE SALARY

Trainee: £30,000
Newly Qualified: £53,000

THE BUZZ
WHAT EMPLOYEES AT OTHER FIRMS ARE SAYING

- "Well respected"
- "High profile for its size, but why?"

GRADUATE RECRUITMENT CONTACT

Jennie Bishop
Graduate Recruitment and Trainee Manager
E-mail: traineerecruit@blplaw.com

THE SCOOP

In 2001, the merger of property firm Berwin Leighton and general commercial firm Paisner & Co created a 122-partner London outfit that did very little to excite the market at the time. How things have changed. Berwin Leighton Paisner is now arguably among the most dynamic law firms in the City—each year its profits and turnover jump substantially, and it continues to lure some of the best partners from its rivals.

More than the sum of its parts

Key to the success has undoubtedly been the scrupulous management of leader Neville Eisenberg, who spotted the opportunity in two sleepy mid-market firms. Berwin Leighton was a leader in real estate, but it was losing ground as the market got more complex: techniques like real estate securitisation were beyond its reach, though it acted for a good client base, including the likes of Tesco and British Land. Paisner & Co was similar in many ways, but fished in the even choppier waters of the City's mid-market corporate and commercial work. Its clients included Great Universal Stores, Forte Holdings and Penguin Books.

On merger, Eisenberg set out a strategy to build a three-dimensional firm, where property's dominance would be equalled by banking and finance, and corporate and commercial. In 2004, a total of 15 partners joined BLP from rivals—chief amongst them the former head of real estate from Clifford Chance, Robert MacGregor—while turnover surpassed £100 million and the average profit for each partner jumped from £425,000 to £570,000, a 34 per cent hike that was one of the biggest increases in the market. Three years in and there is no doubt that the merger is baring fruit: the firm won Law Firm of the Year at *The Lawyer* awards in 2004 and scooped Chambers and Partners U.K. Law Firm of the Year in 2005. The hat trick came with Eisenberg's nomination as Managing Partner of the Year at the *Legal Business* awards in 2005. Eisenberg, a bubbly South African, describes BLP as an "exciting, ambitious, challenging and dynamic organisation", and it's hard to argue.

Practice makes perfect

BLP remains an undisputed leader for property work in the U.K. The firm is now in the first tier of advisers on property finance, planning, projects and property litigation, acting for major clients like Tesco and The Crown Estate.

It has worked on some pretty iconic projects, currently advising on London Bridge Tower—the so-called "Shard of Glass"—the regeneration of Liverpool City Centre, and the redevelopment of Wood Wharf. In summer 2006, contracts drafted by BLP for its largest client, Tesco, have come under investigation by the Competition Commission. The firm admitted that contracts between Tesco and the North Norfolk District Council "prevented the council from selling land to rival supermarket chains." Despite the heat of the investigation, Tesco has declared its loyalty to the firm and claims "there is no reason why our relationship with BLP would be affected."

On the contentious side, the firm recently won a High Court complex titles dispute acting for a company that develops apartments on roof spaces in prestigious mansions in London.

On the corporate side, BLP has made serious efforts to penetrate both private equity work and corporate finance, particularly flotations on secondary U.K. stock market AIM. Legal 500 has placed the firm as the No. 1 legal advisor on AIM work for the last four years. The firm acted for Fat Face Holdings Limited when it was bought by Advent International in 2005 and for The Royal Bank of Scotland in refinancing the buyout of National Car Parks by private equity house Cinven. The AIM market is home to some of the most interesting companies growing up in London: the BLP team recently advised on the float of Raven Russia, a company set up to invest in Russian property, and on the IPO of Cyberscan Technology, a provider of downloadable gaming systems.

When it comes to finance, the firm now counts major institutions like Anglo Irish Bank, Barclays, Close Brothers, ING International, Legal & General, Schroders, UBS and Merrill Lynch amongst its clients. The practice is an established leader in privately funded public projects—both private finance initiatives and public private partnerships. BLP advised the Treasury on the refurbishment of its buildings in Whitehall, and the Home Office on its new HQ, and has recently been appointed to London Underground's panel of legal advisors in relation to its £30 billion PPP contracts for the refurbishment and upgrade of the tube network. The firm is also acting for private sector companies like AMEC and Vinci on such projects.

A third way

BLP has an appetite for doing things differently: in the middle of 2003 the firm embarked on a strategic review, with more than 100 task forces set up to do a bottom-up assessment of how to improve the firm. Every single person in the firm got a say—one result was a client care programme that is seen as one of the best in the City. The bottom-up review is cited by many as evidence the firm really does operate an open-door environment, where good ideas are not only listened to, but acted on as well.

Historically content with being a U.K. mid-market firm, BLP's ambitions have grown along with its size. Though the firm still has only one overseas office, in Brussels, it has recently set up formal alliances with U.S. firm Kramer Levin Naftalis & Frankel, and with Studio Santa Maria in Milan and Rome. Other continental link-ups are on the agenda, with Western Europe a priority, particularly Germany.

Good works

Closer to home, the firm is more committed than most to its charity efforts, and has a committee that nominates one charity a year on which to focus the form's efforts. In 2005, the firm picked The Coram Family, a little-known organisation that raises funds for disadvantaged and vulnerable children in London. The previous year, the Greater London Fund for the Blind was chosen, and the firm raised more than £50,000 for them through events that included a London to Paris bike ride by 50 of the partners and staff.

The firm is a patron of the Hayward Gallery in London and borrows works of art on a regular basis to display in its offices—brightening up the place for clients and visitors.

Recent pro bono projects include the 2012 London Olympic Bid and the new Museum in Docklands. The firm also acts for organisations like The Anne Frank Trust, Camden's "Food for All" programme, Jewish Care and the New Israel Fund.

Bird & Bird

90 Fetter Lane
London EC4A 1JP
Phone: +44 (0)20 7415 6000
www.twobirds.com

OTHER LOCATIONS

Beijing • Brussels • Paris • Düsseldorf • Frankfurt • Hong Kong • Lyon • Madrid • Munich • Milan • Rome • Stockholm • The Hague

MAJOR DEPARTMENTS & PRACTICES

Commercial
Corporate
Corporate Restructuring & Insolvency
Dispute Resolution
EU & Competition Law
Employment
Finance
Intellectual Property
Outsourcing
Privacy & Data Protection
Real Estate
Regulatory & Administrative Law
Tax

THE STATS

No. of lawyers: 483
No. of lawyers in London: 176
No. of offices: 14
Trainee intake: 25 (2006)
Trainees retained: 73% (2005)
Chief executive: David Kerr

BASE SALARY

Trainee: £28,000
Newly Qualified: £45,000

GRADUATE RECRUITMENT CONTACT

Lynne Walters
Graduate Recruitment Manager
E-mail: lynne.walters@twobirds.com

THE BUZZ
WHAT EMPLOYEES AT OTHER FIRMS ARE SAYING

- "Good at IP and branching out"
- "Great for IT & IP but not much else"

THE SCOOP

Founded in the City in 1846 as an IP boutique, today Bird & Bird is an international firm with specialities in eight sectors offering a full service across each. Bird & Bird, or "Two Birds" as it's sometimes known, may have been a start-up darling during the tech boom, but the firm's work for young companies was dwarfed by the work they had been doing and continue to do on behalf of clients such as major telcos and life sciences companies.

Sector specific

Unlike some perceived rivals—think Osborne Clarke and Olswang—Bird & Bird resisted layoffs when times got tough, and continued to invest in an international network now the envy of many of its peers. Like so many of the entrepreneurial law firms in London's mid-market, Bird & Bird has organised its practice by sector. The partners choose to specialise in either aviation and aerospace, banking and financial services, communications, e-commerce, IT, life sciences, media or sport. According to the firm, every time Bird & Bird opens a new office (there are now 14 in nine different countries), it does so with the aim of "replicating [its] full service, full sector approach."

Aviation and aerospace might look a bit odd here, though the firm would no doubt argue it is as high tech as any other sector. Recently the firm won a landmark ruling for the Board of Airline Representatives in Belgium. The firm successfully argued that a 10-year-old tax on every airline flying into Brussels National Airport was illegal.

What dotcom bust?

Bird & Bird can unleash some serious communications expertise. In 2005, the firm managed to convince highly-rated communications partner Graeme Maguire to jump ship from Linklaters. Maguire does telecoms, media and outsourcing work, and slots neatly into the Bird & Bird fold. The team recently worked on the initial public offering of Alternative Networks, one of the U.K.'s leading telecoms resellers.

Bird & Bird continues to make a tidy income from e-commerce work. Bumper fees are not the only concern though: the firm advised Oxfam pro bono on the launch of its online music site www.bignoisemusic.com. In outsourcing, the firm recently acted for Michelin in its €1 billion outsourcing agreement with IBM for all its European and North American IT needs.

Chocolate break

Many of the firm's partners have science degrees as well as legal qualifications, and at the heart of the firm is an IP practice that is one of the best in Europe. The team just advised Texas-based Smith International on a patents dispute with Halliburton, successfully contesting two patents Halliburton owned. On a lighter note, the firm won a case in the European Court of Justice for Nestlé, which was fighting to have its "Have a Break" slogan registered despite opposition from Mars. And in July 2006, Bird & Bird snagged the former head of Eversheds' IP and life sciences department, Sally Shorthose, to boost its own life sciences group.

Then there is the budding sports practice, with clients like the Football Association and the UEFA. The firm also has a team that does sponsorship and film finance work, the impressive client roster of which includes the London Organising Committee for the Olympic Games 2012 and Woody Allen.

International reach

Bird & Bird set off on a programme of international expansion that dented the profits but put some important flags in the ground. With 14 international offices, including three in Germany and two in Italy, it now has a good footprint. In May 2004, the firm opened its 10th international office in Beijing, which, when combined with Hong Kong, gives the firm building blocks for a China practice. The following year, three additional offices were launched in Madrid, Rome and Frankfurt. The firm's German presence has been beefed up to three offices. The idea is that Frankfurt is really the economic hub of the country, and that the Frankfurt office will focus on banking and finance, IT, aerospace and corporate work, while Düsseldorf and Munich continue to stick to the IP, telecoms and media bent. More recently the firm opened a second French office in Lyon. Bird & Bird now has more lawyers outside London than it does in it.

The global network certainly seems to have begun to deliver the large-scale TMT M&A work that Bird & Bird is after. In October 2005, in a deal involving a team of nearly 30 lawyers from all of the firm's 14 European and Asian offices, Bird & Bird advised the telecommunications division of the European Aeronautic Defence and Space Company (EADS) on its acquisition of Nokia's Professional Mobile Radio business. The acquisition created a line of business called EADS Secure Networks, which provides secure telecommunications systems to armed forces and the defence industry.

Strategic growth

Bird & Bird has evolved into a strong mid-market City firm with one of the most targeted strategies out there. Who would believe that in 1999 the firm had 51 partners and offices in London, Brussels and Hong Kong only? The firm now comprises 126 partners, with offices all over the place and a growth line that continues to head in the right direction.

The firm has collected awards for its efforts: Chambers & Partners named Two Birds as its Western Europe Communications/IP Law Firm of the Year 2005; *Legal Business* dubbed the firm TMT Team of the Year 2005; *The Lawyer* honoured the firm as its IP/IT Team of the Year 2005; and *Juve Handbuch* bestowed Bird & Bird with its Law Firm of the Year 2004/5 for Sport.

Cadwalader, Wickersham & Taft LLP

265 Strand
London WC2R 1BH
Phone: +44 (0)20 7170 8700
www.cadwalader.com

OTHER LOCATIONS

Beijing • Charlotte • New York • Washington, DC

MAJOR DEPARTMENTS & PRACTICES

Antitrust • Banking • Business Fraud • Corporate Finance • Corporate Governance • Environmental • Healthcare • Insolvency • Insurance & Reinsurance • Litigation • Mergers & Acquisitions • Private Client • Private Equity • Real Estate • Regulation Securitization • Securities & Financial Institutions • Structured Finance and Tax

THE BUZZ
WHAT EMPLOYEES AT OTHER FIRMS ARE SAYING

- "Well regarded"
- "Scary and American"

THE STATS

No. of lawyers: 583
No. of lawyers in London: 54
No. of offices: 5
Trainee intake: "Dependent on the needs of the business"
Trainees retained: 80% (2005)
London managing partner: Andrew Wilkinson

PLUSES

- Friendly colleagues
- High-quality work

MINUSES

- "Lack of transparency"
- Billable hours pressure

NOTABLE PERKS

- Laptops
- A lively social scene with firmwide social events every six weeks
- Several sporting teams including Netball, Cricket and Football
- Child care vouchers, corporate gym rates, cycle to work scheme, sabbatical programme

BASE SALARY

3rd-year solicitor: £85,000
5th-year solicitor: £117,500
6th-year solicitor: £122,500

GRADUATE RECRUITMENT CONTACT

E-mail: cwtinfo@cwt.com

THE SCOOP

Launched in 1997, Cadwalader's London office was its first outside of the United States. The firm hit the ground running with what remains one of the most successful lateral hires by any American law firm in London, the luring of Andrew Wilkinson from Clifford Chance. Recent high-profile lateral hires include Justin Jowitt and Angus Duncan from Allen & Overy, Christian Parker from Norton Rose and Peter Baldwin from Slaughter & May.

A bigger name now

If Wilkinson was a big name back then, he is an even bigger one now. As the office's managing partner, he has developed a practice in insolvency and restructuring that is stronger than that of most of the Magic Circle, albeit in a different part of the market. When companies run into trouble, the big English law firms have tended to advise either the corporations themselves, or the banks who lent them money. Cadwalader spotted the growing power and influence of unsecured creditors in the process—normally hedge funds and distressed high yield bondholders—and built a practice advising them.

The London office of Cadwalader is one of few with such a niche, and has thus picked up some real headline-grabbing work: we're talking Barings, Lloyd's, Maxwell and British Energy. Basically, if there's a big corporate blow-up in Europe, it's a fair bet that Cadwalader's London office will be involved.

Wilkinson sits on the global management committee of the firm, and is regularly amongst its top billers, as well as outperforming the vast majority of partners in rival law firms across London.

Debt pays

Still, with such a high-profile and lucrative flagship practice, Cadwalader has suffered that most inevitable of downsides—few appreciate that there is more to the firm than just restructuring.

There have been a few false starts with the ongoing bid to diversify the London practice. The firm is enormously profitable and, of course, that means it pays close attention to the bottom line. Thus various practices that have failed to make the grade have moved on: project finance and bank lending amongst them.

This year the City practice has moved firmly into growth mode though, and has attracted a run of strong lateral hires from the leading London law firm competitors. The drive now is in capital markets and structured finance —Cadwalader is a world leader in commercial mortgage-backed securitisations, which it pioneered in the U.S. and is now developing in Europe. Also growing is a strong contentious practice, largely advising financial institutions, and a corporate mergers and acquisitions team that will focus on work for the hedge funds that Wilkinson has managed to develop broader relationships with.

Banking culture clash

There was talk a few years back about moving in to advise the banks, and the London office hired a very high-profile partner by the name of Stephen Mostyn-Williams, who had in the past launched the U.K. finance practice for Shearman & Sterling. Alas it did not work out: Wilkinson's practice sees him regularly locking horns with banks on behalf of his clients, as rival creditors in work-out situations, and thus the firm has rubbed the London banking fraternity up the wrong way. Major U.S. financial institutions may not object to the two practices existing side-by-side, but Cadwalader has yet to convince them over here.

Only three of the firm's major practice areas are yet to be represented in Europe: the health care and not-for-profit work, private client, and securities and financial institution regulation. Certainly the latter seems unlikely to be far off, if the current pace of expansion continues.

City life

The London office of Cadwalader is unusual amongst the U.S. law firms here, being more than 60 per cent are staffed by English lawyers. Associate positions in London are routinely offered to Americans wishing to travel. The firm is also one of the more committed to diversity, and last year held firmwide training on diversity for all lawyers and staff. The firm ranked 39 in 154 for the percentage of minority lawyers in *The American Lawyer* 2005 Diversity Scorecard, and is in the top 25 U.S. law firms for Native American lawyers, and the top 10 for disabled American attorneys, according to *Multicultural Law Magazine*.

Old school do-gooders

The firm was founded in 1792 in New York's Wall Street financial district, and can therefore claim to be one of the oldest law practices in the United States. It remains headquartered in Lower Manhattan for over 200 years, despite many of its competitors moving to Midtown. Committed to the Downtown Manhattan area, Cadwalader took up government-backed incentives to stay in the area post-September 11th, and moved to new space in the World Financial Center for its home base.

Having been rocked by the terrorist attacks, the firm has recently offered its disaster recovery expertise to those affected by Hurricane Katrina, and made significant financial contributions to both the American Red Cross and the Salvation Army. The firm set up a resource directory on its web site for staff and clients who wanted to find ways to help out, and is offering pro bono legal advice to victims. Perhaps most innovative though, are the firm's efforts to provide employment to displaced people, by contacting job banks and hiring New Orleans-based law students for paralegal positions, for example. Like most American firms, Cadwalader takes such efforts very seriously, but its location, just blocks from Ground Zero, has heightened its awareness. Pro bono work since then has included representation of the surviving families of restaurant workers lost in the attacks, and advice and assistance to numerous Downtown small business owners whose retail operations were lost.

The London Pro Bono Committee in conjunction with The Bridge School at Islington and The Almeida Theatre was recently awarded a coveted grant from the Arts & Business Council to be used to fund a joint pro bono initiative. The project will involve specific training for participation in a series of workshops with the children, parents and staff at the Bridge School, the aim of which is to ease the school's transition to its new site later in 2006 or 2007. The grant secured is a significant one, won against fierce competition.

OUR SURVEY SAYS

A friendly place

Asked about the firm's culture, respondents painted a portrait of Cadwalader as a collegiate and congenial place. One junior solicitor describes the atmosphere as "informal and friendly", while another says the West End office is a "pleasant and relaxed" one. An "international mix of associates" contributes to the welcoming atmosphere where ample "opportunities to socialise with colleagues" exist. "The people with whom I work, and the clients for whom I work make my job very enjoyable" reports a third-year whose time is spent doing corporate finance and capital markets work. A senior colleague hailing from Oxford notes the combination of "early responsibility," a "variety of work" and a "supportive environment" as the key elements of job satisfaction at Cadwalader.

Oh, the hours

It is fortunate that the atmosphere at Cadwalader is so friendly because solicitors can expect to spend a fair deal of their time there. The hours can be challenging: "typical city hours" according to a sixth-year. Another senior solicitor describes the time requirement "long hours" that are "very demanding and stressful." "The hours are long," echoes a third-year solicitor, "but not nearly as bad as those worked in some other firms." "The nature of the work is that it can be quite seasonal," says another young solicitor, "and when deadlines are tight there is a lot to get done." Happily, there is a spirit of teamwork, as "people do help each other out a lot." That said, Cadwalader solicitors are paid handsomely for their time. "The salary", reports a senior solicitor wryly, "is what makes it worthwhile." A junior colleague is "happy with the firm's current policy on billable hours, bonuses and other financial incentives," finding little in the way of compensation to grouse over.

High marks for the partners

And what of those doling out the work? Relations between solicitors and partners are reportedly healthy: "the flow of information is good, the partnership fully understand that this is a people business and treat us well", reports a junior solicitor in capital markets. "The firm is very successful in keeping associates informed of firmwide decisions and provides ample opportunity (where appropriate) to participate in such decisions and provide feedback," agrees another junior solicitor. We are assured that "individual partners treat associates as equals and with respect at all times." In addition to respectful partners, junior solicitors can look forward to an "excellent" training program. "The training program", reports an insider, "is at its strongest at the more junior levels; at a more senior level there is less formal training and more coalface learning." If a Cadwalader solicitor cares to identify a specific training need, "the firm has always been good at providing funds for training."

Charles Russell LLP

8-10 New Fetter Lane
London EC4A 1RS
Phone: +44 (0)20 7203 5000
www.charlesrussell.co.uk

OTHER LOCATIONS

Cheltenham • Geneva • Guildford • Oxford

MAJOR DEPARTMENTS & PRACTICES

Employment & Pensions • Real Estate • Company Secretarial • Corporate & Commercial • Construction & Engineering • Corporate Finance • Corporate Tax • Charities • Clinical & Medical Negligence • Data Protection • EU & Competition • Energy • Insolvency • Insurance • Reinsurance • Intellectual Property • Litigation & Dispute Resolution • Healthcare • Rural Business & Landed Estates • Technology • Media & Defamation • Telecommunications • Sport & Leisure • Gaming • Private Client • Family • Personal Injury • Private Capital • Private Property • Trusts & Fiduciary Disputes

THE STATS

No. of lawyers: 268
No. of lawyers in London: 187
No. of offices: 4
Trainee intake: 15 (2005)
Trainees retained: 71% (2005)
Managing partner: Grant Howell

BASE SALARY

Trainee: £28,000
Newly Qualified: £46,000

GRADUATE RECRUITMENT CONTACT

Julia Dalton
E-mail:
   graduaterecruitment@charlesrussell.co.uk

THE BUZZ
WHAT EMPLOYEES AT OTHER FIRMS ARE SAYING

- "Excellent for private client"
- "Stuffy"

THE SCOOP

Charles Russell might not have the most exciting image, but there is more to this apparently sleepy midsized firm than sometimes catches the eye. What started as a family-run, private client law firm has evolved into a more commercial practice fit for the 21st century.

Private practice

Now, 70 per cent of Charles Russell's practice is made of up of corporate commercial work. That doesn't mean private client work has gone though: far from it. The firm hired a team of private client partners from Stephenson Harwood in 2004 to cement its position at the top of that market. Charles Russell used to be the firm of choice for rich Catholic families, and is now ironically one of the best divorce practices about. But though the landed gentry are less central to the firm's strategic direction nowadays, they still feed work into Cheltenham and Guildford, and drive many of the other practice areas. The firm also opened an office in Geneva in January 2006, headed by one of its leading private client lawyers, Catriona Syed.

As any private client lawyer will tell you, the trick is to win corporate work when these high-net-worth individuals either invest in hot, new, young companies, or move into senior positions in public companies. Both should, in theory, deliver a good flow of corporate work, and this is precisely Charles Russell's strategy. In the summer 2005, the firm opened an office in Oxford in a bid to boost its IT, bioscience, publishing and higher education workflow: it claims it can offer Oxford businesses access to City legal services on their own doorsteps.

Where Charles Russell has made real headway in the commercial arena is in its advice to clients wishing to float their businesses on the Alternative Investment Market, London's junior stock exchange. The firm continues to do a lot of IPOs, and not all for tech companies either. The team worked on the listing of gemstone mine operator and prospecting company Gemfields Resources plc, the reverse takeover of pharmaceutical company Lipoxen Technologies Limited by Greenchip Investments PLC and subsequent AIM admission, and advised Puma Minerals Corp., a 40 per cent owned subsidiary of Bema Gold Corporation on its CDN$12.3 million private share placement.

Media counsel for Sven-Göran Eriksson and others

The media and entertainment practice is also growing: clients include ITV and ITV News on compliance work, Channel 4, ntl and a whole host of actors in defamation cases against the press. The firm also acted for three senior Sussex police officers in a breach of confidence claim against Kent Police. In perhaps its most high-profile work, the firm is advising England football manager, Sven-Göran Eriksson.

Proving its institutional ties, the media and entertainment group is also advising the Ministry of Defence's Filming Policy Group on various contracts with media companies, including documentary film makers, film production companies, TV production companies and photographers and journalists. Sports clients now include The Jockey Club and Bolton Wanderers Football & Athletic Club, which the firm advises on general corporate and commercial matters.

Community player

Above all though, with its private client focus, Charles Russell has grown up with a real sense of community, and it demonstrates that more than most. The firm sponsors a number of festivals in Cheltenham, including the Cheltenham Music Festival and the Cheltenham Science Festival—even the Jazz Festival.

The firm's approach to environmental awareness is refreshing: it actually appears to care about the environmental approaches of its suppliers. It recycles its paper and bottles, and uses photocopying paper that is environmentally friendly, promising to replace every tree it cuts down. The vending machines use Fair Trade coffee, the water machines use biodegradable ecologically friendly cups and the archiving boxes are pulped and made into new ones. This is a firm that puts its money where its mouth is.

Going global

Charles Russell opened an office in Geneva, Switzerland, in January 2006. With over 50 per cent of its private client work now being international, Charles Russell says that the office will enable it to capitalise on its highly-rated private client team's existing international capabilities, including significant international trust structuring expertise, whilst offering clients with interests in Switzerland access to U.K. tax expertise and the support of a large U.K. team of English-qualified lawyers.

The firm is also a member of two international groups: the American Law Firm Association (Alfa) out of Chicago, and the Association of European Lawyers.

Alfa comprises 90 firms in the United States and 30 other international firms in Europe, South America and the Pacific Rim. In Europe, the Association of European Lawyers has around 29 members across the continent. Because the relationships with both groups are nonexclusive, Charles Russell markets itself as the independent firm that can either introduce you to overseas advisers, or work with your own choice of foreign law firm. It's a strategy that saves a lot of time and money when compared to the oft-overambitious plans of some other U.K. midsizers, though it has to be said that much of the firm's work remains domestically focused.

Onwards and upwards

There is little doubt that Charles Russell is expanding its range. The firm now derives almost three-quarters of its income from commercial work, a break from its private client past. The most recent expansion was into construction law. The firm hired David Savage from the London office of U.K. firm Hammonds to head its national construction practice, and he will lead a strategic drive into construction law. In theory, the firm says, such a practice is a natural step from the property development, property litigation and commercial work it is already doing. Also set for expansion are the telecommuniations group, which this year hired specialists Victoria Russell and Gabrielle Young, and the employment group, which hired Simon McMenemy to deal with the booming workload in its Guildford office.

Cleary Gottlieb Steen & Hamilton LLP

City Place House
55 Basinghall Street
London EC2V 5EH
Phone: +44 (0)20 7614 2200
www.clearygottlieb.com

OTHER LOCATIONS

Beijing • Brussels • Cologne • Frankfurt • Hong Kong • Milan • Moscow • New York • Paris • Rome • Tokyo • Washington, DC

MAJOR DEPARTMENTS & PRACTICES

Acquisition Finance • Antitrust & Competition (European and US) • Asia • Banking & Financial Institutions • Bankruptcy & Restructuring • Belgian Law • Corporate Governance • Derivatives • Employee Benefits • Energy • English Law • Environmental Law • French Law • German Law • High Yield Debt • Intellectual Property • International Trade • Italian Law • Latin America • Litigation & Arbitration • Mergers Acquisitions & Joint Ventures • Private Clients & Charitable Organisations • Private Equity • Privatisations • Pro Bono • Project Finance & Infrastructure • Real Estate • Russian Law • Securities & Capital Markets • Securities Enforcement • Sovereign Governments & International Institutions • Structured Finance • Tax

THE BUZZ
WHAT EMPLOYEES AT OTHER FIRMS ARE SAYING

- "Brilliant, international, pro bono-oriented"
- "Workaholics"

THE STATS

No. of lawyers: 850
No. of lawyers in London: 65
No. of offices: 13
Trainee intake: 5 (2005)
Trainees retained: 100% (2005)
Firmwide managing partner: Mark A. Walker

PLUSES

- "Pay, prestige, autonomy"
- Integrated international practice

MINUSES

- Tough hours
- Absence of some practice areas such as project finance and securitisation

NOTABLE PERKS

- Every associate has own office
- Gym membership

BASE SALARY

Trainee: £35,000
Newly Qualified: £85,000

GRADUATE RECRUITMENT CONTACT

Glen Scarcliffe
E-mail: lontraineerecruit@cgsh.com

THE SCOOP

Cleary Gottlieb was founded back in 1948 with two offices, one in New York, the other in Washington, D.C. Mr Cleary was a tax lawyer, Messrs Gottlieb and Steen were corporate and business lawyers, and, last but not least, Mr Hamilton was a litigator. Internationalism has been part of the fabric at Cleary Gottlieb since the firm's inception. Mr Hamilton went on to serve, during the Kennedy administration, as director of the U.S. Agency for International Development.

Early into Europe

In 1949, just a year after the firm was founded, it opened an office in Paris. It was thus one of the first American firms to launch in Europe, and did so on the back of advice to the French Government and in particular, Jean Monnet, one of the founding architects of European economic and political integration, on the implementation of the Marshall Plan. Through advising the French government on such a massive programme, Cleary Gottlieb built significant relationships, and sizeable expertise in international debt and equity capital markets.

It was the first firm to hire and train European lawyers, all of whom received some of their training in the U.S., and then was the first American firm to move into Brussels in 1960, when it spotted the opportunity to develop a practice based on what was then the fledgling European community. From the first, Cleary was intimately involved with the integration of Europe, representing the coal and steel community, the European Economic Community and Euratom. Today, the firm's European offices meet the needs of its multinational clients by employing a diverse team of lawyers from more than 50 countries. Cleary Gottlieb is going from strength to strength in Belgium in both its corporate and antitrust practices, with the firm being chosen as Western Europe, competition/antitrust law firm of the year in 2004 and 2005 by Chambers Global. Besides the deal for the Brussels International Airport, in late 2004 the firm got its first matter from Belgium's largest drugmaker, UCB, on the sale of its chemicals business for over $2 billion. The firm also advised on the Telenet IPO in 2005. Cleary Gottlieb acts locally for the Belgian Government, IBM and Coca-Cola. The firm also advised Sony in getting clearance from the European Commission in mid-2004 for its planned merger with BMG, a victory given similar mergers in the music business and other similar industries that have been blocked in recent years as being anticompetitive.

The rest of the continent

Cleary began practicing in Germany in 1991 and was recently chosen German law firm of the year in *JuVe*. The firm's Italian practice began in 1998 and received a significant boost from the lateral recruitment of Italian M&A partner Roberto Casati in 2004; the practice has recently worked on Italian law aspects of UniCredito's business combination with HVB, the largest cross-border M&A deal in the banking sector in Europe, resulting in one of the 10 largest European banking groups.

The U.K. way

In 1971, Cleary Gottlieb opened its doors in the City, but it was not until 1997 that it began to hire English lawyers. It added partners from Lovells and Travers Smith to start its corporate M&A practice, and since 2001, has complemented them with capital markets expertise, finance law and tax capability from other major English law firms. But the strategy has been one of slowly-but-surely, and also one of organic growth. Cleary Gottlieb was one of the first American law firms to promote an English assistant to its partnership in the U.K., and that continues to be the way it hopes to grow. Thus much of its English law recruitment is to the junior ranks, but those individuals are encouraged to aspire to the higher echelons of the firm. Cleary first took on trainees in 1998 and now has a small but well-established programme.

Share and share alike

Cleary Gottlieb is unusual amongst the major New York law firms in that it does not reward its partners according to their performance. All the partners get a share of the profits based on how long they have been in the firm, and every single partner gets a stake. So whether you have a bumper year or not, you will get paid the same as your classmates. Furthermore, whether you are in the highly profitable New York office or the fledgling Cologne operation, you will get the same. That makes for one of the most equitable firms out there, and is said to instil a culture of sharing work. Similarly, all associates are lock-step within each office, thereby, according to the firm, "allowing focus on work and avoiding negative politics or feelings."

Since every Cleary partner is supposedly working towards the same aim of improving the whole firm's performance, rather than just his own, the firm's London operation is largely built on work for clients that originally got to know the firm elsewhere and were subsequently referred to U.K. partners.

All the major investment banks are regular users of the firm's services, as are private equity houses like Texas Pacific. The firm has bagged some major roles on European deals through its strong contacts: it advised Euronext on its bid for the London Stock Exchange as a result of Paris connections, and currently represents Euronext on its proposed merger with the New York Stock Exchange—a deal that would result in the world's first transatlantic securities exchange; worked for Germany's HypoVereinsbank when it was the subject of a £10 billion bid from Italy's Unicredito; and is representing Mittal Steel in its proposed acquisition of Arcelor, with the firm advising on both corporate and competition aspects.

Changing face

Cleary went through something of a generational shift in 2005 or so, after the firm's managing partner in the U.S. Peter Karasz passed away following a four-year battle with cancer. Mark Walker, a New York-based finance partner, was elected to replace him, having been a partner since 1975. As a leading sovereign debt specialist, Walker has a remarkable international practice and has been credited with pushing the firm into further global investment. Hence Cleary only recently opened its doors in Cologne, Milan and Beijing, as reportedly some within the partnership began to fear it was losing its early advantage to hungrier competitors entering the market.

The other great gem of Cleary's European presence is its Russian practice, where the firm has handled assignments for the government since 1991. With an increasing number of Russian corporates now choosing to list on the London Stock Exchange instead of the more regulated New York exchanges, and also beginning to acquire assets outside their home countries, the work has been a boon to the London corporate team.

Cleary strives to be among the most democratic of law firms, and it is that dedication to one-partner, one-vote that some claim has led to such cautious overseas growth. Most of the major decisions of the firm are voted on by the partners, and the managing partner uses committees of partners and counsel to advise him on what to do. Membership of the committees rotates on a three-year basis, and lawyers cannot usually serve more than one term.

GETTING HIRED

Difficult and slow

Cleary Gottlieb's solicitors report that their firm has a strong and extremely competitive hiring program. "In 2005, we had 2,400 applications for five trainee places," reports a mergers and acquisitions specialist. "It's extremely difficult to get hired, either as a trainee or lateral." A fourth-year adds that applicants shouldn't expect the gruelling interview process to be quick, either. "the interview process took ages," he advises.

Here's how the firm describes its own hiring practices: "Cleary Gottlieb offers an informal and collegial working environment that fosters the professional and personal growth of our lawyers. We seek lawyers who are confident in their abilities and creative in their thinking ... We place a premium on openness, diversity, individuality and collegiality, and look for candidates who do so as well."

OUR SURVEY SAYS

Extremely! Fantastic! Challenging! International!

Cleary Gottlieb's solicitors profess to be wildly satisfied with their jobs and their firm.

"The quality of the work is fantastic," reports a second-year solicitor. "The lawyers are more academic and thoughtful than elsewhere," according to an M&A lawyer. The firm offers "extremely high levels of responsibility, especially compared to Magic Circle firms" and "very international work, including a lot of sovereign work," he adds. A tax attorney says that the "work is generally varied and challenging, which makes for an interesting time. The varying work has often put me outside my comfort zone, and through that I have learnt a heck of a lot."

Of course, the enthusiasm isn't universal. A third-year calls the firm a "generally pleasant and comparatively relaxed atmosphere", where attorneys are "granted considerable autonomy", but complains that the "office support is not as comprehensive as it should be."

Phenomenally! Friendly! Relaxed! Enjoyable!

Solicitors also use superlatives generously when describing the firm's culture. "The London office is phenomenally friendly", reports a second-year. "Generally, it appears, the firm only hires people that it likes to work with." A first-year calls Cleary Gottlieb's London office "relaxed, respectful, enjoyable and sociable." A fourth-year says the office is "generally a friendly place with easy to approach people and some colourful characters."

And great partners!

Cleary Gottlieb's solicitors have equally positive things to say about the firm's partners. "Junior solicitors are given tremendous responsibility and respect", enthuses one insider. A tax lawyer adds, "Partners treat assistants well and usually with good humour (no shouting, screaming or ranting in this office). No real feeling of assistants being involved in any decisions though."

All that enthusiasm aside, it's still a large firm

Though the solicitors love their firm, they would still like to be there a little less often, truth be told. They don't blame the firm, however, but rather the profession. "Long hours," complains a mergers and acquisitions solicitor. "Not as bad as some, but longer than Magic Circle firms." A tax attorney adds, "The days are always full, and a 6:30 p.m. departure time feels like a half day."

And, now that you mention it, what's with the training?

One area that could stand to improve, solicitors say, is the firm's formal and informal training. Training is "okay" one tax attorney reports, "but it is often cancelled due to workload. That said, if people ask for training in a particular area, then that training is given." A mergers expert adds, "English law training is mostly on-the-job, but structured training is increasing." Indeed, those who really want more training say that they have no problem getting it. "Extra training opportunities have been provided at my request, and Cleary has paid", says an antitrust attorney.

No complaints about the pay, though

Cleary's solicitors save some of their kindest words for the firm's compensation program. "One of the best things about the firm is that no compensation is dependent on chargeable hours or other targets, including bonuses," reports a second-year. "Salary and benefits are top of the market", adds a first-year, who has "no complaints." A fourth-year says, "I generally feel I earn more than I would at another firm, with the benefit of having no billable hours targets." Another benefit of the firm's compensation system is its effect on pro bono work. "There are no billable targets, so [it's] not an issue," reports a first-year.

Mixed reviews for the office space

The office space is a mixed bag, solicitors say. As one first-year puts it, "Our London office could be in a better building, but the offices themselves are very nice." A fourth-year adds, simply, "Having my own office is good."

Clifford Chance LLP

10 Upper Bank Street
London E14 5JJ
Phone: +44 (0)20 7006 1000
www.cliffordchance.com

OTHER LOCATIONS

Amsterdam • Bangkok • Barcelona • Beijing • Brussels • Budapest • Düsseldorf • Dubai • Frankfurt • Hong Kong • Luxembourg • Madrid • Milan • Moscow • Munich • New York • Padua • Paris • Prague • Rome • São Paulo • Shanghai • Silicon Valley • Singapore • Tokyo • Warsaw • Washington, DC

MAJOR DEPARTMENTS & PRACTICES

Antitrust/competition • Asset Management • Banking & Finance • Capital Markets • Commercial • Construction • Employment/Employee Benefits/Pensions • Environment • Financial Institutions & Markets • Insurance • Intellectual Property • Litigation • M&A/Corporate • PFI/PPP • Private Equity • Private Funds • Projects • Public Policy • Real Estate • Restructuring/Insolvency • Tax

THE BUZZ
WHAT EMPLOYEES AT OTHER FIRMS ARE SAYING

- "Professionally excellent, prestigious"
- "MegaCorp LLP"

THE STATS

No. of lawyers: 3,300
No. of lawyers in London: 1,200
No. of offices: 28
Trainee intake: 130 (2005)
Trainees retained: 95% (2005)
Senior partner: Stuart Popham

PLUSES

- "Steady stream of cross-border mega-deals"
- Excellent facilities

MINUSES

- Long, unpredictable hours
- "Size affects collegiality"

NOTABLE PERKS

- On-site pool and gym
- Games room
- On-site hairdresser

BASE SALARY

Trainee: £31,000
Newly Qualified: £55,000

GRADUATE RECRUITMENT CONTACT

www.cliffordchance.com/careers

THE SCOOP

In 1987, two somewhat non-descript London firms merged. The link-up of Coward Chance and Clifford Turner has long been hailed as the first U.K. merger of equals that really worked: bringing together the two firms' individual strengths in corporate and finance to create a full-service giant. If Clifford Chance was considered large back then, when it leapt into the top five U.K. law firms by dint of size, it is simply gigantic now. Perhaps buoyed by the success of that first merger, Clifford Chance was the English law firm that really grabbed internationalisation by the horns and began hoovering up firms across the world in the late 1990s.

Home is where the heart is

The turn of the 21st century saw Clifford Chance take on its biggest challenge yet, when it merged simultaneously with Rogers & Wells in New York and Punder Volhard Weber & Axster in Germany. Suddenly the firm became the world's largest, with 2,700 lawyers spread across the globe. Integrating those practices was no mean feat.

Unlike its closest rival in terms of size, Baker & McKenzie, Clifford Chance has never tried to shift its centre of emphasis away from its roots, and remains very much a London firm. In 2005, the firm's managing partner, Peter Cornell, announced that he would be spending more time in the New York office—beset as it was with ongoing post-merger teething troubles—but the rest of the management is holed up in the firm's brand new headquarters in Canary Wharf. Cornell took the reins in 2002 and has since sorted out a messy U.S. strategy—which had involved significant expansion, and then retreat, in California. The plan now is to focus attention on the firm's largest clients wherever they operate, and for the most part these are significant financial institutions. In early 2006, the firm announced that Peter Cornell would stand down as managing partner. David Childs took over the position in May 2006.

Three pillars

To call Clifford Chance a finance firm is perhaps unfair these days, though however well Clifford Chance does in M&A tables, rivals will continue to claim it is really a banking powerhouse. Most recently, the firm topped the charts for completed deals both worldwide and in Europe, according to Thomson Financial's M&A review for the first half of 2006. The truth is corporate, finance and litigation are three pillars of an incredibly stable stool. A list of deals would be too lengthy to mention here. Suffice it to say that Clifford Chance is genuinely up there in the largest corporate work (it remains the best firm in the City for private equity work), for dispute resolution, for real estate, for banking and capital markets, and for much, much more. In one month in 2006, the firm acted for eBay in its $2.6 billion acquisition of Skype Technologies; and worked on Gas Natural's whopping €42.5 billion bid for Endesa in Spain. Clifford Chance is currently advising Siemens on the €16bn merger of its network division with that of Nokia to create the Nokia Siemens Networks.

And such strength is now broadly replicated across the globe. The firm received some awful press for pushing associates too hard in the New York outpost—another reason Cornell flew in—but broadly speaking, the partners are a down-to-earth bunch and the firm is right up there amongst the top cabal of law firms in each jurisdiction in which it operates.

Onwards and upwards

Working out where to go next could be a problem, and there are some who worried a year or so ago that Clifford Chance had hit a ceiling. Global revenue came close to touching the £1 billion mark in 2002, but instead came in just shy. Global revenue for 2005 came in at £915 million. But the firm's latest financial results should put the doubts to rest: in May 2006 the firm predicted that 2005-2006 revenue would exceed £1 billion, making Clifford Chance the first British firm to hit the billion-pound mark. Still, that hasn't stopped the management spending some serious money on an external consultancy to look at where it should go from here. The firm broke the mould of professional services firms when it hired experts to look at three scenarios for the world going forward: What if China invades Taiwan? What if America adopts an isolationist foreign policy? Or what if globalisation were reversed? For each scenario, the firm now knows how its clients would be likely to react, and most importantly, what they would expect from their lawyers. It's certainly forward thinking, though one wonders what the partners will think of those consultancy fees if not one scenario comes to fruition.

For now, the firm is focusing some serious energies on cutting costs and getting rid of some of the duplication that remains from the last set of mergers. There is no need for a human resources team in each European office, for example, they say. The result of such clear thinking: Clifford Chance is picking up a healthy stack of awards of late. In 2006, the firm has won the EVCJ Private Equity Law Firm of the Year and Best European Firm (Transactions) in the

PrivateEquityOnline.com awards and it won Corporate Team of the Year at *The Lawyer* Awards 2005 for work on the mammoth restructuring of British Energy. At the 2006 The Lawyer Awards, Clifford Chance was crowned Law Firm of the Year. Clifford Chance was also named Global Banking Law Firm of the Year 2006 in the *Who's Who* Legal Awards and Law Firm of the Year at *IFLR*'s seventh European Awards ceremony. The firm also won Dutch Law Firm of the Year, Securitization Team of the Year, Restructuring Team of the Year, Restructuring Deal of the Year—Parmalat, M&A Deal of the Year—Unicredito/HVB and Project Finance Deal of the Year—Shuaibah Power Plant.

But it's not all mergers and complicated financial transactions. The firm was also appointed official advisor to the Hutton Inquiry, the investigation into the death of Iraq arms expert Dr. David Kelly, and assisted in the independent review surrounding the deaths of four soldiers at Princess Royal Barracks, Deepcut. Clifford Chance is among five firms appointed to the Olympic Delivery Authority's legal panel, and London partner Chris Bates was recently named to the European Commission's securities task force. Clifford Chance was the first U.K. firm to sign up to the Solicitors' Pro Bono Group and Bar Pro Bono Unit's joint agreement, pledging to freely donate a certain amount of legal work each year.

GETTING HIRED

Openminded

If one was to suggest that Clifford Chance is less selective than its Magic Circle brethren, the firm's partners would no doubt object. Yet, Clifford Chance's very own solicitors say as much. Aside from noting the standard expectation of a 2:1 degree level, insiders report that Clifford Chance is a bit more, oh, flexible, than its rivals. "Assuming you have the basic intelligence/skills, [getting hired] doesn't seem to be that difficult," muses a source. "I know examples of people who don't have great degrees for one reason or another but the firm was willing to look past that." Winning an offer is "possibly not as hard as it should be," concedes a colleague, who goes on to note, "The firm is openminded about hiring non-Oxbridge candidates, which is great, but should seek to increase the number of offers to laterals that are accepted—they all get offers from several Magic Circle firms and Clifford Chance should try to up the rate of conversion of offers into hires."

OUR SURVEY SAYS

International intrigue

Clifford Chance's "very open culture" is "friendly" and "less snobby than other Magic Circle firms," claim sources. A number of solicitors credit the "diverse" employee pool of the firm, which has a "greater mix of people than what you find elsewhere." One happy source tells us it's a "pleasure to work in a truly international environment with none of the stuffiness usually associated with City solicitors." The firm is "very internationally-minded", agrees a co-worker, "[and] most lawyers are bilingual."

The firm is also considered "informal, unpretentious, hardworking, [and] cosmopolitan," reports a fan. Another contented solicitor characterizes the firm culture as "supportive, empowering, exciting ... cutting-edge." Social activity at the firm depends largely on the department; some have social committees to plan events, while others lay low. There's "not a huge amount of socialising after the first two to three years' PQE", but the firm does have extracurricular activities for its solicitors, such as sports teams and "an art club." Those who began with the firm as trainees may be a little more social, explains a source, "as you were obviously thrust in at the deep end with 60 other people, and that tends to build a bond between those people."

Work on the cutting edge

The work at Clifford Chance is characterised by its "challenging and cutting-edge" nature, making for a "very interesting, varied, intellectually stimulating job" that offers opportunities early. "Very good variety of work and support to diversify your practice and to develop professionally," says a lawyer of the firm and its cases. "Encourages initiative at all levels. Very good level of responsibility and involvement in all aspects including entertainment and business development." The firm's "top class" tasks "will also give one better and more international deal experience than many other firms," a fourth-year comments. Still, much "depends on the team you work with," cautions a contact; as one attorney explains, "I am not sure banking work can ever be entirely fulfilling, but quality work certainly abounds and we take on complex transactions very early on."

Flex-time over face time

Unfortunately, even with the best of work, the hours at Clifford Chance can take their toll. "The work is very interesting," agrees an insider on his way out, "but I often feel pulled in many different directions so cannot do the work to the best of my ability. Lack of control over hours is a major factor in why I'm leaving." Adds a colleague, "When busy on a transaction I resent the fact that I am assumed not to have any 'me time', even for important personal commitments, and that even on quiet days it is hard to commit to evening plans as something may come in at the last minute." But solicitors appreciate that partners are "compassionate with leave for appointments/deliveries" as well as a host of other "personal matters", and are also "flexible" about part-time schedules. And face time is irrelevant; "as long as you get the work done, no one cares how long you are in the office." Still, the balance between professional and private duties remains wobbly at the firm, though "great efforts are now being made to address this," a solicitor tells us. "However, if you want to get to partnership, you need to put in the hours."

Bridging the great divide

Relations between partners and solicitors are reportedly "very good", with "daily contact and support" and "increased emphasis on keeping people informed." In keeping with this trend, the firm "has established an employee forum which has participants from all business areas (lawyers from each practice area, secretaries, HR, etc.) as a soundboard for firmwide decisions." "Feedback on work/career could be better", and though things between the partners and their underlings are "informal, cordial and generally very good", a solicitor ventures that the reality is that still "there is quite a big ... divide." "They just inhabit a different world," the source explains. Partners are aware, however, that training is an absolute necessity, and they have made CC's "excellent." There are online, day courses and residential training courses', including "two-day long off-site[s]" and "immersion" courses, which often include colleagues from across Europe. And it's not just for beginners; continuing education is also readily available. Informal training is also on tap, but lack of time can make it difficult to take advantage of, and some feel it "would be useful to have mentoring more formalised at a higher PQE level." There can be a sense that such guidance is out of reach, however; says one lawyer, "Very good mentoring and excellent support for fee-earners who are 'rated'."

Money talks

But as is often the way, solicitors measure their partners' true appreciation by their compensation. Many feel that "base salary is too low across the board" and "a shift to a U.S. firm is an increasingly attractive prospect." But the most annoyance is reserved for bonuses, which "are virtually nonexistent as an NQ" and "linked to billable hours and internal grading in a fairly complex formula." "The bonus system works well for me," remarks an attorney, "though many are frustrated with the 'rationing' of higher grades for the quality of their performance." Further explanation reveals that "bonuses are given on a quota system so obviously [they are] only going to go to those the firm is most scared of losing." We're also told by a source who adds that "while in the great scheme of things my salary is good, on an hourly rate I'd be as well off temping." Offers another solicitor, "The only frustration I have is that those working in-house can earn half of my annual salary in one day (bonus payment day) for working fewer hours." The firm itself comments: "[W]e believe that we have the most generous bonus scheme in the sector, we do also recognise concerns about the way in which it is structured. We continue look at ways of improving our approach to reward."

Clyde & Co

51 Eastcheap
London, EC3M1JP
Phone: +44 (0)20 7623 1244
www.clydeco.com

OTHER LOCATIONS

Abu Dhabi • Belgrade* • Caracus • Cardiff • Dubai • Guildford • Hong Kong • London (1 additional) • Los Angeles • Moscow • Nantes • New York • Paris • Piraeus • Singapore • St. Petersburg*
* associate offices

MAJOR DEPARTMENTS & PRACTICES

Aviation/Aerospace • Corporate/Commercial • Corporate Recovery/Insolvency • Dispute Resolution • EC/WTO • Employment • Energy • Insurance/Reinsurance • International Finance • International Trade • IP/IT • Marine/Transport • Property/Construction • Regulatory

THE STATS

No. of lawyers: 420
No. of lawyers in London: 330
No. of offices: 16 (including 2 associate offices)
Trainee intake: 20 (2004)
Trainees retained: 100% (2004)
Senior partner: Michael Payton

BASE SALARY

Trainee: £29,000
Newly Qualified: £50,000

GRADUATE RECRUITMENT CONTACT

E-mail: theanswers@clydeco.com

THE BUZZ
WHAT EMPLOYEES AT OTHER FIRMS ARE SAYING

- "Top dog in shipping"
- "Always the bridesmaid"

THE SCOOP

Clyde & Co was founded back in 1933 by Scottish lawyer Richard Arthur Clyde. He had left a firm of City marine lawyers to start up on his own, and immediately managed to attract instructions from Lloyd's underwriters and insurance companies. Not much has changed since. In 1977 a serious fire badly damaged the London office. But you would expect a firm that makes its living in the cutthroat market of insurance to take all this in its stride, and it did. Ever since 1981, the firm has been on an enviable growth curve, expanding internationally and diversifying its practice whilst always staying true to its insurance and transport roots.

Practice makes perfect

Indeed, Clyde & Co has made its name in the shipping industry, and in insurance and reinsurance. So its practice booms, in large part, when others are having a tough time. The firm was heavily involved in claims arising from September 11th, when it devised a special evaluation scheme that allowed £28.7 billion of claims to be processed more quickly. It also worked on disputes coming out of the collapse of Enron, and was then the first international law firm to enter Iraq after the war, hoping to get a share of the reconstruction work. The firm gained a toehold through an alliance with a local firm—even the plucky guys at Clyde & Co concede it is still too dangerous to put their own lawyers on the ground in the country.

The firm's commercial litigation practice is one of the best in the City, and when it's not disputing insurance claims, it gets involved in other really interesting matters. The firm just launched a claim on behalf of 30 claimants in a dispute about artworks lost in a fire in an East End warehouse in 2005 that hit the headlines. The claimants blame Momart for incorrectly storing the art.

The team also waded in on a dispute about the sales of tickets for the World Cup 2006, representing the Consumer Association in a successful EU claim against FIFA, the Deutsche Fussball Bund and Mastercard. The selling arrangements have now been changed so that football fans across the EU can pay for tickets through bank accounts in their own countries, in their own currency.

Corporate ambition

It's not all disputes work though. Amazingly, the firm's senior partner, Michael Payton, has been in the post since 1984, and his leadership has been characterised by diversification of the firm into more corporate and commercial work. Payton won *Legal Business* magazine's Senior Partner of the Year award in 2004, and despite more than 20 years in the job, continues to push the firm on to new heights.

The strategy is now, Clyde & Co says, to become "the premier law firm in insurance, transportation, trade and natural resources, providing a full service to an international client base." Thus the corporate work has that angle running through it: the firm advised Guardian General on its acquisition of the Zenith group of insurance companies; advised Heritage Underwriting Agency on its proposed merger of Syndicates 1200 and 1245 at Lloyd's; and helped investment trust company Caledonia with its second round of investment in the holding company of the Oval group of insurance brokers.

The firm is fast-developing a technology practice too, and does an increasing amount of work on the secondary stock market AIM. The team just acted on the first float of a Norwegian company on AIM, helping Westhouse Securities on the IPO of Jumpit, which develops rechargeable and disposable batteries for handheld devices. The outsourcing team is doing well too, recently working for Group 4 Securicor on a 10-year outsourcing deal in which Securicor and Alliance & Leicester will together provide Abbey National with cash for its branches and bank machines.

The firm is certainly in expansion mode, and continues to hoover up great partners from its rivals whenever it gets the chance. Most recently, the firm announced a merger with aviation boutique Beaumont and Son, creating an aviation division that will be branded as "Beaumont and Son—Aviation at Clyde & Co." Beaumonts advises the airline industry and its insurers, and works with many of the world's airlines, including start-ups and low cost carriers. The firm needed more resources though, and Clyde & Co happened to be looking for more airline work, so the two should make a good fit. The firm also added some aviation litigation experience on the other side of the pond, when it poached four partners from U.S. firm Condon & Forsyth in June 2006. The move gives Clyde & Co a foothold on American shores, with offices in New York and Los Angeles.

Worldwide

When it comes to expansion, Clyde & Co just can't get enough of international work. The firm's attitude is typified by its work for the WTO: at the end of 2004 it was one of eight law firms to be appointed to the panel of the Advisory Centre on WTO Law, an independent legal aid organisation set up to give representation to developing countries that can't otherwise afford to bring WTO litigation.

The countries that Clyde & Co is interested in are not always the obvious economic centres. At the end of 2004 the firm opened its doors in Abu Dhabi, its third office in the United Arab Emirates, after Dubai and Dubai Media City. Then in summer 2006 came Moscow, adding to the firm's 13-year association with a firm in St. Petersburg. The office will focus on corporate work: the firm says it has a whole host of clients now looking at Russia, and knows Russians seeking to invest abroad.

Clyde & Co is also one of the few firms with two offices in the Southeast of England, with both London and Guildford. Guildford was originally set up in 1969, when office rents in the City were reaching extortionate levels and the firm decided to relocate its back office function, and two partners. It subsequently grew to become the firm's second-largest office, doing all kinds of national and international work with the benefit of a lower cost base. Also closer to home, the firm is one of the founder members of the U.K.'s Solicitors Pro Bono Group, and indeed this year's SPBG chairman is Clyde & Co partner Paul Newdick, the firm's head of employment.

CMS Cameron McKenna LLP

Mitre House
160 Aldersgate Street
London EC1A 4DD
Phone: +44 (0)20 7367 3000
www.law-now.com

OTHER LOCATIONS

Aberdeen • Amsterdam • Arnhem • Beijing • Belgrade • Berlin • Bratislava • Bristol • Brussels • Bucharest • Budapest • Buenos Aires • Casablanca • Chemnitz • Dresden • Düsseldorf • Edinburgh • Frankfurt • Hamburg • Hilversum • Hong Kong • Leipzig • Lyon • Madrid • Marbella • Milan • Montevideo • Moscow • Munich • New York • Paris • Prague • Rome • São Paolo • Seville • Shanghai • Sofia • Strasbourg • Stuttgart • Utrecht • Vienna • Warsaw • Zagreb • Zurich
(list includes associated offices)

MAJOR DEPARTMENTS & PRACTICES

Banking & International Finance • Commercial • Construction • Corporate • Dispute Resolution • Energy • Financial Services • Acquisitions & Disposals • Restructurings • HR Services • Healthcare • IT • Insurance • Projects • Real Estate • Tax

THE BUZZ
WHAT EMPLOYEES AT OTHER FIRMS ARE SAYING

- "Good all-rounder"
- "Not a player"

THE STATS

No. of lawyers: 770
No. of lawyers in London: 530
No. of offices: 8
Trainee intake: 80 (2004)
Trainees retained: 90% (2004)
Managing partner: Dick Tyler

BASE SALARY

Trainee: £28,000
Newly Qualified: £50,000

GRADUATE RECRUITMENT CONTACT

E-mail: gradrec@cmck.com

THE SCOOP

CMS Cameron McKenna attributes its lengthy moniker to two things: first the merger in 1997 of U.K. firms McKenna & Co and Cameron Markby Hewitt, and second its founder membership of the CMS alliance. CMS was set up in 1999 and brings together nine European law firms with the common CMS prefix. Between them they cover 47 cities and boast 575 partners. The English branch launched it all, alongside the German, Austrian, Dutch and Belgian firms, while others have joined later.

Different drivers

It's a pretty joined-up approach, and allows Camerons to boast of an international offering without the hefty financial outlay. The U.K. firm also has its own overseas offices in the Czech Republic, Moscow and Romania, and further afield in Hong Kong. What's more, the presence in Britain extends beyond London to Aberdeen, Bristol and Edinburgh.

Camerons is the 10th-largest law firm in London by turnover, but unlike many of its larger rivals, it is not driven so hard by corporate finance and capital markets. Instead, there are certain sectors where Camerons is a real leader, namely project finance, energy, insurance and financial institutions.

Diverse initiatives

The energy, projects and construction group is one of the firm's leaders, with a client list that includes the big names like Taylor Woodrow, AMEC, Metronet, BP and Alfred McAlpine. The deals list of the last few years is one most competitors would give their eye-teeth for: highlights were acting for National Grid Transco on the £5.8 billion sell-off of its regional gas distribution networks, and working for Metronet on the public-private partnership project for the London Underground. Both tasks kept huge teams of lawyers busy.

For a long time, U.K. retail bank Lloyds TSB was Camerons' biggest client by some margin. More recently however, firm has made diversification—despite the potential risk of alienating Lloyds TSB—a strategic imperative. So far, there have been no signs of trouble with new strategy. In 2004, the firm continued to keep Lloyds as an important customer, and advised it on funding loans to domestic corporates like Ocado—the online supermarket—and financing the management buy-in of DIY retailer Robert Dyas. Elsewhere on the financial institutions side, the firm won a place on the panel of Lloyds rival HSBC last year, and continues to do major transactions for National Australia Bank.

Thanks, Eliott

And then there is insurance, a hot area in 2005 when Eliot Spitzer, the attorney general in New York, decided to investigate the industry and crack down on misbehaviour. Camerons has a roster of clients to die for, and was called in by a number to give a clean bill of regulatory health. The firm's contentious and non-contentious insurance teams are spread across London and Bristol, and cover aviation and aerospace, directors and officers, professional indemnity, and general major insurance and reinsurance work.

In 2005, the firm decided to focus its energies on relationships with 25 to 30 major clients, and hence the big-name client list keeps on growing. The other key panel appointments last year were for General Electric and Accenture, while the firm did a good run of M&A deals for ABN Amro Capital.

Heading east

Despite the existence of the CMS alliance, it's fair to say Camerons' international strategy has had a few incarnations, and the big hiccup came in 2003 when the firm announced it was to refocus its Asian operations. The firm closed Beijing and now does only insurance work out of Hong Kong, which meant some departures and a fair amount of bad press. The Hong Kong office had been full service, and had contributed 5 per cent to the firm's bottom line, but gone were private equity, insolvency and litigation, and instead came what has grown into a very successful targeted office.

The firm shut Washington, D.C. as well, so that investment is now driven into the CMS alliance and a sizeable Eastern European practice. That group of offices—Moscow, Romania and the Czech Republic—is doing well, and in 2005 was awarded Eastern European Law Firm of the Year at the Chambers Global Awards. Deals included the €735 million acquisition of the Bulgarian Telecoms Company, and the sale of Slovenske Elektrarne to Enel, one of the world's largest cross-border electricity deals. The firm built out its Moscow office with the hire of five lawyers from Coudert Brothers when that firm collapsed in 2005.

People power

With work levels all going in the right direction, Camerons spent much of 2004 working out how to better differentiate itself in the crowded mid-tier of the U.K. legal market, and decided the key was to compete on the way it treated its people. Camerons was the first law firm to publish a human capital report, looking at how its staff were looked after and telling clients. The changes are coming from the top down: the firm has restructured its partnership so that everyone with the title of partner now gets a share of the equity. That means Camerons is moving against the trend, as rivals increasingly introduce ranks of "salaried partners", with the title but not the stake in the business or say in the management that the name suggests. Camerons says it is all about improving the culture, and making sure everyone is pulling in the same direction. The firm claims to be different from the rest of the market because it puts "organising, coaching and developing" its people at the heart of the business strategy. Certainly lots of others say the same, but the rhetoric put the firm into the *Sunday Times* list of The Top 100 Companies to Work For in both 2002 and 2003, which is no mean feat.

Part of being good to your people is also about being good to the rest of the community. The firm has a Community Affairs Programme that covers pro bono, employee volunteering and charity giving. Camerons picks a charity each year and matches employee donations, choosing The Samaritans for 2005. There is also a significant smattering of free representation for death row prisoners in the Bahamas, with the firm particularly active at the Fox Hill Prison in Nassau. With an entrenched environmental policy in place as well, Camerons appears to be pursuing the old dream of "doing well by doing good."

Covington & Burling LLP

265 Strand
London WC2R 1BH
Phone: +44 (0)20 7067 2000
www.cov.com

OTHER LOCATIONS

Brussels • New York • San Francisco • Washington, DC

MAJOR DEPARTMENTS & PRACTICES

Antitrust/Consumer Protection • Communications & Media • Energy • Environmental • EU Law & Regulation • Financial Institutions • Food & Drug/Life Sciences • Government Affairs • International Trade • Sport • Technology & Software • Transportation • Litigation • Appeals/Supreme Court • Arbitration & ADR • Insurance Coverage • Intellectual Property • Securities • Trials • White Collar • Bankruptcy & Restructuring • Corporate Governance • Employee Benefits • Structured & Debt Finance • Mergers & Acquisitions • Private Equity • Securities • Taxation • Technology Transactions

THE STATS

No. of lawyers: 670
No. of lawyers in London: 51
No. of offices: 5
Trainee intake: 4 (2005)
London managing partner: John Rupp
London deputy managing partner: Edward Britton

PLUSES

- Closeknit environment
- Strong client list

MINUSES

- "Secretive management decisions"
- Not yet well known in London

NOTABLE PERKS

- One month paid paternity leave
- Frequent trips across the pond

BASE SALARY

Trainee: £30,000
Newly Qualified: £70,000

GRADUATE RECRUITMENT CONTACT

E-mail: graduate@cov.com

THE BUZZ
WHAT EMPLOYEES AT OTHER FIRMS ARE SAYING

- "Solid US firm"
- "Tiny in London"

THE SCOOP

Covington & Burling was founded in Washington, D.C. in 1919 by two lawyers who predicted an era of more pervasive federal legislation, regulation and taxation. How right they were—today the firm has 415 lawyers in America's capital city alone, representing companies from all over the world. Some of these clients still come to the firm primarily for assistance in navigating matters involving the U.S. government. However, the firm now, with five offices and over 590 fee earners, services client needs of all kinds.

Sector focus

Covington's heart, then, is in the regulated industries and public service. The firm opened in London in 1988, its first overseas office, with the ambition of selling such expertise to Europeans. The practice here centres to a large extent on M&A, private equity and other corporate transactions, as well as litigation and international arbitration for a broad number of clients. In addition, the office provides regulatory and policy advice, as well as corporate and dispute resolution expertise, to a large number of life sciences, technology and telecommunications clients. The London office lawyers early on developed special expertise in software and internet policy, antipiracy and electronic commerce. In 2005, the firm won the "Best Achievement in Protecting IP on the Internet" Award at the WORLDLeaders European Awards in London. The firm also advises on intellectual property, transactions and the regulatory environment for both major international pharmaceutical companies and smaller emerging biotechnology groups. Covington consistently earns plaudits for its expertise in life sciences, including being ranked as the No. 1 life sciences firm in the world for 2005 in a survey of industry and private practice lawyers conducted by *Global Counsel*, which assessed a broad range of legal services including corporate partnering, IP, competition, product liability, regulatory and commercial law.

There is capability in London in U.K., U.S. and international M&A and other corporate transactions, international tax planning, antipiracy, U.S. and European food and drug regulatory matters, data protection, litigation and arbitration, and licensing, to name but a few. Like most firms rooted in D.C., many of the firm's strengths lie in its deep knowledge of certain sectors, making the very most of its regulatory expertise. On the antitrust side, it is a clear leader, opening in Brussels in 1990 to offer European law advice hand-in-hand with U.S. law, something clients were apparently crying out for as their businesses butted into lawmakers on both sides of the Atlantic simultaneously.

Client calling

Though Washington remains the heart of the firm, with the bulk of its lawyers, Covington is a very joined-up organisation, with Europe having been the originator of some of its biggest clients. On the tech side, the firm now counts Microsoft as a major client, and that work was initially won in London. An initial instruction to a U.K.-based lawyer at the firm on what seemed like a minor matter was built on, and grew. The client was introduced to colleagues in the U.S., and now makes use of the firm's expertise across many practice areas. Another example of the integrated approach was in the firm's recent representation of Coty Inc. on its $800 million acquisition of Unilever's global prestige fragrance business.

In all, around 75 per cent of the lawyers in Covington's London office are U.K.-qualified, and though it is not a high-profile operation, it has quietly built a formidable team. Hires last year included Anne Ware, a specialist partner in product liability litigation, who joined from Davies Arnold Cooper, and Robert Pietrowski from Coudert Brothers, who is an arbitration specialist. Perhaps the office's most impressive hire, though, came back in 2002, when it attracted the senior vice president and general counsel from GlaxoSmithKline. James Beery brought unrivalled industry knowledge to the London operation, and is a senior of counsel in the office. With such a team, it's little wonder the work keeps flowing.

More than deals

But it's not all about corporations doing deals. Covington is one of the U.S. firms with the strongest government affairs tradition. Keeping up-to-date with the workings on Capitol Hill and in the Executive Branch requires a flow of information in both directions, and the firm regularly loses partners to, and attracts recruits from, high positions in the U.S. government. In August 2005, the U.S. Senate approved Covington & Burling partner John Dugan as Comptroller of the Currency (the official responsible for supervision of the U.S. banking system), after his nomination by President George W. Bush. Just a few months earlier, another Covington & Burling partner—Tom Barnett—had been appointed Assistant Attorney General for Antitrust of the U.S. Department of Justice.

Covington lawyers are amongst the most rounded in the business. They make their money helping clients through strategic and complex issues, and are much more than just transactions people. Indeed, it is striking when you meet a Covington partner that they are more likely to boast about their pro bono work than they are about some mega-billing piece of corporate work, though there are plenty of those too.

Covington is one of only 13 firms to make *The American Lawyer* A-list for three consecutive years (since 2003). That's no easy task—the table pits the top 200 American law firms against each other on the basis of revenue per lawyer, pro bono efforts, associate satisfaction and diversity. The A-list is the top 20—the firms that make money, keep their people happy, treat them fairly and give something back to their communities.

In the public interest

Covington is a real world leader in pro bono legal services. It is consistently ranked as one of the top firms in the U.S. in terms of average pro bono hours logged by its lawyers, and in 2005 it was again ranked as the number one firm in the pro bono area by *The American Lawyer*. The firm does more of this than any other law firm in the United States: with the average lawyer doing 142.9 hours of pro bono each year. The average is 108.1. What's more, if you think that's just the junior associates or U.S.-based lawyers doing the community service work, think again.

The London office of Covington & Burling was one of five firms to be short listed in 2005 for the U.K. Pro Bono Firm of the Year by *Legal Business*. In all, 73 per cent of the firm's lawyers worldwide spend more than 20 hours a year on free work in the community. The list of projects is long, and there is room for only one stunning example here. After the September 11 attacks, the firm was asked by Mayor Rudolph Giuliani to take control of arranging pro bono legal advice for the families of the 417 New York uniformed workers who died in the World Trade Center attacks. The firm recruited a coalition of 15 other law firms, and together they trained more than 100 lawyers to assist the families. Covington worked for 30 families itself.

The firm's public interest work attracts a fascinating caseload that few other commercial law firms can offer. In Germany, Covington successfully defended non-governmental organisation Transparency International, which fights corruption, in a libel claim brought by Slobodan Milosevic in the Berlin regional court. The group had listed the 10 most corrupt political leaders worldwide, and had ranked Milosevic at five for allegedly embezzling U.S.

$1 billion. The court accepted Covington's plea that because the information was sourced from The Associated Press, and Milosevic had never disputed that, the report was based on credible information and due care had been taken. The case brought together the firm's German litigators and partners from London. It's a tasty piece of ground-breaking work, and underscores Covington's commitment to the good guy. It may keep a low profile in the City, but it does the deals, and has a heart. The firm may not always get the billion pound M&A and capital markets work in the U.K., but Covington gets involved in projects that really matter.

GETTING HIRED

Ethos affinity

Covington & Burling's young solicitors say that job applicants should prepare themselves for a particularly rigorous interview process. "Associates are subjected to a multi-round, multi-person interview process and come from a small pool of lawyers with an excellent academic record and who have trained at one of a limited number of admired firms," reports a midlevel finance and capital-markets specialist. "As the firm has only a small number of trainees, it is able to pick only those candidates who not only have excellent academics but who also have a particular affinity with the firm's ethos." A junior corporate solicitor adds, "For lateral hires six to nine [interviews are] the norm" in two to three visits to the office. In addition to seeking out candidates with standout credentials, the firm places a strong emphasis on fit, its solicitors say. Specifically, "We look for people who will get on well with the people they will be working for," according to a senior corporate solicitor.

OUR SURVEY SAYS

All things in moderation

Covington's solicitors report that they are moderately satisfied with their jobs. The lawyers appear fairly evenly split between those who enjoy their jobs and those who do not. One happy fifth-year solicitor states, "I am very well remunerated and as a result of recent senior hires now have a varied and interesting caseload." On the other hand, a less-than-pleased seventh-year offers, "There is a lack of mobility and prospects, and the review process focuses only on partnership even though this is not a realistic goal for many lawyers." The firm reports that "over recent years non-partner career tracks have been expanded and that the review process has been adjusted to better address the various career tracks that are available to lawyers at the firm."

Solicitors call the firm "closeknit", "very open", and "friendly." As one junior solicitor puts it, "People go out of their way to support and encourage those around them." A midlevel solicitor adds, "Professionally the firm is collegial and lawyers are encouraged to share knowledge. As a result of the London office's relatively small size, lawyers and support staff of all levels know each other well and regularly socialise together although there is little pressure to do so." However, a senior solicitor suggests that the firm's culture has its weaknesses. "The atmosphere in the office is friendly and low-key though it can be cliquey," he says. "There is a high standard of professionalism, but not of genuine collegiality. Lawyers often find it difficult to get other lawyers to cover for them, not a great team ethos." The firm itself notes that "difficulty to get cover may be attributable to a lean team, which the London office is trying to address through a stepped-up recruiting effort."

Strong relations; weak training

One of Covington's London office's particular strengths, solicitors say, is solicitor-partner relations. According to one midlevel lawyer, "There is a very high rate of associate participation in recruitment and marketing. The associates are informed of, and to a certain extent, consulted on the business plan for the office and their practice area." Other solicitors, however, suggest they feel they have insufficient input regarding the firm's direction. "Many management decisions [are] shrouded in mystery unnecessarily," says a senior solicitor. "Associates are not given much opportunity to participate in even minor management issues." A junior corporate attorney adds, "One bone of contention is that there is no real input by associates with regards [to] strategic decisions taken by the firm, e.g., on pay and recruitment." In the future lawyers may feel that they have more input in firm matters. In 2005 Covington initiated a firmwide associates' committee, on which two London solicitors sit, along with their peers in the firm's other offices. Partner representatives participate on the committee as well.

Solicitors give the London office's formal training program particularly low marks. A junior corporate solicitor states that "The U.S. associates seem to receive excellent training. This is not replicated in London." A senior corporate solicitor adds that "Formal training can be hit and miss. Much of it is run in-house so if the trainers (partners) are too busy then the training falls away." Interestingly, however, Covington received the "Best Trainer Award (midsized City firm)" at the LawCareers.Net/Trainee Solicitors' Group Training & Recruitment Awards in 2005, based on a confidential survey of 2,400 trainee solicitors in the U.K. The firm also recently hired a director of professional development with a mandate to increase training opportunities for young lawyers at the firm, including in London.

Money matters

The solicitors give their firm middling marks for compensation. One midlevel corporate attorney reports, "Remuneration is significantly above market rate, although it is no longer at the very top of the available range." A first-year solicitor adds, "Compensation used to reflect the London market for U.S. firms of Covington's size, but has recently been cut, causing problems with morale and probably going toward attrition." The firm itself rejects characterisations of the recent move as a "cut." Rather, the firm maintains that it "reduced its salary scale as it applies to new hires and to future year increases for current associates." According to the firm, its compensation policy is intended make "each office's compensation package competitive with the local market for that office. Although this review of local conditions resulted in the firm decreasing its salary scale in 2005 for new hires in London, it also resulted in the firm increasing the London associates' holidays to a total of 25 days (plus Bank holidays) per year." The firm states that it will "continue to monitor the London market to ensure that its total compensation package remains in the top tier of its peer firms."

The hours, perhaps surprisingly, are not as bad as one might expect, according to insiders. "Hours can be demanding, but this is not the case at all times," says an eighth-year attorney. A fifth-year adds, "Generally the hours are not horrific as the U.S.-firm stereotype could lead you to believe. However, they are long and as with most law firms can be unpredictable."

Davis Polk & Wardwell

99 Gresham Street
London EC2V 7NG
www.davispolk.com

OTHER LOCATIONS

Frankfurt • Hong Kong • Madrid • Menlo Park • New York • Paris • Tokyo • Washington, DC

MAJOR DEPARTMENTS & PRACTICES

Capital Markets • Corporate • Credit • Financial Institutions • Financial Products • Global Technology • Intellectual Property • Mergers & Acquisitions • Tax

THE BUZZ
WHAT EMPLOYEES AT OTHER FIRMS ARE SAYING

- "Great"
- "Hardcore"

THE STATS

No. of lawyers: 550
No. of lawyers in London: 40
No. of offices: 9
London managing partner: Paul Kumleben

PLUSES

- "Top-tier clients and interesting work"
- "Cordial, pleasant culture"

MINUSES

- "Unpredictable" hours
- Some complaints about the technology

NOTABLE PERKS

- Free car rides
- Gym stipend

BASE SALARY

1st-year associate: $145,000

GRADUATE RECRUITMENT CONTACT

Bonnie Hurry
Director of Recruiting & Legal Staff Services
E-mail: hurry@dpw.com

THE SCOOP

Topflight Wall Street player Davis Polk & Wardwell has a sizeable City operation; despite the fact the firm does not practise English law. Davis Polk's London office opened back in 1973, so is well-established and here to stay, though yet to join the wave of raids on English law firms for U.K.-qualified solicitors. For the most complex legal work in Europe, however, where there is a seriously chunky U.S. law element, and even sometimes where there is not, Davis Polk is one of an elite band that tends to get the call.

Massive combinations

The office is the firm's largest outside of America, and focuses on the firm's core strengths of capital markets and M&A. The work is pan-European, and reaches beyond to places like India and South Africa, both of which the firm handles out of the U.K. Recent deals include work on massive combinations, like the $6 billion merger between ntl, the U.K.'s largest cable company, and Telewest Global. There is also the $5.4 billion sale by British Nuclear Fuels, a U.K. state-owned company, of U.S.-based Westinghouse Electric to Toshiba. Together with colleagues in Paris, London lawyers are advising the financial advisers to Mittal Steel on its unsolicited €20 billion bid for Luxembourg-based Arcelor.

On the capital markets side, there was a $9.5 billion series of notes offering by the Royal Bank of Scotland, the second-largest bank in Europe, two bond offerings totalling more than $1.4 billion by STMicroelectronics, a French/Dutch semiconductor manufacturer and a €577 million initial public offering by Neste Oil Corporation, a Finnish oil refining, marketing and shipping company.

No English please

Davis Polk takes the view that it does not wish to take the top U.K. law firms on as competition in the London market. Therefore, it has not attempted to hire English solicitors, but instead staffs its office with lawyers from its three U.S. offices—New York, Silicon Valley and Washington—and some London-specific hires. Although all London associates operate as U.S.-qualified lawyers, the office is cosmopolitan: roughly half of London associates are not Americans, representing a range of nationalities. Many received their primary legal education outside of the United States. The office mainly aims to advise European issuers accessing the U.S. and international capital markets or making acquisitions involving the U.S., as well as Americans doing deals in Europe, and it does this very well. Where the work requires local law input, Davis Polk works with a network of so-called "best friends", essentially law firms that equally do not compete with it in New York. The largest of these is undoubtedly Slaughter and May. On the continent, the firm works with the leading independent law firms in each jurisdiction: think Uría & Menéndez in Spain, and Hengeler Mueller in Germany.

While the strategy has served the firm well, it comes under pressure. Many of Davis Polk's biggest rivals—the likes of New York's Skadden, Arps, Slate, Meagher & Flom, and Los Angeles firm Latham & Watkins—have built sizeable London operations that do practise English law, and can thus offer clients a one-stop shop. Furthermore, the English firms are increasingly hiring American lawyers in their own counter-bid to give clients a seamless transatlantic service.

While Davis Polk remains resolute in its dedication to such a strategy, the first sign of a crack appeared this summer, when the firm hired its first non-U.S. lawyer. The addition of Arnaud Peres shook the legal market on both sides of the Atlantic, and he joined the firm's Paris office to launch a French law M&A practice. For six years beforehand he had been a key player in Freshfields Bruckhaus Deringer's French corporate team. While Davis Polk insists that the step is not the first of many, and that France remains an entirely different competitive environment and proposition to London, the hire nevertheless fuelled speculation that a move into U.K. law might follow.

More than deals

Davis Polk has cemented a position at the heart of global corporate boards. In a recent survey by *Corporate Counsel* magazine, Fortune 250 companies ranked Davis Polk second among all law firms as the firm of choice for corporate governance matters. The firm loses a fairly significant number of partners to in-house roles with major corporations—partners have gone to Citigroup, Marsh & McLennan and Morgan Stanley in 2005 alone. Going the other way, the firm had three partners return from public service in the summer, with CIA general counsel Scott Muller, senior Securities and Exchange Commission Executive Joseph Hall, and counsel to U.S. President George W. Bush Charles Duggan all coming back to the fold.

Focus on pro bono

The firm's tight focus and strong U.S. heart builds loyalty. The pro bono programme is also well-established and something to behold: many lawyers volunteer for bar associations, charities, and educational or religious organisations. The firm has mentored more than 275 students through its high school programme since 1993, and sponsors two National Association of Public Interest Law Foundation Equal Justice Fellowships. Davis Polk funds a permanent summer fellowship at the Sanctuary for Families Centre for Battered Women's Legal Services in honour of a former associate who worked closely with the group. London associates have done non-legal work with the His Majesty the Prince of Wales' Trust and community-based charities, working closely with lawyers from other U.S. firms.

GETTING HIRED

No sense of entitlement, please

Hiring for all of Davis Polk's overseas offices is coordinated from the New York office. U.S.-based summer associates are offered opportunities to spend up to four weeks in the London office during their summer. Full-time lawyers, all of whom are N.Y.-admitted, are a mix of those who wish to be based in London for the long term and those who rotate for two or more years from the New York or Menlo Park office. Davis Polk seeks candidates at "top-tier U.S. law schools," and "concentrates at Yale, Columbia, Harvard [and] NYU." But students studying at "second-tier" institutions aren't shut-out completely, provided they "are exceptional in some way." Whether "exceptional" means "brilliant" or "doublejointed" is unclear. We do know that DPW has little tolerance for "arrogant law students who feel entitled to be at a prestigious firm." Anyone with the bells and whistles ("numbers, law review, etc.") can nab the face-to-face; acing it is another thing. "[I]nterviews are more focused on a candidate's character, interest in the law, and whether he or she demonstrates good judgment and fits into the firm's culture," reports one insider. "Associates and partners interviewing a candidate are looking primarily at one thing: Do I want this person on my team?"

OUR SURVEY SAYS

Very social

DPW's London office is "social, cordial and pleasant", according to one source, and "a lovely, gracious, friendly place", from the perspective of another. Vault doubts nicer endorsements could be found at another firm. The warm and fuzzy feelings can be had during activities with co-workers, who "tend to eat lunch together every day" and head out "at least once a month ... for Friday night drinks." Outside of socializing, the firm is reportedly "rather conservative" politically, but "professionally [it] is exceptionally nurturing, pushing their stars to develop and take on as much as possible, as soon as possible." In the scheme of the whole firm, however, the London office doesn't receive as much love as it gives, observes an insider: "The London office is treated as a poor stepsister of the New York office."

On their best behaviour

It's a blessing that DPW lawyers revere their firm, otherwise their "unpredictable" schedules would be tougher to handle. "I think that a lot of time spent in the office could be avoided if projects were staffed less leanly," comments a source. "There is a lot of time spent spinning wheels because there isn't a senior associate to ask questions to." But partners attempt to be fair, doing "everything possible to keep associates' vacation plans and pre-existing personal plans sacrosanct" and offering an "excellent" flex-time option. Partners "try very hard to give part-time lawyers interesting work", ostensibly avoiding the doldrums of document review. Such responsiveness to their lawyers' needs is further proof of partners giving them "tremendous respect", reports one contact. "I've seen no examples of a partner belittling an associate or exhibiting other behaviours (screaming, etc.), which are rumoured to occur at other firms."

Reportedly, "the management committee can be slow to disclose strategic plans, bonuses, and so forth, but the flip-side is that their conservative approach to all things, including hiring laterals, avoids kneejerk reactions to market forces—we do things slowly, but correctly." This includes "exceptionally good" formal training, as well as informal training courtesy of "good teachers who value enthusiastic and interested associates and do all they can to bring the associates up to the next level of sophisticated legal analysis."

The money question

It will come as little shock that the firm's solicitors, like their peers everywhere, gripe about money a bit. According to one insider "compensation is very good. However, in years such as 2005, in which associates generally worked tremendously long hours, it would be nice to see a step-up in compensation to reflect how hard the firm's associates worked."

Debevoise & Plimpton LLP

Tower 42
Old Broad Street
London EC2N 1HQ
Phone: +44 (0)20 7786 9000
www.debevoise.com

OTHER LOCATIONS

Frankfurt • Hong Kong • Moscow • New York • Paris • Shanghai • Washington, DC

MAJOR DEPARTMENTS & PRACTICES

Bankruptcy & Restructuring • Corporate Governance • Executive Compensation • Finance • Hedge Funds • Insurance & Financial Institutions • Litigation • Media & Communications • Technology & Intellectual Property • Mergers & Acquisitions • Private Equity • Real Estate • Securities • Taxation • Trusts & Estates

THE STATS

No. of lawyers: 800
No. of lawyers in London: 85
No. of offices: 8
Trainee intake: 1 (2005)
London managing partner: James Scoville

PLUSES

- High salary
- Approachable partners

MINUSES

- Not much holiday
- "Snowball in hell's chance of partnership!"

NOTABLE PERKS

- Regular events
- Free drinks and biscuits

BASE SALARY

Newly Qualified: £82,000

GRADUATE RECRUITMENT CONTACT

Sandra Herbst
Director of Legal Recruiting
+1 (212) 909 6657

THE BUZZ
WHAT EMPLOYEES AT OTHER FIRMS ARE SAYING

- "Enduring and stylish"
- "Highbrow sweatshop"

THE SCOOP

Debevoise & Plimpton is without doubt one of New York's finest law firms, in a tier with the elite firms like Sullivan & Cromwell and Davis Polk. It opened its doors in 1931, and first came to Europe back in 1964 when it launched its Paris office. The firm was slower than many of its competitors to make a splash in London, but while "conservative" quite understates the firm's investment strategy, it is most definitely making a splash now.

Comings and goings

Beginning in 2004, the firm has gone on a softly, softly hiring spree that has turned the U.K. office into a miniature version of the New York office, where 80 per cent of the firm's lawyers still reside. On this side of the Atlantic the firm focuses remain private equity, insurance and financial institutions, and dispute resolution. The latter took a knock this year when the London arbitration partner, Arthur Marriott QC, announced he was leaving Debevoise, where he had practised since 1997 and was the U.K.'s first solicitor QC. He joined the London office of rival LeBoeuf, Lamb, Greene & MacRae, perhaps because Debevoise here is becoming increasingly transactional in its outlook.

Hires have attracted City attention. There was Marwan Al-Turki, a fund formation and derivatives partner from Baker & McKenzie; Jeremy Hill, who was an insurance M&A partner and management committee member at Ashurst; Peter Hockless in finance from Allen & Overy; and Richard Ward in tax from Bird & Bird. Such a run of laterals won the office a place on the shortlist for Best U.S. Law Firm in London at the 2005 *Legal Business* Awards.

It is certainly worth adding that the growth in rank has also contributed to a growth in quid. According to *The Lawyer*, 2005 brought an unprecedented increase in Debevoise's annual turnover, a whopping 67.5 per cent rise in London revenue up to £32 million—accounting for 10 per cent of the firm's total revenue of £306 million in 2005.

Dealing winners

There is much more to Debevoise in Europe than its hires. Unlike many of its competitors, the firm more frequently makes headlines for the work it carries out rather than its latest partner moves. The trophy client for Debevoise in London, or at least the one that really got things started, was private equity house Clayton, Dubilier & Rice. When that business began investing in Europe, Debevoise could do little but follow. The client has stayed loyal and delivered the firm a tasty flow of work—in 2004 the London practice advised Clayton in leading a consortium that paid € 3.7 billion to buy electrical parts and supplies business Rexel, Europe's biggest ever public to private transaction. In 2003 the office worked on the $2.5 billion initial public offering of China Life, which was one of the deals of the year, and the rest of the client list reads like a bit of a who's who—Prudential, Goldman Sachs, AT&T, JPMorgan, so it goes on.

Debevoise-London recently advised Korea's leading phone business SK Telecom on a $1.03 billion U.S. SEC-registered offering. On the projects side, it is working for Russian airline Aeroflot's subsidiary OJSC Terminal in the design and build agreement for a new terminal at Moscow's Sheremetyeyo International Airport. That will be commissioned next year and will ultimately service some nine million passengers a year. All of which just goes to demonstrate the truly global outlook at Debevoise in London. The international dispute resolution practice also continues unabated under the leadership of American Mark Friedman, who is a leader in cross-border arbitrations. His work includes counselling Central European Media Enterprises in its successful investment treaty arbitration against the Czech Republic, which netted the client a $360 million recovery. He also worked for a European oil and gas company on successful protection of its ownership interest in a Latin American energy joint venture.

City slicker

While at a glance, the London office may be a relatively small cog in the large global wheel that is Debevoise, it nevertheless finds itself working as a hub for the international deals. While training and resources may be thinner on the ground because of its size, the pay package is hefty compared to the larger English firms in the City. The firm is thriving too—profits per partner are in the £1.5 million a year range, which is not to be sniffed at, and London's £19 million turnover makes a good contribution to the global revenue pool.

Debevoise has a good reputation for pro bono, and even runs projects out of the London office, something often neglected by U.S. firms who organise such things from their home base. Here, Debevoise supports a free legal advice project at the Hackney Community Law Centre, while globally the firm is a charter signatory to the Pro Bono Institute's Law Firm Pro Bono Challenge, under which it commits to giving time to pro bono equivalent to at least 5 per cent of its billed time each year. The firm has ranked first amongst New York law firms for its pro bono commitment for the last five years, according to *The American Lawyer*.

We happy few

What's more, the lawyers working at the firm seem to be happy a bunch, despite the obvious long hours and hard work called for by such high-stakes mandates. *The American Lawyer* also conducts an annual associate survey, which this year ranked Debevoise seventh among the top 100 American and global firms for associate satisfaction, the only New York firm to rank in the top 10. It also scored seventh for the Best Places to Work in New York. The firm was also one of the first to sign up to a new initiative this summer to provide corporate clients with breakdowns on the numbers of minority lawyers they employ, in a pact brokered by the New York County Lawyers' Association.

All of which makes it seem a pretty civilized place to work. Some years back there were rumours that Debevoise might broker a merger deal with London's Freshfields Bruckhaus Deringer, and certainly the two firms continue to work closely together, though Debevoise remains stoically committed to its independence. There's no doubt it is a firm in high demand—going places in a very considered manner.

(And, for the record, be sure to pronounce it right in any interviews … it is Debevoyz. If in doubt, check out the demonstration of how to say it on the firm's web site.)

OUR SURVEY SAYS

"Good culture of mutual assistance"

High atop the City's tallest skyscraper, Tower 42, the atmosphere at Debevoise Plimpton's office is best described as "sociable, informal, relatively relaxed." "A little reserved", acknowledges a fifth-year, "but friendly nonetheless." A first-year, perhaps drawing on colleagues' experiences at other large firms finds Debevoise "rather more sedate than a typical U.K. firm." A more senior solicitor in the corporate department appreciates the "good culture of mutual assistance" at the firm, commending the "high quality of lawyer" the work environment cultivates. A solicitor in his fourth year tells us that the firm's members socialize together "but not compulsively", assuring us "there is no 'herd' culture" at Debevoise. A second-year agrees, observing that office socializing is "not 'enforced', so you can pick and choose" whom you'd like to socialize with and when you'd like to do it. The group is a good one, with a neophyte remarking that the London office offers an "enjoyable mix of people." Though "not noticeably political", the firm, we are told, is "left leaning, liberal" to some degree.

But are they happy?

But are people happy at Debevoise? Most seem largely content with their lot despite conveying an assortment of scattered grievances. Asked about his level of satisfaction, one veteran solicitor gave the firm mediocre marks, but qualified them by telling us "the low score is no reflection on the firm but the nature of the job" itself. Another solicitor opined the fact that "the partnership is a little too secretive." This, he warned, indicates that the partners "don't seem to realise that associates who are kept 'in the loop' are more likely to feel fully involved in the running of the firm." A colleague finds the training at Debevoise wanting, but limits his response by noting that it was just his "relative experience rather than a criticism" of the firm or its training programme as a whole. A midlevel solicitor laments the "snowball in hell's chance of partnership!" but appears, like many, resigned to this fate.

NYC still calls the shots

Though the London office is the firm's second-largest, all are aware that Debevoise is still a New York firm. The shots are called from Manhattan headquarters an ocean away, prompting one mid-level solicitor to bemoan the deus ex machina management, commenting that "a little more independence from New York may be appreciated." The transatlantic divide might be to blame for a reported "lack of resources to a large extent" at the London office. A "poor holiday entitlement" is a testament to the fact that Debevoise is indeed an American, rather than European, firm.

Give thanks and be glad

This is not to say that Debevoise solicitors don't have a good deal to be glad about. "The culture and pay" are what keep one veteran at Debevoise. For a fifth-year, it is a triumvirate of allures: "money, good people, good work." Colleagues generally mention "excellent work"; "interesting, friendly people"; "enjoyable deals"; and "extremely approachable partners" among the reasons they stay with Debevoise. Too few too infrequently realize that small gestures go a long way—not so at Debevoise, where solicitors consider the "free drinks and biscuits"; "free dinners"; "taxis home (very flexible policy)" and "frequency of drinks events" chief among the little perks that make working a more pleasant experience.

"Enjoyable deals. Extremely approachable partners."

— *Debevoise solicitor*

Dechert LLP

160 Queen Victoria Street
London EC4V 4QQ
Phone: +44 (0)20 7184 7000
www.dechert.com

OTHER LOCATIONS
Austin
Boston
Brussels
Charlotte
Frankfurt
Harrisburg
Hartford
Luxembourg
Munich
Newport Beach
New York
Palo Alto
Paris
Philadelphia
Princeton
San Francisco
Washington, DC

MAJOR DEPARTMENTS & PRACTICES

Alternative Investment Funds • Antitrust/Competition • Bank Financing & Securitisation • Bankruptcy • Corporate Recovery & Insolvency • Brand Integrity/Counterfeit • Chemical • Commercial Litigation • Construction • Corporate & Securities • Customs & Excise • Defamation • Domestic & International Tax • Employee Benefits & Executive Compensation • Energy • Environmental Law • Environmental Litigation • EU Law • Finance & Real Estate • Financial Services • Financial Services & Securities Litigation • Government Affairs • Health • Immigration • Insurance • Intellectual Property • Intellectual Property Litigation • International Disputes • International Trade • Islamic Finance • Labour & Employment • Latin America • Life Sciences • Mass Torts & Product Liability • Media • Mergers & Acquisitions • Pharmaceutical • Privacy Law • Private Client • Private Equity • Pro Bono • Property/Real Estate • Retail • State Tax • Technology • Venture Capital • White Collar Litigation

THE BUZZ
WHAT EMPLOYEES AT OTHER FIRMS ARE SAYING

- "Good US firm"
- "Unfriendly"

THE STATS

No. of lawyers: 1,050
No. of lawyers in London: 120
No. of offices: 18
Trainee intake: 15 (2005)
Trainees retained: 80% (2005)
London managing partner: Steven Fogel

PLUSES

- High level of responsibility
- "Genuinely friendly culture"

MINUSES

- Some complaints about training
- "Inefficient work allocation"

NOTABLE PERKS

- Taxi rides home
- Three days extra holiday

BASE SALARY

Trainee: £32,000
Newly Qualified: £59,000

GRADUATE RECRUITMENT CONTACT

Lynn Muncey
Senior Human Resources Assistant
E-mail: lynn.muncey@dechert.com

THE SCOOP

Dechert was the first of the transatlantic mergers, and while it took some time to find its feet, it is now increasingly a force to be reckoned with. The first few post-merger years saw some upheaval on this side of the Atlantic. But things are stabilising now, and the combination has set to work focusing on synergies between businesses on both sides of the pond. New office space could be the final injection of energy that the firm needs to start taking on the big boys of the City.

Goodbye to all that

Not so long ago, Titmuss Sainer Dechert was a nice little London firm known for its property practice. It had a long-standing alliance with Dechert Price & Rhoads in Philadelphia, hence the shared moniker, but really it just quietly got on with its work in a little rundown office just off Fleet Street. In 2000, it all changed, with the merger of two firms to create Dechert. Gone was the comfy old-fashioned approach to law, and gone, too, was much of the real estate practice. With a new focus on the bottom line, a drive to increase profitability left many of the property partners feeling this wasn't the place to work, and they opted for pastures new.

Investment in Europe has become de rigueur for the new firm, with partners being relocated over here to boost the financial services practice, amongst others. A Luxembourg office was opened in 2001, again with financial services in mind, and most recently the firm seriously expanded out its Brussels office with a team of five partners from the now-defunct international firm Coudert Brothers. Earlier the firm took 32 lawyers from Coudert in Paris, and between them, the two teams will boost Dechert's offering in M&A, private equity and EU competition on the Continent.

Merged finances

Clearly the strongest synergies from the tie-up are in the immense world of financial services and increasingly Dechert, and the market, are waking up to just what a heavyweight this firm could be. The U.S. arm is a leader for advising on alternative fund formations—the lucrative and secretive world of hedge funds—and in London a team led by Peter Astleford is at the top of the very same game for Europe.

Astleford has been setting up investment funds since the mid-1990s, and alongside Simmons & Simmons, the firm can claim to be a real leader in the space. What's more, it's an increasingly fruitful business to be in—you only have to look at the role of these über-rich hedge funds throwing their weight around in the buyout of Manchester United to know that they are going to be big players going forward.

Not only do they take big stakes in public companies and then try to tell the boards what to do, they have also been known to back companies bringing litigation, in exchange for a chunk of the payout if they win. As an unregulated industry, they are constantly under scrutiny from financial watchdogs the world over, all of which means huge potential work for Dechert.

The strategy now

Historically, Dechert made its money advising the fund managers setting up the funds, and still they do well here. The strategy now, and the struggle, is to get more work out of these managers when they do more interesting things, be it M&A, litigation, real estate investments, whatever. Hence Dechert hired James Croock from Linklaters in 2003. He was a senior M&A partner there, and is now head of the firm's European M&A team, charged with building up both the firm's international dealflow, and its M&A work for established clients.

In 2005, Dechert also added Doug Getter, an M&A partner from the London office of Dewey Ballantine, who had worked extensively for hedge funds and private equity houses, and will continue to drive the firm's efforts in that regard. Then there was the hire of Baker & McKenzie's private equity partner Adam Levin—all of which make it look like things are finally moving. Other partner hires include Clifford Chance funds practitioner Andrew Hougie, Islamic finance and capital markets expert Abradat Kamalpour from Norton Rose and internationally-recognised heavyweight competition/antitrust and telecoms guru Chris Watson from Allen & Overy.

Dechert seems to now have a sensible and feasible strategy, which began to bear fruit, in 2004, when the London office secured its largest instruction to date, advising longstanding client Travelex on its £1 billion sale to funds advised by Apax. That's precisely the sort of work a financial services firm wants to net.

Turning a corner

Still, while the M&A seems to be coming on stream, the firm's finances have begun to reflect the upturn. London revenues for 2005 were £44.6 million, up from £39.5 million in the previous year. Also on the upswing is office space: In November 2005, Dechert moved out of its previous dingy digs into new City space in Times Square, along with major client Mellon Bank. Mellon is a corporate client that the firm hopes to do more work for, so being down the stairs will help. In 2005, Dechert advised Mellon when it bought the 70 per cent it did not already own in Pareto Partners.

There is more to Dechert London than financial services and hedge funds too. The real estate side, though transformed, remains busy—the firm acted for Freeport on the £245 million disposal of four shopping centres to Hermes Pensions Management, and advised GMAC on a number of multi-million pound investments across the U.K.

In restructuring, the firm worked for Rabobank International in a $800 million restructuring of a credit default swap, and on the contentious side, there was work for Countrywide Assured in multimillion pound proceedings against insurers over claims arising from a Financial Services Authority review into pensions mis-selling. The team also worked for Bebb Travel in a challenge to the National Minimum Wage Act, which was successful and brought about a change to U.K. law.

OUR SURVEY SAYS

In the plus column

On the whole, Dechert solicitors rate their satisfaction with the firm as about "average." The firm's strengths, according to its solicitors, include providing junior solicitors with "good experience" and "very high level of responsibility for level of qualification." Moreover, insiders describe Dechert as "friendly and sociable" and "social but professional." According to one junior solicitor, "The financial services group is a stellar department and very friendly (no less than three Christmas parties to attend in as many weeks!)"

Some strained relations

Dechert solicitors, however, give the firm much lower marks for solicitor-partner relations, as well as for Dechert's formal and informal training. "Some partners are very supportive," suggests one corporate solicitor. "Others have no respect or consideration for associates whatsoever." A business-and-finance specialist tell us that the degree of helpfulness "varies from partner to partner, but most will explain whenever not too busy." When the partners prove unhelpful, sometimes formal training will fill the gap, but not always. Another business-and-finance solicitor reports that the program is "very good firm wide, less good in my department."

Solicitors also give the firm fairly low scores for its compensation program and hours requirements. As one first-year solicitor gripes, pay is "not on a par with Mid-Atlantic rates." Another first-year complains that there is "too much work for too few associates" and that the firm maintains "too many partners."

All pro bono hours count

The solicitors are nearly unanimous in reporting that the firm offers a generous pro bono policy. As one junior lawyer reports, "All pro bono hours count towards billable hours goals." However, some say the encouragement to take on volunteer cases is not supported by institutional assistance. "We are made to do pro bono, but receive no support in doing so", complains a junior corporate attorney.

Happy birthday

Solicitors report that they receive the day off for their birthdays. In addition, the firm offers a few other perks, though nothing extraordinary, insiders report. One sure quality-of-life boost is the firm's move to "much-improved" offices. One firm policy that may sound particularly appealing to American-trained attorneys accustomed to stingy vacation plans: attorneys receive "three days extra holiday on top of the usual 25 days."

Denton Wilde Sapte

5 Chancery Lane
Clifford's Inn
London EC4A 1BU
Phone: +44 (0)20 7242 1212
www.dentonwildesapte.com

OTHER LOCATIONS

Abu Dhabi • Almaty • Cairo • Dubai • Gibraltar • Istanbul • Milton Keynes • Moscow • Muscat • Paris • Tashkent

MAJOR DEPARTMENTS & PRACTICES

Banking & Finance • Corporate • Dispute Resolution • EC & Competition • Employment & Pensions • Energy & Infrastructure • Real Estate • Tax • TMT

THE STATS

No. of lawyers: 691
No. of lawyers in London: 510
No. of offices: 12
Trainee intake: 30 (2005)
Trainees retained: 72% (2005)
Chief executive: Howard Morris

BASE SALARY

Trainee: £30,000
Newly Qualified: £53,000

GRADUATE RECRUITMENT CONTACT

Jo Wilson
Recruitment Officer
E-mail: jo.wilson@dentonwildesapte.com

THE BUZZ
WHAT EMPLOYEES AT OTHER FIRMS ARE SAYING

- "Lovely firm"
- "Decreasing in size"

THE SCOOP

In 2000, two of the U.K.'s strongest mid-market law firms combined. The merger of Denton Hall and Wilde Sapte was meant to bring together the strong corporate practice of the former with the supreme banking brand of the latter. What emerged—and the new firm is still very much finding its feet—is a firm known for finance, media, energy and real estate, with a real expertise in the Middle East. The years since merger have been a long and sometimes rocky road for Dentons, with consistent good work but occasional bad news.

A tough run

Denton Wilde Sapte has had a run of bad luck recently. In April 2004, the firm took the tough decision to close its Asian operations, thus ditching offices in Beijing, Hong Kong, Singapore and Tokyo. The idea was to refocus on what was doing well, and to get profits up back at home. The result, though, was a firm divided over its strategic direction, and thus a run of large-scale defections back in London. Denton Wilde Sapte was the unfortunate victim of the largest team move ever to hit the City legal market, when no fewer than 11 partners in the media and IP practice quit for a far more international DLA Piper Rudnick Gray Cary. The one-off cost of closing the Asian operations also meant profits were going to suffer, which did nothing to keep further doubters on board. It's been a tough run, but the upside is that the firm now maintains that its vision is clearer and the remaining partners are now pulling in the same direction. Every one of the offices is profitable, and the roster of clients still includes some big names.

Banking brand

Denton Wilde Sapte's clients roster boasts financial institutions and sizeable corporations, with the list of banks the firm acts for including such U.K. heavyweights as Barclays and the Royal Bank of Scotland. Whatever mishaps the firm has endured since its merger, the Wilde Sapte brand is still well-established in banking circles, and the practice is a go-to name for insolvency and asset finance advice where it rivals the best in the City. On the corporate side, the departures in the TMT practice were a tough blow, but the major clients continue to include the likes of the FA Premier League and Virgin. For the stalwart old-school clients, read Shell, Sainsbury's and General Electric.

The new Denton Wilde Sapte got a replacement chief executive in the shape of Howard Morris in 2005, and he is so far sticking to the firm's tried and tested sector-based strategy, focusing on four areas: energy, transport and infrastructure; financial institutions; real estate and retail; and technology, media and telecoms. One place in which the firm shines is in IT outsourcing, where it is advising on a £4 billion outsourcing contract for the Ministry of Defence. Also on the TMT side, in the summer of 2005 the firm won the first victory against an Office of Fair Trading infringement decision, when the Competition Appeals Tribunal over-ruled its decision and turned in favour of Dentons client the Racecourse Association. The team also advised the England and Wales Cricket Board on the renewal of its sponsorship deal with Vodafone.

The Middle East and elsewhere

Despite its international shenanigans, Denton Wilde Sapte retains one of the strongest Middle Eastern and African practices of any UK law firm, and won the Middle East category at the Chambers Global Awards in 2003, and Africa in 2004. In summer 2005 the firm advised the Ministry of Finance of Oman on the flotation of state-owned telecoms company Omantel, raising approximately £400 million. The company immediately became the largest listed on the Muscat Securities Market in Oman. What's more, the firm advised Dubai International Bank as underwriter on the largest ever bond to be issued in compliance with Islamic law, which prohibits the earning of interest. The $550 million sukuk, as such bonds are known, was issued on behalf of Emirates Airlines.

Elsewhere, the energy and infrastructure practice often works outside of the U.K. The firm worked for Shell on the world's first crude oil exchange-traded fund, worth around $2 billion; acted for Japan's Sumitomo on the acquisition of a substantial stake in a major hydroelectric power plant on the Euphrates in southwest Turkey; and advised Hitachi on its first rolling stock procurement deal in the U.K. Hitachi signed contracts with the Strategic Rail Authority and HSBC Rail for the supply of state-of-the-art high-speed trains to operate domestic services on the Channel Tunnel Rail Link and local lines in Kent.

Community spirit

Denton Wilde Sapte, for all its internal wranglings, has never stopped presenting a united image to the world at large, and that's particularly the case when it comes to pro bono. The firm says, "We quite simply believe it is right to be involved with the community, both through the traditional giving of legal advice on a pro bono basis, and more widely through community-oriented initiatives." As a result, initiatives have included free advice to charities as diverse as the British Motorcyclists Federation and Unicef, and sponsoring the City of London Road Race, which takes place every year. The firm gets its name flagged all over town at the right time of year, with 6,000 City workers usually signing up for the charity run. Then as part of its African commitment, the firm awards a prize each year to the top student at Tanzania's Dar es Salaam University Law Faculty.

Denton Wilde Sapte dramatically rebranded in 2004, and now has a pretty exciting web site bedecked in bright orange and proclaiming an all-new approach to advising clients. The idea is that Dentons knows its sectors, it claims, better than any of its competitors. That message may not have stopped some partners leaving, but there have been new arrivals too: this year the firm has added distinguished IP litigation partner John Linneker from Taylor Wessing. Moreover, according to *RollOnFriday*, DWS plans to double the size of its corporate department over the next five years, adding a dozen partners and another 25 assistants.

Dewey Ballantine LLP

One London Wall
London EC2Y 5EZ
Phone: +44 (0)20 7456 6000
www.deweyballantine.com

OTHER LOCATIONS

Austin
Beijing
East Palo Alto
Frankfurt
Houston
Los Angeles
Milan
New York
Rome
Warsaw
Washington, DC

THE STATS

No. of lawyers: 550
No. of lawyers in London: 35
No. of offices: 12
London managing partner: Fred Gander

MAJOR DEPARTMENTS & PRACTICES

Antitrust & Trade Regulation • Arbitration & Alternative Dispute Resolution • Bank & Institutional Finance • Banking & Financial Institutions Litigation • Bankruptcy Litigation • Compensation & Benefits • Corporate Finance • Corporate Reorganisation & Bankruptcy • Derivatives • Emerging Markets • Employment Law • Energy • Insurance • Insurance/Reinsurance Litigation & Arbitration • Intellectual Property Litigation • Intellectual Property Transactions & Technology • International Litigation • International Trade • Latin America • Leasing & Tax-Advantaged Financing • Life Sciences & Health Care • Litigation • M&A & Corporate Governance • Mergers & Acquisitions • Private Clients • Private Equity • Project Finance • Public Policy • Legislative & Executive Branch • Real Estate • Securities • Sports Law Litigation • Structured Finance • Tax • White Collar Crime & Corporate Internal Investigations

THE BUZZ
WHAT EMPLOYEES AT OTHER FIRMS ARE SAYING

- "Magic Circle US, hardhitting"
- "Strictly Eastern Europe"

PLUSES
- Plenty of early responsibility
- International travel

MINUSES
- Low partnership prospects
- Billable hours pressure

NOTABLE PERKS
- Thanksgiving lunch, St. Patrick's day celebrations and monthly bagel breakfast
- Annual firmwide meeting in New York

BASE SALARY
Newly Qualified: $145,000

GRADUATE RECRUITMENT CONTACT
Julia Sherlock
Head of HR and Administration
E-mail: jsherlock@deweyballantine.com

THE SCOOP

Dewey Ballantine has been one of New York's biggest law firms since back in 1909, and when it was joined in 1919 by the Internal Revenue's first solicitor, Arthur Ballantine, it took an early lead as a preeminent tax practice. The head of the London office today, Fred Gander, is himself one of the few American tax partners based in the City, and the firm is a leader in global tax work. With clients like Nomura, JPMorgan, Deutsche Bank and ABN Amro all sending Dewey London regular work, the firm is gradually transporting its global franchise to these shores.

From '19 to '91

Dewey grew in the 1920s on the back of strength in litigation, and started a corporate practice working for the likes of AT&T, Dillon Read, Standard Oil and the Guggenheim Brothers. The firm was one of the first to start an entertainment practice, acting for Paramount-Lasky, MGM and Westco, and then in the mid-1950s the firm added three-time New York governor Thomas Dewey to the partnership. From here, Dewey Ballantine began acting for both the energy industry—think Phillips Petroleum, Continental Oil and Mobil—and major investment banks like Dean Witter and Paine Webber.

And so the modern Dewey Ballantine was set in motion, a firm that continues to this day to be strongest in tax, energy, and M&A for both investment banks and key industries, including entertainment. In 1991 the firm signed an alliance with London's Theodore Goddard, and together they opened offices in Budapest, Prague and Warsaw. That alliance split up in 1996, when the firm took on sole ownership of the three continental outposts and opened its own London operation. Thus Dewey was relatively late to the U.K. market, but has been in Europe for a while, now having rounded out its operations here with the addition of Germany and Italy, whilst some of the Central European offices closed down or floated off as separate entities in 2005.

City sleeker

Dewey Ballantine has quietly built a strong and stable London office, albeit one that is yet to shake the market particularly. The practice here is strongest for project finance and capital markets, and general finance work. The international capital markets team has had a sensational year closing new listings in the Middle East and North African regions.

Also doing well in the City is the tax team, where Fred Gander is teamed with David Blumenthal from Linklaters so that they can provide English and U.S. law advice, and then there is general M&A.

Dewey, like many other American firms in London, has found it very hard to attract major corporate hires to join its office from the English rivals. On the face of it, the firm should be a leader in corporate work on this side of the Atlantic: it has a table-topping practice in New York, and its continental offices deliver good mandates. But partners are either not convinced by its commitment or find its current resources lacking, so at the moment its M&A deals are normally limited to those referred in from other offices.

Top of the Euro tables

What's more, in the U.S. Dewey play in the big league for advising investment banks on M&A deals. Over there, investment banks have relatively sizeable roles on deals. Also, Dewey has managed to get the investment banks to recommend them to corporations, so increasingly they get to work for the companies on the deals. In the US, the firm's mega deals work included last year helping advise Disney in defending the $66 billion hostile bid for the company from Comcast in 2004, helping the client acquire Pixar, and also advising on its disposal of its radio ABC assets.

Over here, a similar plan has not so far borne fruit, because the investment banks just don't play such a large role on mergers here, so they haven't given Dewey so much work, or sent over so many referrals. Instead, it has come from the companies the firm is working for in America, or elsewhere in Europe.

Having said all that, those sources of work have proved pretty darn fruitful for late for Dewey, and the firm actually topped the European M&A tables by doing some of the biggest work. In Italy, the firm represented a team of investors paying $15.6 billion for a subsidiary of Enel called Wind, one of the largest continental deals ever done.

Continental triumphs

But while Dewey has found it hard to get things to take off in the U.K., it has suffered no such problem elsewhere. Its Italian practice, as the Wind deal shows, is one of the best there is, staffed by partners who moved over from the local office of Simmons & Simmons in 2003. Then in September 2005 the firm rattled the German market when it took two senior M&A partners, one from Linklaters, the other from strong local player Norr Stiefenhofer Lutz.

The firm cut links with its Prague practice in January, despite it having worked for clients like SAB Miller and on the largest ever U.S. direct investment into the country, Central European Media Enterprises buying TV Nova. The firm also pulled out of Budapest, but has a sizeable Polish office, and runs a lot of work in the Central and Eastern European region out of London.

The firm's London office is heavily involved in pro bono over here, and was a founder member of the Community Development Group, which is made up of a number of US law firms operating in London. They are used to pro bono back home and found it lacking here, so by teaming up they felt they could make a greater contribution. Dewey's work includes helping out London's poorest neighbourhoods, and it is also involved in the Solicitors' Pro Bono Group work on a programme called LawWorks for Community Groups.

GETTING HIRED

American standard

It's no secret that nabbing a spot at the London office of a U.S. firm will earn a young solicitor a lot more dough, so getting into white-shoe Dewey Ballantine, for example, is a tough business. U.K. attorneys should find it "very competitive" as they battle each other to win a slot that pays the Big Apple standard. While "most associates in the U.S. offices are hired through the summer associate program, which recruits at top law schools", lateral hiring is the modus operandi in London. Lateral recruits should have professional experience that proves their worth in the form of "experience at another top firm or in a very specialised field." Of course, don't forget top academics, a keenness for business and self-motivation.

OUR SURVEY SAYS

Legal challenge

Solicitors claim it's hard to beat the challenges put forth at Dewey Ballantine, which has a long, storied history abundant with superior work and clients. "Overall I feel that the firm offers extremely high-level work in terms of prestige of the clients and complexity of the legal issues involved", remarks a solicitor. "The quality of the transactions is fantastic and there is great variety", raves a source: "I am able to have a broader practice than many firms would allow." Adds another insider, "I appreciate the access to intellectually challenging work and the opportunities to participate in matters that allow me to work hard and rise to the occasion." And it's not just partners and senior solicitors who get a piece of the action—"this work is completed by associates at all levels", a fact that likely leaves those at the lowest levels of competing firms weeping over their document review.

Lateral snooze

Socialising isn't unheard of at Dewey Ballantine—the office is described as "generally very sociable"—but it happens "probably less than at the average law firm in London (particularly as compared to British firms)", volunteers a solicitor, who blames it on the lateral-heavy atmosphere that has caused "less comradeship within class years." The office is a sophisticated mix of lawyers from a host of international and political backgrounds, though personalities vary from practice to practice with at least one called disrespectful and "very aggressive." "Given the amount of time I am in the office I am thrilled when I have time for my non-Dewey friends and family", sighs a victim of one such group. The "often needlessly stressful" environment is still a point of pride for many of the solicitors on board, though: "Professionally the office is definitely one that I am proud to work in and is respected by both clients and the legal community."

Time is money

In the finest tradition of big-firm law the hours at Dewey Ballantine are brutal. Some people, such as our source who is "generally in the office for at least 45 to 50 hours per week" and finds "the hours are reasonable" in comparison to his prior firms, justify that it is "expected when working with this level of clientele and on complex and time-sensitive matters." Co-workers aren't nearly as forgiving, perhaps because they are even more overworked. "The working hours are extreme", says one. "The hours are extreme", reiterates another, "and you have to fight to take vacations." There is consolation in the form of pounds, however, and lots of them. While there are no pension plan contributions, salaries at the firm are "above market" for the U.K.

Tax contributions

Dewey partners keep their underlings aware of the goings-on at the firm, but don't expect them to contribute to the actual decision-making. That seems to be just fine with solicitors. Although, there are some who would rather receive a modicum of respect instead. While a few sources describe the partners as "professional and approachable", there are others who could not disagree more. Some associates note that some partners approach to associates' workload at times crosses the line. "This behaviour appears to be tolerated by the firm because of the quality and amount of work that these partners bring in." Still, partners do get points for clarity and approachability in the tax department, where "on-the-job training occurs daily" and "partner[s] and senior associates are always available to answer questions and provide guidance." Partners also oversee the monthly (and mandatory) in-house training offerings on tap at the firm.

"The quality of the
transactions is fantastic
and there is great variety."

— *Dewey Ballantine solicitor*

DLA Piper Rudnick Gray Cary

3 Noble Street
London EC2V 7EE
Phone: +44 (0)87 0011 1111
www.dlapiper.com

OTHER LOCATIONS

Austin • Austria • Baltimore • Belgium • Birmingham • Bosnia-Herzegovina • Boston • Century City • Chicago • China • Croatia • Czech Republic • Dallas • Denmark • Easton • Edinburgh • Edison • Egypt • France • Georgia • Germany • Glasgow • Hong Kong • Hungary • Italy • La Jolla • Las Vegas • Leeds • Liverpool • Los Angeles • Manchester • Minneapolis • Netherlands • New York • Northern Virginia • Norway • Philadelphia • Poland • Raleigh • Russia • Sacramento • San Diego • San Francisco • Seattle • Sheffield • Silicon Valley • Singapore • Slovak Republic • Spain • Sweden • Tampa • Ukraine • Washington, DC

THE STATS

No. of lawyers: 3,000
No. of lawyers in London: 430
No. of offices: 54
Trainee intake: 83 in the UK, 21 in London (2005)
Trainees retained: 95% (2005)
Managing partner: Nigel Knowles

PLUSES

- High marks for training
- Appreciative, responsive partners

MINUSES

- Tough hours
- No bonuses

NOTABLE PERKS

- Subsidised canteen
- Concierge services
- Service holiday scheme

BASE SALARY

Trainee: £29,000
Newly Qualified: £50,000

GRADUATE RECRUITMENT CONTACT

E-mail: recruitment.graduate@dlapiper.com

THE BUZZ
WHAT EMPLOYEES AT OTHER FIRMS ARE SAYING

- "Not the regional firm they were!"
- "Not there yet"

MAJOR DEPARTMENTS & PRACTICES

Advertising, Promotion & Trade Practices • Aerospace & Defense • Affordable Housing & Community Development Law • Antitrust & Trade Regulation • Antitrust & Trade Regulation • Aviation • Capital Market • Class Action • Construction • Communications • Copyrights • Corporate & Securities • Corporate Real Estate Portfolio Management • Domain Name Practice • Drug & Medical Device • Electronic Commerce & Privacy • Emerging Growth & Venture Capital • Employee Benefits & Executive Compensation • Energy Oil & Gas • Environmental • Federal Affairs & Legislative • Finance • Financial Restructuring & Bankruptcy • Franchise & Distribution • Franchise & Technology • Franchise Litigation • Fund Formation & Operations • Government Affairs • Government Contracts • Government Controversy • Government Leasing & Compliance • Health Care • HIPAA Privacy & Security • Homebuilding & Master Planned Communities • Insurance & Reinsurance • Insurance Litigation & Coverage • Intellectual Property • International Arbitration • International Franchise & Distribution • International Investment Disputes • International Social Responsibility Advisory Group • International Tax • International Trade • Iraq Reconstruction • Labour & Employment Law • Land Use & Development • Landlord Leasing • Latin America • Legislative Financial Services • Life Sciences • Litigation • Lodging & Timeshare • Media & New Media • Medical Malpractice Defense • Mergers & Acquisitions • Mixed Use Development • Nonprofit & Philanthropy • Nonprofit Organisations • Outsourcing • Patent Litigation • Patent Prosecution • Pesticide • Privacy Litigation • Private Equity • Product Liability & Toxic Torts • Professional Liability • Project Finance • Public Company & Corporate Governance • Public Finance • Public Finance • Qui Tam/False Claims Act • Real Estate • Real Estate Capital Markets • Real Estate Finance • Securities Litigation • Sports Facility Development • State Legislation & Public Policy • Tax • Tax Policy & Legislation • Technology & Outsourcing • Tenant Leasing • Trademark Litigation • Trademarks • Transportation • Trusts & Estates • White Collar Crime • Workout Experience

THE SCOOP

Not so long ago, Dibb Lupton Alsop was a Sheffield law firm with ideas above its station. Managing partner Nigel Knowles spoke of building a top five European practice and most rivals sniggered behind his back. Boy, has he proved them wrong. At the start of 2005 the firm signed a merger that has not only transformed its practice, but has come close to transforming the legal market. The tripartite deal linked DLA, which by now was well on its way to a top five ranking, by size at least, in Europe, with Piper Rudnick of the East Coast of the United States, and Gray Cary of Silicon Valley. The firm's ambitious strategy was acknowledged at *The Lawyer* Awards 2006 when DLA Piper was named Global Law Firm of the Year.

Pesticides? La Jolla?

How things have changed for those partners in Sheffield. Few of them, one assumes, would be able to tell you even where La Jolla is, let alone the names of their partners there and just why they have an office. (It's in California, in case you wondered). How many of them will know quite why they list a specialism in pesticides on their web site is another question.

But whether this firm is yet as joined up as it should be somewhat misses the point of both what it is trying to achieve, and how it is doing. The strategy, as set out by Knowles, is not to compete with the first-tier Magic Circle law firms for international M&A and capital markets work for the world's biggest corporations. Rather it is to service those same clients on their second tier, day-to-day, work, like real estate, employment, intellectual property, and regulatory advice. When you put that together with work for smaller companies on their way up, it begins to make sense.

Avoiding the franchise tag

It is perhaps not a revolutionary strategy—Baker & McKenzie and the now-defunct Coudert Brothers would claim to have spotted the same opportunity many years back. Coudert couldn't make it work, and DLA will have to avoid the accusations of a franchise operation that have dogged Bakers.

Perhaps what sets DLA apart from these competitors is its war chest, though, and its ability to use it. The firm's highest paid partners in the U.K. are paid more than £1 million, largely at the expense of those in the junior ranks who get an increasingly diminished share of the pot. The result is that DLA can attract the best partners in the City to join up, perhaps the most notable being

David Taylor, who was head of real estate at Herbert Smith until joining DLA a year ago.

Dealing rooms

Of all the U.K.'s so-called national firms—the ones that were once rooted in the regions, and have by-and-large grown to be national and pan-European players—DLA has undoubtedly had the greatest success in the City. It has a roster of banking clients that have stuck with it through its expansion and continue to buy its services in some considerable number, with Barclays a fine example, and the rest of the U.K. clearing banks there too. DLA may not be getting Barclays" most complex work, but the volume it gets means the bank is one of its largest clients.

Aside from finance, the two areas where DLA really stands out from the pack at the moment are in the aforementioned real estate, and in technology, media and communications. Piper Rudnick was one of the leading real estate firms in the U.S., and the combination has created what is undeniably one of the strongest forces in international property work. In 2004, the firm showed it is playing with the big boys when it acted for U.S. private equity house The Blackstone Group on its £750 million sale of the Savoy Group to Quinlan Private. Other chunky clients include Axa Sun Life, GE Capital Real Estate and the Unilever Pension Fund, all major property investors. On retail, the firm acts for a whole bunch of high street names, like Boots, Halfords and the Co-op.

Techies and start-ups

On the tech side, DLA was similarly doing well in the U.K. before its combination with Silicon Valley's Gray Cary, and now its story is a pretty compelling one. In England, the highlight has undoubtedly been advising the Department of Health on its £530 million contract with BT to develop a new national network for the NHS in IT and telecommunications. That was one of the firm's largest mandates, and is one of the biggest projects of its kind ever attempted worldwide.

But it's not just the mega-deals where DLA's tech team is shining—one of the first Piper Rudnick partners to relocate to London post-merger was a venture capital partner, and the firm is now devoting serious energies to advising small start-up companies raising funding and expanding their businesses. Like every law firm, DLA would like to advise the next Cisco when it starts in a garage and looks for a lawyer—doing so generally means they stick with you as they grow. The difference at DLA, though, is that they are prepared to do the low-paying early work that the Magic Circle won't do, hence investing in the clients from day one.

Culture shock

There's no doubt that DLA's culture has changed so much in the last few years that it's now impossibly difficult to define. The firm is always ranked in the *Sunday Times* survey of the Best Places to Work, which suggests happy lawyers, but expansion has pushed the centre of power further and further away from the young associate in the U.K.

The firm is decentralised enough, though, that corporate social responsibility programmes are established and taken seriously wherever you are, and London is no exception. The firm will likely invest more in such efforts now that it has such a large American contingent (American lawyers are famously dedicated to pro bono), but the U.K. arm was already doing as much as any of its competitors.

While DLA may always be a small fish in a big pond, the firm's work is challenging and interesting, and all signs indicate that is a firm on the rise. Rivals might suggest that Knowles has bitten off more than he can chew with the latest mega-merger, and certainly integration is now the key. Going forward, Knowles has spoken of floating the firm on the Stock Exchange when laws allow—it's certainly one of the hottest legal stocks around right now.

GETTING HIRED

As you'd expect

No one will be surprised to learn that DLA Piper is seeking presentable, articulate candidates. As one junior solicitor puts it, the firm wants "individual[s] who can be put in front of clients and can communicate well." And for the background of these well-mannered, well-spoken young legal eaglets? Believe it or not, insiders tell us that DLA Piper has "no preference as to university [or] school." Since the firm operates a "recruit to retain" policy, there is "stiff competition for training contracts." Our sources characterize the interview process as "fairly rigourous with a mixture of interviews, written and practical tests and presentations." The firm reportedly takes a broadminded approach: "There does not seem to be any particular degree requirement and any strengths academic, personality- or commercial-wise will be taken into consideration."

OUR SURVEY SAYS

A fairly content bunch

A stone's throw from St. Paul's, DLA Piper's London office is a very "friendly and dynamic place to work." The atmosphere is described as "sociable and unintimidating" but busy, with some departments "very social" and others "very work-driven" with "no socializing or rapport [among] work colleagues." DLA strives to be an "entrepreneurial, very client focused" firm, and is "operated along corporate lines rather than a partners club.' Reflecting on her lot, a young solicitor gushes: "In almost all aspects my work is fulfilling." Another tells us he "enjoys[s] the team" he is in, operating with a "good support structure" and receiving a wide "variety of work." What doesn"t he like? The "hours and high and constant pressure" incident to big firm life. All in all though, DLA Piper's solicitors make a fairly content bunch.

No delusions

And those at DLA have no delusions about working for a City firm, one junior solicitor telling us "nine to five-thirty does not really exist in my department, but this seems to be a common affliction" as far city firms go. Naturally enough, the hours worked at DLA Piper vary "a great deal, from crazy hours to more reasonable depending on department." A fourth-year solicitor reports that "hours are consistently pretty good, although there are occasional flurries of activity where longer hours are required." A second-year realistically notes his "hours could be a lot worse." A junior solicitor practicing intellectual property advises that time spent at the office depends on the needs of each particular department, "and also whether there is a big due diligence project ongoing, which are becoming more frequent." Fortunately, a second-year insider assures us that "when required, you arc expected to work late, [or] the weekend", however, this is "not unless you absolutely have to."

Kudos to the leaders

"Good management. Good treatment of solicitors" a fourth-year tells us plainly. As in the case of hours, solicitor relations with partners at DLA appear to vary "considerably depending on which department" you are in. "On the whole," begins a fourth-year, "with occasional individual exceptions, partners treat solicitors well in the firm." A junior colleague agrees: "I feel that we are kept informed of all the issues affecting the firm, and [partners] do seek our feedback on some issues." But a senior solicitor begs to differ, believing partner "support is now poor." He says while relations "used to be much better", the "working environment [has become] unhealthy" as relations have degraded. Others find that solicitors "are kept informed of decisions, but rarely are we consulted beforehand." Another solicitor disagrees, arguing that solicitors "are kept very well informed of the firm's plans and progress" and citing the information flow as "one of the firm's greatest strengths." It is also worth noting that "there is no formal mentoring system" in place at DLA Piper, and "the amount of informal training tends to be different on an individual basis."

Making a list

Asked what they liked least about their jobs, solicitors at DLA Piper reported a list of grievances more remarkable in its breadth than its depth. The "brain numbing administrative projects," for example, tend to darken one first-year solicitor's days. A fourth-year finds the "red tape and bureaucracy" the worst thing about working at DLA. Another fourth-year takes issue with the "arrogant members in certain teams" along with the "long hours." But without question, virtually all solicitors at DLA Piper share one common gripe: the lack of bonuses. Apparently, DLA Piper does not have a "performance based bonus system which can be frustrating", a solicitor going so far as to say there are "no real incentives to speak of. We all work too hard for little reward." A junior solicitor speaks for his colleagues when he says that while "benefits are fairly good," the fact that there are no bonuses "is a bone of contention for many—who feel we are underpaid compared with other top 10 firms."

> "A friendly and dynamic place to work."

– *DLA Piper solicitor*

Eversheds LLP

Senator House
85 Queen Victoria Street
London EC4V 4JL
Phone: +44 (0)20 7919 4500
www.eversheds.com

OTHER LOCATIONS

Barcelona • Birmingham • Brussels • Budapest • Cambridge • Cardiff • Copenhagen • Doha • Ipswich • Kuala Lumpur • Leeds • Madrid • Manchester • Milan • Munich • Newcastle • Norwich • Nottingham • Paris • Rome • Shanghai • Singapore • Sofia • Stockholm • Valladolid • Vienna • Warsaw • Wroclaw

MAJOR DEPARTMENTS & PRACTICES

Biosciences • Claims Management • Commercial • Commercial Litigation • Competition Litigation • Construction & Engineering • Corporate • Costs • Data Protection • Developers • Early Case Assessment • E-commerce • Education • Employee Share Schemes • Employment Law • Energy • Environment & Regulatory • EU & Competition • Finance • Financial Institutions & Telecoms • Financial Services Litigation • Food • Franchising • Fraud & Asset Recovery • HR • HR Consultancy • Human Rights • Immigration • Insurance • International Arbitration • IP • Investors • IT • IT Litigation • Labour Law • Legal Systems • Licensing • Litigation & Dispute Management • Litigation Support • Local Government • Media • Mortgage Enforcement • Occupiers • Pensions • Planning • Private Equity • Product Liability • Projects • Public International Law • Real Estate • Real Estate Finance • Real Estate Litigation • Recoveries • Reputation Management & Protection • Residential Development • Shipping • Tax • Telecoms • Travel

THE BUZZ
WHAT EMPLOYEES AT OTHER FIRMS ARE SAYING

- "Good quality"
- "Mundane"

THE STATS

No. of lawyers: 1,960
No. of lawyers in London: 310
No. of offices: 29
Trainee intake: 86 firmwide, 18 in London (2004)
Trainees retained: 90% (2004)
Managing partner: David Gray

BASE SALARY

Trainee: £29,000
Newly Qualified: £48,000

GRADUATE RECRUITMENT CONTACT

HR Recruitment Team
115 Colmore Row
Birmingham B3 3AL
E-mail: recruitment@eversheds.com

THE SCOOP

With some 2,000 lawyers, Eversheds is now among the world's largest law firms, a leader by sheer size in Europe. That's quite a feat for a firm that, not so long ago, was best described as a cobbled together collection of regional outfits spread across the U.K. When Eversheds changed is hard to pinpoint, but if you consider the fact that it was only in 2000 that the firm decided to merge its seven separate U.K. profit centres into one business, no one can deny it has transformed pretty quickly.

Multiple mergers

Eversheds has emerged as a fairly joined-up English operation, spanning 10 cities, and balancing regional politics together with a thrusting international ambition. Where else would you find Kuala Lumpur sandwiched on a list of office locations between Ipswich and Leeds? Certainly a strategy of global expansion through acquisition has given the firm a great diet of work of late, though it can leave it exposed to chasing too many opportunities and lacking a clear strategic focus. That said, compare the firm to its national arch-rival DLA, now part of the global super-firm DLA Piper Rudnick Gray Cary, and Eversheds looks positively focused.

Work wise

Eversheds has a sell for the major U.K. companies that are expanding abroad, and for international corporations that are investing in British industry. Competing in a world below the Magic Circle, it's a tough market to be in. The firm hopes to stand apart on the back of client relationship programmes, cost predictability and outstanding service. That model appeals to some of the world's biggest corporations—Eversheds does all the UK work for DuPont, for example. The chemical giant is the sort of client that likes law firms to bend over backwards and "partner" with it, in return for a sizeable chunk of work, and that's just the kind of model Eversheds follows.

Other major Eversheds clients include U.K. financial institutions, like ABN Amro and HSBC, where again there is lots of work to be had. Where Eversheds can really flex its national muscle is on infrastructure projects, and it has got some tasty work as a result. The firm is now a key adviser to Transport for London, but has also advised Land Securities on the £500 million regeneration of Birmingham city centre, with the building of the

Bullring shopping centre, and is working for the London Development Agency on the Olympic City project.

Notable breadth

On the run-of-the-mill corporate side, Eversheds advised shoe retailer Kurt Geiger when it was sold by Harrods to Barclays Private Equity, and acted for pub retailers Greene King buying 71 freehold tenanted pubs from Ridley's. On the juicier mandates, the firm advised the administrators selling MG Rover Group and Powertrain to Nanjing Automotive of China, and worked for Canadian giant Brascan in the disposal of $1.7 billion shares in Falconbridge to Xstrata.

Eversheds does the whole gamut of work, from mega-mergers to the day-to-day employment advice, so a broader practice is hard to come by. Indeed, the firm's human resources practice grew its revenue by 6 per cent to £42 million in 2004 alone. The team won the work to advise British Airways on its pension scheme, wresting it away from City rival Macfarlanes. In recent litigation, the firm helped Bob Marley's family win a long-standing royalty dispute with Aston "Family Man" Barrett, the former bass player from The Wailers, and won an appeal before the House of Lords on behalf of Smiths Docks and British Shipbuilders, in a controversial case limiting the amount of damages available to victims of asbestos-related diseases.

People power

When it comes to its own human resources, Eversheds is making a concerted effort to stand apart from its rivals in the way it treats its people. The firm claims to have been the first major City practice to introduce a comprehensive flexible working policy, and has also introduced a values system whereby all staff are rewarded bonuses for living up to the new standards. These are summed up in six core values that Eversheds hopes to personify: client centred, straightforward, teamwork, mutual respect, accountability and continuous improvement.

The "Lifestyle" policy—as flexible working is known—is open to everyone, and includes a variety of options like part time, remote and shift working, through to extended periods off with career break and sabbatical schemes. The policy was awarded the Best HR Initiative award in 2003 by the European Managing Partners Forum.

Taking responsibility

Of course the other big part of a firm's values is shown by its corporate and social responsibility programmes, where Eversheds claims to be at the forefront. With such a national footprint the firm can get involved in pro bono and charity efforts countrywide—Eversheds works with legal advice centres across the U.K., and is a supporter of Streetlaw UK through a number of its offices. Streetlaw aims to increase legal literacy among disadvantaged or disenfranchised people, such as the long term unemployed, and helps groups who need to know how the legal system works, like women's groups and tenant's associations, who can't afford large legal bills.

Eversheds also encourages its lawyers to get involved in the community, and is active in helping out in various primary and secondary schools. Then there is a pretty active charitable trust: instead of Christmas cards the firm gave £2,500 to Medicins Sans Frontiers and £5,000 to the NSPCC. The firm also matched employee donations to a special appeal for the tsunami victims, and raised £31,500.

Internationally-minded

Eversheds' global strategy cannot be described as anything other than hungry —the firm signed international alliances in Austria, Hungary, Malaysia, Poland, Spain and Germany in 2004 alone. But the merger route is no longer the ideal; the firm is now convinced that non-financially integrated link-ups are the way forward.

When it comes to North America, Eversheds is perhaps a little cleverer than most. On the back of its strong DuPont relationship it has sold its expertise directly to U.S. corporates through nothing short of hard work and determination, and a not inconsiderable number of transatlantic air miles. The firm now sets out its stall as the go-to firm for U.S. corporations investing across the EU, and has as a result picked up the likes of Hewlett Packard, 20th Century Fox, Gap, American Express and TRW as sizeable clients.

Farrer & Co

66 Lincoln's Inn Fields
London WC2A 3LH
Phone: +44 (0)20 7242 2022
www.farrer.co.uk

OTHER LOCATIONS

None

MAJOR DEPARTMENTS & PRACTICES

Charity & Community • Commercial Property • Corporate • Disputes • Employment • Estates & Private Property • Family • Financial Services • Heritage • Immigration & Nationality • Intellectual Property • International Private Client • Media • Pensions • Private Client • Sponsorship • Sports • Tax

THE STATS

No. of lawyers: 150
No. of lawyers in London: 150
No. of offices: 1
Trainee intake: 8 (2005)
Trainees retained: 100% (2005)
Senior partner: Robert Clinton

BASE SALARY

Trainee: £27,500
Newly Qualified: £43,000

GRADUATE RECRUITMENT CONTACT

Donna Davies
Graduate Recruitment Manager
Phone: +44 (0)20 7242 2022
E-mail: graduates@farrer.co.uk

THE BUZZ
WHAT EMPLOYEES AT OTHER FIRMS ARE SAYING

- "Quiet and respectable"
- "Too posh"

THE SCOOP

Farrer & Co is the Queen's law firm, and has advised the Royal Family for more than 70 years. Incredibly, that's pretty recent by Farrers' standards: the firm can trace its history back to the early 1700s, and has occupied the same impressive building on Lincoln's Inn Fields for over 200 years. Since 1769 the firm's moniker has had Farrer in there in some shape or form, and the present name has been firmly entrenched since 1881. Indeed, until 1999 there had always been at least one Farrer in the partnership, and there are still members of the original family in the firm today.

Old School and more

Farrer & Co is as old-school as it gets, but makes good money out of family and private client work, whilst increasingly venturing into corporate work. The private client practice continues to expand, hoovering up the team from Nabarro Nathanson in 2001 when that firm decided to move out of the practice area, like so many others in the City. Like many of its competitors, Farrers has in turn now woken up to the opportunities of cross-selling into the high-net-worth individuals that it deals with on a daily basis, so is targeting work for them when they make corporate finance investments or start up new businesses.

Media matters

Building a corporate practice on the back of private client tends to leave you focused on some niches, and Farrers is no exception. The firm does a lot of funds work for wealthy investors, and then has a healthy diet of venture stuff. Particular specialisms are in sport, media and education: the firm advised the British Olympic Committee on the legal aspects of sending teams to the Games and running the successful London 2012 bid.

On the media side, the firm's litigation practice is right up there amongst the leaders in the field. They act on some massive disputes: think Interbrew v *Financial Times*, or the Jamie Bulger killers against News Group Newspapers. In all they are giving pre- and post-publication advice to organisations that between them put out 750 newspapers and 230 magazines, which makes for a pretty healthy practice. The crossover with the media practice into M&A works well, showing that a sector focus can bear fruit for a firm of Farrers' size if it's done well: the team acted for BMJ Publishing on the sale of its books business to Blackwell, and worked for the sports photography and photo marketing specialist EMPICS when it was bought by the Press Association.

School days

The firm's education work falls under what it likes to call Charity & Community: a practice that also includes a lot of work for not-for-profit organisations. Some of the more interesting work includes the largest charity merger in the U.K., and working for the University of London on the establishment and funding arrangements for a new freestanding college.

On the day-to-day deals side, the corporate team advised on the sale of organic chocolate company Green & Black's to Cadbury Schweppes, and worked on the listing of Serabi Mining, a U.K.-based gold mining company, onto secondary London stock market AIM.

Property in practice

But wealthy individuals don't just do the occasional deal, they buy and sell property, too, and Farrer & Co has built a juicy real estate practice as well. Most of the work crosses over with the leisure practice somehow or another: the property team worked for the National Hockey Foundation in a groundbreaking agreement where it allowed Wimbledon Football Club to use the National Hockey Stadium in Milton Keynes for its home soccer matches.

Then there are hotels: the firm worked for Queen's Moat Houses on the sale of two of its flagship properties, one in Drury Lane in London, the other in Edinburgh, to a hotel property fund.

All of which means there is a nice flow of corporate and commercial work in the firm, even though what really makes it tick is the less cutthroat side of the City's legal community.

Farrers is one of the few major London firms to devote serious resources to arts and heritage work. The firm got involved in some hefty lobbying last year against a European Parliament proposal that would have required educational and cultural institutions to make their information available for resale by private sector businesses. It also puts its own money where its mouth is. Farrer & Co sponsored Art Fortnight London when it started in 2004, and again in 2005. The two-week programme of gallery exhibitions, auctions and other cultural events is aimed at promoting the capital's place on the international art landscape, a project close to Farrer's heart.

Something different

Farrer & Co sets itself apart from the vast majority of London's leading law firms by positioning the firm as one that can advise on both commercial and private matters for clients. Outside of the business sphere there is immigration and nationality advice, personal tax planning advice, family law, drafting wills and handling probate issues, to name just a few.

Institutional clients run the gamut from colleges, charities, universities and sports bodies to art galleries and museums, plus one of the firm's oldest clients is the Queen's bank: Coutts & Co. Back in 1788, the story goes, the then Duke of York asked the firm to advise on his purchase of an estate at Weybridge in Surrey, and the sale of an estate in Allerton in Yorkshire. A big deal at the time, the Duke borrowed the money from Thomas Coutts, and the Farrer brothers lent him some money themselves. From then on, the firm worked with Coutts.

Field Fisher Waterhouse LLP

35 Vine Street
London EC3N 2AA
Phone: +44 (0)20 7861 4000
www.ffw.com

MAJOR DEPARTMENTS & PRACTICES

Banking & Finance • Brands, Technology, Media & Communications • Competition • Construction • Corporate & Commercial • Dispute Resolution • Employment • Pensions • Personal Injury & Clinical Negligence • Private Client & Charities • Projects • Real Estate • Tax

THE STATS

No. of lawyers: 210
No. of lawyers in London: 210
No. of offices: 1
Trainee intake: 16 (2005)
Trainees retained: 100% (2005)
Managing partner: Colin McArthur

BASE SALARY

Trainee: £29,000
Newly Qualified: £47,000

GRADUATE RECRUITMENT CONTACT

Carol Battrick
Graduate Recruitment Manager
E-mail: graduaterecruitment@ffw.com

THE BUZZ
WHAT EMPLOYEES AT OTHER FIRMS ARE SAYING

- "Good firm, good people"
- "Old-fashioned"

THE SCOOP

Field Fisher Waterhouse is one of those trusty mid-tier U.K. law firms that knows what it wants to be, and is getting on and being it. Focus is all in this part of the market, with massive competition coming from all sides. So Field Fisher's response has been to target technology and outsourcing with gusto. Although the firm almost got swept away in the dotcom boom—it was one of the first U.K. law firms to start taking equity in lieu of fees from start-up clients—its steady and solid construction, projects and outsourcing work saved the day.

Tech-tastic

Field Fisher has always been a firm to hide its light under a bushel, a little backward in coming forward. But that's changing: it is one of only a handful of single-office firms in the U.K.'s top 100, and resisting the temptation to invest overseas has also served to stoke a healthy bottom line.

Without doubt the heart of Field Fisher is in its brands, technology, media and telecommunications team, and that's where it can really claim to lead the field. In advertising, the firm advises big names like Petronas, Avis and Specsavers; in telecoms the list of clients is like a who's who: Orange, Hutchinson 3G, ntl and Cable & Wireless, among many others. The firm became an industry darling when it secured the mandate to advise the telcos on the so-called 'unbundling' of British Telecom's local loops, essentially allowing them to compete with the mega-telecoms provider for the first time.

In franchising, the firm acts for Regus, the office services provider, and in IP and IT litigation the group regularly finds itself in the U.K.'s highest courts. Media and broadcasting clients include the Canadian Broadcasting Corporation, Eurosport and the Broadcasters' Audience Research Board, and the firm's trademarks group acts for big names like Apple Computer.

The privacy team is a strong one, but the other great highlight of this practice is the technology team, for which read outsourcing. The firm is on the panel for Accenture, and advised on its groundbreaking outsourcing deal for the Medicines Control Agency, while the team also regularly works for the public bodies on deals, like advising Newcastle City Council on IT procurements.

Old school

But it's not just the brave new world that pays Field Fisher's bills. The real estate practice provides a good solid base and adds a few more household names to the client list: on the hotels and leisure side there is Whitbread and Travel Inn, on the industrial side, ICI and Mitsubishi Heavy Industries. Then there's retail: think House of Fraser, Laura Ashley, Vision Express, Oddbins and Burger King; a veritable high street full of shopping's big names.

Field Fisher is not afraid to get its hands dirty on the projects side either: the firm does quite a lot of pipeline and infrastructure work for the likes of Transco and BP Chemicals. In power projects, the team's work runs the whole way from the North Sea oil rigs, through power stations in Spain, back to the Enfield Energy Pipeline, where the firm advised on construction aspects of laying a gas pipeline recently.

The team also has a certain niche expertise in wind farms, advising a German bank on German wind farms, and a Japanese corporation on wind farm projects in the United States.

Best friends

All of which nicely demonstrates that while the firm won't open outside London, it certainly doesn't mind working farther afield. Field Fisher is a member of the European Legal Alliance, along with six other law firms in Scotland, Ireland, Germany, France, Spain and Italy. Between them they service 21 European business centres, working on a non-exclusive, "best friends" basis that the clients, so far, seem pretty happy with. It's certainly a cheaper way of achieving the international footprint that companies tend to demand from their lawyers these days.

The firm's London office is also home to eight 'country desks,' where Field Fisher brings together lawyers from all practice areas to focus their attentions on work from key jurisdictions. The eight are Scandinavia, the U.S., China, France, Germany, Italy, Spain and Japan.

Growing plans

If all this sounds rather disparate, Field Fisher has identified five key areas in which it wants to focus its growth efforts over the next few years, most of which will come as no surprise. Corporate and finance are obvious, as is brands and technology. The other two, though, are the public sector and regulatory work, where the firm continues to build its name. Field Fisher does a fair amount of public sector work, advising government agencies in public private partnerships, PFI projects and, of course, outsourcing.

The firm created an eight-partner regulatory department in 2005, bringing together EU and competition, telecoms, and public and regulatory groups under one roof. With two new partner hires—Martin Smith from Clifford Chance and James Robinson from Tite & Lewis—it's a strategic cog the firm is well and truly investing in. As a result, revenues from public law and regulatory work grew 35 per cent last year and the team now acts for 20 regulators.

Field Fisher used to be seen as a somewhat sleepy mid-market player on the edge of the City, which had missed the international expansion boat and been slightly burnt by the TMT explosion of the late 1990s. Now, no one could blame the firm for being a bit pleased with itself, and the lack of overseas offices makes it appear slicker and smarter than many of its competitors.

Freshfields Bruckhaus Deringer

65 Fleet Street
London EC4Y 1HS
Phone: +44 20 7936 4000
www.freshfields.com

OTHER LOCATIONS

Amsterdam • Barcelona • Beijing • Berlin • Bratislava • Brussels • Budapest • Cologne • Dubai • Düsseldorf • Frankfurt • Hamburg • Hanoi • Ho Chi Minh City • Hong Kong • Madrid • Milan • Moscow • Munich • New York • Paris • Rome • Singapore • Shanghai • Tokyo • Vienna • Washington, DC

MAJOR DEPARTMENTS & PRACTICES

Antitrust • Arbitration • Asset Finance • Banking • Competition & Trade • Corporate • Dispute Resolution • Employment • Environment • Finance • IP/IT • Mergers & Acquisitions • Pensions & Benefits • Planning & Regulatory • Product Risk & Liability • Project Finance • Public International Law • Real Estate • Restructuring & Insolvency • Securities • Structured Finance • Tax

THE BUZZ
WHAT EMPLOYEES AT OTHER FIRMS ARE SAYING

- "Best global English firm"
- "Sweatshop, but glamorous"

THE STATS

No. of lawyers: 2,350
No. of lawyers in London: 830
No. of offices: 28
Trainee intake: 95 (2005)
Trainees retained: 90% (2005)
Managing partner: Hugh Crisp

PLUSES

- "Great deals, fantastic clients"
- High level of responsibility

MINUSES

- "Intense" hours
- Limited partnership prospects

NOTABLE PERKS

- Subsidized child care costs
- Free taxi after 9:30 p.m., free dinner after 7 p.m.
- On-site gym

BASE SALARY

Trainee: £31,500
Newly Qualified: £55,000

GRADUATE RECRUITMENT CONTACT

Phone: +44 (0)20 7936 4000
Fax: +44 (0)20 7832 7001
E-mail: graduates@freshfields.com

THE SCOOP

In the year 2000, Freshfields kicked off the new millennium with a whole new approach to law: it merged with two German law firms at once to create a firm that now has as much of a presence in that market as it does in the City of London. Linking up with Bruckhaus Westrick Heller Löber at almost the same time as tying the knot with Deringer Tessin Herrmann & Sedemund was a huge leap of faith for a firm that was already well entrenched at the top of the U.K. profession: senior management roles are now shared between English partners and Germans, and much power clearly rests on the continent.

Losing partners, but still profitable

It has not all been an easy ride. Certainly the German M&A market has yet to take off to anything like the extent that was predicted at the turn of the century, and Freshfields has suffered a number of partner departures from both Frankfurt and Munich, largely to the local offices of predatory U.S. law firms.

But Freshfields can now lay a claim to being the most European of the Magic Circle law firms, and with two senior partners, one English and one German, the firm does not think with the London-centric bias exhibited by so many of its rivals. That said, competition from arch-rival Linklaters has got harder to laugh off, perhaps because Freshfields" attentions have been focused elsewhere. Still, this firm remains well and truly ensconced in the Magic Circle of top U.K. law firms, with the highest profit margin of the whole group.

Corporate powerhouse

Freshfields is one of the leading law firms in the world when it comes to public M&A, having adopted a strategy back in the 1990s to target the investment banks as a source of referral work. That focus, mundane by today's standards but positively revolutionary when suggested by then head of corporate Anthony Salz, has been much copied but not bettered. The list of corporate clients thus reads like a directory of U.K. corporates, and is too lengthy to even allude to here. Suffice to say the likes of Tesco provide a hefty fee income, and the Bank of England remains one of the firm's largest clients.

Overlooking private equity?

Where Freshfields was slower than its competitors was in recognising the potential of private equity. The firm took its eye off the ball on that one, busily focusing on the FTSE 100 while these funds amassed huge war chests and started bidding for the U.K.'s household names. Still, Freshfields has belatedly made a play into private equity, and though the market was sniffy about their tardiness at first, has been accepted. The firm scored a breakthrough when it advised a private equity consortium buying Debenhams, and has since won work for key houses like KKR, Apax and Permira, to name just three.

Bruising M&A battles

There were two other great private M&A battles last year: when Sir Philip Green attempted to buy Marks & Spencer, and when Malcolm Glazer audaciously bid for Manchester United. Freshfields emerged from both battles a little bruised: it was instructed by Green on the M&S takeover, but had to stand down after ending up in court over a conflict of interest. The firm had worked on an employment contract for M&S before, so was thrown off the deal. Then there was Manchester United. Freshfields M&A partner Mark Rawlinson, a lifelong fan of the club, did a nice bit of business development and contacted the team after reading about the Glazer bid, only to scoop the instruction to defend against the unwelcome suitor. Sadly it was not to be; Freshfields" defence tactics were thwarted, and the American tycoon walked off with the world's most iconic football club.

Much more than M&A

There is more to Freshfields than just M&A, and in the summer of 2005 the firm restructured its corporate group into sector specialisms for precisely that reason. Now the team will focus on private equity; leisure, technology, media and telecoms; financial institutions; and energy and transport. The firm says the sector focus will help it get closer to clients and better understand the industries in which they operate.

Outside of corporate, the firm has for many years been trying to build a finance practice, with varying degrees of success, a highlight being the first-rate securitisation team. More obvious breakthroughs are in the dispute resolution and real estate teams. The firm worked for Legal & General winning the first appeal against a Financial Services Authority ruling, and worked for Deutsche Bank on a massive pan-European real estate outsourcing project.

Leading lights worldwide

Salz, the firm's head of corporate through much of the 1990s, had been joint senior partner since the mergers, but retired in March 2006, making way for new blood at Freshfields. Salz is larger than life, combining senior partnership in the firm with a role as vice chairman of the BBC and, before that, chairman of the corporate advisory group of the Tate Gallery. He will be sorely missed, not least as one of the firm's biggest rainmakers and architects of international expansion.

When it comes to a global footprint, Freshfields certainly has a larger one than most, and the quality outside London is rarely questioned as it is for others. The Asia practice has been motoring, and Germany reports a busy year, while the firm's Moscow presence also performs well.

Across the Pond

In the U.S., Freshfields is one of the very few English law firms to boast two offices, with outposts in both New York and Washington, D.C. The firm makes no attempt to beat the Americans at their own game, so rather than pursuing American M&A the focus is heavily on finance and antitrust work, at which the offices have proved highly successful.

All in all, two German mergers have transformed Freshfields into by far the most internationally-minded of the major U.K. law firms, though there are some that argue the deals distracted the firm from its home market. With the corporate practice restructuring, change is in the works. As the private equity experience shows, if Freshfields sets its mind to do something, it tends to deliver.

GETTING HIRED

No, really, we're not worthy

Practically a majority of our Freshfields contacts claim that they would never be hired at the firm now, it's become so stringent. It is a tad difficult to ascertain whether this is actually true, or just insincere self-deprecation; alas, we'll never know. But for the intents and purposes of this profile, we can tell you what we do know. The firm takes graduates from "mainly Oxbridge and other top-10 universities" and "good grades are a given", "but most people tend to have something that make their CVs stand out in some way." Surely partners can't (and don't want) to leave the firm in the hands of academic hacks alone: "candidates need to be bright, hardworking, personable and motivated." Add fearless to the list as well, as "the interview process is extremely well developed and rigorous", involving lawyers of all levels. "Associates are encouraged to participate [in the interview process] and are trained in interview technique," we're told.

OUR SURVEY SAYS

Finding one's niche

Working at Freshfields can be a "bit like being at college sometimes", as the firm has "a genuine sense of fun" behind its professional façade. Solicitors can recapture their youth at regularly scheduled events (organised on a monthly and seasonal basis) as well as adventures along the lines of ski trips and sailing outings. Though known for "a very high degree of both sociability and good humour", any pressure to hang out with colleagues is— to the relief of the awkward or misanthropic—nonexistent. And according to a member of the firm's younger generation, "Socially it is possible to find your niche group of colleagues who you get on with", ensuring that no one is completely left in the cold, even if they're more the wallflower type. Older lawyers comment somewhat wistfully that for all of the activity at the firm, it is really "less sociable than previously." In addition to its supposedly fun-loving persona, Freshfields is "reasonably conservative, hardworking [and] professional", but a tax attorney warns that characterising a firm of Freshfields" size is not helpful: "As the firm is so large, it is the culture in the individual's department which is most important. [For example] the tax department is social and largely does not have time for people with egos."

Anti-social behaviour

Freshfields has "excellent deals with high-quality partners," says a solicitor with three years PQE. "Some wobbles, as is only to be expected, but very good all round." Despite being "very happy with the work and culture," wobbles do indeed abound. There is "too much to do and not enough support"—if you have work, that is. "The good work is there if you can get it. The department is riddled with partners who are unwilling to look behind their comfort zone and have relied on the same associates," explains a litigator. One seasoned Freshfields solicitor believes that for senior lawyers, "The only fly in the ointment is the grim partnership prospects." There are also whispers that spirits are down as a greater number of solicitors make for greener pastures in search of better bonuses, more manageable workloads and less "anti-social" schedules.

"Them and us"

"Individual associates may be well regarded but generally there is a 'them and us' culture ... Not enough appreciation is shown by the partners," a source grouses about the state of affairs at Freshfields. Confirms a compeer, "I have witnessed and been in receipt of very poor treatment." Some departments—cheers tax group!—have more approachable partners than others, but overall support and "communications are poor." The one saving grace may be age: "Generally the partners treat associates, particularly as they get more senior, as an important part of the firm." With partnership a long shot, however, "more senior associates may feel more undervalued." Even with the poor treatment taken into account, "there are very few arseholes around, far fewer it seems than at other firms."

The feedback on feedback

"Huge effort" is put into the "very good and thorough programme of training" at Freshfields. "Well organised", "comprehensive and ongoing," the firm encourages the ongoing learning of both legal skills and "personal development." The only dissenter keeps his gripe somewhat tongue-in-cheek: "Sometimes my only complaint is that there is too much, especially since I am frequently asked to give the training." When it comes to informal feedback, however, it doesn't come so easily, depending, as it does, by nature, on the individual partner and the associates themselves. "I am a senior lawyer and have less need of this but my impression from more junior people is that there is a limited amount of informal training and mentoring," offers an insider. A colleague of similar standing has a more optimistic point of view, calling informal training "pretty good." "You can get feedback on most bits of work if you ask for it and, particularly when junior, you get unsolicited feedback. As one of the more senior lawyers I try to do my bit to train," he adds.

Time and effort

With "effectively no part-time program" and hours that "can be very intense at times," Freshfields lawyers are under tremendous stress. But "others seem to get away with doing far less. Ability appears to be punished as the good people are piled up with work while the less dedicated get away with freeloading," mutters someone who is apparently more able than others. Overall "fewer hours would be a good thing," comments a source, "But we're paid to work hard and we knew what we letting ourselves in for, so no real grounds for complaint."

Pond hopping

The real ire is reserved for the newly overhauled bonus system, which has yet to erase the memories of bonuses past, described as "mean." It was only just decided that bonuses be given to those "under two years PQE," we hear, 'but no one has any idea on what basis they are awarded." And no one receives an "entirely discretionary" bonus during the Christmas season as they do elsewhere. (It must be noted that, at the time of writing, the firm was again reviewing its bonus system, with planned changes to take effect 1 May 2006.)

Otherwise, Freshfields solicitors do fairly well, especially when taking into account the fact that "pension/healthcare arrangements are very good." "Undoubtedly very good pay, but I'd rather be paid less and work fewer hours," an overworked insider tells us. For those who would prefer more quid over less time in the office, there's always the Dark Side: "The Americans do offer a great deal more cash ..."

Fried, Frank, Harris, Shriver & Jacobson LLP

99 City Road
London EC1Y 1AX
Phone: +44 (0)20 7972 9600
www.friedfrank.com

OTHER LOCATIONS

Frankfurt • New York • Paris • Washington, DC

THE STATS

No. of lawyers: 525
No. of lawyers in London: 37
No. of offices: 5
Managing partner: Justin Spendlove
Chairperson: Valerie Ford Jacob

MAJOR DEPARTMENTS & PRACTICES

Antitrust • Bankruptcy & Restructuring • Asset Management • Benefits & Compensation • Corporate • Capital Markets • Corporate Governance • Financings • International & Cross-border Transactions • Private Acquisitions & Private Equity • Public Mergers & Acquisitions • Financial Institutions • Intellectual Property & Technology • International Trade • Litigation • Arbitration & Alternative Dispute Resolution • Commercial Litigation • Environmental • Government Contracts • Healthcare Fraud & Compliance • Intellectual Property • Internal Investigations • Qui Tam • Securities & Shareholder Litigation • Takeovers & Proxy Fight Litigation • White-Collar Crime • Taxation • Real Estate • Securities Regulation, Compliance & Enforcement • Trusts & Estates

GRADUATE RECRUITMENT CONTACT

Robert Edwards, Esq.
Director of Legal Recruitment
E-mail: robert.edwards@friedfrank.com

THE BUZZ
WHAT EMPLOYEES AT OTHER FIRMS ARE SAYING

- "Rising star"
- "Boring"

THE SCOOP

Fried Frank first came to the attention of the London legal market in a big way in 2002, when it entered into merger talks with English firm Ashurst. Until then, Fried Frank had been an established player in New York, only dabbling in Europe through an ill-fated securities alliance with Simmons & Simmons and a tiny London office of its own.

Would have, could have

The combination with Ashurst would have created a major force, with international revenues of some £400 million. Both had some strong investment banking relationships, particularly with Goldman Sachs, and both were doing a fair chunk of private equity work, capital markets and structured finance. Together they could have expanded a European network and offered a transatlantic legal service that would have put them on a par with the best of both Wall Street and the City of London. That was the thinking, but alas it was not to be. Despite some serious commitment to the idea on behalf of Fried Frank, the Ashurst partnership decided for the third time in a decade to opt out of a merger that it was close to signing, and both firms went their separate ways. While Ashurst considered its options, Fried Frank emerged somewhat reinvigorated by the experience, and set to work building its own European network.

Midway through the merger talks, Fried Frank elected a new leader in the form of Valerie Ford Jacob, a capital markets partner whose relationships with those investment banks are tight, and who had long been driving the firm to build operations in Europe to service them. When the talks fell through, she promised to build that capability herself, through strategic hires. The plan was not just to win work for the investment banks here, in capital markets and structured finance, but also to work for corporates doing deals here. Those clients include ntl, Telewest, Gallaher, Rio Tinto and Mettler-Toledo, all FTSE 100 companies. Jacob's appointment was the first sign that the firm was now prepared to take international expansion seriously.

London ascendant

The first step to building the London operation came in mid-2004, when Jacob convinced the former managing partner of Ashurst, with whom she had spent many a long hour negotiating, that he should still join Fried Frank. Justin Spendlove signed up, insisting that the vision of the merger they had tried to pull off was the correct move. Spendlove joined as the head of Europe, but within the year was promoted to managing partner of the whole firm. Jacob is now chairperson and Spendlove, who splits his time between New York and London, is running the firm with Jacob. That's a first for a U.S. law firm, and shows how seriously the firm takes its European practice. Since Spendlove's promotion there have been further hires in London, and the office has grown to a reasonable, if still nascent, size. The firm has opened in Germany in the meantime, and has added some more corporate lawyers to its ranks in Paris, where it had previously had only one partner.

Fried Frank has certainly not lacked for work lately. The firm acted for Goldman Sachs as financial adviser to Telecom Italia in its €40 billion merger with Olivetti, and was joint counsel to private equity house Permira when it raised a €5.1 billion fund. In Germany, Fried Frank was US counsel to Procter & Gamble on its acquisition of Wella. Firmwide, from the start of 2001 there have been 420 M&A deals for the firm, both public and private equity, totalling over $863 billion. Other recent deals include advising ntl on its £817 million potential bid for Virgin; counselling ntl on the financing of the £5.1 billion merger with Telewest; and AEA Investors on its $530 million acquisition of Pactiv Corporation's North American and European protective and flexible packaging businesses.

Also over the last five years, the firm has handled 254 public and private debt and equity offerings, plus work for all the major investment banks, each of the Big Four accountants, and most of the large insurance companies. The firm's litigation practice is right up there, as is its restructuring expertise. The recent addition of prominent French attorney Maurice Lantourne, who joins the firm's Paris office along with eight associates, further strengthens the bankruptcy and litigation practices. And in regulatory work Fried Frank is a real leader—Harvey Pitt, the last chairman of New York's Securities and Exchange Commission, was a former Fried Frank partner.

Organic growth strategy

Merger is now well and truly off the Fried Frank agenda, with Spendlove and Jacob both having emerged from the Ashurst experience with a view that sizeable transatlantic link-ups just aren't possible. So organic growth is the order of the day. The firm has one of the largest and well-established Washington, D.C., offices of any New York firm. The client list includes the likes of American Express, Lloyd's of London and Sara Lee, and this is a firm established at the heart of Wall Street.

Chairperson Jacob is also celebrated for her extensive work rescuing, and now running, a suburban New York soccer school for underprivileged children. She is regularly on the pitch surrounded by 13-year-olds at weekends, and managed to convince Nike to stump up serious cash for its survival. The firm as a whole does pro bono work for refugees, death-row inmates, victims of racial and other discrimination, and the disadvantaged.

Gibson, Dunn & Crutcher LLP

Telephone House
2-4 Temple Avenue
London EC4Y 0HB
Phone: +44 (0)20 7071 4000
www.gibsondunn.com

OTHER LOCATIONS

Brussels • Century City • Dallas • Denver • Los Angeles • Munich • New York • Orange County • Palo Alto • Paris • San Francisco • Washington, DC

MAJOR DEPARTMENTS & PRACTICE AREAS

Administrative Law • Antitrust & Trade Regulation • Appellate & Constitutional Law • Business Crimes & Investigations • Business Restructuring & Reorganisation • Capital Markets • Consumer Class Actions • Corporate Transactions • Crises Management • Emerging Technologies • Employee Benefits • Environment & Natural Resources • Executive Compensation • Financial Institutions • Global Finance • Government & Commercial Contracts • Insurance & Reinsurance • Intellectual Property • International Trade & Customs • Labour & Employment • Legal Malpractice Defence • Litigation • Media & Entertainment • Public Policy • Real Estate • Securities Litigation • Tax • Telecommunications

THE STATS

No. of lawyers: 823
No. of lawyers in London: 46
No. of offices: 13
London Co-Partners-in-Charge: James Ashe-Taylor and Andrew Thomas

PLUSES

- High salary
- Open environment

MINUSES

- Difficult hours
- Little support

NOTABLE PERKS

- Subsidised cafe
- Individual marketing budget
- Annual retreat
- Moving expenses

GRADUATE RECRUITMENT CONTACT

Elaine Palmer
London Office Administrator
E-mail: epalmer@gibsondunn.com

THE BUZZ
WHAT EMPLOYEES AT OTHER FIRMS ARE SAYING

- "Top league"
- "Too small in London"

THE SCOOP

Founded in 1890 in Los Angeles, Gibson, Dunn & Crutcher got its break when it won the work advising the Southern Pacific Railroad. It remains a firm very much rooted in L.A., in contrast to certain local rivals (e.g. Latham & Watkins) which now have a distinctly global flavour. In the 1960s and 1970s, the firm opened outposts in Paris and London and then soon after came Washington, D.C. and New York. Gibson Dunn was once described in the L.A. press as harder to get into than the CIA, and the firm takes a certain delight in its tough and exhaustive hiring processes.

Second Spring

Today, Gibson Dunn has 13 international locations, having opened Munich and Brussels in a European expansion begun in 2002, but the heart remains in L.A. The London office is the focus of much internal attention of late, with the appointment of new management and a renewed focus on lateral hiring after a few years of neglect. The firm started targeting English law in 2000 when it hired Stephen Ball, the former general counsel of Nomura, Judith Shepherd, former head of corporate finance at Stephenson Harwood, Alan Samson and Andrew Thomas. Though a big name in the market, Ball did not deliver clients, and ultimately left the firm two years later to return to an in-house role. Shepherd, Samson and Thomas, however, stayed and became the foundation of Gibson Dunn's build-out of the corporate, real estate and finance groups as well as delivering the credibility to enable the office to handle transatlantic deals. Since then the firm has, like so many other American firms in London, focused attention on winning cross-border M&A work, boasting as it does a first-rate M&A practice in the United States, and adding and further deepening its bench in finance and capital markets.

The American way

Back at home, Gibson Dunn is one of the top law firms for both M&A and litigation. It is also a leader in antitrust work and restructuring, and in all those three areas it is now aiming to replicate its success in London. The firm has been a bit slow to make a huge impression in the City, despite American partner Paul Harter's work for trophy client Investcorp on the private equity side, which has always delivered serious deal flow.

However, in the first six months of 2005, the firm made a surprise appearance as second in the U.K. M&A rankings, thanks in large part to a busy run of deals in the corporate and real estate markets, where it is particularly strong. The firm added real estate private equity partner Alan Samson from Nabarro Nathanson in 2000 (as the firm's first U.K. partner), and he has proved a serious rainmaker for the office. Between March 2005 and February 2006, the real estate practice has advised on transactions totalling over £10 billion in value, and this has secured for the office a solid reputation in the market as the "go to" U.S. firm with the leading stable of major opportunity fund and real estate private equity fund clients.

Onward and upward

Since the middle of 2005, this steady flow of M&A and real estate work has been boosted by the arrival of a U.S. capital markets practice, run by Alan Bannister, who joined from Clifford Chance. Also new to the London office is James Ashe-Taylor, who was the head of antitrust at Crowell & Moring in Europe before joining up with Gibson Dunn in London and Brussels.

The firm has continued its recent growth this side of the Atlantic with the hire of Jones Day's finance partner, Tom Budd, and a litigation team from Clifford Chance led by Philip Rocher. Rocher joined with three associates and the group now counts 10 lawyers. The firm points to this addition of a litigation practice as evidence of its commitment to developing a "full-function" London office, a feature distinguishing them from most other U.S. firms in London. All of which means the office has increased both in size and visibility in the market and, more to the point, now has a number of the support functions necessary to attract the elusive English M&A hires. One senses that if this firm were to get the right corporate stars in London, it could really grab more headline deals. Judith Shepherd recently netted the instruction to advise First Reserve Corporation, an established client in America, on its £470 million sale of U.K. natural gas producer Caledonia, just demonstrating what the combination can do when it is really motoring.

Culture club

The firm's pro bono efforts are recognized as exemplary, and Gibson Dunn won Pro Bono Law Firm of the Year from the Public Law Center in the U.S. In the U.K., Gibson Dunn is also engaged in wide-ranging pro bono efforts. In 2006, the firm sponsored The Courtauld Institute of Art MA Scholarship: the scholarship is awarded to an American MA student at the Courtauld Institute of Art, London, in the academic year 2006/2007. Each year between 30 to 40 American students take part in the Courtauld Institute of Art's courses, and its alumni are significantly represented at a senior level in many of the major museums and galleries across the U.S., encouraging intellectual exchange in art history between the U.S. and the U.K. This scholarship is awarded on the basis of academic excellence and will support the fees of a post graduate student who might not otherwise be able to undertake further study.

In addition, Gibson Dunn partner Nicholas Aleksander acts as general counsel for Medicinema, a non-profit organisation which installs and operates cinemas in public hospitals for the benefit of long-term patients and their families. He is also a member of the Executive Board of JUSTICE (the British section of the International Commission of Jurists). In addition, partner Andrew Thomas and associate Tariq Mahmoud volunteer with Young Enterprise London, a part of the national Young Enterprise network and the International Junior Achievement movement led by businesses to help promote and develop entrepreneurship in schools.

GETTING HIRED

Extremely difficult

"By reputation," begins a senior solicitor, "it's meant to be extremely difficult to join Gibson Dunn." Indeed, be prepared to run the gauntlet to get into Gibson. High standards and an intense, thoroughly exhaustive interview process make the firm seem impregnable to outsiders. "The interview process consists of many rounds, many interviews and can take a long time to complete," advises an insider. Another source breaks down the process, telling us "there were numerous interviews with at least seven partners, a handful of associates, submission of two pieces of written work product and the provision of two references." Another solicitor corroborates the extensiveness of the interview process, noting "the applicant has to go through several series of interviews with at least a dozen partners and associates." "The firm is focused on academics," says another solicitor. "I have been told that they only let in candidates whose academic grades are in the top 5 per cent." (While the firm itself agrees, of course, that it does "require strong academic credentials," it points out that the "top 5 per cent" criterion is inaccurate.)

OUR SURVEY SAYS

Meeting the target

Lawyers at Gibson Dunn describe the firm culture as "very friendly", and one of "openness to diversity." A junior solicitor values the firm's "open-door policy", while a senior colleague finds the atmosphere "open and transparent." There is a spirit of camaraderie at Gibson, as "highly committed" "lawyers form a good team and make every effort to be sociable." A young solicitor who gives Gibson good marks in most areas believes the "work/life balance is the main problem with job satisfaction." He goes on to explain that "long hours are not necessarily reflected in billings", as "at a small firm, there is a greater involvement in non-chargeable activities." Another junior solicitor explains simply that billable "targets need to be met." Therefore, one has to expect "long hours of work", but, fortunately, work hours that are "all very interesting." Speaking of which, a fifth-year solicitor agrees "the hours have been very long." However, "associates who have been here longer have more settled hours."

Relations between solicitors and partners appear solid for the most part, though one solicitor acknowledges that the quality of the solicitor/partner relationship "depends entirely on the attitude of the partners." That being the case, "communications between partners as a whole and associates as a whole could be a lot better." Another solicitor finds "generally, partners treat the associates very well," but cautions that "there are always one or two individual exceptions to this rule." As far as training goes, partners endeavour to ensure that "associates are fully implicated in the transactions" according to a first-year solicitor. The same person also notes that there is an "organisation of trainings, which count for the CPD."

A marketing budget of one's own

Solicitors can look forward to being granted "plenty of responsibility" and working on "good, high-profile deals with a small, friendly team." This, along with remuneration that is "very competitive", the "high quality of the work", "plenty of social gatherings," and good "ambiance" make working at Gibson professionally fulfilling. The firm is aware that law is a service industry, and that some clients demand round-the-clock service, so Gibson provides its attorneys with "a laptop, BlackBerry and mobile phone, which does help with late night working out of the office when necessary." In line with this spirit of generosity, Gibson also gives each solicitor "a marketing budget under his/her own control."

Transatlantic tension?

There are relatively few complaints coming out of Gibson Dunn. One solicitor suspects that "there may be some political tensions between partners", specifically as to "U.S. vs. U.K." management style and direction (It must be noted that the current co-partners-in-charge in London are both U.K. partners.) An insider complains that the "bonus structure is not transparent at all." A colleague does not enjoy the "long hours" and is disheartened by the "slight feeling that many of the associates are only in it for the money and will not remain with the firm in the long term." A colleague agrees, hinting at "employee selection/retention practices" being a problem, but elaborating no further. Another associate advises Gibson Dunn to distribute hours "more evenly" and to recognise "other activities (not just billing and pro bono) in hours targets."

Hammonds

7 Devonshire Square
Cutlers Gardens
London EC2M 4YH
Phone: +44 (0)87 0839 0000
www.hammonds.com

OTHER LOCATIONS

Aosta • Beijing • Berlin • Birmingham • Brussels • Hong Kong • Leeds • Madrid • Manchester • Milan • Moscow (joint venture office) • Munich • Paris • Rome • Turin

MAJOR DEPARTMENTS & PRACTICES

ADR/Mediation • Arbitration • Asset Based Lending • Banking & Finance • Brands & Trade Marks • Business Immigration • Business Recovery & Insolvency • Business Risk & Fraud • Commercial Agreements • Construction • Copyright, Designs & IP • Corporate • Corporate Governance • Data Protection • Dispute Resolution • E-commerce • Employment • EU, Competition & Trade • Finance Law • Financial Services & Markets • Information & Communications Technology • International Benefits • IPOs & Secondary Offerings • Joint Ventures • M&A • Media & Communications • Outsourcing • Patents • Pensions • PFI/PPP • Planning • Private Equity • Projects • Property • Safety, Health & Environment • Sport • Tax • Venture Capital

THE STATS

No. of lawyers: 800
No. of lawyers in London: 190
No. of offices: 16
Trainee intake: 40 (2004)
Trainees retained: 75% (2004)
Managing partner: Peter Crossley

BASE SALARY

Trainee: £20,500
Newly Qualified: £46,000

GRADUATE RECRUITMENT CONTACT

E-mail: graduaterecruitment@hammonds.com

THE BUZZ
WHAT EMPLOYEES AT OTHER FIRMS ARE SAYING

- "Top regional player"
- "Shambolic"

THE SCOOP

Things have not been going particularly swimmingly for Hammonds of late, it has to be said. After more than 100 years of stability in Bradford, the original AV Hammond merged in 1988 with another law firm in its home city, Last Suddards, and embarked on a strategy of dramatic growth. Hammonds Suddards moved its headquarters to Leeds and began to target international expansion, becoming the first law firm outside of London to open for business in Brussels in 1990. A year later the firm opened in the U.K.'s capital city, and then in 1993 Manchester was added to the list.

Merger in the Midlands

In 2000 came the next transformative merger, when Hammond Suddards merged with Midlands-based Edge Ellison, hoping to expand its UK client list and increase its London presence with the addition of Edge's established offices. The enlarged practice saw the international marketplace as the way to go, and set about hoovering up firms across Europe: in 2001, the firm acquired both a French firm and a German firm, and opened for business in Hong Kong. In 2002 there was an Italian merger, and then subsequently joint ventures in Moscow and a Madrid acquisition. With 800 lawyers, the firm rebranded as Hammonds in 2004 and now finds itself in the top 100 list of global law firms ... not bad for a firm from humble Bradford beginnings.

Costly exercise

Still, international expansion does not come free, and Hammonds has suffered a dramatic drop-off in profitability as a result. Furthermore, it has proved difficult to keep the best people onboard in London, particularly given a significant majority of the firm's opinion formers are based in Northern England, and don't always see the merit of the costly City presence. That said, though profits may be tumbling, Hammonds has some good practices of which it should be proud. The energy team, for one, is doing some good work: earlier this year it advised Prime Infrastructure of Australia buying Channel Islands-based International Energy Group for £200 million, while at the end of 2004 it worked for EdF Energies Nouvelles on a £100 million joint venture for the design, operation and construction of an offshore wind farm near Liverpool. The firm won Legal Adviser of the Year at the Renewable Energy Awards for its work on the financing and development of wind farms.

Also doing well is the Hammonds' work on the Alternative Investment Market of the London Stock Exchange, known as AIM. Hammonds advised Rurelac, a British company that develop rural electrification for Latin America, on its listing on the market, the first utility to join AIM. It also acted for the first AIM debut for a pure nanotechnology company in Europe, advising Oxonica, which develops commercial products based on nanotechnology.

Overall, Hammonds is the archetypal national law firm, able to offer the whole gamut of legal services to the medium-sized corporation or the U.K. clearing banks. With strong partners in all the support disciplines, such as tax, employment, IP, the firm can also boast a strong public sector toehold, particularly in public private partnership (PPP) and private finance initiative (PFI) projects. In April this year, Hammonds was appointed by Partnerships for Schools to work on the Building Schools for the Future initiative. The firm will advise on the roll-out of £2.2 billion of investment into school buildings over the next 15 years.

Care in the community

Hammonds has a charitable trust that donates £70,000 a year to a variety of good causes, funded by annual contributions from the firm's partners. Beneficiaries include The Macmillan Cancer Relief, the National Autistic Society, the British Wheelchair Sports Foundation, the NSPCC and Shelter. Each U.K. office gets involved in community work as well—in London the firm works to support a local primary school, while in Yorkshire the offices work with three local charities, The Yorkshire Post Hidden Disabilities Appeal, Martin House Hospice and The Leeds Childrens' Holiday Camp.

Then there's the firm's pro bono work, supporting the Paddington Law Centre, and working for Pro Help, an organisation putting lawyers and community projects together. The firm gave pro bono advice to the Thorn EMI Pensioners Association, preventing a £50 million surplus from the fund being transferred to Thorn's owner Nomura, and is a patron of the Construction Industry Relief and Assistance for the Single Homeless. Hammonds advises the charity's management on things like Articles of Association, liabilities of trustees and insurance matters.

Broad appeal

While Hammonds also boasts clear strengths in a number of niches, like sports, advertising, and media, some would argue it is lacking the money-making strength in key areas like corporate and finance. What's more, the lucrative sports practice has suffered some tough publicity of late, with the firm forced to defend itself against a £150 million negligence claim being bought by the Football League. The row surrounded Edge Ellison's role, back in 2000, negotiating for the League in a deal with OnDigital, where the League claimed the firm failed to protect its interests. Hammonds denied all the allegations, and in June 2006 won a High Court battle when the League's claim failed.

Still, the management has been changed, with litigator Peter Crossley taking over as managing partner and current senior partner Richard Burns standing down in April 2006. Equity partners, faced with disappointing results at the end of the financial year in April 2005, were asked to commit to Crossley for the foreseeable future. Whilst there were inevitable departures, a surprising number signed a "lock-in" to stay on, and the firm now hopes to build on the network it has in place, and a national brand to take it through the current dip and out the other side.

Herbert Smith LLP

...ouse
... ...reet
London EC2A 2HS
Phone: +44 (0)20 7374 8000
www.herbertsmith.com

OTHER LOCATIONS

Bangkok • Beijing • Brussels • Hong Kong • Moscow • Paris • Shanghai • Singapore • Tokyo

Associated offices:
Amsterdam • Berlin • Budapest • Frankfurt • Jakarta • Munich • New York • Prague • Stuttgart • Warsaw

MAJOR DEPARTMENTS & PRACTICES

Corporate • Dispute Resolution • Finance • Employment and Trusts • EU and Competition • Intellectual Property • Real Estate • Tax • IT & Communications

THE STATS

No. of lawyers: 1,100
No. of lawyers in London: 800
No. of offices: 21 (including our associated offices)
Trainee intake: up to 100
Trainees retained: 93% (2005)
Senior partner: David Gold

BASE SALARY

1st-year Trainee: £31,000
2nd-year Trainee: £35,000
Newly Qualified: £55,000

GRADUATE RECRUITMENT CONTACT

Kerry Jarred
Graduate Recruitment Manager
Phone: +44 (0)20 7374 8000
E-mail: graduate.recruitment@herbertsmith.com

THE BUZZ
WHAT EMPLOYEES AT OTHER FIRMS ARE SAYING

- "Top class for litigation"
- "Pointlessly aggressive"

THE SCOOP

Herbert Smith has a reputation as the No. 1 litigation firm in the City. In a fight, this is the firm you want on your side. In 2005, high profile litigator David Gold was elected senior partner, so it is certain that keeping the dispute resolution practice at the very height of its game tops the firm's list of priorities.

Litigation innovation

Herbert Smith has launched an in-house advocacy unit; in other words, it hired two Queen's Counsel away from the Bar and moved them into its own offices. Both will have to requalify as solicitors in order to become partners at the firm, but don't let that fool you into thinking this is not a radical move. Though officially solicitor advocates, of which there are a number around the City, these two will remain advocates first and foremost. They will not handle cases, but will be instructed by Herbert Smith partners just as they were at the Bar. The advantage, the firm argues, is that they are just down the hall and willing to work through the night if a case demands it. And the client gets one bill at the end of it, which is much more palatable for those international corporations who just don't get the English split legal profession.

This novel arrangement is not for everyone, and there will still be huge bet-the-farm disputes where clients will demand the most specialist independent barrister that money can buy. Herbert Smith (Herbies as their solicitors are affectionately known) does not mind that possibility, insisting this is just about giving clients another option. What's clear is that despite being at the top of the litigation tree, Herbies are not afraid to innovate and push the boundaries of the way law is practised in this country.

Such an attitude has won the disputes department numerous accolades - not least the *Who's Who Legal* "Global Commercial Litigation Law Firm of the Year 2006" award and *The American Lawyer*'s U.K. Litigation Team of the Year award—as well as some instructions to die for. 2005 saw the firm represent Sir Philip Watts, the former chairman of Shell, in his much-publicised argument with City watchdog the Financial Services Authority over Shell's misstatement of oil reserves last summer. The team also advised the U.S. Securities and Exchange Commission in securities fraud proceedings in the Isle of Man, which culminated in the repatriation to the United States of approximately $200 million—the largest ever such recovery by the SEC.

It also advised Eurotunnel on the termination of its contract with an external supplier.

More than disputes, honestly

But this round-up will already have irritated the average Herbie, as the firm spends a significant amount of time emphasizing to the rest of the world that it is not just a litigation practice. And well it might. Whilst maintaining its position at the top of the contentious league tables, the firm has quietly built a corporate practice that now genuinely rivals the best in Europe. Such success has seen U.K. legal publication *Legal Business* brand the firm the sixth member of the City's so-called Magic Circle, something the other five would no doubt dispute.

Still, Herbert Smith topped mergermarket's U.K. M&A tables for the first half of 2005, and ranked fifth for European deals in the same period. The highlight was undoubtedly advising Fortune Brands from the U.S. on its joint £7.4 billion bid, alongside Pernod Ricard, for Allied Domecq, and there was also work for Britannic on its £1.8 billion merger with Resolution Life.

On the IPO front, the firm's Asia practice had a record 2005 advising on the Hong Kong market's top two deals of the year—China Shenua Energy's $3.3 billion offering, and the record-breaking $9.2 billion listing of state-owned China Construction Bank. The latter was the largest stock market listing seen to date in Hong Kong and was the world's largest IPO for four years. Herbert Smith's work on the deal resulted in their winning the 2006 *Asian Legal Business* Award for the "Equity Market Deal of The Year."

The firm has a client list that firmly positions it in sixth place in the U.K.: think BP, AOL Time Warner, BSkyB, PricewaterhouseCoopers, Credit Suisse, Goldman Sachs, Hollinger International, Vodafone … so it goes on. While clearly not the first firm to attempt to make as much money from transactions as it does from disputes, Herbert Smith is one of few to succeed in achieving preeminence in both in the U.K. The firm's model is the New York law firms, where litigation and M&A sit side-by-side and essentially feed off each other. Herbert Smith claims that the increasing strength of regulators on both sides of the Atlantic plays into its hands, as clients must now consider the litigation risks of every deal before they do it. That doesn't convince everyone, but if the profits are anything to go by—the firm ranks third in the country for average profits per partner—Herbert Smith is doing something right.

Allied strategy

One of the things that sets Herbert Smith apart from the rest of the market is its unique—some would say unusual—approach to international strategy. The firm has its own overseas offices in Brussels, Paris, Moscow (winner of the 2004 *Legal Business* award for the Best European Office), as well as an extensive network of offices covering the Asian region in Bangkok, Beijing (winner of the 2006 *Legal Business Award* for Asia Pacific Firm/Office of the Year), Hong Kong, Shanghai, Singapore and Tokyo. However whether a result of last-mover disadvantage or considerable foresight, the firm did not invest in its own presences in Germany or the Netherlands. Instead, Herbert Smith set up an alliance in 2002 with Germany's Gleiss Lutz and Dutch firm Stibbe, a tripartite link-up that involves the firms working increasingly closely whilst maintaining independence. Such an approach is undoubtedly cheaper than investing in your own outposts all over the place, and when the M&A market dropped off, there were certainly some international firms that looked at Herbert Smith with a dose of envy. Still, the firm continues to face criticism of its arguably disjointed approach, even while the deals keep coming. The three firms worked together for PwC Consulting on the separation of PricewaterhouseCoopers' worldwide management consulting businesses in 50 countries, and then the U.S.$3.5 billion sale of the consulting businesses to IBM, for example.

Wall Street chums

In the U.S., the firm's strategy differs from others in that it has refused to open an office and has instead opted for close associations with some of Wall Street's finest. Thus impressive referrals have come from the likes of Cravath, Swaine & Moore and Paul Weiss Rifkind Wharton & Garrison; Herbert Smith worked with the latter for Hollinger International on the sale of The Telegraph Group last year.

The London, Hong Kong and Moscow offices are home to the U.S. securities law team, a group within the firm's corporate department. The U.S. securities practice specializes in cross-border mergers and acquisitions, international capital markets transactions, securitisation, venture capital and private equity matters, some of their recent transactions include work with TomTom on its €540 million IPO and listing on Euronet Amsterdam and with Goldman Sachs on the HK$1.54 billion IPO and listing on the Hong Kong Stock Exchange of China Yurun Food Group.

So far, Herbert Smith has managed to position itself as the good all-rounder, and its international strategy teamed with the simultaneous contentious/non-contentious approach seems to be coming good. Throw in one of the best reputations in the City for diversity—Herbert Smith both monitors the progress of minorities and welcomes part-time partners—plus good community sponsorship programmes and pro bono involvement, and whether the firm is Magic Circle or not, it's certainly one of the top players.

Holman Fenwick & Willan

Marlow House
Lloyd's Avenue
London EC3N 3AL
Phone: +44 (0)20 7488 2300
www.hfw.com

OTHER LOCATIONS

Hong Kong • Nantes • Paris • Piraeus • Rouen • Singapore • Shanghai

MAJOR DEPARTMENTS & PRACTICES

Admiralty • Air, Rail & Road • Alternative Dispute Resolution • Arbitration • Aviation • Banking • Commercial Litigation • Commodities • Company Finance • Competition • Corporate & Financial • Crisis Management • Employment • Energy • Engineering • Environmental • Fraud • Insolvency • Insurance • International Trade • IP • IT • Logistics & Multimodal • Marine • Mediation • Personal Injury • Professional Negligence • Property • Reinsurance • Ship Finance • Shipping • Transport • Travel & Leisure

THE STATS

No. of lawyers: 210
No. of lawyers in London: 140
No. of offices: 8
Trainee intake: 8 (2004)
Trainees retained: 60% (2004)
Senior partner: Roderick O'Sullivan

BASE SALARY

Trainee: £28,000
Newly Qualified: £50,000

GRADUATE RECRUITMENT CONTACT

Graduate Recruitment Department
Phone: +44 (0)20 7264 8333
visit www.cvmailuk.com/hfw to apply online

THE BUZZ
WHAT EMPLOYEES AT OTHER FIRMS ARE SAYING

- "Shipping excellence"
- "Haven't heard from them in years"

THE SCOOP

Holman Fenwick & Willan is a slightly rare beast in the City of London, in that its practice remains heavily dominated by just two practice areas, the twin engines of litigation and insurance, which account for a mammoth 80 per cent of its revenues. The core of the firm is in shipping, in all its guises, but while its rivals – think Clyde & Co, Ince & Co and others – have diversified, Holman Fenwick still derives a relatively miniscule 10 per cent of its billings from corporate work.

Change in the offing?

Reportedly, the firm's current drive is to diversify out of contentious work and make more money for the rest of the practice from those trusty shipping clients. Thus there was the hire of a ship finance partner from Stephenson Harwood, and then in summer 2005, the former assistant legal director and assistant company secretary from P&O joined the firm. Mark Wandless has a strong logistics, shipping and ports experience, but is essentially a corporate and commercial lawyer, boosting Holman Fenwick's transactional team.

Work experience

Holman Fenwick's biggest case in 2005 was acting for Brandywine, a reinsurance company, which won a Court of Appeal decision brought by a Lloyd's syndicate about the Exxon Valdez disaster, with Brandywine arguing that the costs of cleaning up after the oil spill were not covered under the insurance policy. It was one of the longest-running cases to affect the so-called run-off market, and had been rumbling through the courts for nine years: the original oil spill was way back in 1989. Such a high-profile case demonstrates just how entrenched in this industry Holman Fenwick is, and the firm was certainly one of the first to recognise the benefits of "sector focus", now all the rage in London law firms. Holman Fenwick can track its history back over 100 years, and decided relatively early on to target insurance, transportation, trade and finance.

Thus the firm's clients now fit pretty neatly into one of five categories: ship owners and operators, ports and shipyards; insurance underwriters and brokers; commodity houses and traders; energy companies and oil traders; and banks and other financial institutions. The business seems to be serving the firm well, with revenue reaching £52 million this year, putting the firm into the top 40 in the U.K. Major clients now include Qatar Gas Transport

Company, Smit Internationale, China Ocean Shipping Company, HSH Nordbank, Ace, Rio Tinto and Tsakos Shipping & Trading. The firm may not be one of the sexiest mid-market players, but it is stable and free from any identity crisis, which is more than can be said for a lot of its rivals. Hence profits continue to rise, with the average partner bagging more than £300,000 for the first time this year.

Global power

Holman Fenwick began its international expansion in 1977, opening first in Paris, and then in Hong Kong a year later. The Paris office is now home to both English and French lawyers, specialising in reinsurance, international trade, cross-border disputes and contracts matters. Hong Kong remains the firm's key Asian presence, and is its largest overseas office with some 30 lawyers. No surprise that the core drivers are as they are for the rest of the firm, but the maritime practice is a particularly bumper driver out there. Singapore and Shanghai have since been added to the offering.

In Europe, the 1990s saw the firm add Rouen and Nantes to the roster of outposts, in 1994 and 1997 respectively, though the two still share just five lawyers between them. Their significance, the firm says, is their ability to service French clients beyond the country's capital. And then there is Piraeus, in Greece, a hub that no self-respecting shipping firm can live without. Opened in 1993, the office provides litigation support and consultancy, and does everything for the shippers, most importantly hull and cargo claims, charter party disputes, collision, salvage and total loss claims, and commodity-related matters.

Flying high

While eminently low profile, there is no shortage of innovation going on at Holman Fenwick in its chosen niche. Just as arch-rival Clyde & Co merged with aviation boutique Beaumont and Son, so Holman Fenwick has its own air link-up. Two years ago the firm signed a formal alliance with boutique legal practice Gates & Partners. That firm is one of the most established in the industry, advising airlines in the worldwide deep vein thrombosis litigation, and regularly acting for British Airways. Thus it ties in nicely with Holman Fenwick's general transport and insurance direction. The firm is growing organically too—this year it promoted five of its assistants to the partnership, which, given the total is only 86, was a pretty sizeable growth message.

By all accounts, Holman Fenwick is a firm that keeps itself to itself, and is as publicity-shy as it is possible to get in the client-driven world of law firms. Rumour has it that the working hours are not nearly as bad as they might be elsewhere in the City, and the culture is supposedly relatively friendly and relaxed. That culture, plus all the first-tier work in transport and insurance—most of it on the contentious side—Holman Fenwick seems to have found itself an enviable niche in the market.

Ince & Co

International House
1 St Katharine's Way
London E1W 1UN
Phone: +44 (0)20 7481 0010
www.incelaw.com

OTHER LOCATIONS

Dubai • Hamburg • Hong Kong • Le Havre • Paris • Piraeus • Shanghai • Singapore

MAJOR DEPARTMENTS & PRACTICES

Aviation • Business & Finance • Commercial Disputes • Energy • Insurance & Reinsurance • Shipping & Trade

THE STATS

No. of lawyers: 220
No. of lawyers in London: 150
No. of offices: 9
Trainee intake: 9 (2006)
Trainees retained: 91.6% (2005)
Senior partner: Peter Rogan

BASE SALARY

Trainee: £28,500
Newly Qualified: £48,500

GRADUATE RECRUITMENT CONTACT

Claire Kendall
Personnel Manager
E-mail: recruitment@incelaw.com

THE BUZZ
WHAT EMPLOYEES AT OTHER FIRMS ARE SAYING

- "Niche leader"
- "Aggressive"

THE SCOOP

Alongside Clyde & Co and Holman Fenwick & Willan, Ince & Co sits at the very top of the market for shipping law advice in the U.K. The firm can trace its roots back to 1870, and even then founding partner Francis Ince was a shipping lawyer through and through. In the 1940s the firm was one of the first in London to hire new young partners to grow the business—until then law firms had largely expanded through adding family members or people that could invest significant new capital. Then in the 1960s Ince & Co started to hire foreign lawyers, and opened its first overseas office in Hong Kong in 1979. Singapore followed in 1991, and Piraeus, the shipping market's capital, in 1993.

A global footprint

Then in 2000 came another spate of dramatic expansion, starting with the moves into Shanghai and Hamburg. A year later came the decision to take over the Paris and Le Havre offices of rival Constant & Constant. That firm was a shipping specialist as well, so the fit was obvious. Thus, Ince & Co has grown into a firm with a global footprint, remaining focused on the core areas of shipping and trade, insurance, aviation, energy, business and finance, and general commercial disputes.

Ince & Co does things a little differently. Instead of dividing its lawyers into practice areas, the sector focuses are well and truly embedded at the firm. Young Ince lawyers can be called on by any of the partners to help out, which means they are developing generalists who are not, the firm says, pigeon-holed into narrow specialisms like acquisition finance, for example, as they would be at larger practices.

The firm divides into six core business strands, including a shipping and trade group. That team covers everything from ship casualties, through EU and competition, to cargo recovery and defence for the industry. In 2004 the firm won the *Legal Business* award for Shipping Team of the Year, following its advice to the owners of the Prestige, which had hit violent storms off the Spanish coast in 2002. The oil tanker sunk and the oil spillage caused major pollution and environmental damage, with an ongoing clean-up cost over the ensuing years of some £588 million, making it one of the largest ever. These are the kinds of cases you work on at Ince & Co.

Shipping news

One of the biggest shipping areas is maritime insurance, and from that base, the firm has developed a market-leading insurance and reinsurance team, both marine and non-marine. Here the firm globally acts for those who provide insurance, those who broker it and those who buy it. Then, from its shipping and transport routes, the firm moved into aviation law, another area where it is now a specialist. The firm's litigators in the area are amongst the best there are, and the aviation team includes the former legal director of Emirates.

In energy, the firm has long been a leader in oil and gas, but is increasingly moving into renewables. In commercial disputes, the firm is just at the top of the game. Indeed, in 2002 a Commercial Court working party announced that between them, Ince & Co and Clyde & Co were doing more than half the cases coming before that court. Perhaps not surprising, given the bulk of the cases there are in insurance, maritime and commodity disputes, but still a pretty good show. Moreover, the firm has ranked in the top five when it comes to rankings of firms for reported shipping litigation cases since 2002: in 2002 it did 10 cases, nine in 2003 and a bumper 13 in 2004, keeping it well up against the competition.

There is then a steady business and finance group, covering restructuring and insolvency, intellectual property, employment, real estate and private client, amongst other things. And finally, somewhat originally, there is the Emergency Response Unit, manned 24 hours a day, 365 days a year, to give rapid legal advice when there's a disaster.

Growing business

Ince & Co may have an incredibly stable business, and it may prefer to get the work done than talk about it, but it is nevertheless expanding at quite a pace. In the last few years it has been gobbling up ship finance partners from its rivals like they are going out of fashion: first from Sinclair Roche & Temperley, and then from Norton Rose. In 2004, the firm even appointed its first business development partner in a bid to generate more work and new clients. Indeed, it's all change at the firm, which moved into new London offices this summer after more than 33 years at the old abode. It is now right next to Tower Bridge, with great views of the City and Canary Wharf.

That has reportedly led to a boost in morale, which, when combined with a China boom in the shipping industry and some major reinsurance disputes work, meant that the financial year that ended in 2005 was a good one for the firm. Ince & Co is acting for reinsurers Cox and Cotesworth in a case called

Aon 77, one of the biggest reinsurance cases ever, which centres around an insurance policy covering energy risks brokered by Aon, underwritten by five Lloyd's syndicates and reinsured by Cox, Cotesworth and Euclidian.

With major clients including Ace Aviation, Gard Services, Nordisk, Transocean and Vitol, Ince & Co is a firm well and truly embedded in its industry. With growing work in non-contentious shipping, like ship finance, it isn't just the firm's London premises that are going places.

Psst...
Need a Change in Venue?

Use the Internet's most targeted job search tools for law professionals.

Vault Law Job Board
The most comprehensive and convenient job board for law professionals. Target your search by area of law, function, and experience level, and find the job openings that you want. No surfing required.

VaultMatch Resume Database
Vault takes match-making to the next level: post your resume and customize your search by area of law, experience and more. We'll match job listings with your interests and criteria and e-mail them directly to your inbox.

For more information go to www.vault.co.uk/law

V/\ULT
> the most trusted name in career information™

Irwin Mitchell

150 Holborn
London
Central London EC1N 2NS
Tel: +44 (0)87 0150 0100
www.irwinmitchell.com

OTHER LOCATIONS

Birmingham
Leeds
Madrid
Manchester
Marbella
Newcastle
Sheffield

THE STATS

No. of lawyers: 310
No. of lawyers in London: 80
No. of offices: 7
Trainee intake: 40 (2004)
Trainees retained: 50% (2004)
Senior partner: Michael Napier

MAJOR DEPARTMENTS & PRACTICES

Acquisitions, Mergers & Disposals • Adjudication • Administrative & Public Law • Advertising & Marketing • Agency & Distributorship • Arbitration • Asset Management • Banking • Business Crime • Commercial Contracts • Commercial Dispute Resolution • Commercial Litigation • Commercial Property • Company Secretarial • Company Structure & Restructuring • Construction & Engineering • Contentious Probate • Conveyancing • Corporate Finance • Credit Management • Criminal • Data Protection • Debt Recovery • E-commerce • Education Litigation • Employee Benefits • Employee Share Plans & Share Options • Employment • European Law • Family • Financial Services • Flotations • Franchising • Group Actions • Health & Safety • Housing • Information Technology • Insolvency • Insurance • Intellectual Property • Joint Ventures • Judicial Review • Landlord & Tenant law • Partnerships • Pensions Litigation • Pensions Trustee Services • Personal Injury • Planning • Private Equity • Professional Negligence • Property Litigation • Public Companies • Public Sector • Regulatory • Retail Property • Sport • Takeovers & Mergers • Venture Capital • Wills & Trusts

THE BUZZ
WHAT EMPLOYEES AT OTHER FIRMS ARE SAYING

- "Good at what it does"
- "Provincial"

PLUSES
- Supportive and friendly colleagues
- "Excellent quality of work"

MINUSES
- Modest salary
- "A lot of the time it is like being in school"

NOTABLE PERKS
- Firm contributes to private health care

BASE SALARY
Trainee: £18,000

GRADUATE RECRUITMENT CONTACT
Jane Horton
Graduate Recruitment Partner
E-mail: jane.horton@irwinmitchell.com

THE SCOOP

That Irwin Mitchell ranks in the top 20 of the U.K.'s leading law firms by revenues is testament to that good old British tradition of diversity, for the firm is almost unlike any other. Founded 90 years ago in Sheffield, it has grown rapidly from humble roots in the personal injury business. Irwin Mitchell is divided into four divisions: IMbusiness and Private Client, insurance services, IM Personal Injury, IM Asset Management and IM Private Client. Then there are two offices in Spain and a London-based travel litigation group—the largest of its kind in the country—that joined the personal injury team in 2003 through a merger with City firm Lorenzo Zurbrugg. It specialises in representing mainly claimants in accidents that happen abroad. Few, if any, firms can boast of a more varied practice.

Personal injury and beyond

Personal injury is where Irwin Mitchell originally made its name. It's a volume business, processing claims on behalf of injured parties, but it makes a profit even though the margins are being squeezed. It's an oddity amongst top U.K. law firms: recent cases range from recovering £1,100 for a man injured by a poorly maintained crane, through to acting for a group of people who suffered heart attacks which they claim resulted from taking Vioxx, and who are bringing a class action in the U.K. against pharmaceuticals giant Merck.

Having realised that such business may not be the most lucrative around, the firm decided in the mid-1990s that it may be more sensible to start working for the insurers, as well as the insured. Clients there now include Direct Line, Churchill, esure and Eagle Star; evidence that such a strategy of advising both the company and its customer could in fact pay off. The private client department is divided into four areas—you're getting a feel of just how huge and disparate this firm is now: family law; conveyancing; wills and trusts; and criminal law. The criminal law practice is probably the most interesting, as again it's something you won't find in your average top U.K. law firm. It is one of the departments on which the firm was founded, and so it stays around, and is amongst the leading defence teams in the north of England through its offices there.

No fear of controversy

The criminal defence work crosses neatly over with the firm's fraud and white-collar crime practice, which is one where Irwin Mitchell is truly top notch. The practice sits in the IMbusiness division and has done some cracking, albeit controversial, cases. The team advised Mohammed Abacha, the son of the deceased Nigerian dictator, in a High Court dispute about whether the family stole millions of pounds from Nigeria. Other work in the business crime team includes work on the long-running BCCI litigation, and on the Jubilee Line extension fraud case, one of the most expensive fraud prosecutions ever brought in the U.K.

This kind of work forms the basis of Irwin Mitchell's London presence. The firm only opened in the capital in 1995, and merged in 1998 with debt recovery and insolvency specialists Braby & Waller. Thus even though the firm's IMBusiness section can turn its hand to almost any corporate and commercial work, the fact remains that around 80 per cent of the firm's income is derived from litigation, be it insurance, insolvency or negligence.

Assets under management

The final department at the heart of Irwin Mitchell is IM Asset Management. The firm is one of very few to have opted to set up its own asset management arm when regulations changed a few years ago, and this part of the practice is essentially ring-fenced outside of the legal firm. It is regulated by the Financial Services Authority, rather than the Law Society, but offers clients advice on their investments, with lawyers on hand to help if necessary.

Here the fit is probably obvious: that guy who got a windfall from being hit by a crane needs to know what to do with the cash, and Irwin Mitchell is there to help. Then of course it can help you with buying and selling property, or reorganising your assets in the case of family breakdown, for example. The firm's profits are right up there with its London rivals, even though Irwin Mitchell is essentially a northern firm. The profit margin may be a rather modest 23 per cent (at Slaughter and May it is 44 per cent), but that doesn't matter if the cash is well managed. Just over 300 of the firm's 800-plus fee-earners are qualified lawyers, the rest being paralegals and the like, which goes some way to explain how the firm runs its leverage.

Pro bono publico

There is one other area where Irwin Mitchell truly leads the profession, and that is in pro bono work. The firm's senior partner Michael Napier was recognised in this year's New Year's Honours list for his work promoting pro bono, and is the Attorney General's pro bono envoy. Lawyers in the firm spend a total of 5,000 hours a year on pro bono, giving free legal advice to individuals and community groups who lack the means to pay, and where public funding is not available. A lot of the work is done through co-ordination with the Citizen's Advice Bureaux and Law Centres, while other corporate pro bono advice is given to charities and the like.

The firm set up its own charity in 1997, called 101 Donations, which gives to a whole host of charities. Irwin Mitchell has a dress-down day every week for which the staff donates, and that goes into the pot, as does around £14,000 a year from the employees, donated through a Give As You Earn scheme.

GETTING HIRED

Not just talk

"At IM we believe we are a different kind of law firm," reads Irwin Mitchell's web site. "We encourage individuality and embrace natural flair. We promote positive thinking and will listen to new and unusual ideas." Rhetorically, at least, the firm is open to innovation, appearing to distance itself from the stuffed shirt image of the profession. One IM solicitor tell us that the firm's spiel isn't lip service: "No, we're pretty openminded really. That's a good thing—there are no prejudices about qualifications or education. If you know your stuff and you are interesting and have a good way about you, you're in with a chance. I think the recruitment and interview process is pretty good actually. We seem to get good people here."

OUR SURVEY SAYS

IM social club

Solicitors at Irwin Mitchell appreciate that "the firm is excellent, providing good quality work and training" as well as "a friendly working atmosphere with an open plan policy." "People are the best part of the firm", they enthuse, and the "sociable" London location has "a small ... contingent of Friday night pub-goers" who enjoy blowing off some steam at the end of the week. For those who want to be part of the club but would rather not give up the first night of the weekend, never fear; "there are many social activities where all members of the firm are encouraged to interact."

Pleasant partners and strong training

Solicitors report that partners are "personable, pleasant people" on an individual level. "I have nothing but praise for the partners in my department," reports a source in the personal injury practice, "as they are excellent lawyers and positive, encouraging and inspiring people to work for." They place "great emphasis on legal training, which is of high quality," and informal training is also strong. Says an insider, "I am fortunate to work for patient supervisors who regularly give me time to supervise and assess my work and give me guidance and informal hints on how to deal with clients, situations, problem files, etc."

On the other hand, some IM insiders resent the partners who "keep themselves and their decisions to themselves." One lawyer tells us that "politically, the assistant solicitors and support staff tend to resent the partnership as 'taking all the profits for themselves' and not giving staff the support they need or the salaries they feel they deserve." A colleague complains that partners" behaviour makes working at Irwin Mitchell "like being in school."

North and South

Despite the widespread good will among IM solicitors, there are those in the London office who can't shake the feeling that they're the redheaded stepchildren of the firm. "The firm's head office is in Sheffield, so the London office gets treated like an expensive and irritating relation sometimes," explains a litigator. Adds another source, "Sheffield holds all the power and this is resented by the London office."

The daily grind

Like anywhere else, "There is a requirement to work the hours needed to get the job done," an attorney tells us. "If you want to progress your career you have to be prepared to work hard at it and put in the hours." There are times when hours can be "generally pretty good", but the sheer volume of work can make such a schedule close to impossible. "I work long hours partly through choice and partly because I feel I have to in order cope with the volume of work and in order to obtain promotions," comments a litigator. Thankfully, a new "flexi-time policy ... has recently been introduced", perhaps liberating some of the more stressed-out types at IM.

Jones Day

21 Tudor Street
London EC4Y 0DJ
Phone: +44 (0)20 7039 5959
www.jonesday.com

OTHER LOCATIONS

Atlanta • Beijing • Brussels • Chicago • Cleveland • Columbus • Dallas • Frankfurt • Hong Kong • Houston • Irvine • Los Angeles • Madrid • Menlo Park • Milan • Moscow • Munich • New York • Paris • Pittsburgh • San Diego • San Francisco • Shanghai • Singapore • Sydney • Taipei • Tokyo • Washington, DC

MAJOR DEPARTMENTS & PRACTICES

Antitrust & Competition • Business Restructuring & Reorganisation • Capital Markets • Complex Commercial & Multi-jurisdictional Litigation • Corporate Criminal Investigations • Employee Benefits & Executive Compensation • Energy Delivery & Power • Government Regulation • Health Care • Intellectual Property & Technology • International Litigation & Arbitration • Issues & Appeals • Labour & Employment • Lending, Structured Finance & Derivatives • Life Sciences • M&A • Oil & Gas • Private Equity • Products Liability, Personal Injury Torts & Health Litigation • Real Estate • Securities & Shareholder Litigation • Tax

THE BUZZ
WHAT EMPLOYEES AT OTHER FIRMS ARE SAYING

- "Good firm, great deals"
- "Very average"

THE STATS

No. of lawyers: 2,200
No. of lawyers in London: 180
No. of offices: 29
Trainee intake: 20 (2005)
Trainees retained: 100% (2005)
London partner-in-charge: Russell Carmedy

PLUSES

- Relaxed environment
- High level of responsibility

MINUSES

- "Laddish culture"
- "The lack of clear information about partnership decisions"

NOTABLE PERKS

- Good maternity benefits
- Everyone has their own office

BASE SALARY

Trainee: £39,000 (trainee salary increases every 6 months: £41,000, £45,000, £50,000)
Newly Qualified: £60,000

GRADUATE RECRUITMENT CONTACT

E-mail: recruit.london@jonesday.com

THE SCOOP

The London office of Jones Day is the result of perhaps the most controversial transatlantic merger yet, when the American giant took over the City corporate finance boutique Gouldens in February 2003. Gouldens was the mid-tier firm that no one thought would ever give in to the temptations of the Yankee dollar, but sure enough, the partners were convinced that their business would be better off as part of a global megafirm, and they put their hands up. Gouldens, which lost its name within months of the merger, is now part of one of the largest and most profitable firms in the world. The firm ranks ninth in the world by turnover, and is pretty well up there for partner pay too—the average partner took home nearly a million dollars last year.

Gouldens, RIP

Gouldens was known for its entrepreneurial spirit, and for high salaries, high profits and a unique approach to trainees. All four remain as part of its new profile: the firm still pays more than any other for trainees, and instead of rotating youngsters to four six-month seats, trainees are forced to seek out their own work and are not assigned to one partner or one practice area. It's pretty radical, but the firm says it develops well-rounded lawyers, even if it's not for the fainthearted.

While the cultural fit of Gouldens and Jones Day may have been tough—many partners voted with their feet as the City outpost was dramatically restructured—the business fit was obvious. Both firms were strong in corporate finance, with a healthy dose of litigation and real estate thrown in. For Gouldens, the chance to offer clients a cross-border capability, and hence get a slice of the bigger M&A, was too much to resist.

Corporate powerhouse

Among the firm's recent major deals, Jones Day has acted for the institutional and management shareholders of Arlington Securities plc on the sale of its entire issued share capital to Macquarie Goodman Group Limited for a base consideration of £163 million and further consideration of up to £20 million. The firm also won its first major piece of work for WL Ross & Co., an existing client of the U.S. practice, in connection with its successful bid for the insolvent Collins & Aikman European Group and its $600 million operations in Belgium, Czech Republic, Germany, Netherlands, Slovakia, Spain, Sweden and United

Kingdom. This deal was short-listed as Restructuring Deal of the Year by *International Financial Law Review*.

On the real estate side, where the old Gouldens was always a leader, the firm still acts for what was once that firm's largest client, Pillar Properties (now part of British Land). In March 2005 a team worked for them making four retail park investments, totalling some £795 million. It also does a lot of work for Hercules Income Fund and Hercules Unit Trust. The firm is currently acting for a number of international real estate funds not only structuring the funds worldwide, but also investing the funds in U.K. real estate.

New growth areas

Gouldens used to do a huge amount of stock market work on London's Alternative Investment Market (AIM) and in 2005 Jones Day advised some of the increasing number of U.S., European and Asian companies coming to AIM—a trend that is likely to continue as the market grows. Recent transactions include advising U.S.-based biotechnology and aquaculture company Aqua Bounty Technologies, Inc. on its £20 million IPO and Beximco Pharmaceuticals, the first Bangladeshi company to obtain a quotation or listing in London, or, indeed, anywhere outside of Bangladesh.

One area of growth for 2005 has been the private equity practice, which has won work from a number of major players including Morgan Stanley, WL Ross & Co., one of the most profitable restructuring focussed private equity houses in the U.S., and Riverside, the most active private equity house by number of deals in the U.S. which is now breaking into the U.K. market.

The Jones Day finance practice has also seen recent growth, winning a number of significant deals for major banks. These deals include acting for JPMorgan Chase in a €3.5 billion acquisition financing for the Abertis-led consortium in connection with its successful bid to acquire the SANEF autoroute in France and for Morgan Stanley Real Estate Fund on the $386.8 million acquisition of Executive Offices Group from Soros Real Estate Investors and founder Peter Kershaw.

There are few firms in the City where you get a mix of entrepreneurial emerging company work and mega-M&A, but for now Jones Day is one of them. The energy work is also streaming in, not least as a result of the new Moscow office, which delivered the BP-TNK instruction, for example.

Culture clash

There is little doubt that the merger in London has been a rocky one. The departure of the former joint managing partner of Gouldens, Charters Macdonald-Brown, to set up his own intellectual property firm, was some evidence of discomfort, as was the move by the office's highly-rated tax team to the London practice of Fried, Frank, Harris, Shriver & Jacobson.

But putting together an individualistic firm like Gouldens and a monolith like Jones Day was never going to be easy, and some dissenting voices have since found happier homes. The renewed Jones Day London can get on with doing the tastier instructions for mega-clients—there's no denying that the firm is seeing the benefits of an increased client base and global footprint.

As an originally American law firm (though these days over 600 of its lawyers are based outside the U.S.), Jones Day has a bigger commitment to pro bono than most of its English counterparts. All Jones Day lawyers worldwide are encouraged to get involved and live up to the exemplary work of the U.S. practice, which acts on behalf of diverse needy clients. Speaking of clients, Jones Day has been recognized Number One for Client Service, from the BTI Consulting Group, Inc., Survey of Fortune 1000 corporate counsel, in 2002, 2004 and 2005. In 2004, Jones Day's score for service surpassed that of its closest follower by 37 per cent, and in 2005 the firm was honoured as a member of the BTI Client Service Hall of Fame.

GETTING HIRED

Must fit in

Jones Day, of course, requires stellar credentials. The firm's solicitors, however, say that applicants should be more concerned about their character and personality. "We are quite fussy about the sort of personality we hire—there has to be a fit," reports a fifth-year. "Otherwise we are openminded as to background, but at trainee-level we tend to recruit outgoing, academically solid candidates with plenty of personality." A seventh-year adds, "With trainees, we look to hire independent, smart people who want to think for themselves and who are mature beyond their years." The firm itself professes to look for "individuals who are motivated to skill development and professional growth," as well as those "whose academic record and professional and personal experiences demonstrate their commitment and drive to constant growth in a dynamic professional marketplace." Applicants should be looking for a firm that emphasises a team environment and should want responsibility for assignments "that are often intellectually challenging and that have direct, significant consequences for many of the world's most prestigious clients." During the interview process, the hiring partners do not rely on a set of predetermined questions, but rather try to establish a relaxed, in-depth conversation about a topic of mutual interest.

OUR SURVEY SAYS

Profess to be pleased

Jones Day's solicitors profess to be rather pleased with their jobs. "I do my job because I really enjoy it," reports a senior solicitor. "I am able to develop my practice with support from my colleagues both here and overseas and I work for a wide range of clients, with full opportunity to develop client relationships." It's not all sweetness and light. but those who do complain do so more about their chosen profession rather than their employer specifically. The job can be very "high pressure" and "aggressive", says another senior solicitor, but the firm does indeed provide a "very high quality of work."

Culturally—a nice mix

Solicitors call the firm "friendly", "supportive", "down-to-earth", and "slightly maverick", with "plenty of personalities." A senior litigator puts it like this: "The firm is relatively relaxed, in the sense that if you do your work well, your personal life is no one else's concern. People are generally supportive and keen to assist in new ventures. It is not very hierarchical ... Generally, yes, we do socialise with other lawyers and with the other staff." A junior litigator adds that the firm is "generally nonhierarchical", with a "good amount of mixing between departments and in particular between people of different levels of qualification." There is a "general feeling that the U.K. partners are looking after the interests of associates," she says.

Partners: individually fantastic; collectively maybe not so much

Jones Day's solicitors have nothing but kind words for the firm's individual partners, though they feel that the firm itself has a few institutional issues to resolve. "The partners I work with treat both solicitors and trainees with a lot of respect," reports a midlevel solicitor. However, he adds, "The firm management and the partnership as a whole is not able to allow us to participate in firmwide decisions, and is not particularly good at keeping us informed." A senior labour specialist agrees. "On a one-to-one basis, partners treat the associates very well—this is not a hierarchical place, and associates and trainees are trusted to get on with their jobs and seek help when appropriate … In terms of the larger management decisions, we are not always kept well informed … There is no feeling that information is purposefully being kept from us, but it does not always trickle down from those who know, often because they are too busy and do not seem to put a high priority on communication."

Formal training? Not here

The firm's solicitors say that this is not the place to work if one desires tons of formal training. "The firm complies with the Law Society's CPD requirements, but does little beyond that in the way of training," reports one midlevel solicitor. "Most of my learning has been on the job." A junior solicitor adds that formal training is 'fairly poor', but that 'a conscious effort is being made to improve this." A first-year solicitor says that she relies mostly on informal training: "Partners are generally very good at discussing strategy and in my experience provide very good mentoring to the more junior solicitors.'

Great compensation and reasonable hours

Essentially, no one complains about the pay at Jones Day. "Salary itself is very good", according to a senior solicitor, although she adds "I am concerned about the erosion of other benefits, particularly maternity benefits." One especially appreciated aspect of the compensation plan, according to a midlevel attorney, is that there is "very little emphasis made on meeting target hours, although it does impact on pay." A first-year adds, "The hours can sometimes be long, but certainly no longer than at other firms in the City (and significantly less than at some).'

This senior solicitor's comments seem to represent the consensus. "The hours are not bad—there is no hours culture, in that if you are not busy, it is not held against you if you go home," he reports. "However, if the work is there, you are expected to do it, and sometimes this means late nights—if I couldn't cope with that, I would never have become a City lawyer."

Kilpatrick Stockton LLP

One Canada Square
Canary Wharf
London E14 5NZ
Phone: +44 (0)20 7154 6000
www.kilpatrickstockton.com

OTHER LOCATIONS

Atlanta • Augusta • Charlotte • New York • Raleigh • Stockholm • Washington, DC • Winston-Salem

MAJOR DEPARTMENTS & PRACTICES

Construction & Public Contracts
Corporate & Business
Employee Benefits
Environment, Energy & Land Use
Finance
Financial Restructuring
Government Relations
Intellectual Property
Labour & Employment
Litigation
Real Estate
Tax/Trusts & Estates
Technology

THE STATS

No. of lawyers: 450
No. of lawyers in London: 40
No. of offices: 9
Managing partner: Jeb Jeutter

GRADUATE RECRUITMENT CONTACT

Lea Whiteside
E-mail: lwhiteside@kilpatrickstockton.com

THE BUZZ
WHAT EMPLOYEES AT OTHER FIRMS ARE SAYING

- "Solid mid-tier"
- "Still struggling in London"

THE SCOOP

Kilpatrick Stockton was formed in 1997 through the merger of Atlanta-based Kilpatrick & Cody, and Petree Stockton of Winston-Salem. Though both had been well-established names, the combined entity is new to this world, and it's fair to say its European experience has been one of finding its feet. The firm has had an outpost in London, and another in Brussels, ever since the 1980s, but it pretty much kept its head down, and then was a victim of a number of raids by rival American firms here after its merger.

Scandinavian satellite

Still, in 2001 the combined firm showed its first signs of serious investment on the Continent when it opened in Stockholm. Scandinavia is not an obvious jurisdiction for hungry U.S. law firms, but it is the home of a sizeable venture and technology market, and is increasingly attracting considerable private equity interest. Being one of very few international firms in Sweden, Kilpatrick has made the best of it and gets some interesting work through its doors there.

Things really kicked off for Kilpatrick in Europe in 2003 though, when the little-known firm shocked the U.K. market with its acquisition of the local branch of Altheimer & Gray. Altheimer was a small Chicago law firm, which had invested heavily in a 15-partner London office that was almost full service. The investment, it seemed, was beyond its means, and the firm folded, leaving its U.K. contingent homeless. Kilpatrick stepped into the breach, and took on the team to bolster its own offering over here, principally in small corporate venture work, projects and public-private partnerships, telecoms and real estate.

Outgrowing the office

Such a big acquisition meant Kilpatrick outgrew its Mayfair offices and relocated to a swanky HQ in Canary Wharf. Two years on, though, and the cracks started to show. A number of the old Altheimer partners left for pastures new, and the Kilpatrick management announced a restructuring of the U.K. operation that the firm said would realign the London business with its U.S. practice. What does this mean exactly? Well, it suggests that the Altheimer acquisition proved just that little bit too much to swallow. But it also means that the firm is remaking the London office into a mirror image of its U.S. self, leaving the bulk of Kilpatrick lawyers to peddle their wares on the job market while the IP folks carry the burden of rebranding. (There are grumblings, however, that room may be made for arbitration and labour practices). In the meantime, the Kilpatrick situation is doing little to rehab already-strained Anglo-American relations in the legal world: 'Frankly,' writes The Lawyer.com, 'it's another example of remote management from the U.S. causing the break-up of a previously reputable U.K. team.'

Practice what you preach

Back home in Atlanta, Georgia, Kilpatrick is known as a top-rate firm for intellectual property advice, and that is something it will now focus on in London. Also strong back home is international arbitration and global infrastructure work, though the latter will not be developed here for now. The plan now is to build on IP, employment, arbitration and corporate support, so, reportedly, the firm's real estate and project finance capability here is likely to be shown the door. After the Altheimer acquisition, the firm did make considerable hires in the areas it now hopes to focus on, most notably taking a pair of highly rated IP partners from Simmons & Simmons, one of whom was based in New York and launched the American firm's office in Manhattan.

Also welcomed was an arbitration partner from Clifford Chance, and an employment partner from the City office of Scotland's McGrigor Donald. This firm is certainly not afraid to invest, and is hoping that its renewed focus will now channel energies into the right direction. The firm's clients are an impressive bunch of names: it is one of the few firms to make the elite DuPont legal panel, and acts for BellSouth, Krispy Kreme Doughnut Corporation, Office Depot, PepsiCo, RJ Reynolds Tobacco, Smith & Nephew and Sara Lee, to name but a few.

Nice range

In London the firm's deals are not always huge—one recently announced was acting for MITIE Group buying The Watch Security for £8 million—but that just demonstrates the range on offer here. The firm also worked for Russo International Venture and MGM Productions Group, successfully defending a $16 million arbitration award against Aeroflot Russian Airlines. In 2004, Kilpatrick advised Carillion Private Finance and Prime LIFT Investments on the contract for the Birmingham and Solihull LIFT project, which could see a £100 million investment in the region over the next 20 years.

Elsewhere, the firm's telecoms instructions are not to be sniffed at. London has worked for BellSouth on the $20 billion sale of its stake in German telephone company E-plus to KPN, and worked for U.S. telecoms group PTEK on various acquisitions in the U.K., France and Switzerland. It acted for mobilePosition, a Swedish telecoms service provider won out of the Stockholm office, on its $80 million acquisition by SignalSoft, and worked for a U.S.-based e-commerce company in a $500 million acquisition of nine companies in eight jurisdictions across Europe, though it can't disclose any more detail than that, sadly.

Giving back

Kilpatrick's London operation is now pretty ensconced in the London legal community, and where the name was unknown five years ago, it is now established. Appointments such as the panel place for Partnerships for Schools, where the firm is one of only 12 firms working on the Building Schools for the Future framework, show that the market thinks its operation credible. There the firm won out in a competition of more than 30 vying to advise local authorities choosing private sector partners to help them meet government secondary school investment targets.

As a firm, Kilpatrick is active in giving back to the community, and that spirit is extended to pro bono efforts in London. Unsurprisingly, given its roots, the firm made some chunky donations to help the New Orleans region in the wake of Hurricane Katrina. On a more day-to-day basis, the firm just gave $100,000 to the Oklahoma Medical Research Foundation to create a small animal magnetic resonance imaging facility, allowing the state for the first time to study the cells and organs of genetically engineered mice and rats at near-microscopic levels. If the firm's latest announcement on employee benefits is anything to go by, its employees are well looked after too. Late in 2004 the firm said it would help employees get health coverage for obesity treatment, something rarely on offer (and presumably just coincidental to the Krispy Kreme representation).

Kirkland & Ellis LLP

30 St Mary Axe
London, EC3A 8AF
Phone: + 44 (0)20 7469 2000
www.kirkland.com

OTHER LOCATIONS

Chicago
Los Angeles
Munich
New York
San Francisco
Washington, DC

THE STATS

No. of lawyers: 1,000 +
No. of lawyers in London: 53
No. of offices: 7
Recruitment partner: Matthew Hurlock

MAJOR DEPARTMENTS & PRACTICES

Advertising • Antitrust & Competition • Appellate Litigation • Asset Finance & Securitisation • Biotechnology • Capital Markets • Class Action • Commercial Litigation • Construction Litigation • Corporate Finance • Corporate Governance & Counselling • Data Security & Privacy • Derivatives • Employee Benefits • Employment & Labour • Energy • Energy Transactions • Environmental • Financing & Secured Transactions • First Amendment & Defamation • Franchise & Distribution • Fund Formation • Government Contracts • Healthcare • Information Technology Transactions • Initial Public Offerings • Insurance Coverage Litigation • Intellectual Property • International Arbitration & ADR • International Trade • Internet & E-Commerce • Investment Management • ITC Proceedings • Leveraged Acquisitions • Marketing & Promotions • Mass Tort & Toxic Tort Litigation • Mergers & Acquisitions • Mezzanine Finance • Outsourcing • Patent Infringement Litigation • Pharmaceutical & Life Science • Private Company • Pro Bono • Product Liability Litigation • Real Estate • Restructuring • Securities & Shareholder Litigation • Strategic Alliances • Tax • Technology & Service Procurement Arrangements • Technology Transactions in Financial Services • Telecommunications • Telecommunications • Trademark & Copyright Litigation • Trademark Licensing • Trusts & Estates • Venture Capital & Private Equity • White Collar Criminal Defence

THE BUZZ
WHAT EMPLOYEES AT OTHER FIRMS ARE SAYING

- "Another rising US firm, highly respected"
- "Aggressive, long hours"

PLUSES

- "Small office environment with the support of a large firm"
- Great training

MINUSES

- Tough hours and demanding clients
- "Frustrating expenses system"

NOTABLE PERKS

- "Home leave allowance for trips back to the US"
- Dinner after 7, cars after 8 in the winter and 9 in the summer

BASE SALARY

Newly Qualified: £70,000

GRADUATE RECRUITMENT CONTACT

Caroline Nunn
Attorney Recruitment & Training Manager
E-mail: cnunn@kirkland.com

THE SCOOP

Chicago-based Kirkland & Ellis is one of the 10 most profitable law firms in the world, holding its own against stiff competition from both Wall Street and London's Square Mile. It makes its money by being a world leader in its four chosen practice areas of focus: private equity, intellectual property, litigation, and insolvency and restructuring.

Century-old newcomer

The 100-year old firm came to London in 1994, initially with a group of American partners working for some of its largest private equity clients. Those clients, the likes of Bain Capital and Madison Dearborn, were starting to invest their vast war chests in European assets, and were setting up their own London offices and European funds. Kirkland followed to help them structure both their money pots and their investments. Even before the firm added U.K. law capability to London in 2001, the firm would advise these American institutions on their deals, simply calling on local lawyers to help out where necessary.

Despite that, though, the firm decided in 2001 that it was going to invest in an English law practice, and it has become a pretty sizeable one. The office is now 53 lawyers strong, but there are big-name U.K. partners in all the key areas of the firm's international practice: restructuring, IP, finance, tax and litigation are all here alongside the private equity practice, which still goes from strength to strength. The firm recently poached some high-profile talent from a couple of Magic Circle firms, including private equity partners Raymond McKeeve and Graham White from Linklaters, and Stephen Gillespie, Allen & Overy's leveraged finance star. At the same time, one of the office's founding partners, Stuart Mills, announced that he would be leaving Kirkland in September to return to the U.S.

With private equity again in mind, the firm opened its second European office in 2004, when it moved into Munich with a partner from the local arm of Clifford Chance. Again the work is for those trusty longtime U.S. clients, and as their businesses expand across Europe, it seems only natural that Kirkland will follow.

Working capital

On the private equity side, then, Kirkland's London-led deals are not to be sniffed at. The firm advised London-based CVC Capital Partners raising

Europe's largest private equity fund, at €6 billion. In summer 2005, the firm represented Bain Capital in connection with its acquisition of FCI, Areva's connectors subsidiary, for €1.067 billion. The firm also worked for Madison Dearborn buying German equipment manufacturer Sirona, and won its first deal for U.K. buyout fund Change Capital Partners last year when it worked on the £115 million secondary buyout of the Hillarys Group for them. In Germany the firm has won work for U.K. fund Candover, thanks to the hire of Volker Kullman from Clifford Chance.

In restructuring, the firm hired Lyndon Norley from the top workouts group at Cadwalader, Wickersham & Taft to kickstart its City operation. London mandates already include work on the European administration of Collins & Aikman, a major producer of vehicle flooring and acoustic components, and the biggest U.S. company to file for Chapter 11 protection in 2005. Norley is working for Kroll, the administrators of the group's European branch.

Building London litigation capability

On the contentious side, the firm is building a London capability on the back of a U.S. practice that is at the top of its game. It recently hired a team from the London branch of New York's Shearman & Sterling. Back home, work includes advising Motorola, which is defending an environmental class action; as national trial counsel for General Motors; and the firm secured a $64.5 million win for Cable & Computer Technology for claims of fraud and breach of contract against Lockheed Martin. Here, partners serve as arbitrators and advocates in arbitrations sponsored by the International Chamber of Commerce, the London Court of International Arbitration and other European arbitration bodies.

In IP, the firm won $46.5 million for Honeywell after Hamilton Sundstrand wrongly used two of its patents in the production of aircraft auxiliary power systems, and represented Hermes in the reversal of a ruling that would have allowed the continued sale of knockoffs of the famous Hermes leather goods.

Finally, let's not forget the firm's public M&A practice, which, though overshadowed by the renowned private equity team, is nevertheless top-notch. Here we're talking work for General Motors spin-off Hughes Electronics in its $26 billion merger with News Corporation, and for TWA in its $4.2 billion merger with American Airlines. There's also BioChem Pharma's $4 billion link-up with Shire Pharmaceuticals.

Growing gains

As the build-out of London, and now Germany, has continued, so too has the firm's commitment to integrating into the local legal community. In 2005, the firm hired Francis Neate as of counsel in London—he is a former head of litigation at Slaughter and May, and one-time general counsel at Schroders. Nowadays he is the chair of the International Bar Association, which obviously takes a fair bit of time, but Kirkland has taken him on in part for his vast English legal experience, which it feels will benefit its junior ranks as it expands in London.

The firm moved in 2006 to new office space in the City's high-profile Gherkin building, at 30 St. Mary Axe, which will make it the envy of many contemporaries. The move down the street (out of the Natwest tower) will give it space for expansion.

In the States, the firm has a good commitment to pro bono activity and giving something back to the community, and it's keen to transport that ethos over here. It is also one of the firms most forthright about its diversity initiatives, so though it demands hard work of its lawyers, it's actually a pretty nice place to be. In 2004 one of its American partners was appointed as co-chair of The Lawyers' Committee for Civil Rights Under Law, which is a pro bono civil rights and anti-racism group set up by John F. Kennedy.

GETTING HIRED

A realistic glimpse of the future?

Kirkland & Ellis is proud of the difficulty of its interview process. Solicitors call the program "extensive" and suggest that candidates remember "that both partners and associates must approve of a candidate." "The key is having the right experience or interest," says a U.S.-trained associate from the firm's London office. "Best grades from the best school are meaningless if you are not interested in finance and private equity work (though, the office is diversifying by acquiring other specialty practices, such as arbitration)." Though there is no current U.K. trainee program, the firm itself professes to offer its U.S. summer associates a "realistic view" of their potential future as lawyers: "Our summer associate program is filled with challenging client matters, substantive training sessions and exciting social activities. Summer associates are given the tools to succeed in the 'free market' system, during their summer at the firm with assistance from both a partner and associate mentor."

OUR SURVEY SAYS

What more could you ask for?

Kirkland & Ellis' solicitors evince a remarkable degree of satisfaction with their jobs. "Associates at all levels are provided with very substantive and meaningful work and, for the most part, the work is interesting and our clients are very intelligent," reports a midlevel associate. "I'm much more satisfied here than at my previous firm," says a recent transfer. "Lots of responsibility and client contact. Lack of hierarchy means deal knowledge and opportunity to learn are greatly improved." A second-year solicitor raves, "The office environment is supportive, friendly and relaxed. Associates have real input into the direction of their training, with individual CPD budgets, a "free market" working system, and "no strict team structure."

Somewhere between "genuinely friendly" and "very friendly"

Solicitors call Kirkland & Ellis "fun", "supportive", "very friendly", "genuinely friendly", and "nonhierarchical with respect for home-life and life outside the firm friendly." There is a lot of "socialising horizontally between U.K. and U.S.-trained attorneys and vertically between partners and associates," according to one fourth-year. A third-year adds, "The firm is very grown-up compared to Magic Circle firms ... No one will raise an eyebrow about what time you arrive—unlike my last firm where I was criticised for arriving at 9:45 a.m. despite having been in the office until 4:30 a.m." A second-year solicitor calls Kirkland "the best of both worlds", featuring a "small-firm culture with huge infrastructure and reputation of the firm at large."

Pretty perfect partners

Insiders—believe it or not—also have only kind words for the partners. "All of our partners are easily accessible and do not mind one bit a casual or professional visit from associates," reports one corporate lawyer. "Partners are generally very bright and some partners go out of their way to provide solid on-the-job training," echoes a colleague. Another K&E solicitor reports that "share and non-share partners alike are very approachable." A junior insolvency specialist adds, "I have only been at the firm a short while, but so far everyone I have encountered has treated me with respect and equality."

Training: typical weakness a strength

Kirkland & Ellis' solicitors even rave about the firm's formal training, a frequent source of complaint at other firms. They call it "organised", "open to individual needs," and "regular and comprehensive." "Kirkland has the best formal training program hands down," claims a fourth-year. The in-house training programs, he adds "are fabulous for those associates that truly care about our practice." One additional reason for the praise: each solicitor's $5,000 per year budget for outside training.

The informal training is equally effective, solicitors say. "The partners with whom I have worked have all been great teachers," reports one junior solicitor. "There are one or two partners here that are not focused on teaching associates, but, given our free-market system, associates tend to avoid working for them."

Compensation commentary

Kirkland & Ellis' solicitors may have an issue or two with their compensation, but the general consensus is that there is "good basic pay" and "adequate" end-of-year bonuses. "People always think they are getting paid too little for the amount of hours worked. I agree with this statement at times, but not always," reports one insider. "Bonuses tend to reflect quality and quantity of work, and vary accordingly. Kirkland tends to be more of a meritocracy than other peer group firms."

Long, but flexible

If Kirkland & Ellis is the "best of both worlds"—a big-time firm with a small-firm feel—its hours requirements appear to represent a little of each world, depending on the solicitor. But generally, solicitors say, one should simply expect to work hard. "Kirkland is not a lifestyle firm and nobody joins Kirkland under false pretences," according to one midlevel attorney. "I believe associates here work as many hours and as hard as our peer firms (e.g., Simpson Thacher and Sullivan & Cromwell). Like our peer firms, we offer around-the-clock, top-notch service. We do not aim to be a McDonald's or Tescos of legal practice." A seasoned corporate lawyer says, "The firm works long hours, but is very flexible about whether those hours are worked in or outside the office." A second-year adds, "While the hours can be bad, it is rarely for sustained or long periods of time."

Kirkpatrick & Lockhart Nicholson Graham LLP

110 Cannon Street
London, EC4N 6AR
Phone: +44 (0)20 7648 9000
www.klng.com

OTHER LOCATIONS

Boston • Dallas • Harrisburg • Los Angeles • Miami • New York • Newark • Palo Alto • Pittsburgh • San Francisco • Washington, DC

MAJOR DEPARTMENTS & PRACTICES

Arbitration • Banking • Commercial Litigation/Dispute Resolution • Competition • Construction & Engineering • Corporate Finance • Corporate Tax and VAT • Employment Financial Services and Funds • Healthcare & Pharmaceuticals • Information Technology • Insolvency & Restructuring • Insurance Coverage • Intellectual Property • Music Rights • Planning and Environment • Private Equity/Venture Capital • Projects/PFI/PPP • Real Estate • Real Estate Finance • Real Estate Litigation • Sport and Sponsorship • Telecoms • Travel and Leisure

THE STATS

No. of lawyers: approximately 1,000
No. of lawyers in London: 142
No. of offices: 12
Trainee intake: 10 (2005)
Trainees retained: 60% (2006)
Administrative (Managing) Partner: Antony Griffiths

PLUSES

- "Good work/life balance"
- Approachable partners

MINUSES

- "The amount of admin involved in billing"
- No canteen for associates (until summer 2006)

NOTABLE PERKS

- Associate symposium in Pittsburgh
- Firmwide 1st-year Academy in Pittsburgh
- Car rides if working late

BASE SALARY

Trainee: £28,000
Newly Qualified: £49,000

THE BUZZ
WHAT EMPLOYEES AT OTHER FIRMS ARE SAYING

- "Nice firm"
- "Middling"

GRADUATE RECRUITMENT CONTACT

Apply online at klng.com (and then by entering the UK graduate recruitment pages)

THE SCOOP

On 1 January 2005, Kirkpatrick & Lockhart sealed one of the largest transatlantic law firm combinations to date when it tied the knot with London's Nicholson Graham & Jones. Combined, the two firms have approximately 1,000 lawyers, 142 of them based in London.

Hands across the water

Kirkpatrick & Lockhart's institutional history arose following WWII, when seven lawyers returned from their war responsibilities to launch Pittsburgh-based Kirkpatrick, Pomeroy, Lockhart & Johnson. The firm began its growth in 1981 when merging with Washington, D.C.-based Hill, Christopher & Phillips, increasing its ranks to 120 lawyers. In the last 20 years they have added nine offices and a whole raft of lawyers to hit the 800-lawyer mark pre-combination with their London colleagues.

Nicholson, Graham & Jones, for its part, was a well-regarded London full-service operation that had been around for 100 years, advising City corporate financiers and small companies on their deals. As their cultures and practices were complementary, the two firms were well suited for a match. Hence, the tie-up.

Combination drivers

The two areas where K&LNG now plans to expand operations on this side of the Atlantic, beyond the mainstream corporate, litigation and real estate stalwarts, are in investment funds work and insurance coverage disputes. Both are large for the firm as a whole, and were the apparent drivers for transatlantic expansion. The firm's key clients will be the likes of DuPont, Halliburton, Alcoa and United Technologies on the corporate side, while the bank clients include the likes of Bank of America, Merrill Lynch, Wachovia and Fidelity Investments.

Though little known in London prior to the January 2005 combination, Kirkpatrick does boast one of the leading investment funds practices in the United States, advising on the set-up of a huge number of mutual funds, hedge funds and private equity funds. This was a small business for Nicholson Graham, but it was there, and it is something that is taking off in London as American hedge funds, in particular, look to spend their cash on European assets. Hence that is one area where the combination of two and two really could make five, and where the competition is sparse.

Growth plan

With the combination now settling in, the firm's growth plan is to increase the number of lawyers in London long term. In the first two years the London operation will gradually move towards the American way of doing things, with partners increasingly being paid according to merit instead of the U.K. system of lock-step, which pays according to seniority.

There are also ambitions to grow on the Continent, though the firm is yet to stake its colours to the mast and name either when or where it will open its first Continental outpost. Still, if the last 20 years of growth stateside are anything to go by, you get the feeling the firm will soon start motoring.

Already Kirkpatrick has got its City expansion under way. First up was the hire of Trevor Nicholls from Mayer Brown Rowe & Maw, where he was a construction specialist. He brought with him work on infrastructure projects including Newcastle Hospital, North Staffordshire Hospital, Leicester Hospital, Surrey County Council and Swindon Schools, perhaps demonstrating that joining up with the Americans has not dampened the appetite for U.K. domestic work. The firm's London arm was already working on a public-private partnership deal referred to it from the U.S., involving Kellogg Brown & Root and the Mexican government.

More hires

The next hire was Addleshaw Goddard IT partner John Enstone, and then there was Allen & Overy senior associate Jonathan Lawrence, who joined as a partner focusing on offshore trusts and securitised financing; Martin Lane, previously a partner at Pinsent Masons, arrived shortly afterward with a particular view to assisting the development of K&LNG's standing with City institutions such as investment banks, brokers and accountants. He was followed by Ian Fraser (share schemes tax partner) and Kevin Dean, (international M&A partner). More recently three lateral senior associates, Jeremy Davis and Ed Smith from Jones Day, and Kathryn Thomas from Shearman Sterling have also been promoted into the partnership. Meanwhile, back in the U.S., K&LNG added a white-collar crime practice, a California Unfair Competition Law practice, and, most recently, a stem cell technology practice. The firm bolstered its private equity and intellectual property teams and also opened an office in Palo Alto, all going some way to demonstrating this is a firm that just won't stand still.

Deal maker

In London, the work levels have had a nice shot in the arm from Kirkpatrick's weighty U.S. corporate practice. The clients here continue to include Sky Capital, Henderson Global Investors and Laing O'Rourke, with other major clients like the London Underground already on the roster.

There are also some niche practices that you won't find in your average American law firm, like a pretty well-renowned sport group that advises the Ryder Cup, a travel and leisure group, and an electoral law team that advised on the introduction of postal ballots and handled the only petition for a European parliamentary election.

The K&LNG London corporate team worked for A.S. Watson Limited's acquisition of Merchant Retail Group plc, IB Daiwa Corporation's acquisition of Lodore Resources Inc and the SHS Group Limited takeover of Merrydown plc.

Wrestlers v. Pandas

The firm also represents the National Greyhound Racing Club on its rules and disciplinary procedures, and advises World Wrestling Entertainment in a long-running dispute with the Worldwide Fund for Nature over the use of the initials WWF.

All of which makes for a pretty diverse practice, where you get the feeling that no two days will ever be quite the same. Whilst benefiting from the might of a large U.S. firm behind it, Kirkpatrick is nevertheless well established in the U.K., so things like its graduate training programmes and pro bono efforts have been up and running for a long time.

For more than five years, the firm's lawyers have participated in regular open legal surgeries at the Battersea Law Centre, giving assistance and representation to individuals without access to law in areas such as housing, employment and welfare rights. That effort was recognised at the recent Young Solicitors Group Pro Bono Awards, where Marc Sosnow, London coordinator of the firm's pro bono activity, received £1,000 for continued commitment and support at the centre.

GETTING HIRED

Picky, picky

Just about every firm claims to be the most selective of the selective, the most elite of the elite, and K&LNG is no different—give us the "2:1 honours degree from Oxbridge or red-brick university and A-levels equivalent to 26 UCAS points", its partners cry, while also demanding laterals "with previous commercial experience." Before we lump K&LNG with all the rest, however, we must divulge that the firm does separate itself from the pack, and we're not referring to its attempt to amp up BigLaw's funk quotient (if there is any) with nontraditional ampersand placement. Rather, K&LNG insiders can point to numbers to prove the degree of difficulty to getting a trainee placement at the firm. "I was recruited as a trainee and the process is very competitive. At the time there were around 2,000 applicants for 10 places," recalls a solicitor. My, my. That's tough. The firm may be picky, but it is not cruel, continues the same source, who tells us that "the process itself was relatively painless and the open day for applicants is an excellent way of allowing you to see the firm and for them to see you face-to-face outside of the interview room."

OUR SURVEY SAYS

Mutual appreciation

K&LNG solicitors are able to lend their talents to "varied, very satisfying" work in a "very nice culture" with a "motivating and friendly working environment" that encourages being "academic and individualistic." Considered "laid-back", K&LNG is noteworthy for its "very open and approachable supervisors" who are happy to make note of a job well done, rather than focus on the negative. "The work I do is appreciated and I will always be thanked and praised for a good job which is not the experience of many contemporaries at other firms," raves one former trainee. "My working hours are manageable and the fact that I have a life outside work is never forgotten." Communication appears to be key at the firm, where the atmosphere is "completely open door" and there is "good support from partners." Comments a source, "You are left to get on with the job but with support, backing and encouragement."

Cross training

Of course, part of this support comes in the form of training, about which the firm's solicitors can't say enough. The "excellent and broad ranging" formal training includes monthly seminars, and solicitors "are encouraged to go to outside events and seminars," explains a source. And partners want to make sure that what they offer is actually helpful, says a lawyer: "Feedback is requested on all internal seminars.' However, the high marks for such training are a recent phenomenon, and not everyone agrees. "It's not been consistently good," sighs an insider who appears sympathetic to the difficulties faced by large firms on this front. "The problem with department training is that trying to cover the range from partners to trainees in a lunch hour can lose focus." A colleague agrees, but is more optimistic: "Hopefully things will improve with the appointment of an individual responsible for HR and development." K&LNG does have a "very good mentoring scheme," according to one solicitor, but many of the firm's lawyers feel that it is not up to snuff. The quality "is variable" and "very poor in some cases," we're told, due in part to the fact that mentors do receive formal training, but "the quality of mentoring depends on the will of the mentor to get involved." Others feel that "there is a good culture of helping each other out, and taking time to explain things," rendering the need for formal mentorship redundant.

The English patient

Solicitors also praise partners for being "receptive" and "patient', and making sure "individual associates are treated well and with respect.' Though there is debate about the firm being "hierarchical" or 'not too hierarchical', there is a consensus that "treatment of associates … is entirely respectful, proper and cordial." Partners do leave associates out of the loop somewhat, but this is improving with the implementation of "a symposium of junior members of the firm where associates can air their opinions, and the regularly scheduled 'Questions for Tony' (the managing partner in the London office), which helps keeps us involved in what is going on."

Hanging out

"Caring, human" and "co-operative," K&LNG does have a social element, but there is more of a "close-knit" culture among trainees, particular departments and specific seniority bands. There are some planned social events and sports teams, but such activities do not dominate as they do at peer firms. It also avoids cliques: "The firm"'s culture tends to be inclusive and open both in professional and social terms," explains a lawyer. While people seem content with the firm's steady, relaxed socialising, others have a more burning desire. As one attorney tells us, "We do socialise but it would be better if we did so more."

Punching in

It may be that with the emphasis on balancing work and the rest of life, there isn't the need to socialise like mad, as they do at firms where they don't see anyone but each other. At K&LNG "you're expected to work hard but to also have a life outside work" and "to make the most of free time." There is no face time, and "the culture of the firm is such that you are expected to stay late when the work dictates that it is necessary to, not just to be 'seen' to be staying late." Of course hours can be "unpredictable", as they "are always subject to the client's needs", but, depending on the department, hours can be considered "reasonable" for the field—that is, if you consider 8:30 a.m. to 7:00 p.m. reasonable. However, "when things aren't so busy, it is not frowned on to leave at 6ish", and flexible schedules "are encouraged." "It can get a bit busy at times," allows a solicitor. "But life's like that." Others who are concerned about the firm "becoming less people-focussed and more target driven" are watching how the firm's recent merger unfolds: "It will be interesting to see whether our target hours increase following the merger ... I am trying not to be cynical about the effect of merging with a U.S. law firm and the adverse impact that can have on targets and hours needed in the office. We'll see."

Trade-offs

Like clockwork, the true complaints are saved for compensation. One insider gripes, "The salaries are just within the average bands for a City practice, let alone an international practice." But some solicitors see it as a trade-off; says one, "My understanding is that we get paid slightly less than the big City firms but are expected to put less in." Sadly, everyone seems to be aware that "the firm's bonus scheme is a joke and little recognition is given to the amount of time spent by people doing non-billable work. The "generally small" bonuses do not "provide much incentive to work beyond the minimum."

GO FOR THE GOLD!

ET VAULT GOLD MEMBERSHIP
ND GET ACCESS TO ALL OF VAULT'S
WARD-WINNING LAW CAREER INFORMATION

- Access to **500+ extended insider law firm profiles**

- Access to **regional snapshots** for major non-HQ offices of major firms

- Complete access to **Vault's exclusive law firm rankings**, including quality of life rankings, and practice area rankings

- Access to **Vault's Law Salary Central**, with salary information for 100s of top firms

- Receive **Vault's Law Job Alerts** of top law jobs posted on the Vault Law Job Board

- Access to complete **Vault message board archives**

- **15% off** all Vault Guide and Vault Career Services purchases

more information go to
ww.vault.co.uk/law

VAULT
> the most trusted name in career information™

Latham & Watkins LLP

99 Bishopsgate
London EC2M 3XF
Phone: +44 (0)20 7710 1000
www.lw.com

OTHER LOCATIONS

Brussels • Chicago • Frankfurt • Hamburg • Hong Kong • Los Angeles • Milan • Moscow • Munich • Newark • New York • Reston • Orange County • Paris • San Diego • San Francisco • Shanghai • Menlo Park • Singapore • Tokyo • Washington, DC

THE STATS

No. of lawyers: 1,800+
No. of lawyers in London: 130+
No. of offices: 22
Trainee intake: 10-15 trainees (2008)
Trainees retained: Figures not yet available: first intake March 2006
London managing partner: Andrew Moyle

MAJOR DEPARTMENTS & PRACTICES

Corporate
  Communications • Corporate Finance/Securities • Equity Capital Markets • Health Care • IP • Life Sciences • Public Company Representation • Public M&A • Private Equity • Technology Transactions • Outsourcing Venture & Technology
Environment
  Land & Resources
Finance
  Banking • Bankruptcy • Project Development & Finance • Energy • Structured Finance • Real Estate
Litigation
  Antitrust & Competition • Appellate • Communications • Employment Law • Entertainment • Sports & Media • Government Contracts • Health Care • Life Sciences • Insurance Coverage • Intellectual Property & Technology • International Arbitration • Securities & Professional Liability • Torts • White Collar & Corporate Compliance
Tax
  Benefits & Compensation • International Tax • Tax Controversy • Tax-exempt Organizations • Transactional Tax

THE BUZZ
WHAT EMPLOYEES AT OTHER FIRMS ARE SAYING

- "Best of the US firms to work for in London"
- "Think they're better than everyone—why?"

PLUSES
- Great pay package
- "Relaxed flat organisational structure"

MINUSES
- "Gruesome" hours
- No cafeteria

NOTABLE PERKS
- Espresso machine
- Monthly associate pizza lunches

BASE SALARY
Trainee: £35,000
Newly Qualified: £88,044

GRADUATE RECRUITMENT AND TRAINING MANAGER
Tracy Davidson
Trainee Coordinator
Phone: +44 (0)20 7710 1000
E-mail: london.recruitment@lw.com

THE SCOOP

Among the best American law firms working in the Old Smoke, there is no denying that Latham & Watkins has become one of the City's major players. Founded in Los Angeles back in 1934, the firm was a relative newcomer to London when it opened its doors over here in 1990, keeping a low profile as a project finance boutique for a few years before expanding its operations.

The merger that never was

In 2001, Latham entered merger talks with London stalwart Ashurst, in an ambitious attempt to pull off a market-shaking merger. By all accounts, those discussions went into some detail, and many will tell you it is one of the greatest law firm mergers that never was. Both sides abandoned the idea in 2002, citing the cultural difficulties of putting such different organisations together. Latham bounced back, however, immediately announcing a Plan B: To build and expand its own full-service operation on this side of the Atlantic.

So began a programme of lateral hiring in London that has taken the office to more than 130 lawyers practicing everything from banking and finance, competition, corporate, employment, litigation outsourcing, real estate and tax law. Capitalizing on its resources and prestige, Latham has managed to attract some of the City's finest laterals. European expansion has been a success as well, with continental offices in Brussels, Frankfurt, Hamburg, Milan, Moscow, Munich and Paris. By establishing a European presence, Latham has become a force on a global level, with more than 1,800 lawyers practising in 22 offices worldwide.

A truly global partnership

Though founded in L.A. Latham is now arguably the only global law firm that can genuinely claim to be without a headquarters. It may not have heralded from New York, but its office in the Big Apple is now bigger than its office in L.A. Meanwhile, its chairman is based in San Francisco and its executive committee members are dotted across the globe including one in London—former office managing partner David Miles—who was recently elected to the executive committee. So no one office reports to another, with London reportedly given just as much autonomy and power as any of the sibling offices in the U.S. This sense of unity and partnership extends to those just joining the firm; in fact, every partner who joins has to do a world tour—literally—and is interviewed by as many as 100 Latham lawyers before it is agreed that he or she can join, while associates have a say in which of their contemporaries are promoted to partnership. And partners are paid not on the basis of seniority, as they are at U.K. firms, nor on the basis of the hours billed, as in most U.S. firms; rather it is based on the work they generate for themselves and their colleagues, so Latham partners actually get the same incentive for giving their partners work as they would have for hoarding it themselves.

No denying financial focus

Known for work on high-yield debt—an American asset class that is still fairly new to the U.K.—Latham found a capital markets niche over here and has grown it. The firm also acts for private equity clients including Carlyle, though it will not deny that it is essentially a finance firm, having built its practice on the back of investment banks, first in L.A. and then New York, and successfully transporting those links to London.

Recently Latham has been quite busy, advising on the restructuring of British Energy, a precedent-setting deal for the industry, and assisting some of the banks on the restructuring of Gate Gourmet, the catering company at the heart of the British Airways strikes in the summer of 2005. It also worked for the financiers in the sale of Wind of Italy to Weather Investments, currently one of the largest leveraged buyouts globally, and advised Charterhouse Capital Partners LP on the sale of Coral Eurobet, one of the world's leading betting and gaming operators, to Gala for £2.18 billion. Latham's finance department advised Cablecom, Switzerland's largest cable television service provider, in its landmark CHF1.425 billion financing. On the arbitration side of things, Latham's London public international law team advised the government of Barbados on the first ever international maritime delimitation arbitration, and in projects, the office worked for the Export-Import Bank of the United States and the Italian Export Credit Agency SACE on the financing of two liquefied natural gas production facilities in Qatar. Commercially, Latham's London lawyers worked for E.ON Kernkraft, the nuclear subsidiary of German utility company E.On, on its nuclear reprocessing contracts with British Nuclear Fuels Group. Its outsourcing team recently advised Scottish Widows Investment Partnership (SWIP) on the renewal of its investment operations outsourcing arrangement with State Street Corporation. The deal still remains one of the largest in Europe, covering the administration of assets in excess of £87.5 billion.

Commitment to the community

Latham brought the U.S. commitment to pro bono with it upon arriving in London. The firm's admirable efforts resulted in the office giving more than 3,000 pro bono hours in 2005, amounting to over 30 hours per attorney. Among its signature causes are Rosetta Life, a charity that uses film- and videomaking with its palliative care patients; North London's Roundhouse Theatre, which is currently fundraising for the redevelopment of its youth performing arts venue; women's volunteer organisation the Junior League of London; and Learning for Life, which works with South Asian organisations to provide educational opportunities for those traditionally marginalised, such as girls, the disabled and refugees.

Industry respect

For some, no good deed goes unpunished; for Latham, no good deed goes unnoticed. The firm has received praise far and wide, with accolades from Chambers and the Legal 500 directories as well as *The Lawyer*, *Project Finance* magazine and *Legal Business*. Latham was noted in the top tier of Legal 500's *Corporate Law Firms in London* for expanding quickly into mainstream U.K. practice and building up bigger teams than their rivals. Most recently, *International Financial Law Review* recognised the firm as having the Debt and Equity-Linked Team of the Year and the Debt and Equity-Linked Deal of the Year, and *Project Finance* magazine awarded the office two Deal of the Year accolades. In addition, a number of partners have received recognition in the likes of *The Lawyer*'s Hot 100, as well as top-tier rankings in *Chambers* and *Legal 500*. This string of accolades joins the long list of praise on the other side of the pond that includes *The National Law Journal*'s Hot Defense List and *The American Lawyer* A-List.

GETTING HIRED

Making the cut

Any "smart, self-starter who is willing to be a work horse" will fit in perfectly at Latham & Watkins. Anyway, such characters are likely the only people who want it so badly that they would be willing to sit through "three sets of interviews" involving some 12 lawyers, with the "final interview lasting circa three hours." And it doesn't end there. "All interviewers write ... reviews which are then considered before making the decision to hire," explains a source. If these so-called "reviews" are a mixed bag? Good luck. "If one person expresses reservations, you may not receive an offer," a solicitor tells us. "The firm is managed by consensus and this includes all associates having a say in relation to recruitment." Ways to reduce your chances of being ousted from consideration include being academically inclined ("I think it would be difficult for someone who didn't have at least a 2:1 to get a job here.") and being easy to deal with ("Laid-back and friendly people are the norm and anyone that is arrogant or unfriendly will not make the cut"). Though the process sounds terribly daunting, Latham is merely selective, not cruel; they try to make the "extensive interviewing ... as painless as possible." 2006 will be the first year the firm takes on trainees, having so far only hired qualified English lawyers from U.K. law firms.

OUR SURVEY SAYS

"A wealth of human talents and experience"

Because Latham attracts and chooses the academic sort, the satisfaction of the firm's solicitors is inevitably intertwined with the responsibility of the job and the stimulation of the work involved. "The work here is of an excellent quality and I am doing jobs that are above my level of qualification which provides great job satisfaction," raves a member of the banking practice. Aside from the "good levels of responsibility," it helps that there are "excellent working facilities, top-quality secretarial support, outstanding IT support (with literally worldwide resources) ... [and] a wealth of human talents and experience." A third-year appreciates that "I get to work in the way that I want and am allowed free rein to achieve the best results for my clients—a perfect combination." "As a profession and a career, law is never going to set my world on fire", adds a colleague, "but having worked elsewhere I cannot ever imagine working in another law firm."

Humane society

Despite their "hardworking" approach, Latham lawyers are "friendly" and "easy-going", sharing a "good camaraderie" in the "relaxed, laid-back" and "inclusive" firm. It is "the nicest place I have ever worked", brags a source, whose co-worker raves that "Latham's culture is the best thing about it. It is extremely open and meritocratic and treats attorneys like adults." The "very humane environment" is light on politics, focusing instead on "genuine interest in" and "respect of everyone." This translates into a social environment that includes "monthly pizza lunches and breakfasts [that] always bring out the crowds" as well as plenty of impromptu gatherings outside of the office.

The great wide open

An additional perk to the "very open culture" is the "pretty transparent" partnership "which encourages participation at all levels in the development of the practice and the office." An associates committee—"at least half of which are associates"—is just one way that solicitors are allowed to take part in firm management. Partners—who "seem like senior associates" rather than superiors—"seem to genuinely value input", allowing underlings to take part in the recruiting and hiring process and offering "a free flow of information (including financial)" that is described as "unbelievable" by one impressed solicitor. Though there are a couple of the inevitable "bad eggs," overall "the partner/solicitor relationship is as good as it could be", with candid communication and a "very flat management structure."

Mixed reports on mentoring

Formal training in Latham's London office is reportedly "evolving and improving as the firm grows in size", with "training via online conferences" and "an off-site 'academy'" in which all offices participate. Latham does have a formal mentoring program matching solicitors and partners, and there are those who feel it could also use a makeover. "Partners here are very poor on mentoring and would rather just focus on bringing deals in," grouses one source. However, this is far from a universal view: one happy mentee tells us, "My formal mentor has been extremely proactive when I have approached her with issues and she has helped to address some of these. The partner that recruited me is more of an informal mentor and is very supportive."

Working hard for the money

Face time is not an issue at Latham, which has "hours as demanding as any leading law firm," but doesn't expect one to stay into the wee hours of the morning for the appearances" sake. Of course the 1,900-hour billable goal keeps solicitors busy, but "the culture is to be flexible when you are less busy"—including working from home. When the pressure is on the hours are "ridiculous', even 'killer', but Latham solicitors have no illusions and whine minimally about them; as an insider points out, "Hours are high but you are aware of this when you take the job."

This attitude could lead some to call Latham attorneys well adjusted, but it is more likely that they're simply well compensated. Latham solicitors are "rewarded accordingly" for their lengthy days with "NYC rates", shares a source, "Who would complain about that?" On the always-contentious topic of bonuses, some Latham London insiders report that "bonuses are primarily based on billable hours" and that "[t]here is a bit too much emphasis on billable hours rather than quality of work in calculating bonuses." On the other hand, a colleague disagrees, "The salary is competitive and our bonuses really are a bonus. There are no complaints here." According to the firm itself, the evaluation process for bonuses "looks at commitment to the community, the support of one's peers, and contribution to business development."

Lawrence Graham LLP

190 Strand
London WC2R 1JN
Phone: +44 (0)20 7379 0000
www.lawgram.co.uk

OTHER LOCATIONS

London (1 additional office)
Monaco

MAJOR DEPARTMENTS & PRACTICES

Capital Raising • Outsourcing • Real Estate • Risk & Regulation

THE STATS

No. of lawyers: 280
No. of lawyers in London: 272
No. of offices: 3
Trainee intake: 18 (2005)
Trainees retained: 81% (2005)
Managing partner: Penny Francis

PLUSES

- "Not too bad" hours
- Relaxed environment

MINUSES

- Unpopular bonus scheme
- Part-time schedules discouraged

NOTABLE PERKS

- Profit-related bonuses
- Gym

BASE SALARY

Trainee: £28,000
Newly Qualified: £48,000

GRADUATE RECRUITMENT AND TRAINING MANAGER

Vikki Horton
Graduate Recruitment Officer
Phone: +44 (0)20 7759 6694

THE BUZZ
WHAT EMPLOYEES AT OTHER FIRMS ARE SAYING

- "Technically superb"
- "Seen as an also-ran"

THE SCOOP

Lawrence Graham is part of the resurgent London mid-tier legal market, a firm that has for a long time been ignored by the larger players but which lately has been nipping at their heels. The reasons are manifold, perhaps chief amongst them the fact that for a firm like Lawrence Graham, grounded in real estate, there was little choice but to face up to some serious strategic decisions when the corporate market dipped a few years back.

Revamped strategy

Lawrence Graham was one of many to realise that the dotcom boom was not going to deliver all that it had promised. The real estate practice, of course, offered much-needed stability at the time, and the firm's to-die-for client list kept things on an even keel. At that point the firm elected the former head of real estate, Penny Francis, to be firmwide managing partner, and she is reportedly a refreshingly energetic force within the practice. She realised the firm had to shape up if it were to survive, and also that the key to doing so was in playing to its strengths, not just property but also private client, where the firm advises more billionaires than any other City rival.

The strategy now is to get at corporate work through these two pillars of the practice, and it seems to be working. Lawrence Graham's profits have rocketed over recent years to a more-than-respectable £405,000 per equity partner, putting it in the upper echelons amongst its City peers. Untroubled by overseas offices, bar one outpost in Monaco for the private client work, the finances are looking bright, and a move into new offices in 2006 is being heralded as the last step in Lawrence Graham's transformation from West End real estate practice to true City player.

Client care

Lawrence Graham's list of real estate clients makes for a pretty formidable roster, amongst them Scottish & Newcastle, Legal & General, Hermes Property Asset Management and Axa. Multiplex and Development Securities were new clients secured in 2004, both of them significant. The firm advised the Globe Pub Company in a deal to buy 364 managed pubs from Scottish Courage for £345 million, and it is working for Centros Miller on the proposed development of the Canal Corridor North, a plan for a £100 million mixed use scheme to redevelop 10 acres in Lancaster City Centre.

Aside from the run-of-the-mill, albeit large, real estate work, Lawrence Graham is also increasingly playing with the big boys in complex real estate financing deals. It acted for Redevco on the £325 million securitisation of the majority of its U.K. real estate portfolio, which comprises 53 investment properties across the country. Then there was work for GMAC Commercial Mortgage Europe on senior and mezzanine facilities totalling more than £107 million, and the provision of equity funding for the acquisition of Vintners Place in London. On the corporate side, the plan now is to build on real estate opportunities, like working for real estate companies and funds buying assets, and to play on strengths from the private client side.

Where to put that money?

With such a glut of wealthy individuals on the books, Lawrence Graham has more opportunity than most to advise them on the start-up businesses either founded or backed by their high rolling clients. From the real estate side comes an expertise in outsourcing, and that was boosted in 2005 by the merger with Tite & Lewis, formerly the legal arm of Ernst & Young. And from the private client side, with the expertise in early stage business, comes an expanding amount of work floating companies on the Alternative Investment Market, London's junior stock exchange.

Lawrence Graham's corporate group is now picking up some big deals. It just acted for China's largest copper producer, Jiangxi Copper, on its sale of HK$880 million of new shares to investors, and it advised independent oil and gas company Knightsbridge Petroleum on the U.S. $460 million sale of its Venezuelan and Colombian oil production and exploration assets to French-listed oil company Etablissements Maurel & Prom.

Greyhounds, glass towers and gadgets

The private client team at Lawrence Graham is genuinely invested in and looked after, as evidenced by the acquisition of Eversheds" Monaco practice a few years back. In 2005 the firm won Private Client Law Firm of the Year at the High Net Awards. The firm also works in areas like housing associations advice, and shows no sign of neglecting these less than fashionable areas as it tries to transform its image. The firm has abundant retail expertise as well, which means assistants are regularly working for big household names. The firm was appointed to work for the Gadget Shop on its administration, for Wembley plc when it sold its greyhound racing business, and for Debenhams when it bought eight Allders stores out of administration.

In early 2007 Lawrence Graham will move into a flashy designer glass building overlooking the Thames at More London, on the South Bank. It's bound to give the firm a new lease on life and keep it motoring up the league tables—the firm's real estate expertise means it negotiated a great deal on the rent for its current office space, and you can bet it's pulled off a similar coup this time around.

Sure enough, Lawrence Graham is not as international as many of its competitors, and for young lawyers looking for cross-border work, this is probably not the place to go. But the firm has not missed the globalisation wave completely; it has close relationships with like-minded firms across Europe, which have proved sufficient for clients and far less costly for partners. This is a mid-tier firm that has quietly transformed its image, its work and its profits, and the slow and steady approach suggests it's been done in a sustainable way, too.

GETTING HIRED

The skills that pay the bills

Lawrence Graham makes no bones about the need for candidates to be of robust academic standing. Though partners apparently have little or no preference for one's field of study, it is, as ever, necessary to have attained at least a 2:1. The firm does understand, however, that it cannot depend on academics alone, and the right personality traits carry a good deal of weight. In addition to brain power, "team players" are also held in high esteem, so those with such experience—sports or otherwise—have an edge. Final necessity? Humour. It's definitely appreciated. Should one find one's self with none of the above, there may still be hope; a solicitor indicates that it's "hard to fill jobs in some areas as pay is too low."

OUR SURVEY SAYS

"Really nice people"

The folks at Lawrence Graham seem to be keenly aware that their satisfaction is most related not to pay, quality of work or ease of schedule, but to the genial culture of the firm, thought of as "very friendly and sociable." Solicitors—most considered "really nice people," according to one—do spend time together outside of the daily grind and manage to maintain the same approachability professionally. Lawrence Graham is "quite laid-back [and] very open door," and "everyone is keen and is committed to getting the work done within demanding deadlines. There is lots of support." While some believe that times have changed and the firm "used to be much more collegiate", Lawrence Graham is overwhelmingly characterised by insiders as a place where lawyers are "helpful to each other," rather than populated by the backbiters found elsewhere.

Cross training

Though there is some concern that the firm is "more concerned in teaching us networking skills than refreshing our legal knowledge," Lawrence Graham appears to be on the right track in the training department. "The training is absolutely excellent," a solicitor in the property practice tells us. "There is good general training, legal updating, market awareness and other appropriate skills for the job. This is now being tailored to the individual's needs." Partners are also on hand for more learn-as-you-go methods. "As I am a senior solicitor, I can obtain all the advice, help and assistance I require if I ask," one seasoned insider explains. And at least one attorney has "had a mentor partner since my trainee days."

Keeping mum

That isn't to say that the accessibility of partners makes them more forthcoming on firm issues. The "secretive partnership," like many others, tends to keep more sensitive information to themselves. "There are some attempts at letting the staff know about matters," a solicitor explains, "but it tends to be sporadic and this is an area where there is room for improvement."

Money woes

"Work enjoyable, low prospects, pay well below market" is how a fourth-year unceremoniously summarizes Lawrence Graham, and on the pay front, plenty of colleagues agree. "Hugely undermarket," a solicitor comments. "Our pay here is low," says another. "Bonus was insulting." Ah, yes, bonuses. Even those get little respect. A source explains that the "Bonus system merely keeps us in line with basic remuneration in like firms and is discretionary. Very divisive." "I worked like hell this year and was not rewarded for it," rages a seventh-year. At least one solicitor, however, will happily trade money for sanity: "I am happy with my salary level as I have a life outside work," the insider tells us.

Be "reasonable"

That's right, though Lawrence Graham attorneys may earn less than those at equivalent firms, they actually have lives—by legal standards, that is. Hours are still "quite long", but "very reasonable for the job." "By the very nature of the job, the hours are long but I think that they could be worse in other firms!' exclaims an eighth-year. "Fairly standard" schedules may abound, but, unfortunately for working mothers, "Part-time working is not encouraged." It "is frowned upon," confirms a contact.

LeBoeuf, Lamb, Greene & MacRae LLP

No. 1 Minster Court
Mincing Lane
London EC3R 7YL
www.llgm.com

OTHER LOCATIONS

Albany • Almaty • Beijing • Boston • Brussels • Chicago • Hartford • Houston • Jacksonville • Johannesburg • Los Angeles • Moscow • New York • Paris • Pittsburgh • Riyadh • San Francisco • Washington, DC

MAJOR DEPARTMENTS & PRACTICES

Bankruptcy & Debt Restructuring
Corporate & Finance
Energy & Utilities
IP Licensing & Assignments
Legislation & Public Policy
Real Estate
Tax
Technology & Intellectual Property

THE STATS

No. of lawyers: 650+
No. of lawyers in London: 80 (excluding trainees and legal assistants)
No. of offices: 19
Trainee intake: 10 in each year from 2007
London managing partner: Peter Sharp

PLUSES

- "Approachable and supportive partners"
- "A fascinating diet of work"

MINUSES

- "Being joined to a BlackBerry"
- Some complaints about training

NOTABLE PERKS

- Orientation/training in New York

BASE SALARY

1st-year Trainee: £33,000
Newly Qualified: £65,000

GRADUATE RECRUITMENT AND TRAINING MANAGER

E-mail: traineelondon@llgm.com

THE BUZZ
WHAT EMPLOYEES AT OTHER FIRMS ARE SAYING

- "Decent, growing"
- "OK"

THE SCOOP

LeBoeuf Lamb is one of the most established U.S. law firms in London, but it is also one of the most low profile. Though it has a strong office peopled by a great staff of mostly U.K.-qualified lawyers, it falls under the radar of many legal commentators simply because what it strives to do is different to many of its competitors—instead of setting out to be the top M&A law firm in the world, or act for the most investment banks, LeBoeuf Lamb has made a real success of a sector-based approach.

Like Clyde

The firm is old-school New York, set up there in 1929, and focused on energy, utilities and insurance. It is the U.S. equivalent of firms like Clyde & Co in London—very strong in litigation but doing everything for major corporations in the industries on which it focuses. In London, its office is close to the Lloyd's building, at the very heart of the insurance industry. Together with its Moscow office, it also has a command of the energy industry over on this side of the pond that is hard to match outside the Magic Circle.

The deals say it all really. The team has advised Chinese oil and gas companies on recent key transactions, including CNPC International Ltd wholly controlled by China National Petroleum Corporation, on its historic first joint acquisition with Oil and Natural Gas Corporation (ONGC) of India of Petro-Canada's Syrian assets; acted for Endemol N.V. and Telefónica S.A. on the U.S. Rule 144A and U.K. governing law aspects of Endemol N.V.'s €281 million IPO on Euronext Amsterdam; and represented Lancashire Holdings Limited on its formation and $1 billion IPO, which included a U.S. private placement, equity offering in the U.K. and debt offering of trust preferred securities to U.S. investors and subordinated notes to European investors.

Lured to LeBoeuf Lamb

Such a focus has gained recognition in the relevant sectors of the London legal market, and LeBoeuf Lamb has been quietly adding to its partnership over here in the last few years. Most recently, the office got a major boost with the hire of arbitrator Arthur Marriott QC, who was one of the first solicitors to become a Queen's Counsel back in 1997. He had been a partner at U.S. rival Debevoise & Plimpton until he was lured by LeBoeuf Lamb, and moved with another arbitration partner, Deborah Ruff.

Norton Rose's insurance chief, Francis Mackie, joined in spring 2006. He is a highly rated litigator who headed up the insurance litigation team and non-contentious insurance group at the London firm, with clients like Axa Global and Swiss Re.

Such high profile hires were in addition to that of an intellectual property practice in the form of Marija Danilunas, who was previously the global head of IP at U.K. law firm Hammonds. Then the hires of John LaMaster, who had been the London managing partner for Vinson & Elkins in the days before that Texas firm become best known as "Enron's law firm," and Christopher Prior, also of Vinson & Elkins. Both of these new hires are energy specialists.

Few would fault those that hopped over to LeBoeuf, especially in light of the firm's incredible success since 2005. As *The Lawyer* reported in March 2006, LaBoeuf posted some impressive numbers for 2005, including a staggering 43 per cent increase in U.K. turnover over 2004's revenue. The partners didn't fare too poorly either—profit per equity partner rose from £389,000 in 2004 to £650,000 in 2005—an unprecedented 67 per cent increase. If those numbers aren't validating—well, we don't know what is.

Work around the world

Whilst quietly expanding its numbers, LeBoeuf Lamb has been expanding its workload as well. The firm won one of only six places on the global panel for insurance giant Zurich last year, but that was the more standard of the appointments. LeBoeuf Lamb London was drafted in by the Mozambique government to investigate and audit the accounts of the formerly state-owned bank Banco Austral, working closely with its outpost in South Africa.

And then on the corporate side, there was work advising on the €485 million multi-jurisdictional acquisition of adidas's winter sports equipment business, Salomon, by Finnish company Amer Sports Corporation, just showing there is more to this firm than energy and insurance, despite those proving highly lucrative drivers. What kicked off 2006 in style was advice to CNOOC, the Chinese oil and gas company, on its largest international transaction ever, when it spent $2.3 billion taking a 45 per cent stake in the offshore Akpo field in Nigeria from South Atlantic Petroleum.

The firm's Russian practice works very closely with London, and is regularly awarded for its efforts. The firm was a flagship advisor to Yukos, the Russian oil company that was set to merge with Roman Abramovich's Sibneft before Putin's government arrested its leader on suspicion of tax evasion. That heralded the end of Yukos, but though it was a major client for LeBoeuf Lamb, the firm was able to fill the gap by chasing other work for investors going into Russia and the CIS.

Such instructions have brought rewards—LeBoeuf Lamb won Reinsurance/Insurance Law Firm of the Year in 2005 for the fourth year running from insurance bible *Reactions* magazine, was named No. 1 for Energy Transactional and Regulatory work in New York by Chambers and Partners and was recognised as Africa Law Firm of the Year at the Chambers Global Awards 2005.

Pro bono

The London office of LeBoeuf Lamb is pretty committed to pro bono, in line with the whole firm's extensive efforts. Lawyers are encouraged to work on public interest projects, and associates can count up to 200 hours of pro bono work as billable for the purposes of compensation, which can come in useful.

The firm's projects include work preventing the eviction of low-income tenants, obtaining political asylum for people coming to the U.S. seeking refuge from persecution, and obtaining relief for prisoners who have been denied medical care.

Pioneers in organic growth

The London graduate recruitment programme has been up and running for 10 years, with LeBoeuf Lamb as one of the few that recognised early on that there was real value in growing organically, as well as through those big name lateral hires. Young solicitors can specialise in corporate, litigation, energy or insurance, obviously, but also finance, telecoms, media or infrastructure projects—all hot areas for the office.

The practice is one of the few amongst the American firms that can offer such a strong litigation seat, as most are far more M&A-centric. Because of its sector focus, LeBoeuf Lamb is just as strong on the corporate side as it is in contentious work, which can attract recruits. There is also work in the usual disciplines of tax, competition, real estate, IP/IT, employment, insolvency, and international trusts.

LeBoeuf Lamb is a truly global law firm, focused in London on advising overseas clients going about their business, rather than here to nab work for U.K. corporates, as most U.S. firms are.

GETTING HIRED

The right stuff

When it comes to recruiting, "high calibre candidates" are, predictably, favoured; according to LeBoeuf Lamb solicitors. "You would be lucky to get in with less than a good 2:1 degree" cautions one insider. "It is very competitive", agrees a colleague, who adds that in addition to "obvious examples of academic excellence [there needs to be] a real commitment to wanting to work at the firm in the types of work we do." Once you think that you are LeBoeuf Lamb's type, it might be wise to start honing those interview skills, as each potential trainee faces "two rounds of interviews by at least four partners in all besides [the] head of recruitment."

OUR SURVEY SAYS

Satisfaction guaranteed?

LeBoeuf Lamb may be most notable for how "interesting" its lawyers find everything about it: the work, the people, the clients. A few call these things "good" and "great", but "interesting" outstrips them both by a long shot. "Generally my job satisfaction is down to the type of work that I do, and the people that I work with," a litigator tells us, seemingly speaking for all of LeBoeuf Lamb's London solicitors. When the work is high quality, the atmosphere "hugely rewarding" and "collegiate", the firm's approach "professional", and everything else "interesting," how could anyone not be satisfied with a position at LeBoeuf, Lamb, Greene & MacRae?

The long and short of it

"The work and the people are great," chirps a sixth-year, "however the hours can be very long." Yet, LeBoeuf Lamb solicitors appear so grateful for the quality of work, the people at their firm and the lack of a "strict hourly target" that they can deal: "With responsibility come the hours. Acceptable," a novice states plainly. A colleague adds that any complaints about long days and nights go out the window "when viewed with my salary." After all, "for a U.S. firm the hours are reasonable in return for better compensation." And "face time is a rarity, as there are no unneeded hours." "If there is work to be done, then you need to stay to do it," says a source, "otherwise you can go home. The partners are generally flexible as to working hours as long as you are doing the work required of you. For example, you can easily work at home if you need to, or come in late if, say, you are waiting for a repair person to get to your house in the morning." An isolated gripe is that work distribution is uneven. As one disgruntled corporate solicitor tells us: "There is an attempt at central planning of associates" work flow but it does not appear to be working and there is a huge discrepancy in the work received by different associates."

At work and at play

LeBoeuf Lamb "is professional, respectful and polite" along with "relaxed", but undoubtedly work comes before play at the "hardworking, but not frenetically so" firm. "Everybody has to work hard, and everybody does because they are very self-motivated. That encourages a friendly and sociable atmosphere," a source explains. "Lawyers tend to get in earlier than at U.K. firms and work hard during the day so they can leave and have a life outside work," adds a peer. "As a result, there is not much banter in the corridors." It must be that they're conserving their energy for "regular Friday drinks" and "firm-organised drinks" alike, as well as their families and extracurricular interests. Though hardly cliquey, LeBoeuf Lamb solicitors tend to socialise "within each specific group rather than across the firm as a whole."

Partner participation

"Friendly and down-to-earth" partners who are "generally good in relations with associates" also contribute to the firm's pleasant tone. Those at the top "are very good to work for in general," states a solicitor. "All of them seem to provide good feedback and none are difficult to work with." Unfortunately, despite being approachable and offering solicitors "large degrees of responsibility," partners receive low marks in terms of sharing firm news and information with their minions and addressing solicitors" concerns. A third-year clarifies that "there is little associate involvement in firm activities outside of normal client work." They also have work to do in the training department; though there are "some training seminars", there is "no structured programme." Having said that, the firm, unlike many, willingly pays for its lawyers to attend external training courses. The "mentoring scheme [is] rarely used, leaving solicitors to approach partners who they work for rather than mentors chosen for them" for any assistance.

Fair trade

Insiders at LeBoeuf Lamb assess their salaries as "good but not superior", figuring that it's a fair trade-off in light of the "pretty moderate" billing requirements and "the relatively unpressurised working environment." Bonuses are on "a sliding scale, starting at 1,800 hours" with "small extra increments per 200 additional hours", but "should also reflect the quality of the work provided by the solicitor," comments a lawyer. Expats wish there were a COLA in place, but other than that, there just isn't much to complain about says an attorney: "I am very happy with my salary."

Linklaters

One Silk Street
London EC2Y 8HQ
www.linklaters.com

OTHER LOCATIONS

Belgium • Brazil • China (mainland) • Czech Republic • Dubai • France • Germany • Hong Kong • Hungary • Italy • Japan • Luxembourg • Netherlands • Poland • Portugal • Romania • Russia • Singapore • Slovakia • Spain • Sweden • Thailand • United States

MAJOR DEPARTMENTS & PRACTICES

Asset Finance • Banking • Capital Markets • Corporate/M&A • Employee Incentives • Employment • Environment & Planning • EU/Competition • Financial Markets • Intellectual Property • Investment Management • Technology, Media & Telecommunications • Litigation and Arbitration • Pensions • Private Equity • Projects • Real Estate & Construction • Restructuring & Insolvency • Tax

THE BUZZ
WHAT EMPLOYEES AT OTHER FIRMS ARE SAYING

- "Ultimate blue chip City practice"
- "Large and impersonal"

THE STATS

No. of lawyers: 2,000
No. of lawyers in London: 800
No. of offices: 30
Trainee intake: 130 (2005)
Trainees retained: 86%+ (2005)
London managing partner: Tony Angel

PLUSES

- "Great people and cutting-edge work"
- "High pay"

MINUSES

- Long, unpredictable hours
- Demanding clients

NOTABLE PERKS

- Generous marketing budget
- On-site gym, salon, dry cleaner, doctor, dentist, physiotherapist
- Flexible work arrangements

BASE SALARY

Trainee: £31,300
Newly Qualified: £55,100

GRADUATE RECRUITMENT AND TRAINING MANAGER

Claire Cherrington
Head of Graduate Recruitment
Phone: +44 (0)20 7456 2000
E-mail: graduate.recruitment@linklaters.com

THE SCOOP

In 2006, there is no doubt that Linklaters is at the very top of its game. What's more, of the six Magic Circle firms, it is increasingly emerging as the one to beat, after a blip in performance in 2003. Linklaters broke the £1 million PEP barrier for the first time, with the average equity partner pocketing some £1.06 million for the 2005-06 year, putting the firm hard on the heels of Slaughter and May, whose PEP was only slightly higher at £1.12 million. Linklaters is a corporate firm, through and through. Its business is driven by a fantastic franchise in both M&A and capital markets, where it regularly tops league tables both for the U.K., Europe and the world.

Follow the Angel

Linklaters' corporate focus means it took a hefty hit when the market tanked in 2001 and 2002, but the firm was quick enough to spot what it had to do, and turned it round. Under the leadership of the highly personable tax partner Tony Angel, the firm slimmed down its partnership by scrapping the underperformers, and honed its business plan to focus on the cream of the global work.

As a result, the numbers picked up, and Linklaters stole a march on a number of its competitors, who belatedly underwent very similar restructurings. In 2006, the firm could point to tangible evidence of its success: a 16 per cent increase in turnover, to £935 million, and a 25 per cent increase in PEP. Some of that revenue will even trickle down to lowly associates: Linklaters kicked off the latest round of salary increases when it boosted newly qualified lawyers' salaries to £55,100 effective May 2006. What's more, throughout the tough times, Linklaters continued to invest in the parts of its business that were perceived as weak, most notably its finance team. The firm has quietly built a banking practice that is now established as the third player in the City's finance market, alongside Clifford Chance and Allen & Overy.

Deal magic

Then there was overseas investment, which could have halted, but instead kept motoring through the tough times. Linklaters made sensible moves into Asia, particularly Japan, in those years. Another priority of Linklaters has been the development of the New York office. In 2003, the firm brought in a four partner litigation team from Shearman & Sterling. A steady stream of lateral hires followed, taking the office to full service with banking, restructuring and corporate capability.

When it comes to doing the corporate work, there are few that can beat the sheer scale of the deals going on at One Silk Street. The biggest clients are the likes of BP, JPMorgan, Barclays, the Royal Bank of Scotland and Vodafone, all of whom send whopping deals the firm's way on a regular basis.

In 2004, key deals included advising Centrica on its £1.75 billion sale of the Automobile Association, and work for National Grid Transco on the £1.1 billion acquisition of Crown Castle UK, a broadcasting transmission company. In mining, the firm advised long-standing client Gold Fields in defence of the £8 billion hostile takeover bid by rival Harmony, with U.S. litigation aspects being handled by the new team in America.

Here, there and everywhere

Across Europe, the deals are good and feed more work into London. The Paris office led the *mergermarket* league tables there, which rank advisers on M&A deals, with the highlight being advice to Sanofi-Sythelabo on its bumper acquisition of Aventis. In Germany, the firm worked on four of the five largest M&A deals, and Linklaters is the only Magic Circle firm to have a presence in Sweden, where it worked on seven of the 10 largest deals, including the top four.

The Asia practice is doing well, too, with work for China Mobile on the acquisition of 10 provincial mobile phone operators in a deal that topped U.S. $46.6 billion in value, and then in Singapore there is work for BP and Temasek.

Beyond M&A

But there's more to the firm than just M&A. When the restructuring was going on, many speculated that Linklaters would drop things like real estate and litigation from its roster of services, but in fact nothing of the sort occurred. It is true that the emphasis has been placed firmly on the corporate and finance side, but all the support areas still receive resources and investment. A big growth area in 2005 was the telecoms, media and technology team, where the firm worked for BT on a whole host of regulatory approvals, advised Vodafone and T-Mobile on deals, and worked for Barclays Capital, CSFB and RBS on Apax and Permira's $1.5 billion buyout of Inmarsat, the international satellite service provider. The firm is currently acting for Australian investment firm Babcock & Brown on the financing of its €2.4 billion bid for Irish telecoms company eircom.

Any kind of attempt at a comprehensive outline of the Linklaters workload is impossible, but suffice it to say, if you want good work in any City practice area, you'll get it here. The firm has been jostling with arch-rival Freshfields Bruckhaus Deringer for years for the global corporate crown, and after coming from behind, it can now probably lay a pretty good claim to it.

Say it loud: pink and proud

In 2002, Linklaters rebranded and changed its image. Gone was the dull branding that characterised every other firm that it competed with, and in came pink. No one at the firm will deny that the partners took a bit of a double take, but the magenta branding and clever wordings have embodied a new spirit of confidence. Other internal developments include the election of a new senior partner: on 1 October 2006 former Head of Corporate David Cheyne will succeed Anthony Cann who will retire on 30 September after 37 years with the firm.

The firm is one of the better Magic Circle firms for both involvement in community affairs, action on pro bono, and diversity commitment. It was the first to allow partners to work part time without penalising them, something still frowned on by many of the competition, and it was also an early signatory to City commitments to diversify the legal market by targeting youngsters outside the traditional Oxbridge hunting grounds.

Impressive pro bono

Its community projects are varied and well established—with staff being actively encouraged to support local community partners through pro bono work and other employee volunteering and by the firm awarding funding. In London, the firm provides volunteers to cover sessions at the Royal Courts of Justice Advice Bureau and other law centres, and acts on death row appeals from Jamaica that end up in the House of Lords.

In the U.S., the firm supports a variety of organisations and programmes including the "Everybody Wins" national literacy programme, while in Hong Kong the firm sponsored the fit-out of a training room at Hong Chi Shan King Centre's TEACH programme for autistic children.

GETTING HIRED

The anti-mould

"2:1, excellent academics in general, nice people to hang out with, personable, good with commercial issues, adaptable, not easily fazed by big jobs, the best of their class, but generally nice people I think," goes a solicitor's breathless (and rather idealistic) list of favoured characteristics. It "helps if you are from Oxbridge" and overall "the top five universities make up the vast majority of lawyers" at the firm. However, the firm recruited from more than 35 universities in the U.K. in 2005 and a source cautions that 'there is no mould candidates have to fit into; the firm wants to recruit the best, but who is best is widely defined: it is anyone who has achieved something special in his life, whatever the discipline. The aim is to have a diversified workforce with creative people who make things happen. "After all, it takes more than grades to make it through Linklaters" "very thorough interview process, including application screening, written IQ test, [and] two interviews (one including a prepared case study)."

OUR SURVEY SAYS

The fantastics

Despite being a member of the overworked Magic Circle, Linklaters is a "fantastic place to work", filled with "exceptionally talented individuals" and copious amounts of "really good, high-end work" assignments. "The work is very interesting and challenging, and I feel like I'm learning something new every day," chirps a solicitor who is still wide-eyed despite being three years PQE. "I get to work with some of the most intelligent people I've met doing work that challenges me every day," echoes a sixth-year.

The downsides to the "high-calibre" work and people are "unpredictable timing" and "depressing" schedules that can leave solicitors stranded at work until the wee hours, along with the bad attitudes of certain clients. "I generally enjoy the work and responsibility I am given, although it is sometimes slightly demoralising when the time and effort involved is not recognised by clients," grumbles a source, who nevertheless feels that "on the whole clients are very appreciative." And no Linklaters attorneys are raving about the wonderful prospect of attaining partner status: "Shame there's no future here," emotes one (barely). "The up-or-out policy makes life very uncertain."

Working stiffs?

For a firm of such prestige and standing, one would expect the Linklaters culture to be a bit stiff. Yet it is thought of as "supportive", "relaxed", and, hitting a more maternal chord, "protective of its people." "Linklaters is a very professional firm but with a friendly culture," comments a seasoned lawyer, who debunks the stuffy myth. "In my 10 years here I have seen it become quite liberal and embracing." The firm has a "good, laid-back culture, overlaid on a slightly blue-chip backbone that although conservative can be surprisingly progressive," a peer agrees. While Linklaters uses its approachability for good within the office, actively embracing an open-door policy and encouraging socialising, it also extends outside the office, as the firm is "very committed to pro bono and charity and to involving its lawyers in this." Put it all together and the firm has amazing star power: "People here are dedicated to being excellent at what we do and there is a real sense of common purpose—to be the best law firm in the world. That said, there is a very friendly and collegiate feeling in the corridors. The place is just full of nice people."

Cake Thursday thinking

And because the "collegiate" Linklaters avoids the usual cast of big-firm characters, instead striving for the "nice" gene in its lawyers (though some credit the laid-back vibe to the "large number of Antipodean lawyers"), socialising at the firm is present "without it being prescriptive." "Social and fun loving" with "good, regular social events for all staff and families", the firm structure encourages solicitors to spend time with their own departments and "seniority bands." There are also regular perks for the firm at large. Case in point: "We have just had a department retreat in Cannes which was great fun (no work involved)," recounts an insider. Another source tells us that Fridays are reserved for the "group drinks trolley" while there are "cakes on Thursday." No word on Weight Watchers Wednesdays as of yet. Clearly, though, Linklaters knows how to create a "really good balance of hard work and rewards' as well as 'a close community, despite its size."

It's busy at the top

As some departments work "reliably until 6:30", others find that "it is not unusual to be in the office past 11 p.m. several nights a week," and the unpredictability is a killer. (We pity you, leveraged finance). But there's no need to stick around twiddling one's thumbs. "We work hard, long hours but that is the deal if you are working at a leading law firm," clarifies one lawyer. "And the culture is not that people are expected to put in face time—if you are not busy then you leave the office." One pragmatic colleague summarizes: "You cannot expect to do the most interesting work on the most interesting deals (and get paid at the top of the market) without putting in some tough hours."

A few solicitors manage flexible schedules, but there are complaints that the "part-time programme exists in theory only, unless you are a PSL or work in the employment department." The corporate department gets slammed with accusations that "there is little or no willingness at partner level to consider flexible work arrangements for non-family reasons … for family reasons the attitude is only marginally better." And "with an intense focus on chargeable hours" having developed over the past several years, it likely won't change anytime soon, though the extra focus has been "reflected in bonuses."

Oddballs out

"There is always the oddball partner who thinks he can treat associates as slaves, but generally very friendly" is the overall consensus of Linklaters solicitors, who also find that most partners are "professional" and "take great interest in the development and well-being of their associates." But it may be slightly more complex than that: "Treatment of individuals is excellent," a solicitor specifies. "I have never seen a partner lose his/her temper or show any disrespect. Treatment as a group is shoddy: we're an expendable resource who work to keep the partnership profits high, but are booted out when we get too qualified." "Ah, yes, particularly in litigation partners … treat trainees as though they are a commodity resulting in many of them feeling demotivated." For now, though, lawyers will have to be satisfied with partners who are affable face-to-face and make "a real effort … to attend all departmental social events en masse!"

Support system

Insider reports on training and mentoring are mixed, as some departments have a structured scheme and others do not. But everyone agrees that the information and knowledge is there to access. The benefits of the slightly "haphazard" mentoring system at Linklaters "often depends on how proactive the solicitor is—what you put in is what you get out," says an attorney, but others feel that "the friendly relations between partners and associates really mean this is a natural result," not something that needs to be sought out. "No gripes at all," we hear. "Mentors are allocated and can be contacted as and when you wish. Informal training is excellent too, as sitting in a room with someone more qualified means that you automatically learn things every day." There are whispers that mentoring gets kicked down to senior associates, as partners are "generally very busy." Strangely, some solicitors feel that receiving mentoring reveals some deeper meanings about members of the firm. It's "seen as unnecessary if you're any good," cracks a cocky source, whose co-worker gives it a more exclusive spin: "Good associates receive very good support."

Fortunately for Linklaters, its previously "appalling" training has made quite the turnaround in recent years, becoming "structured and well organised" and "taken very seriously." In addition to being "organised across various practice areas", "top-notch" training is also offered "on demand online", with additional offerings focusing on "more alternative training—e.g., the workplace skills seminar includes sessions on interpreting body language and networking at cocktail functions," mentions a participant. "A week's intensive training on qualification, group lunches every fortnight, training days externally approximately once a month, new series of training sessions at six months qualified," catalogues a lawyer.

Bringing home the bacon

"Firmwide I do not think that those who work seriously hard hours in London and elsewhere receive the recognition, bonuses or share of the profits their hard work and commitment brings in," observes an associate, and it's not an isolated opinion. Bonuses, which are awarded at 1,700 hours "provided you have a 'Very Good' in your assessment", are "calculated using a combination of total utilisation (billable hours, pro bono, etc.) and overall rating (VG, E, etc.)." But the wide-ranging belief is that "really high billing associates tend to get a pretty poor marginal return for the extra hours."

Though Linklaters solicitors are aware that compared to the average worker they earn impressive salaries, the sense is that they are undervalued in their own and comparable industries. "Given that we are expected to work investment bank style hours and lifestyles the contrast with what our clients are paid and what we are paid is frustrating," a contact tells us. It all comes down to the partnership carrot," another analyzes. "Moderate salaries for associates was fine when the partnership track was shorter and when partnership was assured for those who were still with the firm at the right age. Now that your future depends much more on the business case lottery, there is huge uncertainty. I am generally a person who likes to take risks, but to gamble with your whole career is too much for many."

Lovells

Atlantic House
Holborn Viaduct
London EC1A 2FG
Phone: +44 (0)20 7296 2000
www.lovells.com

OTHER LOCATIONS

Alicante • Amsterdam • Beijing • Berlin • Brussels • Budapest* • Chicago • Düsseldorf • Frankfurt • Hamburg • Ho Chi Minh City • Hong Kong • London (2 additional) • Madrid • Milan • Moscow • Munich • New York • Paris • Prague • Rome • Shanghai • Singapore • Tokyo • Warsaw • Zagreb*
*Associated offices

THE STATS

No. of lawyers: 1,622
No. of attorneys in London: 800+
No. of offices: 26
Trainee intake: 90 (2005)
Trainees retained: 91.2% (2004)
Managing partner: David Harris
Hiring Graduate Recruitment Partner: Lawson Caisley

THE BUZZ
WHAT EMPLOYEES AT OTHER FIRMS ARE SAYING

- "Real quality—underrated"
- "Boring, staid and conservative"

MAJOR DEPARTMENTS & PRACTICES

Banking
Business Restructuring & Insolvency
Capital Markets
Competition and EU Law
Corporate Commercial
Corporate Finance
Dispute Resolution:
    Administrative & Public Law
    ADR
    Corporate & Commercial Bank
    Financial Services & Regulatory
    Insurance & Reinsurance
    International Arbitration
    International Fraud & Insolvency
    Investment Bank & Funds
    Pension & Trust Fund
    Product Liability
    Projects, Engineering & Construction
Employment, Share Incentives & Executive Compensation
Energy, Power & Utilities
Engineering & Construction Projects
EU & Trade
Finance
Financial Institutions
Intellectual Property
Insurance & Reinsurance
Pensions
Private Equity
Projects (Engineering & Construction)
Project Finance
Real Estate
Share Incentives & Executive Compensation
Tax
Technology, Media & Telecommunications

PLUSES

- Friendly culture with approachable partners
- Pro bono work encouraged

MINUSES

- High turnover
- Tough hours

NOTABLE PERKS

- Sleeping pods for late-night snoozes
- In-house gym
- Dry cleaning concierge service
- Fees and maintenance for LPC studies

BASE SALARY

Trainee: £31,000
Newly Qualified: £53,000

GRADUATE RECRUITMENT AND TRAINING MANAGER

Clare Harris
Graduate Recruitment Manager
Phone: +44 (0)20 7296 2000
Fax: +44 (0)20 7296 2001
E-mail: recruit@lovells.com

THE SCOOP

Lovells' penchant for mergers and lateral hires has broadened its staff, its range of expertise and its overseas presence, with particularly explosive growth since 2001. Lovells now ranks as the fifth-largest law firm in Europe and one of the largest in the world, its 26 offices spanning Europe, Asia and the United States, and it fancies itself as a full-service business law firm providing a full menu of services.

What's in a name?

Curiously, although Lovells has undertaken a number of mergers through the years—with Lady Hamilton's law firm, Haslewoods, in 1966; with banking and financial powerhouse Durrant Piesse in 1988; with Germany's Boesebeck Droste and Dutch firm Ekelmans Den Hollander in 2000; and with France's Siméon & Associés in 2001—the firm's name has shrunk even as its appetite for expansion has remained unslaked. Like Bono, it now goes by just a single moniker: Lovells.

Lovells' London roots go back to 1899, when John Spence Lovell set up his own legal practice at Snow Hill. Reginald White and Charles King later joined him to form Lovell, White & King, which then moved to Holborn Circus, Fleet Street and finally Holborn Viaduct. The firm has resided there since 1977; a recent move to Atlantic House in 2003 kept it in the neighbourhood, albeit in decidedly posher digs. Management shake-ups and sagging revenues in 2005 haven't aided its bid for top-tier status, but the firm's new executive team is currently working on a policy overhaul that, with luck, may provide a key to the pearly gates.

Taking the heat in the Big Smoke?

And growth is just what Lovells needs at the moment. No, not a new office in Ouagadougou or a merger in Myanmar; what the firm needs now is a fatter bankroll, not a bigger payroll. Following several years of overflowing coffers, Lovells' profits per equity partner allegedly plummeted 21 per cent over the 2004-2005 year, and turnover sagged 3 per cent, to £366 million; the dip in revenue was reportedly steepest at the head London office. Management blamed the cutthroat London legal market (this was news to them, apparently), as well as the costs associated with restructuring the partnership (Lovells decided in December 2004 to shed a number of global equity partners). Although the firm has only just undergone a major leadership change—John Young took over as senior partner in May 2004, and David Harris replaced long-time managing partner Lesley MacDonagh one year later—further shake-up may be in order.

On the other hand, the firm may already be on the road to recovery. In 2006, the firm posted a 34 per cent increase in PEP (yes, you read that right) over the last year. Lest anyone get complacent, however, managing partner David Harris has reportedly urged partners to work harder to sustain that profitability, increasing their overall annual target to 2,200 hours.

Wanted: Cash cows

Harris told *The Lawyer* in November 2004 that he's focusing on generating revenue and boosting utilisation rates rather than downsizing, but the firm's loss-making operations in Asia (does it really need that Ho Chi Minh City office?) could well be a ripe target for the cost-cutting axe. Another merger, possibly with a U.S. firm, is also a distinct possibility, but Harris and his team will need to bolster Lovells' balance sheet beforehand. That said, the management team, in the form of the international executive, has recently been overhauled itself; in October 2005 it was reduced from 14 to 11 in a bid to facilitate decision-making on strategic issues. The sharpened focus on revenue has also led to the introduction of new yardsticks to gauge the profitability of clients and portfolios, with the aim of prodding partners to eschew less lucrative cases in favour of cash cows. Lovells denies that the new system will also be used to cull unprofitable partners, however. Other measures recently voted through include restructuring the firm as a limited liability partnership and shifting from a pure lock-step model to a more actively managed system of remuneration. Although Senior Partner John Young told *Asian Legal Business* that 'we will not be abandoning lock-step,' he conceded that 'we are a very different firm from the one for which our lock-step system was originally designed.'

Lovells has also restructured its corporate group, whose turnover allegedly sank 5 per cent in 2004-2005. Teams are now more specialised, the better to advise clients such as Waitrose (on its acquisition of 19 Morrisons stores, announced in March 2004), Swiss Re (on its £333 million acquisition of Life Assurance Holding Corp. in July 2004), and Japan's Kao Corp. (on its £170 million acquisition of Molton Brown in August 2005). Other recent cases have included advising SABMiller on its £4.75 billion merger with Bavaria, the second-largest brewer in South America. Announced in July 2005, that deal should go a particularly long way toward buoying the fortunes of the mainstream corporate practice, calling for celebratory pints all round.

Merck work

The firm is also active in product liability, defending pharmaceutical company Merck, for example, against Vioxx claims as well as group litigation brought on behalf of children allegedly rendered autistic by the MMR vaccine. Not exactly heart-warming work, but who said law was a popularity contest? Certainly not Andrew Foyle, whose work on behalf of British American Tobacco has landed him in hot water with both the Aussie and U.S. authorities regarding his advice to the tobacco giant on "document retention" —i.e., the shredding of papers detailing the nasty health effects of smoking. Although Foyle argued that his advice was protected by blanket privilege, the High Court gave the U.S. Justice Department the go-ahead to question him.

GETTING HIRED

Varying degrees

The rumour among Lovells associates is that "CVs are supposedly ranked on a point system which favours certain universities," but apparently it wasn't always that way. "Traditionally, Lovells has been quite openminded about the candidates it recruits," shares a source. Why the change? "Now, largely due to the thousands of applications we get, we tend to go for safe bets, i.e., a 2:1 degree from a red brick university." Should you maintain some hope in spite of your lacking the above requirements, there are always the other characteristics that the firm appreciates: determination, a true desire to practice law, and strong communication skills on and off the page. The first step is to log on to www.lovells.com/graduates and fill in an online application form. If you are successful you'll be invited to one of the firm's assessment days. There are no first interviews—candidates will be asked to complete a test to examine their analytical and critical thinking ability, followed by a group discussion exercise on a business-orientated case study, as well as a more classic interview with two partners. Getting the chance to personally present your case is not so easy, however: "You have to fill in a long form and then, if invited, come in for an assessment day with psychometric testing and role-plays, as well as more classic interviews," details someone who survived to tell the tale. And get hired, of course.

OUR SURVEY SAYS

Multicultural

Lovells is so mammoth that its solicitors find it difficult to capture a single image of the firm, as much depends upon one's own experiences. Because "different teams have different cultures" it is hard to know what everyone's habits are socially, for instance. Some call the firm all business, while others find it warm and cosy. But the majority feel that "the firm lives up to its reputation for being very friendly and supportive", "open" and "approachable." "Other big firms are often described as factories, especially in corporate or finance," we're told. "Lovells is quite a relaxed firm where the quality of your work and the atmosphere in the office appear to be given higher priority than your billable hours." "Generally partners are very approachable and there isn't the same level of competitiveness and one-upmanship I sense from lawyers at some other firms," adds a co-worker. Though many lawyers think of Lovells as an apolitical "meritocracy ... [where] good people are recognised and rewarded", others warn that "some groups [are] very hierarchical."

Social skills

Things run the gamut socially, also due to the firm's size. Though one solicitor's "general experience is that the lawyers socialise together now and then outside of the annual events organised by the firm," it's really up to individual departments, with each one planning its own events, such as litigation's weekly Friday afternoon tea. Still, states a first-year, "the firm is so big, I couldn't say that there is a good social network." For some it has less to do with size than personal feelings: "I rarely mix intra-firm (except at ever more common leaving drinks), or even go out with my department," a second-year notes snidely. "I have a good bunch of mates from my intake who are much less boring than the average."

Variety and quality

No one doubts the fantastic quality of work at Lovells, and many find it hugely satisfying. "There is a good variety of work and you are pushed to try new things and take on new challenges and responsibilities but rarely without adequate support," gushes an IP newbie. A seasoned corporate lawyer enthuses about the "top-notch work, excellent colleagues and an inclusive atmosphere." That's not to suggest that everything is perfect. "Generally I enjoy my job and gain great satisfaction working with very pleasant clients on interesting deals, however that is often undermined by a lack of support from partners and having more responsibility than I might expect at my level of qualification," sighs a first-year who apparently feels slightly out of his depth. "[The] quality of work is generally very good", concedes an attorney in mid-career, "but 'high profile' cases can sometimes mean being a very small cog in a very big wheel which can become frustrating."

Balancing act

"I enjoy my work by and large, I just wish it didn't take over my life as often as it does," muses a source. It is said that Lovells "goes out of its way to achieve a happy balance whenever possible", but there are a number of complaints of "unnecessary pressure to stay late" when there is actually little or nothing to do. "I think there is a bit of an unspoken rule that requires you to stay in the office past 5:30 p.m. even if you have finished your work." Whether or not there is work to be done, solicitors spend "too much time in the office", "often work[ing] well past nine in the evening, and occasionally weekends." There can be flexibility regarding schedules, a contact tells us, but another describes the firm's part-time scheme as "not great, although probably as good/better than the competition."

Adding it up

For a large, prestigious, international, corporate law firm, Lovells is a wee bit skimpy on pay, but solicitors don't take it to task very much; they're just grateful that relatively speaking, "you don't have to sell your soul at Lovells." The firm does face annoyance on the topic of bonuses, "which few people achieve": they must surpass their billable hours guideline of 1,700, after which bonuses are awarded in 100-hour increments starting at 1,800 hours. The lucky and industrious solicitors who get that far receive "bonuses of 10, 15 and 20 per cent at 1,800, 1,900 and 2,000 hours." But a lawyer notes this doesn't really amount to much: It's "not very inspiring to earn an extra £6,000 for spending an extra five hours in the office every day for a year."

Hits and misses

Lovells solicitors feel that they are left somewhat in the dark regarding firm decisions and news, sometimes finding themselves the last to hear the gossip. Word is that the firm is improving in this area: "With the recent introduction of a new managing partner, firmwide communications have been very good," a corporate source divulges. There also appears to be a polite (and sometimes impolite) distance kept from minions, as seen at many firms of comparable size. A first-year offers this terse assessment: "Many partners are completely indifferent to junior solicitors. Some very encouraging, and a small minority downright rude." But solicitors are unexpectedly understanding of their overlords' lack of mentoring and informal training. They're "too busy most of time," says one lawyer; "Where possible partners generally explain amendments, etc., but this is obviously subject to timescales, etc.," comments another. On the other hand, Lovells' well-respected formal training is "excellent", providing a "good support network for trainees," who have both mandatory and elective programmes to complete. Additionally, "the firm provides for attendance at various outside training," we hear. "For example, all IP lawyers attend the University of Bristol IP diploma course within the first year and a half of qualification." "The in-house training at Lovells is excellent", concludes a solicitor, "and is seen as an essential part of a lawyer's development rather than a luxury addition."

Macfarlanes

10 Norwich Street
London EC4A 1BD
Phone: +44 (0)20 7831 9222
www.macfarlanes.com

MAJOR DEPARTMENTS & PRACTICES

Advertising & Marketing • Agriculture & Estates • Asset Management • Charities • Commercial Property Occupiers • Competition/EU • Construction • Contentious Construction • Contentious Intellectual Property • Contentious Property • Contentious Regulatory Practice • Corporate • Corporate & Commercial Litigation • Corporate Tax • Debt Finance • Development & Investment • E-Commerce • Employment & Employee Benefits • Environmental • Franchising • Hotels & Leisure • Immigration & Nationality • Information Technology & Outsourcing • International Tax & Trusts • Investment Funds & Financial Services • IPOs • Litigation & Dispute Resolution • Lloyd's • M&A • Non-contentious Intellectual Property • Pensions • Private Banking & Professional Trustees • Private Client • Private Equity • Property • Property Finance • Residential/ Housing • Retail Occupiers • Trust & Probate Litigation • Trust Administration • UK Trusts & Estate Planning • Wills, Probate & Post-death Tax Planning

THE STATS

No. of lawyers: 270
No. of lawyers in London: 270
No. of offices: 1
Trainee intake: 25 (2005)
Trainees retained: 93% (2005)
London senior partner: Robert Sutton

BASE SALARY

Trainee: £31,000
Newly Qualified: £55,000

GRADUATE RECRUITMENT AND TRAINING MANAGER

Louisa Hatton
Graduate Recruitment Officer
E-mail: gradrec@macfarlanes.com

THE BUZZ
WHAT EMPLOYEES AT OTHER FIRMS ARE SAYING

- "Excellent midsize"
- "Old-fashioned"

THE SCOOP

Macfarlanes is somewhat unique amongst the U.K.'s top 50 law firms, as the only one to play at the top of the market without a single overseas office or, perhaps even more surprisingly, any formal network of alliance partners across the continent. Instead the firm works entirely, and devotedly, with the best law firms available in any jurisdiction at any one time—nothing formal, nothing written down, and no obligation. Sure, there are firms it knows better than others, but that's about as close as it's going to get.

Bucking conventional wisdom

So, the conventional wisdom would go, Macfarlanes must be doing mainly domestic work, right? Wrong. Somehow or other, this firm is one of the five most profitable in London, according to industry magazine *Legal Business*, and its clients are from all over the world.

The highlight for Macfarlanes in 2005 was undoubtedly its mammoth instruction to advise Pernod Ricard, the French drinks conglomerate, on a £7.4 billion takeover of U.K. rival Allied Domecq—the kind of deal that rarely goes to a firm without overseas offices. But Macfarlanes had worked for the client in the past, and the kind of loyalty that this practice inspires is something most rivals can only dream of.

Core values

Loyalty and collegiality pretty much sum up this firm, to the extent that they're probably ingrained on the trainees as they walk through the door. An incredible 65 per cent of the current crop of partners trained at Macfarlanes, a pretty phenomenal retention rate. This is not a place given to expansion, and lateral hires at partner level really are very few and far between. Macfarlanes shocked the City in 2004 when it hired Tom Speechley, an acquisition finance partner, from the London office of Norton Rose, and Bronwen Jones, an acquisition finance partner in the London office of Kirkland & Ellis, in a bid to boost its banking offering. Whilst Jones is a borrower specialist, Speechley acts almost exclusively for acquisition finance banks.

The firm had to do something—its debt finance team was weak compared to larger rivals, and the private equity clients were screaming. But Speechley and Jones have slotted in as if they'd been there their whole careers, and cultural equilibrium has reportedly been restored once more.

Deal junkies

The ethos at Macfarlanes is a clear one—size ain't everything. Just because you've got fewer than 300 lawyers, and they're all based in one office, doesn't mean you have to accept doing second-rate work.

Sure enough, the roster of clients and transactions is the envy of much bigger players. On the public M&A side, as well as Pernod Ricard, there was work for France Telecom buying shares in Wanadoo for €6 billion, and for publisher Centaur Communications on its £145 million sale to Centaur Holdings.

On the corporate side, though, it is private equity for which Macfarlanes is most well known. The firm has been acting for clients like Alchemy, 3i and Scottish Equity Partners since private equity was a new invention, and it keeps getting the work. In 2005, the team advised Alchemy selling Four Seasons Health Care for £775 million, and worked for Odeon Cinemas on its £400 million sale to Terra Firma Capital Partners.

Private equity borrowers

The private equity market has changed substantially in the last decade, and it's certainly true that the market has run away from Macfarlanes a bit. As deals have got larger they have gravitated toward the larger U.K. and U.S. law firms, such that it is here more than anywhere else that this firm's practice can look very much mid-market and English.

The banking team was brought in to support those private equity clients when they needed to borrow money for the bigger deals, and to do that, you need to earn your spurs with the banks to get credibility. Speechley et al. have done very well here since 2004—in 2005 they acted on 15 deals for private equity borrowers, and advised banks including Royal Bank of Scotland, NIB Capital Bank, Barclays, Bank of Ireland and Mizuho Bank.

Beyond corporate

But there is a lot more to Macfarlanes than just corporate work. The firm is equally committed to its private client practice—something rarely seen amongst the City law firms nowadays—and through trusts and estates work, private banking, immigration and wills and probate work, yet more of those all-important relationships are generated. This is how the firm gets so ensconced in the Square Mile; it acts for the wealthy individuals on their personal stuff. When those guys then do deals, they're introduced to someone else down the hall.

Macfarlanes is strong on the real estate side too, and has a fantastic fund formation practice that not only feeds private equity, it generates work setting up property investment vehicles, and plugs into the private client team too.

Then there is the litigation practice, which is well known for construction disputes, intellectual property and competition. Highlights of recent years include work for the Formula One team Jaguar Racing in Commercial Court proceedings against a former driver, and work for Marlwood Commercial against Viktor Kozeny in a large dispute about the privatisation of Azerbaijani state-owned enterprises. See, told you it wasn't all London-based.

Friends indeed

Macfarlanes aims to differentiate itself by offering clients a partner-led service, and then building strong relationships. Because it doesn't make lateral hires at partner level too often, it is pretty good at promoting from within, though inevitably that does mean it's pretty tough to get through the door in the first place.

The firm is pretty committed to its community, and picks a charity each year to be the focus of fundraising efforts. At the moment it is Fairbridge, a charity dedicated to helping young people in deprived areas of the U.K. It supports 13- to 25-year-olds in 15 disadvantaged areas, including Kilburn, Hackney and Kennington in London, where it has centres. Macfarlanes will organise fundraising activities, some people will run the London marathon for the cause, and they'll provide all-round support.

The hours at Macfarlanes are no more sociable than those you'd expect at a much larger firm, and in many ways it is tougher—these guys work just as hard as the big boys, but without the back-up of huge teams. Still, you'll sure get a chance to shine if you sign up here, and the work is as good as any London firm will offer. And if stay long enough and work hard enough, you'll also get a chance to share in some of the highest earnings in the City: according *The Lawyer*, Macfarlanes partners posted the third-highest profits of the top 50 firms in 2005-2006—the firm's PEP of £945,000 puts it ahead of Magic Circle favorites Freshfields, Clifford Chance and Allen & Overy. Hey, sometimes it pays to be different.

Mayer, Brown, Rowe & Maw LLP

11 Pilgrim Street
London EC4V 6RW
Phone: +44 (0)20 7248 4282
www.mayerbrownrowe.com

OTHER LOCATIONS

Berlin • Brussels • Charlotte • Chicago • Cologne • Frankfurt • Houston • Los Angeles • New York • Palo Alto • Paris • Washington, DC

(The firm also has an alliance with leading Italian law firm Studio Legale Tonucci, an association with the Mexican firm Jauregui, Navarette y Nader and trade consulting offices in Shanghai and Beijing in China.)

MAJOR DEPARTMENTS & PRACTICES

Antitrust & Competition • Appellate • Asia • Bankruptcy • Biotech • Chemicals • Collateralised Debt Obligations (CDOs) • Company Secretarial • Corporate & Securities • Corporate Governance • Derivatives • E-commerce • Employee Benefits & Executive Compensation • Employee Share Incentives • Employment & Labor Law • Energy & Natural Resources • Entertainment & Media • Environment • Finance • Financial Regulatory • Financial Restructuring & Bankruptcy • Financial Restructuring & Insolvency • Financial Services • Global Trade • Government • Government Contracts • Healthcare • India • Information Technology • Insurance & Reinsurance • Intellectual Property • International Arbitration • International Trade Compliance • Investment Management • Israel • Latin America • Legislative • Litigation & Dispute Resolution • Natural Resources (including Mining) • Outsourcing • Pensions • Pharmaceutical & Life Science • PPP/PFI & Infrastructure • Private Equity • Private Investment Funds • Pro Bono • Product Liability • Professional Practices • Project Finance • Property Rights • Public Law • Rail • Real Estate • Regulated Industries • Securitisation • Sports • Tax Controversy & Transfer Pricing • Tax Transactions & Consulting • Telecommunications & Media • Venture & Technology • Wealth Management

THE BUZZ
WHAT EMPLOYEES AT OTHER FIRMS ARE SAYING

- "Nice place, the most successful transatlantic merger"
- "Wannabe"

THE STATS

No. of lawyers: 1,400
No. of lawyers in London: 261
No. of offices: 13
Trainee intake: 25-30 per annum
Trainees retained: 88% (2005)
London managing partner: Paul Maher

BASE SALARY

Trainee: £29,000
Newly Qualified: £50,000

GRADUATE RECRUITMENT AND TRAINING MANAGER

Maxine Goodlet
Graduate Recruitment Manager
E-mail: mgoodlet@mayerbrownrowe.com

THE SCOOP

When America's Mayer Brown & Platt merged with London mid-sized Rowe & Maw in February 2002, it was the first deal of its kind and the market wasn't quite sure what to make of it. At first glance, this was an odd marriage —Mayer Brown & Platt was a firm known for structured finance in Chicago, generating a huge amount of money from litigation, and with only limited interest to date in Europe. Rowe & Maw, on the other hand, was a small but pretty impressive corporate boutique with some first-rate clients and, apparently, all to play for.

What was that about?

Many industry observers asked, if it must do an American merger, why didn't it choose an M&A firm? But four years on, the deal appears to have worked pretty well. There have been very few partner departures in London, and some significant lateral hires and promotions, and the U.K. arm of the combined, enormous, entity looks to have retained the autonomy that was so important to the partners.

In fact, the two halves of the firm remain merged only in name, as for legal and tax reasons they have opted not to form a single partnership—rather two LLPs. Still, there were symbolic successes for Rowe & Maw from the off—it got its full name into the title of the combined firm, and it has stayed there, and it currently has two partners onto the influential 13-partner board that runs the ship worldwide.

Still an English culture

With more than 1,400 lawyers, Mayer Brown is one of the largest firms in the world. In London, the operation is the largest of any international firm with a U.S. emphasis practising here. (It is worth pointing out that it really riles the U.K. partners to call it a U.S. law firm—they say their culture here is just that of an English firm. And this contention appears increasingly to be more than just rhetoric.)

The office is full service and a genuine leader in a number of practice areas. For the first couple of years post-merger there was a sense of wait-and-see, but there are now clear signs that the London branch is getting access to bigger clients, better work, hiring better partners and getting better results.

Double Dealing

It was shared client Marconi that bought Mayer, Brown, Rowe & Maw together in the first place, and it seemed at the outset that may have been all they had in common. But history has shown otherwise, and the combined entity has made serious headway in all the key areas: notably finance, M&A, dispute resolution, finance, real estate and TMT.

For the legacy Mayer Brown & Platt, securitisation had been the original lynchpin of its European strategy, so linking up with a firm that had no capability in the area was not on the face of it ideal. But the former head of Mayer Brown & Platt's London office, Ian Coles, took charge of the finance practice in Europe and set about rectifying the situation. Adding to the established six partners, recent hires into the London finance group include energy specialist Samantha Hampshire from Baker Botts, real estate finance partner Stephen Bower from Addleshaw Goddard and structured finance and securitisation partner Dominic Griffiths, formerly at White & Case. Together the finance team has worked on numerous transactional firsts, brought in some significant recent client wins and are very much in the ascendancy.

2 + 2 + Maher = 5

On the corporate side, clients include the likes of Reuters, Cable & Wireless, Monsanto and ICI, which is where the firm's star corporate partner and senior partner of the European practice, Paul Maher spent the early part of his career. In one recent transaction, Maher led the Mayer Brown team advising Cambridge Antibody Technology Group (CAT) on its £702 million recommended takeover by AstraZeneca.

The dispute resolution team is doing well, and on the contentious side the client list extends to Bank of America—which was one of the legacy Mayer Brown's largest clients—plus AstraZeneca, AXA, The Football League and Unilever.

In real estate, the firm's link-up has taken the already strong London team up a notch, such that it is frequently advising American investors coming into the European market. The firm just advised U.S. financial services group TIAA-CREF on its purchase of two of the buildings at Canary Wharf from the Canary Wharf Group for £206 million, for example. This ties in nicely with the German real estate team doing similar work for the client in Germany.

The common thread, to a certain extent, is a stand-out practice acting for media organisations and technology groups, be they in life sciences or in communications. Maher's history at ICI has helped, but the combination of strong outsourcing practices on both sides of the Atlantic is just one of many examples of two and two adding up to five.

Hands across the water

Every effort has been made to keep the London office of the merged firm looking and feeling like an English law firm, and certainly there has been no evidence of mass defections from the junior ranks, as has happened in other similar link-ups.

The U.K. arm has a strong and proactive community involvement programme —lawyers staff legal advice lines for the mental health charity, Mind, and civil rights group Liberty. Pro bono projects include seconding a lawyer to the Low Pay Unit, to advise individuals on low incomes and lobby the government on related issues, and supervising BPP Law School students at an advice clinic.

Again, there has been transatlantic co-operation here too—the London office has worked with other parts of the firm on projects including assistance to a start-up university for disadvantaged young women in Bangladesh, and helping a small organisation that works with Indonesian villagers to get established as a U.K. charity and company. A recent initiative is to develop pro bono projects in the firm's Brussels office for English and American lawyers based there.

A merger of equals?

Mayer Brown had looked for a long time for a U.K. merger that would finally establish it on this side of the Atlantic, and Rowe & Maw was attractive for its compact London-only structure. Mayer Brown had its own small offices in Paris and Germany, but again, they needed development and were lacking impetus from a London hub.

Because the Americans needed the deal, Rowe & Maw was able to put its foot down and insist that it wasn't taken over: though it may have been a sixth of the size of the U.S. arm, it did not want to be subsumed. Four years on and it seems to have achieved just what it set out to deliver—a strong London culture that is now part of a huge law firm, welcoming American referrals on a regular basis and working on bigger deals than it ever could on its own. Mayer, Brown, Rowe & Maw was the first link-up of its kind; others will still try hard to emulate it.

McDermott Will & Emery LLP

7 Bishopsgate
London EC2N 3AR
www.mwe.com

OTHER LOCATIONS

Boston • Brussels • Chicago • Düsseldorf • Los Angeles • Miami • Munich • New York • Orange County • Rome • San Diego • Silicon Valley • Washington DC

MAJOR DEPARTMENTS & PRACTICES

Banking and Finance
Corporate
Employment
Energy
EU Competition
European Telecom, Media & Technology
Financial Services & Funds
Information Technology
International Dispute Resolution
IP, Media & Technology
M&A
Pensions & Incentives
Tax
US Securities

THE STATS

No. of lawyers: 1,000+
No. of lawyers in London: 78
No. of offices: 14
Trainee intake: 3 per year
London managing partner: David Dalgarno

BASE SALARY

Trainee: £31,500
Newly Qualified: £60,000

GRADUATE RECRUITMENT AND TRAINING MANAGER

Aine Wood
Senior HR Officer
E-mail: graduate.recruitment@europe.mwe.com

THE BUZZ
WHAT EMPLOYEES AT OTHER FIRMS ARE SAYING

- "Strong employment group"
- "Underexposed"

THE SCOOP

When international law firm McDermott, Will & Emery opened in London back in 1998, it certainly did so with a bang. The City practice was launched with a spectacular raid on Simmons & Simmons—McDermott hired the head of corporate finance William Charnley, the head of tax Peter Nias, and senior banking partner Graham Rowbotham. From the outset, the plan was to do something different from every other American law firm on this side of the Atlantic.

Just another English law firm

McDermott wanted to be big and it wanted to be full service here, and fast. There were to be no American lawyers based here; instead the idea was to create an office that looked just like the average English law firm, and the plan was to hire 250 leading U.K. lawyers within five years. Things started well. First there was a raid on Baker & McKenzie for the firm's star head of employment, Fraser Younson, putting in place a serious labour practice not normally seen at American law firms in London. Next came big hitters John Reynolds, a litigator from Herbert Smith, an IP lawyer Larry Cohen from Hammonds.

Full service and first rate

Despite some comings and goings, the office is indeed full-service now, with a first-rate employment and pensions team, and leading partners in tax, corporate, international dispute resolution, IP/IT, banking and finance, and competition.

While the strategy has changed a little, out of 78 lawyers in London only three practice U.S. law. One of these, Scott Megregian (who heads up the EU competition practice), was originally based in the firm's Washington, D.C., office. The range of work going on in the London office of McDermott Will & Emery is possibly the widest of any U.S. law firm of a similar size in the U.K.

David Dalgarno, who is the current London managing partner, is a member of the firmwide management committee that gives London a voice in all decisions, which isn't always the case at similar firms.

Dealmakers

The firm's corporate work covers mega-mandates like advising Aldersgate Investments on its £2.1 billion proposed joint acquisition of Duelguide, through to smaller work like acting for Principal Hotels on the acquisition of the George Hotel in Edinburgh for £21.5 million. The corporate department's mantra is to service its clients on whatever they need doing, and they do not buy into the vision of some others that say smaller deals should be sent elsewhere.

The firm has a healthy practice for start-ups and emerging companies, working recently on two admissions to London's junior stock market, the Alternative Investment Market (AIM). The firm saw both Cyberscan Technology and Trading Emissions through to float, in both cases working for the company's nominated adviser. Andrew Caunt and Andrew Croxford joined last year from Allen & Overy to grow the equity/capital markets capability. The most recent partner addition of Nick Terras from SJ Berwin demonstrates the firm's commitment to building its structured finance and hedge fund practices.

Employment stands alone

The employment practice works on stand-alone instructions, as opposed to doing support work for the deals being done by the corporate team, as other similar teams might. The group is busy advising investment banks and also does well working on things like company reorganisations and restructurings, and helping institutions navigate data protection issues with their employees.

Clients of the intellectual property, media and technology group include Hitachi, SanDisk, Rohm & Haas, Static Control Components and Formula One. There is also a one-stop shop for patent prosecution and trade marks, which is unusual for a City firm. On the competition side, the firm worked for Lockheed Martin, the U.K. defence company, on the regulatory aspects of its acquisition of Insys Group, which supplies military communications systems and the like to clients including the Ministry of Defence.

Rounded practice

All of which makes for a practice that enables young lawyers to throw themselves into a whole variety of practices and a diversity of interesting projects. To find an office the size of McDermott's in London that allows such opportunity is pretty rare. Growth remains the strategy with 30 partners and nearing 80 lawyers in London.

The London office is, however, backed up by a chunky practice stateside that is one of the largest law firms in America. The firm works for 75 per cent of the Fortune 100 and more than 50 per cent of Fortune 500 companies, and wins regular awards for its pro bono work. At the end of 2004 the firm's Silicon Valley office was honoured by the Legal Aid Society of San Mateo County, for example. Work includes a $100,000 donation by the firm's charitable foundation to enable First Book, a children's literacy project, to distribute more than 500,000 books to low-income families across the U.S. The firm also won the Circle of Humanitarians Award from the American Red Cross for its tsunami relief donation.

McDermott has managed to transport that pre-eminent brand to this side of the Atlantic, although there have been knocks along the way. But since the 1998 launch in London, it has made its way successfully into Germany and Belgium, and retains a presence in Rome.

McGrigors

5 Old Bailey
London EC4M 7BA
Phone: +44 (0)20 7054 2500
www.mcgrigors.com

OTHER LOCATIONS
Belfast • Edinburgh • Glasgow

MAJOR DEPARTMENTS & PRACTICES
Banking & Finance
Commercial Litigation
Competition
Construction
Corporate
Dispute Resolution
Health & Safety
Human Rights
Intellectual Property
People Services
Planning & Environment
Projects
Public Law
Public Policy
Real Estate
Tax Litigation
Technology
Urban Regeneration

THE STATS
No. of lawyers: 320
No. of lawyers in London: 80
No. of offices: 4
Trainee intake: 15 (2005)
Managing partner: Colin Gray

PLUSES
- Relatively relaxed, entrepreneurial culture
- Reasonable hours

MINUSES
- No secretarial support after 5:30 p.m.
- Scottish management does not always understand London-specific issues

NOTABLE PERKS
- Daily lunch vouchers
- Subsidised gym
- Ability to buy up to 5 extra days of holiday each year
- Opportunities for secondment

GRADUATE RECRUITMENT AND TRAINING MANAGER
E-mail: graduate.recruitment@mcgrigors.com

THE BUZZ
WHAT EMPLOYEES AT OTHER FIRMS ARE SAYING

- "Good quality firm"
- "Tedious negotiators"

THE SCOOP

The story of McGrigors in London is quite a tale. The Scottish firm has had a presence south of the border since the early 1990s, but England had always very much played second fiddle to the heart of the practice up north. Then, in 2002, it shook the London market all of a sudden, announcing a merger with KLegal, the London legal arm of accountants KPMG.

Huge in Scotland

McGrigors, as the largest law firm in Scotland, had for a long time been frustrated in its attempts to expand its business. There are a limited number of international clients based in Edinburgh and Glasgow, and those that there are have established relationships with the Scottish legal elite. Continuing to expand, and attract the best talent out of universities, is a perennial problem for all of those firms, with budding young lawyers so often lured to the City.

So, as a result, McGrigors signed a deal with KLegal. KPMG had launched its own law firm in London back in 1999, and was busily building a full-service operation that could team up with the accountants when required, to offer clients a one-stop-shop approach. The atypical firm had made some nice hires, not least the former managing partner of the London office of New York's Weil, Gotshal & Manges, Nick Holt, and the former general counsel of British Telecom, Alan Whitfield.

Unfortunate timing

But KPMG was frustrated by organic growth, and wanted a more significant legal presence that extended beyond the capital. And so the two firms merged —at the time of the deal, KLegal had 100 lawyers in London, and a turnover of around £15 million. McGrigors had a small London presence, and a firmwide turnover of nearer £35 million. The link-up was to create by far the largest accountancy-tied law firm, handing KLegal the resources it craved and McGrigors the City presence it needed.

Alas, as the deal went live at the start of 2002, so Enron collapsed and Arthur Andersen followed, in a worldwide scandal that threw into question everything accountants did for clients beyond audit. Suddenly clients weren't so keen on instructing an accountancy-tied law firm, and the combination started to look doomed. Both clients and key partners deserted.

By the end of 2003, the formal ties to KPMG were ended, and the firm has now moved into fresh office space of its own in the capital. Many of the old KLegal partners have moved on, and McGrigors is left with an 80-lawyer City operation all of its own.

Fresh start

Despite its various incarnations, McGrigors remains a strong firm north of the border and has an enviable client list to mine down in London. The list of clients that once attracted KPMG still stands: the two major Scottish banks, Royal Bank of Scotland and Halifax Bank of Scotland; Boots; BP; BT; Hilton Group; McDonald's; The Ministry of Defence Procurement Agency; Scottish Power, and the Post Office. Those are just the highlights of a list of blue-chips using the firm regularly.

In London, the real estate practice has been one of the real successes, an area that was strong in both of the legacy firms and has combined successfully. One of the early wins for the property group was acting for Scottish entrepreneur Tom Hunter on his ultimately unsuccessful bid for Selfridges—a perfect example of McGrigor relationships teaming up with KLegal's London prowess.

Also strong is the tax litigation practice in London, which was set up by KLegal to make the most of the obvious crossover between the accountant and its lawyers in the field, and which has performed well. Then there is the good flow of corporate work, particularly in the small to mid-market, where the firm holds its own.

Old ties pay off

The relationship with KPMG may no longer be formal, but it is nevertheless lucrative. KPMG can still, of course, refer work to the law firm, just as it does to other law firms and just as every other accountancy firm does. McGrigors has the advantage of having spent many hours developing strong relationships with the key individuals in the potential money pit, and can thus expect more than its fair share of referrals.

Nowadays, McGrigors' revenue is at about £46 million, having dropped dramatically after the KPMG fallout, but rallied again this year. The firm is still the largest of the Scots, and ranks at 46th in the top 100 U.K. law firms by turnover, according to industry magazine *Legal Business*.

Moving on from the merger

Thus, for all its ups and downs, the firm has not done too badly out of the KLegal merger. Clients, by and large, stayed loyal, and the presence in London is now large enough to be taken seriously. The only downside is the international footprint—KLegal was just the London arm of a global legal network run by KPMG, and thus a huge attraction of the tie-up was access to those international referrals and relationships.

Today, KLegal International is but a disparate collection of once-united law firms scattered across the globe. McGrigors does its fair share of cross-border work, and undoubtedly more than it did pre-merger, but works through best friends relationships with other firms. One good example of work was acting on the employment issues faced by Switzerland's flagship airline SWISS as it restructured; another is the firm's work for Rexel preparing a vendor due diligence report on Rexel in connection with its €3.7 billion disposal of shares by Pinault Redoute.

Full circle

McGrigors has almost gone full circle since the turn of the century, starting as a Scottish law firm, morphing into a global legal arm of an accountant, and now largely back to where it started. It has walked away from a KPMG encounter with its pride intact, and while remaining a leader in its home nation, has expanded its horizons with some success. It has been an eventful few years, but the firm has a strong culture, a loyal client base and no less ambition as a result. One awaits the next exciting instalment in its history.

GETTING HIRED

"Ability and enthusiasm"

Of course McGrigors has academic qualifications, but keenness and nous carry a good deal of weight themselves. "We look for students who have ability and enthusiasm", writes the firm, which also prefers candidates who are "able to show that you are a team player, interested in continuous learning, and have strong technical skills." When it does come down to academics, McGrigors likes "good GCSEs and three Bs or equivalent at A-Level for London-based trainees." In Scotland, meanwhile, those with "top level passes at both Standard Grade and Higher level" are preferred and in both other locations the firm desires a "realistic estimate of a 2:1 at degree level." That said, if A-Level and Higher level grades are lacking and one's marks improved with age and learning, the firm is willing to give a second look. And while many firms seem to seek out interchangeable drones to fill their ranks and treat candidates accordingly, McGrigors chooses to take the respectful route, shares a solicitor: "The interview was tough but fair and they were very prompt in giving feedback. I felt I was wanted from the start, and treated as an individual." The firm must be on target; its "newly qualified retention rates across the U.K. for 2005 were 73 per cent."

OUR SURVEY SAYS

Beneficial benefits

"They pay me. That's all I'm interested in," quips a solicitor in the corporate finance practice. Surely the steady, "market rate" pay check is good enough for anyone—except, perhaps, for the attorney who complains that remuneration is "low for contribution of effort and time." This may be true for some, but, says one, compensation is "perfectly fair for the job I do—we are paid almost comparably to top 10 City firms but without the amount of stress. Billing targets are sensible." Indeed they are, coming in at "1,400 hours annually, with a 90 per cent utilisation rate." Vault also hears that "There is a good non-financial, flexible package to choose from, which includes additional holidays (which you have to pay for), health care, pension, life insurance and other incentives." There are also bonuses, which "are generally good, particularly if the firm has had a good year, as it had last year [2005]."

Live and let work

Aside from their salary and benefits appreciation, McGrigors solicitors enjoy "great support and huge level[s] of responsibility", especially when it comes to "allowing all levels of lawyers to pursue and develop client relationships." Not so shocking then to discover that the firm is "open door, friendly, professional" and "entrepreneurial." According to some it has taken the firm some time post-merger to get to this point, as it "faced major challenges after its splitting up from KPMG. However, in the past two years the firm has gone from strength to strength and is up-and-coming. In certain areas—real estate, tax litigation, banking, projects—the firm punches above its weight and there is a team culture in the firm that most lawyers seem to like."

Despite the team culture, optional social activities leave little pressure to join the gang for drinks. For those in the firm's "mixed bunch" who do like a pint or 10, "there is a strong social culture, with events organised by the firm as well as by department or informal Friday drinks." Though the varied personalities coupled with the firm's merger not so long ago can make things slightly "fractious", it is also called—with an abandon uncommon among the legal establishment—"a hell of a lot of fun!"

Punching the clock

It's definitely not fun when attorneys are working "typically ... very long hours", though "the firm doesn't share the macho culture of many other City firms", offers a source. "At present my working hours are perfect", says a relieved solicitor, who doesn't "know whether any fee-earners work part time." Some do have varied schedules, though: "I have specific working time requests ... and this is a high priority for everyone I work with. I have never been made to feel that I was causing difficulty at all", a grateful solicitor shares.

Reliable partners

Though specific treatment of solicitors "depends on [the] individual", general "communication from the partners to lower levels is very good and takes the form of e-mails, weekly update and monthly meetings." A lawyer tells us that "partners actively seek to involve solicitors in the future planning of the firm. There are quarterly roadshows from the senior partners to update staff on the thinking of the board, where it is possible to share this at this stage." Those at the top are also "excellent about giving feedback informally", and provide each solicitor with a "Performance Manager" and a mentor, which continues "at a more senior level" as NQs progress with their careers. They also provide respectable training at the "trainee/NQ level, but [it] tails off significantly after that", a problem they are currently trying to remedy. Altogether, it works pretty well, says a contact: "Partner/solicitor relationships in my department are the best I have ever experienced."

Milbank, Tweed, Hadley & McCloy LLP

Dashwood House
69 Old Broad Street
London EC2M 1QS
Phone: +44 (0)20 7448 3000
www.milbankeurope.com

OTHER LOCATIONS

Frankfurt • Hong Kong • Los Angeles • Munich • New York • Palo Alto • Singapore • Tokyo • Washington, DC

MAJOR DEPARTMENTS & PRACTICES

Bond Restructuring • Capital Markets • Information Technology & Outsourcing • Intellectual Property • International Tax • Leveraged Finance & High Yield • Mergers & Acquisitions/Private Equity • Project & Asset Finance

THE STATS

No. of lawyers: 520
No. of lawyers in London: 48
No. of offices: 10
London managing partner: Phillip Fletcher

NOTABLE PERKS

- Firm retreat
- Cake on Friday
- Subsidized software for home PC users

BASE SALARY

Newly Qualified: £83,333

GRADUATE RECRUITMENT AND TRAINING MANAGER

Philippa Thornton
Legal Personnel Coordinator
E-mail: pthornton@milbank.com

THE BUZZ
WHAT EMPLOYEES AT OTHER FIRMS ARE SAYING

- "High-quality, high-intensity work"
- "Patchy in London"

THE SCOOP

Milbank opened in London more than 25 years ago, and was one of the first New York firms to hire English lawyers when it became possible to do so back in 1994. Milbank started off with a bang—it took two highly rated project finance partners from the London practice of Magic Circle firm Clifford Chance, Kenneth MacRitchie and Nick Buckworth. Suddenly the firm that was so well known for its international project finance capability was able to offer both English and American law advice: the London office was run by an American expert in project finance, Phillip Fletcher.

Bouncing back

Alas, the office grew to a reasonable size—some six partners—but was quickly the victim of its own success when New York rival Shearman & Sterling took three of those partners to launch its own U.K. law practice. With other departures, the office depleted by 1996 to just Fletcher, and so the process began again.

Milbank is a very successful firm on Wall Street, and is among the most profitable law firms in the world. So if things don't work the first time, it makes darn sure they do in the second attempt. By 2000 the office was back on track, through a combination of strategic reviews, lateral hires and reother locations from elsewhere in the firm. No longer as concentrated on project finance, the firm drafted capital markets capability in from New York and Singapore, it added tax and securitisation capability with hires from Cadwalader Wickersham & Taft in London, and it relocated M&A partner Michael Goroff into London.

Goldman link & Freshfields scoop

Goroff has exceptional links to Goldman Sachs, and quickly achieved steady deal flow. Things really started motoring, though, when Milbank scooped up Freshfields Bruckhaus Deringer's London M&A partner Tim Emmerson. His move was one of only a handful by Magic Circle corporate partners to the City practices of American law firms. Immediately, this became the hire to beat amongst U.S. firms in London.

Indeed, much of Milbank's European growth of late has come at the expense of the Magic Circle. Emmerson was followed by capital markets partner Andrew Brodie and outsourcing partner Laurence Jacobs, both from Allen & Overy, and intellectual property partner David Perkins from Clifford Chance.

In 2001, Milbank expanded into Germany, sending two American partners to Frankfurt, and in 2005, leading German banking and acquisition finance lawyers Rainer Magold and Christina Ungeheuer joined the practice. Munich followed in 2004, when three partners joined from Freshfields, including the firm's joint head of private equity. And so the firm was well and truly back up and running in Europe, and the deals have been flowing ever since.

Deal dream

For Emmerson, a lot of the attraction of joining Milbank stemmed from its more manageable size—the firm has a little over 130 partners, compared to more than 500 at Freshfields. Emmerson thought he'd have a voice, and he'd be able to build a business from scratch. And so he has.

One of Emmerson's largest clients was one he shared with Goroff and Milbank, the aforementioned Goldman Sachs. Together the pair of M&A partners could offer the client transatlantic advice on anything they needed, and they hit the ground running straight off, working for the bank on Philip Green's massive hostile bid for retailers Marks & Spencer in Emmerson's first year at the firm. The bid did not succeed, but it was one hell of a mandate for a nascent U.K. M&A practice, and put Emmerson on the map.

Private equity and project finance

Soon afterwards, Milbank secured its first work for major U.K. private equity player Apax Partners, when it advised them on their billion-dollar buyout of satellite group Inmarsat. Later the firm worked for the U.S. vulture fund Cerberus, when it was investing in BoxClever, as well as for the Sainsbury's family.

All the while, the project finance practice has continued unabated, the European team consists of three project partners in London: Phillip Fletcher, John Dewar and Cathy Marsh, as well as the aforementioned Magold and Ungeheuer in Frankfurt. The practice covers the EMEA (Europe, Middle East, Africa) region and the team was named Eurpoean Project Finance Firm 2005 at the *International Financial Law Review* Awards. Fletcher's work includes representing parties involved in the first independent power projects in Portugal, Italy, Hungary and Turkey, working on a petrochemicals project in Saudi Arabia, and doing a groundbreaking liquefied natural gas project in the Middle East. He's also done power projects in Indonesia and Korea, infrastructure projects in Scandinavia, and work for underwriters in capital markets issues for power and coal mine projects.

Complement the Big Apple

Newest to Milbank's fold are the outsourcing and intellectual property practices, both of which complement strong groups back in New York. Laurence Jacobs, the outsourcing partner, came with an excellent pedigree, having worked on a massive IT outsourcing for the National Health Service, which was one of the biggest the industry had ever seen. His clients include Barclays, EDS, Equant, HSBC, JPMorgan Chase, Lloyds TSB, RBS, T-Systems and Unisys, and his brief now is to help multinational companies in all aspects of their global outsourcing strategies.

And then there is IP. Perkins was nearing retirement age at Clifford Chance, and was a beneficiary of the fact that New York law firms like Milbank will quite happily keep productive partners working well into their sixties. He is a litigator, and was the founder, and for a long time the leader, of the IP team in Europe at Clifford Chance. Now he does multi-jurisdictional patent and trademark litigation alongside colleagues in the firm's other offices.

Culture Club

Milbank has gained a reputation for a collegiate culture that no doubt has served to attract so many Magic Circle refugees to the fold. These defectors perhaps can hope that, because of the firm's size, the partnership is truly run by the partners.

Though the London office does not offer training contracts, it actively recruits newly-qualified lawyers who have been well trained elsewhere and want a new challenge. Fletcher is reportedly committed to advancing pro bono efforts on this side of the Atlantic, too, in line with the culture back at HQ, and has worked with other American law firms in the capital to get combined initiatives up and running.

Nabarro Nathanson

Lacon House
Theobald's Road
London WC1X 8RW
Phone: +44 (0) 20 7524 6000
www.nabarro.com

OTHER LOCATIONS

Brussels • Sheffield

MAJOR DEPARTMENTS & PRACTICES

Banking • Charities • Commercial Litigation & Dispute Resolution • Company & Commercial • Compulsory Purchase • Construction & Engineering • Corporate Finance • Corporate Governance • Corporate Real Estate • E-Commerce • Education • Employee Share Schemes • Employment • Energy • Environment • EU & Competition • Health & Safety • Health Claims/Personal Injury • Healthcare • Information Technology • Intellectual Property • Mines & Quarries • Pensions • Pensions Litigation • Planning • Private Equity & Venture Capital • Projects/PPP/PFI • Property • Property Litigation • Public Equity • Public Sector • Rail • Tax • Telecommunications • Transport

THE STATS

No. of lawyers: 440
No. of lawyers in London: 400
No. of offices: 3
Trainee intake: 30 (2005)
Trainees retained: 85% (2005)
London managing partner: Nicole Paradise

BASE SALARY

Trainee: £30,000
Newly Qualified: £53,000

GRADUATE RECRUITMENT AND TRAINING MANAGER

E-mail: graduateinfo@nabarro.com

THE BUZZ
WHAT EMPLOYEES AT OTHER FIRMS ARE SAYING

- "Quality outfit"
- "In a rush"

THE SCOOP

Nabarro Nathanson is, essentially, a real estate firm. It has one of the best real estate practices in the City, and like so many others in that space, its strategy is now to diversify beyond that solid groundwork and become a leading commercial firm for U.K. plc.

Broadening horizons

Certainly Nabarro is making a good stab at just that. It has grown to 100 partners in three offices, and has been pretty aggressive in its lateral hiring of late. The corporate practice is not one to be sniffed at, even though it is well and truly overshadowed by the money and profile generated by the property guys. But on the downside, and there inevitably is one, the firm has suffered the loss of some real rainmakers to American law firms coming into London, and it sometimes struggles to compete as its real estate clients start looking for complicated financial structures to go alongside the brick and mortar deals.

Nabarro was once aligned with American firm Weil Gotshal & Manges, until that firm made its own way into Europe and the Nabarro international strategy looked somewhat exposed. Today it puts a lot of time and effort into building relationships with a number of American law firms and, more crucially, their clients. It sees an opportunity to nab inbound investment work, but again, it is not the only firm to have thought of it.

In Europe, Nabarro now has fully signed up alliances with French firm August & Debouzy and Gassner Stockmann & Kollegen in Germany, while the firm's own tiny Brussels office handles competition work when the need arises.

Part of a resurgent midmarket

Still, the overarching view is of a midmarket U.K. law firm doing domestic deals. The firm did make good progress building an IT practice in the late 1990s, only to see it suffer disproportionately in the dotcom crash. In 2005, the firm closed its office in Reading, one homeland for the tech industry in the U.K., and the corporate partners servicing that market, including work for Oracle, returned to the head office.

But the mid-market in the U.K. is resurgent, and the hungry firms are finding the big deals can indeed head in their direction. Nabarro is one that is quite hungry, but is yet to totally convince the market it has the appetite for greater things, though it clearly has the best of intentions.

Property proper ...

The firm's real estate clients read like a who's who of the industry: Jones Lang LaSalle, Land Securities, Quintain Estates, Great Portland Estates, and many more. The work is good too—the firm acted for Land Securities on the acquisition of retail warehouse specialist and supermarket investor Lxb Properties for £360 million in the summer of 2005, and advised Great Portland on £76 million of City investment deals in the same month.

For LaSalle, the firm acted on a £43 million Kings Cross office buy, and it has advised on copious U.K. shopping centre developments this year. On the inbound American side, the firm nabbed work to advise Whole Foods Markets, the American natural and organic food specialist, on its acquisition of part of the listed Barker's department store in High Street Kensington, a real landmark deal given the retailer's ambition for the U.K. marketplace.

... and property spin-offs

From property work spins a multitude of disciplines, and Nabarro has them all. There is property finance and property litigation, planning and environment, then projects, PFI and PPP, to name but a few. Of these, the projects team is probably the most renowned, and the firm's work on PFI and PPP projects since their inception makes it a market leader; it has done more than £7 billion of public/private deals. In 2005 Nabarro saw a record level of activity in the spring, and closed seven PFI deals in April, three in the housing sector and four in education.

But there really is more to Nabarro than real estate and its spin-offs. The corporate practice has done well riding the wave of smaller companies looking to list on the Alternative Investment Market, where its highest-profile client is corporate finance house Numis Securities. Other sizeable corporate deals include working for Priory Healthcare on its sale to ABN Amro, acting for the shareholders in the sale of Canon Avent to Charterhouse Capital for £320 million, and working for Land Securities on the £300 million sale of its interest in the Telereal joint venture.

Toeholds in private equity and government

The firm is increasingly getting a toehold in private equity by advising management teams in management buyouts. It took the management role in the £552 million sale of Partnerships in Care, the £335 million sale of Innspired Group to Punch Taverns, and on the £177 million sale of the Tatteshall Castle Group. And beyond those most crucial lynchpins of real estate and corporate, Nabarro has its fair share of interesting add-ons that serve as a useful reminder that it has not always had such a clear vision of where it wants to be.

In Sheffield, the firm opened an office in 1996 to consolidate what was by that point a reasonably-sized North of England network, including offices in Doncaster and Hull. Doncaster was run by the former in-house legal team at British Coal, and those individuals brought with them work defending British Coal in some major personal injury claims. Nowadays the cases rumble on, and Nabarro Sheffield advises the Department of Trade and Industry in its defence, with the largest case being brought by miners claiming injuries caused by working conditions. Though an unlikely practice for a City firm, such government and local government work has served the firm well. Also of note is a first-rate pensions and employment team based in London, where the firm really holds its own against some hungry competitors.

Place to be

By all accounts, the management of Nabarro is young and energetic, and that gives the firm an enthusiasm that isn't always evident amongst some of its stuffier rivals. That leadership has transformed Nabarro Nathanson from sleepy property firm to dynamic City player of late. There is a way to go before it really has the competition worried, but all signs are that this could be a challenger of the future if its keeps up the good work. Moreover, the firm's slick offices reportedly feature a great coffee house.

Norton Rose

Kempson House
Camomile Street
London EC3A 7AN
www.nortonrose.com

OTHER LOCATIONS

Amsterdam • Athens • Bahrain • Bangkok • Beijing • Brussels • Dubai • Frankfurt • Greece • Hong Kong • Jakarta • Milan • Moscow • Munich • Paris • Piraeus • Prague • Rome • Singapore • Warsaw

MAJOR DEPARTMENTS & PRACTICES

Arbitration • Banking • Competition • Regulatory & EC • Corporate Finance • Dispute Resolution • Employment • Pensions & Incentives • Financial Services • Intellectual Property & Technology • Real Property • Tax

THE STATS

No. of lawyers: 1,000
No. of lawyers in London: 600
No. of offices: 21
Trainee intake: 60 (2005)
Trainees retained: 80% (2005)
London managing partner: Deirdre Walker

BASE SALARY

Trainee: £30,000
Newly Qualified: £55,000

GRADUATE RECRUITMENT AND TRAINING MANAGER

Ruth Edwards
E-mail: grad.recruitment@nortonrose.com

THE BUZZ
WHAT EMPLOYEES AT OTHER FIRMS ARE SAYING

- "Good all-rounder"
- "Had better days"

THE SCOOP

Norton Rose occupies the most difficult part of the London legal market, the awkward position just beneath the Magic Circle. As a result, it has had a tough time recently, finding itself with the global footprint, and thus cost, to match the top six, but the income, and therefore profits, that don't quite match. Norton Rose is nothing if not resilient however: the firm was bombed twice in the 1990s, and while such incidents might have destroyed less collegiate firms, Norton Rose endured and managed to get things back to normal.

Strong banking brand despite defections

The arrival of American law firms in London has meant the crème de la crème of London lawyers can move elsewhere for a lot more money. What's worse, Allen & Overy made a massive raid of Norton Rose's first-class banking team in 2002, when it lured four of the firm's brightest stars away. For A&O the move was as much about knocking out a competitor as it was about its own expansion, but for Norton Rose it was a nasty reminder of just how important it is to keep up with the market if you don't want to lose people.

In 2005, Norton Rose suffered again, when a team of securitisation partners left to join Baker & McKenzie in London. What is perhaps reassuring for the firm is that, despite all this, its brand remains one of the strongest in the City —even three years after the A&O defections, many bankers still talk of Norton Rose as a banking firm, albeit rather lacking in banking lawyers.

Norton Rose appears to be striving for an image change in order to convince clients to continue handing over big instructions. The latest plan is for a sector-based approach, in which the firm will capitalise on its significant weight in areas like transport and insurance.

Sector-specific

Norton Rose was once known as a shipping firm and from that grew asset finance, insurance, an international practice and a specialism in transport. So many of these areas have taken on a dynamism of their own now, and the firm is still a leader in most.

In insurance, the firm advised the U.K.'s fastest growing motor insurer, The Admiral Group, on its £711 million London Stock Exchange listing last year, and also acts for a host of underwriters, P&I groups, Lloyd's syndicates and brokers.

In transport, the firm is a real leader in rail work, with clients like rolling stock groups HSBC Rail and Porterbrook, the Office of the Rail Regulator, and the financiers for Tubelines, which runs part of the London Underground. The firm extends the rail work internationally too, working with Dutch, Belgian and French state rail operators, and for manufacturer Alstom in Asia. The Thai government even retained Norton Rose to work on the proposed privatisation of Thai Railways.

On the finance front

In finance, HSBC remains a loyal and long-standing client of the firm, and other areas of finance are doing well. The firm has a niche in Islamic finance, designing specialist structures that comply with Islamic law, which forbids the earning of interest. Norton Rose advised the Islamic Bank of Britain on its launch in the U.K. last year, the first Islamic retail bank to launch in any Western country.

The corporate practice at Norton Rose continues to hold its own. One major win in 2004 was the mandate to advise Nestle, the food company, on all its corporate work. Otherwise, most of the work is for financial institutions—such as the two key M&A mandates for HSBC buying Marks & Spencer's Retail Financial Services arm, and for ISIS on its £1 billion merger with F&C Asset Management, one of the country's top five.

Global gamble

Norton Rose followed the pack in the 1990s and, in hindsight, probably opened more offices than it really needed. Chief Executive Peter Martyr is now focusing time and energy on making the international network deliver for London. 2004 saw the Cologne office break away and join CMS Hasche Sigle. Norton Rose had taken the office from Gaedertz just a few years back, as an entrée into Germany, but it has since moved into Frankfurt and Munich, where it seems to find more synergies.

The firm's Asia practice does well, as does the Middle East, where the Islamic finance practice in Dubai and Bahrain is firing on all cylinders. In Hong Kong the firm won *Legal Business* Asia Pacific Office of the Year in 2005 for its outstanding work.

Globally, the firm is more committed than many to action in the community, and works hard to get involved in projects rather than just signing cheques. Norton Rose works closely with a group called Barretstown, which helps children recovering from serious illness. The firm took a view that worldwide it would focus its fundraising efforts on children and medicine. In Bangkok, for example, it began supporting two AIDS-related charities.

Doing well by doing good

Closer to home, the firm works pro bono for the Citizens' Advice Bureau, the Tower Hamlets Law Centre, the Free Representation Unit, and the Environmental Law Foundation. In 2005 one of the firm's associates, Gemma Garner, won The Young Solicitors' Group Pro Bono award for individual contribution.

What Norton Rose lacks in profits, it makes up for in collegiality and loyalty. Many of the partners, and many of the clients, have stuck with the firm through thick and thin, and with new management installed, it now looks like the firm will pull through.

Psst...
Need a Change in Venue?

Use the Internet's most targeted job search tools for law professionals.

Vault Law Job Board
The most comprehensive and convenient job board for law professionals. Target your search by area of law, function, and experience level, and find the job openings that you want. No surfing required.

VaultMatch Resume Database
Vault takes match-making to the next level: post your resume and customize your search by area of law, experience and more. We'll match job listings with your interests and criteria and e-mail them directly to your inbox.

For more information go to www.vault.co.uk/law

VAULT
> the most trusted name in career information™

Olswang

90 High Holborn
London WC1V 6XX
Phone: +44 (0) 20 7067 3000
www.olswang.com

OTHER LOCATIONS

Brussels
Thames Valley

THE STATS

No. of lawyers: 248
No. of lawyers in London: 224
No. of offices: 3
Trainee intake: 20 (2005)
Trainees retained: 87% (2005)
Managing partner: Jonathan Goldstein

MAJOR DEPARTMENTS & PRACTICES

Banking & Insolvency
Commercial Dispute Resolution
Corporate
  Company Secretarial Services • Fundraising /Initial Public Offerings • Funds Formation • Joint Ventures • Mergers & Acquisitions • Reconstructions & Reorganisations
Data Protection
Employee Benefits
  Employee Tax • Pensions • Share Incentives
Employment
EU & Competition
Information Technology
Intellectual Property
  Commercial IP • Copyright & Database Litigation • Patent Prosecution • Patent & Trade Secrets Litigation • Trade Mark & Design Litigation • Trade Mark & Registered Design Prosecution
Judicial Review & Public Law
Media Litigation
Outsourcing
Private Equity/Venture Capital
Property
  Construction • Development • Finance • Investment • Litigation • Management • PFI/Outsourcing • Planning & Regeneration
Tax

THE BUZZ
WHAT EMPLOYEES AT OTHER FIRMS ARE SAYING

- "Meejah darling"
- "Horn-rimmed lefties"

BASE SALARY

Trainee: £30,000
Newly Qualified: £53,000

GRADUATE RECRUITMENT AND TRAINING MANAGER

Victoria Edwards
Apply online at www.olswang.com

THE SCOOP

Olswang is one of the youngest law firms in the London market, and has the bright, upstart image to go with its age. The firm did not set-up until 1981, and to be fair it has already been through various incarnations since then. The plan from the outset was a media and communications boutique—a firm that knew its sector so well that the clients would be queuing up.

Bursting bubble

And indeed they did: through the early 1990s and beyond Olswang grew with rapid pace and success. But then the dotcom bubble burst with spectacular repercussions for the whole legal market, and Olswang was hit pretty hard. It was one of the few law firms to make lay-offs, and did a hefty amount of navel-gazing. The result was only a slight shift in emphasis, with the firm choosing in 2003 to take on a sizeable real estate practice from the disintegrating London practice DJ Freeman.

Ch-ch-changes

That was Olswang transformation number one. The second is going on before our eyes now, with the firm ditching its old independent boutique image and lining up international links with gusto. In summer 2005, Olswang signed an alliance with American 1,400-lawyer firm Greenberg Traurig LLP, hoping to achieve a risk-free entry into the U.S. market by building referral relationships. Now there are talks about France, Germany and India as the strategy takes on more than a hint of likeness to that of the firm's rivals.

But Olswang is genuinely different from pretty much every law firm in London, not least because of its incredibly enthusiastic and enigmatic management. Jonathan Goldstein was only 32-years-old when he took over the leadership of the firm in 1998. He had been a partner for four years by that point, and had been with the firm for a grand total of six. No one can deny he's guided the firm through the seven tough years of his tenure with some panache. In 2006 Olswang posted an impressive 21 per cent rise in revenue and a 31 per cent increase in PEP, according to *The Lawyer*.

Dial O for Olswang

Whatever the economy has thrown at it, Olswang has stayed dedicated to its core media, telecoms and technology client base. The list of major corporations that the firm works for reads like a who's who of TMT: Channel 4, the BBC, HBO, Bloomberg and M&C Saatchi to name a few. Recent deals include advising M&C Saatchi on its £67 million AIM flotation, working for O2 on setting up a mobile network in partnership with Tesco, and advising the record trade association BPI on a new licensing structure for online music.

Through a specialist approach, the firm has won some big corporate clients too: it scooped its first job for U.S. private equity house The Blackstone Group when it advised on the purchase of national cinema chain Cine U.K. The team also won the mandate to advise The Tchenguiz Family as part of a consortium bidding for the Somerfield supermarket chain—its first corporate transaction for the client.

Beyond media

Real estate has settled in at Olswang like a duck in water, with clients including The Rotch Group and Minerva, the latter being a long-standing client of Goldstein's. The firm has combined strengths to advise on deals like the sale of Warner Village's cinema circuit.

On defamation, Olswang partner Geraldine Proudler is arguably the best in London, and was called in by Marks & Spencer head Stuart Rose when he got involved in a libel spat with Goldman Sachs.

And then there is the sports practice—the firm is working for FIFA on the sale of its media rights for the 2010 World Cup, and represented the Rugby Football Union in its deal with Sky to broadcast the Zurich Premiership and various England internationals. Other clients of the group include Eurosport, the ICC, and retailer Sports World.

While lacking the straitjacket formality of some City law firms, Olswang has managed to convince many on the London legal scene that it can in fact handle the most complex work they can throw at it.

Going places

In 2002, Olswang moved into a smart new office space in Holborn, near the West End. While close enough to the City to be feasible, the firm has a purpose-built HQ that is more media than law—there is Sky TV and a Starbucks in the entrance hall, and the building glows yellow through the night, making it pretty easy to find. That move was a credit, once again, to Goldstein, who signed a smart and unique deal with Minerva whereby Olswang committed to the space and Minerva procured the financing.

Also "outside the box" was the firm's decision to launch its own corporate finance house, LongAcre Partners, just as the market for IPOs began to bottom out. LongAcre is now doing successful deals, having been through some tough times.

Goldstein instils a great culture of entrepreneurialism, hard work, and fun at the firm, as evidenced by the firm's garnering position 18 in *The Sunday Times* 100 Best Companies to Work For 2006, the top London-based law firm on the list for the second year running.

The chairman leads by example: though he has four small children, he finds a lot of time for charity work—most notably on the board of Jewish Care—and advises three of the firm's largest clients. He is also a keen Tottenham Hotspur fan—the firm has a box at the team's stadium.

In March 2006 Olswang turned 25 and for its silver jubilee year the firm voted to support Fairbridge, a charity that works with young people to give them the motivation, confidence and skills they need to change their own lives. Through firmwide and individual challenges and events, Olswang aims to raise £250.000 for Fairbridge.

Orrick, Herrington & Sutcliffe LLP

Tower 42, Level 35
25 Old Broad Street
London EC2N 1HQ
Phone: +44 (0)20 7562 5000
www.orrick.com

OTHER LOCATIONS

Hong Kong • Los Angeles • Milan • Moscow • New York • Orange County • Pacific Northwest • Paris • Rome • Sacramento • San Francisco • Silicon Valley • Taipei • Tokyo • Washington, DC

MAJOR DEPARTMENTS & PRACTICES

Acquisition Finance
Arbitration & Litigation
Banking, Trade & Asset Finance
Capital Markets
Competition & European Union Law
Corporate & Corporate Finance
Employment & Benefits
Energy & Project Finance
Global Bankruptcy & Debt Restructuring
Investment Funds
Private Equity
Real Estate
Structured Finance & Securitisation
Tax

THE STATS

No. of lawyers: 850
No. of lawyers in London: 50+
No. of offices: 16
Trainee intake: Up to six places per year.
Trainees retained: 75% (2005)
London managing partner: Martin Bartlam

BASE SALARY

Trainee: £28,000
Newly Qualified: £55,000

GRADUATE RECRUITMENT AND TRAINING MANAGER

Lorraine Parker
Phone: +44 (0)20 7422 4718
E-mail: lparker@orrick.com

THE BUZZ
WHAT EMPLOYEES AT OTHER FIRMS ARE SAYING

- "Going places"
- "Bonds, bonds, bonds"

THE SCOOP

Orrick traces its roots back to the middle of the 19th century, when it was founded in San Francisco. Early clients included the Pacific Gas & Electric Company, and the first two San Franciscan investment banks. The firm was famous in the early days for its work on municipal bonds, and is best known stateside for its work on the issuance of the bonds that helped finance the construction of the Golden Gate Bridge. In recent years, Orrick has embarked on a course of aggressive global expansion, which has not been at the expense of its home strengths.

West Coast roots & London ambition

From its strong roots in finance on the West Coast, the firm has expanded to become an international player. The first office outside California was New York in 1984, then came Washington, D.C. in 1993, London in 1998, Tokyo in 1999 and Seattle in 2000. Since the turn of this century, the focus has been very much on Europe, with the firm making a splash to enter Paris in 2002, then adding Milan and Rome, and finally slotting in Moscow in 2004. The year 2005 also saw the firm more than double the size of its London outpost, with the addition of virtually all of Coudert Brothers' London office, and merge with French M&A and litigation powerhouse Rambaud Martel in Paris. The firm opened offices in both Hong Kong and Taipei in 2004, as well, as part of the expansion of its Asia practice. Approximately 25 per cent of the firm's lawyers are now based outside the United States.

For the London practice, things have not always been easy. Despite opening in 1998, ambitions early on were to secure a merger with a mid-market, full-service U.K. law firm, and thus establish Orrick as a player in one fell swoop. Alas, despite numerous merger talks that included quite serious discussions with Bird & Bird, no compatible partner could be found. A stream of arrivals and departures characterised the practice here until 2002, when Orrick hired the Paris office of London firm Watson, Farley & Williams, to finally make a mark in Europe.

Hoovering up Coudert

The Paris team brought with them good work for great clients, including Vivendi, Renault and EADS, and the energetic partners there injected some impetus to the European network. Next came a new managing partner in London, Adrian Harris, who seemed determined to make it work. Italy was signed up in 2003. However, it was in 2005 that the firm finally got the London hires that it needed to stop its City office appearing the weak link in an otherwise convincing operation on this side of the Atlantic. These included an English law financing team from Jones Day and the arrival of the team from Coudert Brothers.

Orrick had discussed merger, albeit briefly, with international rival Coudert Brothers. When that firm collapsed spectacularly at the start of 2005, Orrick quickly snapped up its London and Moscow teams. The Hong Kong arrivals are also Coudert refugees. In 2005, Orrick added 34 lawyers to its London operation from Coudert Brothers. The new team adds specialisms in banking, mergers and acquisitions, employment, emerging markets and commercial property litigation to the Orrick offering, which has to date been largely finance-driven. The firm is seeking to grow its business in London through a combination of lateral partner and associate hires and well as building its home-grown talent through its graduate recruitment program. Martin Bartlam succeeded Harris as London office leader from the beginning of 2006.

London to go

The office is now a full service practice and building a growing reputation for its finance, corporate and real estate practices. Regular clients of the London office include Merrill Lynch, Goldman Sachs, Deutsche Bank, Bear Stearns, Société Générale, SC Johnson, Total, Telenor and Capital Shopping Centres.

The firm has always done well in securitisation work worldwide and therefore in London. Orrick lawyers advised the managers on a U.S.$1 billion securitisation of U.K. credit card receivables last year, Dynamic Credit Partners on a U.S.$1 billion CDO and acted for another group of managers on a U.S.$765 million mortgage-backed securitisation for an Australian issuer in Europe. It also has a growing acquisition finance practice and advised Merrill Lynch on its mezzanine financing and equity participation in 3i's purchase of National Car Parks from Cinven.

Perhaps the biggest opportunity for the firm in London now, though, is on the corporate side. In the last few years Orrick, so long a finance firm, has aimed to boost its corporate practice in Europe and the U.S. It has done so through various acquisitions in Paris, including its combination with Rambaud Martel, and in Silicon Valley, where it now has one of the best teams for advising start-up companies that emerge there and then expand internationally. Few law firms can offer such clients a global footprint, and being able to offer European start-ups access to Silicon Valley financiers, and vice versa, gives Orrick a fairly unique selling point.

Baxter in charge

The chairman of Orrick is Ralph Baxter, a celebrated leader who has been at the helm since 1990. It was he who first envisioned the firm growing internationally, and diversifying away from municipal bonds into much, much more. He has done well to achieve a large part of that vision. Baxter is one of a rare band of law firm leaders that is not afraid to do something a little different, and that was evidenced in 2002 when the firm became the first to open a global operations centre, outsourcing the day-to-day administrative functions to a centre in West Virginia. There are no lawyers in the office, it is just a support outlet, housing the technology, finance and human resource operations, and document and transcript production services. The idea, perhaps obviously, is to save money, but because it is staffed 24 hours a day, seven days a week, it is also an efficient way of ensuring clients and lawyers always have access to the necessary back-up.

The firm has a culture and dedication to community that is often typical of its San Francisco roots. But it works as hard as a tougher New York player, and appears to have got the balance right. *The American Lawyer* ranks it No. 1 in its midlevel associates survey for the Best Places to Work, which measures job satisfaction at law firms in New York. The firm is ranked eighth nationally.

At the same time, Orrick ranks in the top 10 for seven of the league tables in the magazine's Corporate Scorecard, which measures practice area performance. Perhaps the most notable ranking is its ninth place for advising U.S. corporations on their equity issues, while the firm is still No.1 in the country for advising underwriters on municipal bond issues. The firm's structured finance practice is recognised as one of the world's leaders. The firm also has made its mark in litigation. Both *The American Lawyer* and *The National Law Journal* name Orrick as one of the top defence firms in the U.S., as Orrick lawyers have won major trial victories for clients in major product liability trials, securities class-action suits, accounting fraud cases, employee class-action discrimination suits and patent infringement cases.

Osborne Clarke

One London Wall
London EC2Y 5EB
Phone: +44 (0)20 7105 7000
www.osborneclarke.com

OTHER LOCATIONS

Bristol
Cologne
Munich
Silicon Valley
Thames Valley

THE STATS

No. of lawyers: 330
No. of lawyers in London: 80
No. of offices: 6
Trainee intake: 20 (2005)
Managing partner: Simon Beswick

GRADUATE RECRUITMENT AND TRAINING MANAGER

Paul Mathews
Training Principal
Apply online at
www.osborneclarke.com/careers

THE BUZZ
WHAT EMPLOYEES AT OTHER FIRMS ARE SAYING

- "Up and coming"
- "Not a London player"

MAJOR DEPARTMENTS & PRACTICES

Acquisition Finance • Agricultural Land • Arbitration • Asset Finance • Banking & Finance Disputes • Business Immigration • Competition • Construction Litigation • Consumer Regulation • Corporate Advisory • Corporate Finance • Corporate Lending • Corporate Real Estate • Corporate Tax • Development • Directors & Owner Managers • Employee Incentives • Employment • Energy & Environmental Disputes • Environment • Estate Administration • Financial Services Regulation • Health & Safety Advisory • Health & Safety Disputes • Industrial Relations • Information Technology & Telecoms Contracts • Intellectual Property & Licensing • International Disputes • International Tax & Trusts • Investment • IP Disputes • Joint Ventures • Legal Audits • Licensing • Major Contract Disputes • Marketing & Brand Management • Media Finance • Mergers & Acquisitions • Outsourcing • Pension Disputes • Pensions • PFI Project Finance • Planning • Privacy & Data Protection • Private Equity & Venture Capital • Professional Negligence • Public Procurement • Real Estate Disputes • Real Estate Finance • Real Estate Tax • Restructuring Turnaround & Insolvency • Sales Channels • Shareholder & Partnership Disputes • Sponsorship • Tax & Trust Compliance • Technology & Telecoms Disputes • Trusts & Estates Disputes • Wealth Management & Preservation

THE SCOOP

Osborne Clarke, once a regional law firm based in Bristol, is now an international phenomenon. Getting there has been a fairly rocky road, but back in the 1990s the firm decided it would focus on technology, media and telecoms, and it has done so with much success. The firm has its own three offices in the U.K., having branched out into London in 1987 and grown considerably since. The third outpost is in the Thames Valley, the high-tech name for Reading, and was opened in 1998 as an extension of the firm's brand in Bristol, and an inroad into the abundance of technology and telecom companies that make the area their home.

California Dreamin'

Beyond the U.K. is where things get interesting—Osborne Clarke expanded aggressively in the latter half of the 1990s, and put its own flags on the ground in Germany and, somewhat surprisingly, Silicon Valley. Elsewhere the firm operates through an international alliance, which is a joint venture of best friend firms that was founded 20 years ago and has been expanded since, now including 12 other offices on the continent.

The dream ticket at Osborne Clarke, though, is undoubtedly the trainee seat in the firm's Californian office. This firm is the only English one outside the Magic Circle to have a presence on the West Coast of the U.S., and while it is a strategy that may have made some rivals titter, it has proved entirely smart. The doors were opened in 2000, when a partner went off to ply his trade: the idea was never to hire local American lawyers, but rather to use the place as a way of meeting technology companies that were looking to expand in Europe and needed pan-European legal services.

The sell was to offer these companies the Osborne Clarke alliance, with an English partner on their doorstep who they could get to know, and could trust to be on hand, in their time zone, throughout a deal. So the office is not about billing, it's about relationships. The staff of three or four spends its entire time wining and dining the local venture capitalist community, seeking referrals from Silicon Valley law firms, and getting to know general counsel on the ground. To nobody's surprise, the biggest battles amongst trainees come when the three-month Palo Alto seat becomes available.

Bubble trouble

There's no denying that Osborne Clarke picked probably the worst possible time to decide to expand into Silicon Valley—the year 2000 was the very year the bubble burst and the dotcom boom ground to an unsightly and dramatic halt. At the same time, the firm had over-expanded in the U.K., and had far too many people dependent on the very same business stream over here. It's all well and good to be focused on an industry such as technology, but the age-old adage about all your eggs and one basket is always worth remembering.

The firm grew from 300 to 400 lawyers in the space of a year in 2000, and by mid-2001 it was clear it had over-expanded. In the course of 2002, 25 partners were either asked to leave or upped sticks of their own accord, and a new managing partner, Simon Beswick, fought to get the spiralling costs under control. That he did, all the while insisting that the work was there, and the clients were loyal, it was just the recruitment that had gone astray.

Tech and more

Indeed, the client list is not to be sniffed at, and many of the big names come to the firm at least in part because of its West Coast connections. The tech clients are there to see: Yahoo!, Vodafone, Motorola and VeriSign, for example. The firm just worked for Friends Reunited, the well-known reunion web site company, on its £120 million sale to ITV, and advised U.K. market research company MORI on its £88 million sale to Ipsos.

Much of the work is for the backers of these young companies, and venture capital is a big thing. Here the firm advises 3i, as it has for many years, as well as Barclays Private Equity and Close Brothers Private Equity. The firm then has a weighty practice taking companies public, and regularly works with stockbrokers KBC Peel Hunt, Evolution Securities and Charles Stanley & Co.

There is more to Osborne Clarke than tech. Above all else, it is a canny commercial firm that, perhaps because of its regional roots, has grown up aiming to do everything it can for a client. The employment team is strong—clients include Lazard, P&O Ferries, Nomura, International Power and Imperial Tobacco—and the banking team goes from strength to strength. On the finance side, the roster of clients is good: think Bank of Scotland, Barclays, Lloyds TSB and Royal Bank of Scotland, all the major U.K. clearing banks are here. Then there is a real estate team and a projects practice that are not to be forgotten.

History in the making

Osborne Clarke traces its heritage back 250 years, and there were some who thought that the end was nigh in 2001. But the firm came through the rocky patch, stuck to its strengths, and did not bail out of the entrepreneurial Silicon Valley practice that is now delivering so many hot relationships to Europe.

The firm operates its own charitable fund, through which the partners donate £85,000 a year to good causes, which have in London included the Royal Marsden and Great Ormond Street hospitals. The commitment to pro bono is also alive and well.

Osborne Clarke has managed to maintain the entrepreneurial approach that saw it become the first regional firm to attack corporate work in London, and then the first English firm into the Valley. It still feels like a small Bristol-based firm—the matey culture is obvious to all who walk through the door—but the work is far, far better.

Penningtons Solicitors LLP

Bucklersbury House,
83 Cannon Street,
London EC4N 8PE
Phone: +44 (0)20 7457 3000
www.penningtons.co.uk

OTHER LOCATIONS
Basingstoke
Goldalming
Newbury

MAJOR DEPARTMENTS & PRACTICES

Banking & Finance • Business Recovery & Insolvency • Clinical Negligence • Commercial • Construction • Corporate • Dispute Resolution • Employment • Environmental • European Law Group • Family • Family Business • Immigration • Intellectual Property • IT & E-Commerce • Multilaw • Offshore Tax • Personal Injury • Private Client • Professional Regulation • Property • Social Housing • Travel & Tourism

THE STATS

No. of lawyers: 200
No. of lawyers in London: 80
No. of offices: 4
Trainee intake: 13 (2005)
London managing partner: Lesley Lintott

GRADUATE RECRUITMENT AND TRAINING MANAGER

Andrea Law or Tamsin Kennie
Phone: +44 (0)14 8379 1800
E-mail: gradpost@Penningtons.co.uk

THE BUZZ
WHAT EMPLOYEES AT OTHER FIRMS ARE SAYING

- "Solid old style firm"
- "Who?"

THE SCOOP

Penningtons is one of the most low-profile firms in the U.K.'s top 100—though sizeable by any measure, few outside of its corridors know a great deal about what it does. But to ignore it is to miss out on one of the smartest law firms in the Southeast of England. Originally a private client practice, Penningtons has expanded beyond its sector, largely on the back of the very same private clients who, as wealthy individuals, have gone on to call on the firm for corporate advice, real estate advice and a host of other matters.

Marketing to the Cousins

One thing that Penningtons does especially well is market its services to American law firms in London, many of whom have established themselves as corporate players but are yet to add the support areas that are so crucial on many big deals. For these firms, Penningtons has become a first port of call, and it will provide real estate advice, commercial, IP and IT guidance to the American firm's clients without trying to steal the corporate work, as so many others might.

The firm may not be the most profitable in the region—the average partner earned £125,000 last year, but the business is growing at a steady rate. There was investment in smart new premises in Newbury and Godalming in 2004, and the firm has been on an expansion drive of late that has seen a host of new partners signing up.

Tea, radio and Tory infighting

In May 2005, Penningtons added a corporate partner from Weil, Gotshal & Manges to its London office, Gerald Cranley. He specialises in M&A and venture capital, particularly in the health care sector, and thus fits in well with what Penningtons hopes to build. He was the third partner to join the expanding team in six months, with two other partners joining Newbury and Godalming. On the healthcare side, the firm has a thriving clinical negligence practice, so it hopes to build some of those relationships into corporate work.

There's no denying that deals have been flowing: the firm worked for Indigo Travel buying Getaway Holidays, advised Williamson Tea Holdings on the disposal of its subsidiary Borelli, which owned 19 tea estates in Assam, India, and worked for Sunrise Radio in the acquisition of three separate radio stations and a refinancing.

Major financial services clients include Allied Irish Bank, the Bank of India and Morley Fund Management, but the firm is perhaps the most famous for its representation of the Conservative Party. The firm advised the party in summer 2005 when rogue MP Howard Flight threatened to issue an injunction against leader Michael Howard because he moved to deselect the MP.

Coup sue

Certainly, much of the firm's work is far more colourful than run-of-the-mill corporate work—Paris-based partner Henry Page was advising the president of Equatorial Guinea on a civil action arising from an alleged conspiracy to overthrow the government of the oil-rich African state last year.

The firm represented the Bank of India in a spin-off of the massive BCCI litigation against the Bank of England, and in its immigration practice, Penningtons was the firm responsible for advising *Big Brother* reality TV contestant Makosi Musambasi in a case that gripped the tabloid newspaper readership for much of summer 2005. Makosi was Zimbabwean and was facing deportation after her working visa was curtailed when she gave up her job as a nurse to appear on the TV show. Penningtons convinced the court that it would be dangerous for her to return to the country, and she was allowed to stay on as a refugee.

And then there is the slightly less exciting, but just as prestigious, real estate practice. In 2005, Penningtons added a construction partner from Denton Wilde Sapte, and the firm's Godalming office worked for the trustees of Heart and Stroke Trust Endeavour on the construction of a new wing at the Royal Surrey County Hospital.

Training triumph

As a relatively small law firm considering the competition, Penningtons aims to differentiate itself by offering clients a genuinely partner-led service. That does not mean, though, that assistants don't get responsibility—the firm's make-up is such that there is almost one assistant per partner, so young solicitors will get to work at a pretty senior level right from the get-go.

The firm was nominated this year for the annual lawcareers.net Trainee Solicitors' Group Training award, as best medium city firm trainer. The firm's training course is based on the idea of giving young solicitors as much client contact and responsibility as possible, whilst all the time making sure there is senior support on hand when it's needed.

Penningtons prides itself on being able to offer a serious work/life balance, although there's no doubt that its solicitors have to work downright unsociable hours on occasion, just as is the case with every other City law firm. There is, however, a pretty active sports and social committee, made up of solicitors, trainees and support staff, which a firm this size can manage quite successfully, and there are also two firmwide socials a year, so solicitors get to know the people in other offices.

Wondering what it's like to work at a specific employer?

Read what EMPLOYEES have to say about:
- Workplace culture
- Compensation
- Hours
- Diversity
- Hiring process

Read employer surveys on THOUSANDS of top employers.

VAULT
> the most trusted name in career information™

Go to www.vault.co.uk

Pinsent Masons

Dashwood House
69 Old Broad Street
London EC2M 1NR
Phone: +44 (0)20 7418 7000
www.pinsentmasons.com

OTHER LOCATIONS

Birmingham
Bristol
Brussels
Dubai
Edinburgh
Glasgow
Hong Kong
Leeds
Manchester
Shanghai

THE STATS

No. of lawyers: 900
No. of lawyers in London: 310
No. of offices: 10
Trainee intake: 55 (2005)
Trainees retained: 90% (2005)
London managing partner: Martin Roberts

MAJOR DEPARTMENTS & PRACTICES

Adjudication • Alternative Dispute Resolution • Banking & Finance • Central Government & Central Government Agencies • Commercial Contracts • Competition & European Union • Construction • Corporate • Corporate Recovery & Restructuring • Data Protection & Privacy • Dispute Resolution & Litigation • E-Commerce • Employee Share Plans • Employment • Environmental Law • European Union • Financial Services • Forensic Accounting • Freedom of Information • Health • Health & Safety • Information Law • Information Technology • Insolvency: Insurance & Reinsurance • Intellectual Property • International Arbitration • International Construction & Energy • International Dispute Resolution • Local Government • Media • Mines • Minerals & Landfills • Oil & Gas • Outsourcing • Outsourcing, Technology & Commercial • Pensions • Planning & Environmental • Private Equity • Product Liability & Recall • Projects • Property • Property Litigation • Regulatory & Trading Law • Reinsurance • Tax • Technology • Trade Marks & Designs • UK Construction & Engineering • Universities

THE BUZZ
WHAT EMPLOYEES AT OTHER FIRMS ARE SAYING

- "Excellent reputation"
- "The odd couple"

PLUSES
- "Excellent training"
- "No long hours culture"

MINUSES
- Post-merger cohesion issues
- Some unpopular HR policies

BASE SALARY
Trainee: £28,000
Newly Qualified: £48,000

GRADUATE RECRUITMENT AND TRAINING MANAGER
E-mail: graduate@pinsentmasons.com

THE SCOOP

The 2004 merger of Masons and Pinsents did not surprise anyone in the market, as both firms were clearly in need of a deal. Pinsents was eager to expand its footprint in London, having sat on the sidelines as arch-rivals DLA and Eversheds expanded beyond their regional roots with slightly more direction than Pinsents had exhibited. Masons, on the other hand, was a firm that was absolutely first-rate for construction law work—indeed it was one of the best in the world—but was having trouble holding on to its clients when they started looking to do corporate and commercial work.

Sector leader

So, on paper, it may not have been the most exciting deal in the world, but it did seem to make sense. Pinsents got an expanded London brand and a roster of construction clients, Masons got an opportunity to forge much deeper relationships with the clients it already had, and a chance to take a crack at the Pinsents client base.

Since signing, it's fair to say the new firm has not set the world alight. The combined firm is the 15th largest in the U.K., with six offices across the U.K., and others in Shanghai, Hong Kong, Dubai and Brussels. Pinsent Masons is a national firm rather than an international one, and it has a pretty smart strategy to be the leading "sectoral" firm—it focuses on so-called Chosen Markets, including energy and utilities, financial services and insurance, government, infrastructure and construction, manufacturing and engineering, real estate, and services and technology.

The idea is not new, but it is certainly more developed here than it is elsewhere. Essentially, partners focus on industries rather than just on practice areas. Because they know the business of their clients that much better, Pinsent Masons hopes to be able to give legal advice in a better context, and clients seem to have signed up.

Client culture

On the energy side, then, Pinsent Masons won new client National Grid Transco in its first year post-merger, which was a pretty cracking start. There is also work advising the European Bank for Reconstruction and Development, for Caledonian Environmental Services, for the Government of Sri Lanka on the privatisation of water services, and for Alstom, who the firm defended in a trial against a $188 million claim for an alleged breach of a joint venture agreement in Mexico.

In banking, the firm works for the Bank of Scotland, Barclays, HSBC and the Royal Bank of Scotland, so it has the big U.K. banks sewn up pretty well. It advised Bank of Scotland financing the £120 million acquisition of Karen Millen and Whistles by Iceland's biggest retailer, Baugur, which was a headline deal.

The government team works for more than 20 departments and agencies, and is appointed to the panel of advisers to central government. There is also work for more than 80 local authorities, and then experience on more than 50 major transactions for local housing authorities. In health, the firm has done 60-plus policy, commercial and project deals for the Department of Health, the NHS and health care trusts, and the firm has advised 30 of the country's universities over the years.

Marriage made in heaven

But whilst on the face of it, this was the deal to shake the market, the cultural side of the link-up has proved less easy. The two firms had very different cultures, one entrepreneurial and go-getting regional, the other more reserved and considered in the City. They were also in different buildings in London, meaning the joining of two offices is called for fairly imminently.

For now the key thing is to raise morale and get everyone pulling in the same direction, all of which will be made a lot easier if the financials are going in the right direction. The signs are good so far, and beyond the National Grid win, there has been new work for supermarket chain Morrisons as well, and auto group DaimlerChrysler.

The firm elected a new senior partner in 2005 in the form of Chris Mullen, a former head of both the employment, pensions and tax department, and of the financial services and insurance chosen markets group. With a pensions law background, Mullen also has his feet firmly on the ground of the day-to-day needs of the firm's clients. He has his work cut out for him, but this is a firm with a good brand and all to play for—the national law firms in the U.K. are currently the ones undergoing the most transformation and really positioning to challenge the Magic Circle.

GETTING HIRED

If you've got the grades, you've got (most of) the goods

Pinsent Masons avoids the trap of favouring specific universities, keeping a remarkably open mind about where its candidates were educated and whether or not they have studied law. The firm does expect a certain level of academic success, however: a minimum of a 2:1 and "300 UCAS points across 3 A-levels, excluding General Studies." But prospective trainees and lawyers face an additional challenge in the form of human resources, recalls a Pinsent Masons solicitor, with little detail: "My interview for the NQ job was particularly unappealing, because the HR manager also sat in on the interview as well as the partners from my prospective department, and she asked what I thought were unfair questions." Aside from the above qualifications and the ability to charm HR, the firm is also "looking for flexibility" in trainees as they move among different seats during their training, taking part in the "secondment programme where lawyers within Pinsent Masons spend time in our alliance firms in Europe."

OUR SURVEY SAYS

Merger woes?

Pinsent Masons' solicitors are saddened that post-merger "the firm is not the same as it used to be." It's dead obvious that a merger will cause a bit of chaos, but in this case it appears to be causing more than the usual growing pains. Reportedly, much of the problem rests on the division of the London office, which "is still multi-site", and with the bureaucracy that is the human resources department. "Some HR policies are highly patronising and do not reflect the fact that we are responsible professionals," fumes a litigator, who feels that the poor treatment extends outward from there to trainees and staff. Cheapness also makes the list of complaints; "Good work is not rewarded by bonuses or extra holiday, particularly for support staff," and extras—the usual perks of working a corporate job that can require long-hours—are nonexistent, with gym membership recently axed.

On the bright side

Thank goodness for "varied clients and work" as well as "excellent lawyers," otherwise Pinsent Masons solicitors might wonder what the point of it all is. "The good atmosphere" of the "friendly" firm includes occasional drinks, particularly on Friday, and firm events once in a while. But once again the merger has transformed the one-time "work hard and play hard" environment into something altogether quieter.

Bonus? No.

There are "too many hours at the firm [and] no option to work from home," a solicitor tells us, but this is not a universal view. Other insiders tell us that the Pinsent Masons partners are not at all the slave drivers that preside over rival firms. Partners reportedly "encourage solicitors to leave on time when they are not busy as they appreciate that at other times people work long hours." Though "paid well", solicitors are baffled as to why "a good financial year for the firm doesn't translate into good pay rises"—or bonuses for that matter. According to the firm, the bonus system is being renewed.

Lonely at the top

Partners receive mixed reviews, most likely due to the fact that their behaviour "varies wildly between departments." Some find partners "approachable" as well as good listeners, and "excellent at keeping staff informed of all decisions." They also provide "lunchtime training on specific issues" and "informal training is constant." Others, however, consider the management more "hierarchical", than necessary. "Even some of the partners feel disenfranchised," one source shares.

Reed Smith LLP

Minerva House
5 Montague Close
London SE1 9BB
www.reedsmith.com

OTHER LOCATIONS

Century City • Falls Church • Leesburg • Los Angeles • Midlands • Munich • New York • Newark • Oakland • Paris • Philadelphia • Pittsburgh • Princeton • Richmond • San Francisco • Washington, DC • Wilmington

THE STATS

No. of lawyers: 1,000+
No. of lawyers in London: 74
No. of offices: 18
Trainee intake: 8 (6 in London, 2 in the Midlands in 2005)
Trainees retained: 86% (2005)
London managing partner: Tim Foster

BASE SALARY

Trainee: £28,000
Newly Qualified: £49,000

GRADUATE RECRUITMENT AND TRAINING MANAGER

Rani Grewal
Recruitment Coordinator
Phone: +44 (0)20 7556 6893
E-mail: rgrewal@reedsmith.com

MAJOR DEPARTMENTS & PRACTICES

Advertising & Marketing • Advocacy • Antitrust • Competition & Regulatory Litigation • Appellate • Arbitration • Associations • Aviation Litigation • Banking • Bankruptcy & Commercial Restructuring • Benefits • Class Action Defence • Communications • Construction • Consumer Financial Services • Corporate Services • Debt Recovery • E-commerce • Employment • Energy & Natural Resources • Environmental Law • Executive Compensation • Export • Customs & Trade • Financial Services • Financial Services Litigation • Fraud • French Group • German Group • Government Contracts • Government Relations • Health Care • Higher Education • Homeland Security • Immigration • Information Technology • Infrastructure & Grants • Insurance & Reinsurance • Insurance Recovery • Intellectual Property • Internal Investigation & Government Enforcement Defence • International Distribution • Investment Management • Japan Business Team • Labour • Life Sciences Transactions • Litigation • Mergers & Acquisitions • Non-profit • Pro Bono • Product Liability • Project Finance • Public Finance • Real Estate • Risk & Liability • School Law • Securities Compliance & Litigation • Securities Offering & Transactions • Tax • Tax Controversy • Technology • Trusts & Estates • Venture Capital

THE SCOOP

Before 2001, no one had heard of U.S. law firm Reed Smith on this side of the Atlantic. The firm, which began in Pittsburgh way back in 1877, was one of the largest U.S. players without a presence in Europe when it decided to remedy the situation through merger. In January 2001 the firm linked up with City boutique Warner Cranston, a tiny firm that was punching above its weight in the crowded U.K. market. In June 2006, Reed Smith and U.K. firm Richards Butler agreed to merge effective 1 January 2007. The 1,300-lawyer firm will be known as Reed Smith in most other locations, though in London it will operate as Reed Smith Richards Butler.

The perfect candidate

Warner Cranston was a firm of less than 30 partners, founded in 1979, but many of its lawyers hailed from much larger City-law backgrounds. Together, they were hoovering up a decent share of corporate work, and at the same time they boasted considerable expertise in employment and business immigration, and had a good property team.

In many ways, Warner Cranston was the perfect U.S. merger candidate, being small and easy to integrate, while at the same time established and well respected. Before the merger, half of the firm's income came from overseas clients, and the team had indeed talked to a number of suitors before settling on Reed Smith. Reed Smith, though, was one of the few genuinely interested in Warner Cranston's Coventry operation.

That had been added in 1986, at the behest of clients, and worked in commercial property, litigation, employment and corporate law, with a particular specialism in international inward investment. Reed Smith has an office based in the Midlands that positions it uniquely to advise international corporates investing in the region's industry, and also to advise Midlands-based companies expanding abroad.

Goodbye old W.C.

For the first few years, the U.K. arm of Reed Smith was called Reed Smith Warner Cranston, but the old firm's name has now been confined to the history books. In its place is an integrated international operation, focusing on the combined sector strengths of health care, financial services and technology. Integration has been steady and uneventful—there have been no walkouts of note, and instead, five years later, the new practice is very much in growth mode.

Integration was helped by the fact that Reed Smith embraced the London management culture from the outset. Soon after the merger, two London-based executives joined the senior leadership team of the firm—Mark Dembovsky was Warner Cranston's chief executive and is now firmwide chief strategic officer, while London-based David Duckhouse is chief financial officer. Such an approach puts the U.K. operation at the heart of the firm's business. Moreover, the merger with Richards Butler will make the London office, with more than 300 lawyers, the firm's largest. Despite the inevitable changes such a union will bring, the fact that Reed Smith's current U.K. managing partner, Tim Foster, will continue in that role should provide some continuity.

Working well

The year 2005 was probably the most dynamic for the merged firm since the knot was tied. The opening in Munich was the beginning of what is hoped will be a major European expansion programme, and hires in London meant dealflow significantly increased. Paris also joined the roster of offices at the end of the year, when four partners from French M&A firm Rambaud Martel signed up to head the new office.

The firm added capital markets partner Giles Beale from Hammonds in 2003, and he has now established a solid reputation for the firm in U.K. equity capital markets work, particularly for smaller companies arriving on the Alternative Investment Market (AIM), London's secondary stock market. He has floated companies including Billing Services Group, March Networks Corporation and Basilea Pharmaceutica.

Reed Smith is a sector-led firm, with established focus in both financial services and pharmaceuticals. Those are the two areas that are now the priority in London, and in November of 2005 the firm added a two-partner life sciences team from Bird & Bird to extend the biotechnology group into Europe. John Wilkinson, who was Bird & Bird's head of life sciences transactions and regulations, joined Reed Smith along with corporate partner Nicola Maguire.

Even more additions

The firm also bolstered the London finance team at the end of the year, bringing in banking specialist Leon Stephenson as a partner from the U.K. office of Cleary Gottlieb Steen & Hamilton, where he was an associate. He is admitted to practice in London, New York and Paris, and will help a drive to act for more banks in Europe. Reed Smith works for 28 of the top 30 American U.S. banks, but is still working on translating that across the Atlantic.

2006's hires follow three big-name additions from the year before—Marcus Rutherford in media litigation from Kendall Freeman, Vinay Ganga in project finance from Cadwalader, Wickersham & Taft, and Richard Perkins in real estate from Denton Wilde Sapte.

London's client list already includes some big names, with the likes of Mellon Financial Corporation, Sara Lee and Tate & Lyle working with the firm on a regular basis.

Growth spurt

Europe is just a bit-player in Reed Smith's increased global presence, with a run of significant mergers shaping the firm since the turn of this century. In 1999, the firm merged with Virginia's Hazel & Thomas, a firm known for real estate development and state and local government relations, then in 2001 there was a group from New York's McCaulay Nissen Goldberg & Kiel. After Warner Cranston, 2003 saw the addition of a group from Shanks & Herbert in Washington, D.C., in intellectual property, and then the combination with California's Crosby, Heafey, Roach & May, which added five offices on the West Coast and strengthened capabilities in product liability, mass torts, appellate advocacy, media and entertainment and technology. Then in 2004 came the link-up in New York and California with advertising and marketing firm Hall Dickler, more evidence Reed Smith is going places.

Leading the diversity debate

In London, the firm is an active convert to diversity in recruitment, and with its U.S. approach it is genuinely leading the debate about equal opportunities and inclusiveness for the London legal market. A number of the firm's larger American clients are now choosing legal advisers in part on the basis of their diversity initiatives, and Reed Smith is communicating that approach to both clients and competitors over here.

The firm in the U.S. is a charter signatory to the American Bar Association's pro bono challenge, and in 2004, 60 per cent of its US attorneys did pro bono work, which, when valued at normal billing rates, was worth $5 million. Reed Smith was one of only two law firms in the nation acknowledged by Georgetown Law Center's Pro Bono Institute for providing "extraordinary disaster relief efforts" to Hurricane Katrina victims in the fall of 2005.

GETTING HIRED

"Solid, reliable, intelligent people"

"I think the firm's interview process is fair," declares an insider. Perhaps it has something to do with the fact that Reed Smith is not one of those firms that hammer candidates to prove their worthiness. Rather, they seek solid, reliable, intelligent people. Yes, of course, decent marks are an advantage (a "2.1 is expected"), but other practical factors are heavily weighted. A solicitor tells us that "technical ability is an obvious [necessity] but also real personalities go down well," so poseurs need not apply. Any such behaviour will likely be sussed out eventually during the firm's rigorous four-interview process. You've read correctly: four. There are "two formal and two more informal" interviews, giving candidates the opportunity to show off their legal acuity, impeccable manners and wit. The first set are with "the senior managers of the team [you're] applying for—the second with the rest of the partners in the team." Laterals take note: most come from "high calibre national/London firms at all levels."

OUR SURVEY SAYS

"Down-to-earth"

It's quite basic: Reed Smith "is a good firm to work for." There are plenty of "varied, interesting and challenging" legal tasks and "very interesting projects" performed by a coterie of "friendly and very professional" solicitors, making the firm an "easy culture to work in," according to a source. It starts at the top, apparently, where "down-to-earth" partners encourage "the firm's structure [to be] pretty flat" and the office to be "relaxed", "approachable" and "pleasantly social." The result is "a very professional but friendly firm where all lawyers know each other." The latter does not necessarily mean that lawyers are spending their after hours together getting rowdy with the vigour of football hooligans, however; rather, the "sociable atmosphere" is a cordial, internal courtesy that does not venture out of doors. Solicitors reports there was a time when the culture of the firm had a greater focus on social activities (though "there is the opportunity to play in sporting teams run by the firm," says a source), "but it has lost that edge over the past year or so." An insider speculates that the shift can be traced to the "recent exodus of many younger lawyers."

Got a life

It may also be that with a "sensible hours culture," Reed Smith lawyers are too busy paying attention to their children, indulging their extracurricular activities and visiting their aged parents to concern themselves with hobnobbing with their colleagues. "The length of the average working day is pretty reasonable," one contented insider writes. "I generally work from 8 a.m. to 6 p.m. most days. There are times when we have to work longer hours but these are dictated by clients' demands. As the general working day is not too long we can usually cope well with additional hours." "Long hours are expected when workload requires", adds a colleague, "but not otherwise." Once again it appears that it is the choice of management to treat their solicitors well, rather than mock their efforts and crush their spirits: comments a contact, "I have a lot of work but the firm does take care to ensure that no one is overloaded."

Partnering up

Characteristic of a firm of its kind, Reed Smith does not look to solicitors for input in firmwide decision-making. They are "not very regularly informed" either, meaning they only hear about decisions when they've been made (better late than never, we suppose). Overall, though, solicitors seem to be understanding of partners' choice to keep things to themselves. Case in point: "Information about strategic decisions is given, but like most people more information earlier in the decisions making process is always a plus (although for confidentiality reasons may not be given as early as we would like)." But partners make up for their lack of information and brainstorming sessions by working to maintain what one solicitor describes as a "very productive relationship." "Most partners treat the solicitors [with] respect" and "in general, communication and support is good." In the rare case of troublesome partners, however, there's room for improvement, muses a lawyer: "The partnership does not always deal with matters as it should and prefers to keep a head in the sand approach when dealing with partners who are not towing the line."

Formal support

One more spot where the firm falters a bit is informal training. It's not that such training or mentoring is completely nonexistent; it's just that it requires a bit of initiative on the part of the would-be mentee. "The support and training is there if requested," explains a source. Confirms a co-worker, "I receive help when I ask for it, and I have no problems or issues asking for help, but it is not necessarily offered." An insider who "would appreciate more informal training" notes that "the firm has a mentoring policy but this appears to apply only in the U.S." Thankfully formal training "provided by the firm is second to none," proclaims a lawyer. "It is the best training I have encountered in a law firm." "The internal university ... [has] some interesting internal and external seminars and training programmes" but still has "room for improvement, particularly in property."

The payoff

So what can one earn at a firm with appreciative partners, manageable hours and decent training? "Pay [that] is about average for London. It is not a "U.S." salary but reflects the lower hours requirements." There is some disappointment among solicitors, with complaints that "billable targets can be difficult to achieve" and that "the recent pay review has been disappointing." Bonuses, which are attainable at 1,650 hours with a "profit share bonus" available at 1,500 hours, are also sore subject. "Bonuses [are] not well handled," gripes a solicitor. "There is a bonus for meeting chargeable hours targets but the kind of work which some associates do (i.e., bitty work and not transaction work) means that some generally fail to meet these targets. There are other bonuses, which are apparently intended to reward these associates for good effort but awards are never as high so they have less incentive to work for bonuses. This has been raised with management but they don't accept that there is an issue."

Reynolds Porter Chamberlain LLP

Tower Bridge House
St Katharine's Way
London E1W 1AA
www.rpc.co.uk

OTHER LOCATIONS

Devon

MAJOR DEPARTMENTS & PRACTICES

Commercial Property • Construction and Engineering • Corporate and Commercial • Dispute Resolution • Employment • Health Law • Insurance, Reinsurance and Professional Liability • Intellectual Property • Media & Technology

THE STATS

No. of lawyers: 270
No. of lawyers in London: 260
No. of offices: 2
Trainee intake: 15 (2005)
Trainees retained: 90% (2005)
Senior partner: Tim Brown

BASE SALARY

Trainee: £28,000
Newly Qualified: £50,000

GRADUATE RECRUITMENT AND TRAINING MANAGER

E-mail: training@rpc.co.uk

THE BUZZ
WHAT EMPLOYEES AT OTHER FIRMS ARE SAYING

- "Friendly, ambitious"
- "Plodding"

THE SCOOP

Reynolds Porter Chamberlain is best known for its insurance litigation practice, which is amongst the very best in the country. As well as insurance, though, the firm has a strong media practice and a corporate practice which is increasingly making its presence felt in the crowded London market. Though there are no overseas offices, the firm is a focused one, which has made a run of lateral hires on the back of a clear idea of where it wants to go.

Movin' on up

The firm has a London office in its new premises near Tower Bridge. The move comes as the firm changed to a limited liability partnership (LLP). There is also an outpost in Tiverton, Devon, which helps generate substantial insurance revenues on the back of a lower than usual cost base.

Reynolds Porter Chamberlain is not a huge firm, but it nestles neatly into the top 50 U.K. law firms by revenue, and has one of the highest profit margins around, with a tasty 36 per cent of money billed being pure and unadulterated profit.

In 2005, Reynolds Porter hired a whole bunch of new partners to increase its market share in key areas—Pinsent Masons insurance partner Miriam Bartlett joined the regulatory and brokers team, while Ron Nobbs joined the construction group from Masons. He followed in the footsteps of Michael Blackburne, who had joined in July 2004 as the head of construction litigation from Addleshaw Goddard. The firm has also hired Ashurst IP partner Jeremy Drew as a partner in its Intellectual Property group. Drew specialises in U.K. and international IP disputes, with a particular emphasis on technology. The move brings RPC's IP/IT practice to 10 partners and follows the hire of Hammonds U.S./U.K.-qualified patent and trademark specialist Kathy Harris in 2005.

Growth has been steady and considerable of late, but this is certainly a firm on the right side of the expansion curve. In 2003 Reynolds Porter merged with niche insurance firm SJ Cornish, which did lower-end insurance work and brought with it the Tiverton office. Lateral hires have continued apace ever since and also included Simmons & Simmons litigation partner Jane Howard, who joined the professional liability team.

Media darlings

The biggest clients of Reynolds Porter span its core areas too—Associated Newspapers and HMV Group on the media side, then WS Atkins, Brit Insurance, Hiscox Insurance and Markel International on the insurance side.

Certainly the media practice is where the sexiest work comes from—working for Associated Newspapers the team acted on some of the biggest cases of 2005, including the controversies surrounding suspended police officer Christopher Miller, and Cherie Blair confidante Martha Greene. The firm has also acted for The Telegraph Group, the Mirror Group and *The Guardian* in recent years, and bolstered the team with the addition of David Hooper and his team from Pinsents, along with his client, the publisher Bloomsbury.

For HMV, RPC won a pitch in 2004, which saw it appointed as a lead adviser to the music retailer, advising on general commercial issues. That is further evidence of an expanding corporate group which is starting to get noticed; the firm also made the panel of Vivendi. The team just advised Daily Mail and General Holding on its £48 million offer for Fastcrop, owner of primelocation.com, an estate agent web site. More high-profile, though, was the work advising Bob Geldof's AIM-listed company Ten Alps Communications on its acquisition of 3BM TV, a leading British independent factual TV production company. RPC has done well at cross-selling corporate services to its existing, often media, clients.

Harry P. and the National Elf

On the insurance front, the firm continues to be at the forefront of developments. In early 2005, RPC turned down an appointment to the panel of the National Health Service's Litigation Authority panel, despite having been a go-to firm for the NHSLA for seven years. Instead the firm will focus on acting just for the insurance industry—it had found conflicts often arose when its insurer clients decided to take actions against the NHS in clinical negligence cases.

Without a doubt the most important work the firm did, though, as far as the average man on the street is concerned, was securing an injunction on behalf of Bloomsbury and J.K. Rowling, preventing *The Sun* and anyone else from releasing information about the new Harry Potter book ahead of its launch in summer 2005. The paper had been offered stolen extracts, but new partner David Hooper stopped their publication.

Big picture

Though domestic in focus, Reynolds Porter does act for a raft of international clients, and services them in contentious and non-contentious matters through its membership of legal network Terralex. The firm was a founder member of the network, which covers law firms in over 140 jurisdictions and has been in existence for more than a decade. RPC is the only English member, and all others are vetted before they are allowed to join and seek referrals.

The firm is reportedly a nice place to work, with many insiders saying the doors generally shut about 5:30 p.m. and people head for home—there aren't too many stressful late nights here, though they'll obviously muck in if a client demands.

The mix of juicy media work and sensible lucrative insurance instructions makes for a well-balanced firm, unlikely to lurch from busy period to famine in the way that larger M&A-focused rivals might. With work/life balance something the whole firm cares about, there are quite a few rivals who could take a leaf out of its book, though those lawyers will make sure they don't see it a moment before publication.

Richards Butler LLP

Beaufort House
15 St Botolph Street
London EC3A 7EE
www.richardsbutler.com

OTHER LOCATIONS

Abu Dhabi • Beijing • Brussels • Greece • Hong Kong • Muscat • Paris • Piraeus • São Paulo

MAJOR DEPARTMENTS & PRACTICES

Banking • Competition & EU • Corporate • Data Protection • Defence • E-Business • Employment • Energy • India • Information Technology • Insolvency & Restructuring • Insurance & Reinsurance • Marine Insurance • Intellectual Property • International Trade & Commodities • Trade Finance • Korea • Litigation & Dispute Resolution • Media • Outsourcing • Pensions • Real Estate • Shipping • Admiralty & Casualty • Marine Casualty Response • Ship Finance • Sport • Tax • Telecommunications

THE STATS

No. of lawyers: 390
No. of lawyers in London: 230
No. of offices: 9
Trainee intake: 20 (2006)
Trainees retained: 80% (2006)
London managing partner: Roger Parker

BASE SALARY

Trainee: £28,000
Newly Qualified: £48,000

GRADUATE RECRUITMENT AND TRAINING MANAGER

Mark Matthews
Graduate Recruitment Officer
Phone: +44 (0)20 7772 5821
E-mail: radrecruit@richardsbutler.com

THE BUZZ
WHAT EMPLOYEES AT OTHER FIRMS ARE SAYING

- "Consistently good"
- "Middling"

THE SCOOP

Richards Butler is one of the most successful full-service commercial law firms in the U.K., positioned neatly at the heart of the mid-market. The London mid-market is fiercely competitive, what with the bigger firms fishing in it, the smallest English law firms reaching up, national U.K. players arriving on the scene, and American law firms increasingly taking a chunk of the work. Richards Butler is all too aware of the new entrants on its patch. But while many competitors still refer to the firm as a shipping firm that had its heyday in the 1980s, there is actually still a strong business here. And now the U.K. firm has joined up with one of the U.S. interlopers: in June 2006 the partnership voted to merge with Reed Smith effective 1 January 2007. The 1,300-lawyer firm will be known as Reed Smith in most other locations, though in London it will operate as Reed Smith Richards Butler.

Heart and soul

Shipping, international trade and international dispute resolution work continue to be the heart and soul of Richards Butler, and in many ways the full-service approach has served it well. The difficulty is building a corporate practice in such a firm—it is all very well having the litigation capability to support the firm when the market is down, but where are the M&A practice and the capital markets team to reap the rewards when boom times return?

Richards Butler has spotted this problem and has been doing a fair bit of navel-gazing of late. The young and dynamic managing partner Roger Parker is all too aware of the issues he has inherited, taking over a firm with fingers in so many pies that is hard to know where to devote resources for growth. There have been a number of partner departures, often to the more lucrative American law firms in London, and, with the impending Reed Smith merger, the firm itself has finally managed a link-up with a U.S. player.

And going forward

As far as Parker is concerned, his ambition for Richards Butler is to make sure it is at that top table of international law firms that will no doubt emerge over the next decade. To do that, he concedes, requires more corporate work and a larger international footprint, probably including the Americas. Alas, merger talks with New York's Proskauer Rose ended with no deal in 2005, so it was back to the drawing board. But it didn't take long to find another partner; after a few months of intense discussions, the partners at Reed Smith and Richards Butler agreed to merge. The new firm as a whole will be led by Reed Smith's current managing partner, Greg Jordan, though Parker will join the senior management team and serve as the firm's European managing partner.

Now the firm will continue to look for greater penetration of key practice areas and sectors, namely disputes and transactions in media, real estate, shipping and transport, financial institutions, and international trade and commodities.

Sectors

In media, the firm's client list is a good one, and includes the likes of the BBC, Channel 4 and MTV. The film finance team is one of the best in the City, and the defamation practice is also a strong one: the firm sued Victoria Beckham for malicious falsehood, won the largest anti-piracy case and acted for film director Robert Altman.

In real estate, the firm also takes its fair share of mega-deals, acting for Parkview International on the Battersea Power Station redevelopment for starters, which at four million square feet is one of the biggest of its kind in Europe. It also worked for Microsoft on the sale and leaseback of its Thames Valley HQ, and for Land Securities Trillium on the BBC property outsourcing.

And more sectors

Next up is shipping and transport, where the firm is clearly at the top of the game. Richards Butler is a leading shipping firm and its entire international network is geared to advising the industry on anything it demands, be it contentious or non-contentious. The firm's Hong Kong office, for example, has the pre-eminent practice of its kind in that centre. But shipping work can be hard to make money from in this day and age, and, crucially, shipping clients aren't easily sold corporate services.

For financial institutions, though, Richards Butler has made some headway in differentiating its service offering from what clients can buy elsewhere around the City. The firm is on the panels for many of the major banks, partly as a result of its ship and asset finance work, partly through film finance, and a little through real estate. What it is now offering those banks is first-rate litigation capability, and what's more, Richards Butler claims to be one of the few firms in London that is not afraid to sue the major banks on behalf of its clients.

This is a tough strategy to both explain and, more importantly, to market. The targets are corporates who might, at some point, decide to sue a major investment bank. Richards Butler can't, and doesn't want to, sue the U.K. commercial banks that are its clients, but it can sue the big investment banks that so many of the larger law firms dare not offend.

Also on the financial institutions side is a serious insurance capability, built largely on the back of shipping, and then a professional indemnity practice working for the likes of PricewaterhouseCoopers.

Going global

The fact that half of the firm's revenues hails from litigation is more reminiscent of an American law firm than any of its U.K. rivals, and undoubtedly made it attractive to Reed Smith as a merger partner. The international practice is also more than stellar, with the Asian footprint second to none. That's another problem though, as the Hong Kong office is a separate profit centre and will not, necessarily, come as part of any merger, despite undoubtedly proving much of the attraction for a suitor. As of 15 June 2006, Richards Butler and Reed Smith reported that discussions with Richards Butler Hong Kong were still ongoing.

Still, it is perhaps unfair to criticise Richards Butler for its motley collection of practice areas, when so many other firms would give their eye teeth for such a mix. The struggle, though, must be to grow the corporate work done for these clients, and to find a reason to sit at that top table of global law firms in 10 years' time.

Shearman & Sterling LLP

Broadgate West
9 Appold Street
London EC2A 2AP
www.shearman.com

OTHER LOCATIONS

Abu Dhabi • Beijing • Brussels • Düsseldorf • Frankfurt • Hong Kong • Mannheim • Menlo Park • Munich • New York • Paris • Rome • San Francisco • São Paulo • Singapore • Tokyo • Toronto • Washington, DC

MAJOR DEPARTMENTS & PRACTICES

Antitrust • Asset Management • Bank Finance • Bankruptcy & Reorganisation • Capital Markets • Commodities • Corporate Governance • Criminal Law • Environmental • Executive Compensation & Employee Benefits • Financial Institutions Advisory • Futures & Derivatives • Global Oil & Gas • Insurance • Intellectual Property • International Arbitration • International Trade & Government Relations • Latin America • Litigation • Mergers & Acquisitions • Outsourcing • Private Client • Privatisation • Project Development & Finance • Property • Regulation & Enforcement • Sports • Structured Finance • Tax

THE STATS

No. of lawyers: 1,000
No. of lawyers in London: 130
No. of offices: 19
Trainee intake: 8 (2005)
Trainees retained: 100% (2005)
London managing partner: Kenneth MacRitchie

BASE SALARY

Trainee: £36,500
Newly Qualified: £72,000

GRADUATE RECRUITMENT AND TRAINING MANAGER

Kirsten Davies
Graduate Recruitment Officer
Phone: +44 (0)20 7655 5082
E-mail: kdavies@shearman.com

THE BUZZ
WHAT EMPLOYEES AT OTHER FIRMS ARE SAYING

- "Superb"
- "Sweatshop"

THE SCOOP

Shearman & Sterling has been in London since 1972, and is hence one of the largest and most Anglicised of all the American firms in town. With 130 lawyers here, it has a significant full-service office that is aggressively chasing all types of deals for European clients. The firm came to London because it wanted to act for European companies when they were listing, or raising money, on the U.S. stock markets. That U.S. securities work was its way into such U.K. corporates as British Telecom, and also gave it a great reputation with the American investment banks, which are so crucial to the success of any serious law firm in London.

First league project finance

Shearman's first English hires over here, though, were in project finance, and that is an area where Shearman continues to be in the first league. Again, that's a practice that delivers great relationships, and London managing partner Kenneth MacRitchie has advised on some of the biggest deals around.

Since MacRitchie and his partner Nick Buckworth arrived at the firm back in the mid-1990s, a concerted effort has been made to build an English practice. Shearman, like many of its competitors, wasted a bit of time consumed by the idea that it would only hire partners from the Magic Circle, but once it got going there was no stopping it. Of late the arrivals have included: Peter King, one of the top M&A partners at Linklaters; Julian Tucker, a capital markets partner from Allen & Overy; and Ian Nisse, the former managing partner of Ashurst.

In theory, Shearman aims to advise the clients that it used to work for on U.S. securities, and grow those relationships into providing English law advice, too. In fact, much of the English work is now free-standing, and generated here rather than through U.S. relationships. Still, the arrival of Peter King allowed Shearman to scoop work advising MM02, the mobile phone operator, on its corporate restructuring in 2004, which involved both U.S. and U.K. securities advice, and would previously have been done by Shearman in conjunction with an English law firm.

Working on the railway

Certainly Shearman is one of the few U.S. firms that is making a real mark on corporate Britain. The firm represented Merrill Lynch and Goldman Sachs on the flotation of Yell, the telephone directories business, for £1.3 billion, and advised banks CSFB and Morgan Stanley on their part in arranging the finance for a private equity house to buy high street retailer Debenhams.

Shearman is, at its heart, a finance firm, with Citigroup as its largest client historically. In fact, Citigroup shares a building with Shearman in New York. But still, that banking work is putting Shearman into major pieces of work on this side of the Atlantic, both transactional and non-transactional. Another example is advising the European Investment Bank on the £2 billion project for the rehabilitation, upgrade and maintenance of the Jubilee, Northern and Piccadilly lines as part of the London Underground public-private partnership.

Such work on major projects has reaped the firm many rewards in the U.K., including International Deal of the Year from *Power Finance & Risk* magazine, Middle East Power Deal of the Year from *Project Finance* magazine, and Legal Adviser of the Year from *Infrastructure Journal*.

Versatile presence

But the office is much more than just project finance and corporate work now, with leaders in antitrust, asset management, capital markets, banking and leveraged finance, employment, financial service, IP, arbitration, property and tax. Having all those areas covered means the firm can handle anything that is thrown at it now, pretty much, without having to ask English law firms to support it, as it would have in the past.

The firm's recent deal experience includes advising Citibank as a strategic outsourcing partner to Winterthur Financial Services, with Winterthur transferring £7 billion worth of assets in fund accounting and administration functions to Citibank, and advising Nokia on the €16 billion merger of its network business with that of Siemens. And on the real estate side, the firm worked for Berkeley Homes in the sale of its subsidiary, The Crosby Group, to Lend Lease Europe for £250 million.

English way

As far as the culture is concerned, for a long time Shearman had a reputation for keeping its English and U.S.-qualified lawyers separate in London, such that there were almost two ghettos of lawyers who wouldn't work together. That environment has gone now, by all accounts, and the twinned approach of selling integrated U.S. and U.K. advice to clients is starting to kick in.

The office, though, is peopled by enough English lawyers to give it the feel of any of the major English law firms, albeit on a smaller scale that allows assistants and trainees a more hands-on involvement in the work. The partners are anxious to increase the number of U.K. trainees coming through, so that growth going forward will not just be through lateral hires but also through some organic expansion.

What's more, the English partners have worked hard to ensure the systems and back-ups that are commonplace in the big U.K. firms are all available (they can often be lacking in the London offices of U.S. firms), so you are not going to feel like you are stepping into a start-up practice.

MC hours

That said, along with the feel of a Magic Circle law firm, and partners that hail from Magic Circle law firms, come the hours that go with that, too, and then some. This place is, after all, still part of a big New York firm, and they expect you to work hard when the deals come in.

There have been some partner departures over the years, but that is nothing to write home about given the length of time the firm has been here. The loss of the arbitration practice to Kirkland & Ellis last year was a blow, but Shearman still has good arbitration people in its continental practice and plans to carry on doing the work Shearman is not only well ensconced in London, but is also one of the leading American law firms across continental Europe, so chances are the its lawyers will be working on a deal with German partners just as often as they will be coming across the Yanks.

GO FOR THE GOLD!

GET VAULT GOLD MEMBERSHIP AND GET ACCESS TO ALL OF VAULT'S AWARD-WINNING LAW CAREER INFORMATION

- Access to **500+ extended insider law firm profiles**

- Access to **regional snapshots** for major non-HQ offices of major firms

- Complete access to **Vault's exclusive law firm rankings**, including quality of life rankings, and practice area rankings

- Access to **Vault's Law Salary Central**, with salary information for 100s of top firms

- Receive **Vault's Law Job Alerts** of top law jobs posted on the Vault Law Job Board

- Access to complete **Vault message board archives**

- **15% off** all Vault Guide and Vault Career Services purchases

For more information go to www.vault.co.uk/law

VAULT
> the most trusted name in career information™

Sidley Austin LLP

Woolgate Exchange
25 Basinghall Street
London EC2V 5HA
www.sidley.com

OTHER LOCATIONS

Beijing • Brussels • Chicago • Dallas • Frankfurt • Geneva • Hong Kong • Los Angeles • New York • San Francisco • Shanghai • Singapore • Tokyo • Washington, DC

THE STATS

No. of lawyers: 1,550
No. of lawyers in London: 100
No. of offices: 15
Trainee intake: 3
London managing partner: Drew Scott

BASE SALARY

Trainee: £30,000
Newly Qualified: £65,000

GRADUATE RECRUITMENT AND TRAINING MANAGER

Isabel Tabraham
Legal & Graduate Recruitment Manager
Phone: +44 (0)20 7360 3600
E-mail: itabraham@sidley.com

MAJOR DEPARTMENTS & PRACTICES

Alternative Dispute Resolution • Antitrust • Automotive Safety Litigation & Regulation • Banking & Financial Transactions • China Transactions • College & University Law • Communications • Corporate • Corporate Reorganisation & Bankruptcy • Corporate Securities • Data Protection & Information Security • Employee Benefits • Employment & Labour • Energy • Environmental • EU Law • Financial Institutions • Food & Drug • General Appellate • Government Contracts • Government Relations • Healthcare • Hong Kong Corporate • Immigration • Information Law & Privacy • Information Law & Privacy • Insurance • Insurance • Insurance Corporate • Intellectual Property • International Dispute Resolution • International Investment Funds • International Trade & Dispute Resolution • Investment Company & Investment Adviser • Investment Products & Derivatives • Latin America • Litigation • London Transactions • Postal Services Practice • Privacy • Private Clients • Pro Bono • Public Finance • Real Estate • Religious Institutions • Religious Institutions • Securities Enforcement • Securitisation & Structured Finance • Tax • Transportation • Trusts & Estates

THE BUZZ
WHAT EMPLOYEES AT OTHER FIRMS ARE SAYING

- "Know their stuff"
- "Underexposed"

THE SCOOP

Chicago's Sidley & Austin opened in London way back in 1974, and had a decent-sized office focusing on structured finance until, in 2001, it merged with New York firm Brown & Wood. It is undoubtedly one of the most significant all-American combinations of the last decade, and its impact on the London market was pretty seismic too.

A real competitor

Sidley had always had a sizeable corporate practice in the U.S., and a decent spread of capital markets work. Though its London office was focused on securitisation and complex structured finance, it was not such a focus in the U.S. until the merger. Brown & Wood, like Sidley's London office, was ensconced in the debt capital markets, and it had its own small London office doing that work, too. Thus the link-up of the two London teams gave the combined firm some 80 lawyers in the City, and as most of them were in structured finance, the firm was suddenly a real competitor to the Magic Circle law firms in its chosen market.

The first year of merger was a very difficult one, for Sidley Austin Brown & Wood had been housed in the World Trade Center, and was thus left homeless on 11 September 2001. With hindsight those events probably cemented a relationship between the two firms that could have taken longer to build—dealing with such a crisis pushed all thoughts of internal ructions very much to the back of the mind.

Serious growth

In London, the firm immediately committed to some serious European growth. For a firm of its size—the combined entity is one of the largest law firms in the world—an 80-lawyer London office was just not enough. The target was a more substantial team on the ground in the City, expansion beyond its comfort zone in finance, and moves into Continental Europe.

For the first four years post-merger, there is no doubt that London grew by leaps and bounds, but the rest of Europe lagged, and growth there didn't come as quickly as it would have liked. Still, last year saw the firm open its doors in Germany and Brussels, and there is also an outpost in Geneva and moves afoot to add Italy to the roster. The patience has paid off.

London lights

Post-merger, just about the first thing that Sidley did was add two real estate finance partners from Denton Wilde Sapte, and since then the number of commercial mortgage-backed securitisations that the team has worked on has rocketed. The list of investment banks that Sidley works for reads like a veritable who's who—think JPMorgan, Morgan Stanley, Deutsche Bank and all the rest.

The other additions to the securitisation team have really shown that the firm is at the top of the London market, and it is not taking its eye off the ball. First came the Clifford Chance head of securitisation, John Woodhall, and then an asset finance and securitisation partner from Linklaters, Richard Hughes. Matt Denning, from Baker & McKenzie, also joined the fold.

Downside of a good rep

If Sidley has a downside, it is that it has such a reputation for structured finance that its other practice areas are overlooked. The addition of a corporate restructuring practice in the form of a partner from what was Pinsents has been a big success, and another corporate partner from what was once Wilmer Cutler & Pickering has also strengthened London.

On the continent, the corporate practice has had the necessary investment—the Brussels office is now run by the brilliant Stephen Kinsella, who used to be at Herbert Smith, and the Frankfurt team is peopled by two former Lovells capital markets transactions partners.

Sidley continues to struggle to build its corporate practice in London, and though the firm is nothing short of a huge success here, that is the one thing that is missing. It is a badly kept secret that the firm talked merger with some U.K. firms at one point, including SJ Berwin, in a bid to add corporate in one fell swoop, only to decide that such a deal would be dilutive and doubtless add more baggage than the firm wanted.

Sidley has a fantastic reputation for corporate work in the U.S., and is one of the leading advisers to the Fortune 500 in corporate transactions. But here it is known principally for finance, and that has to change. Still, with hires now regularly coming from the very cream of the English law firms, it will surely not be long before an M&A rainmaker signs up.

Culture club

There were teething problems in London when the two firms linked up, not least because the cultures were vastly different, and there were two separate offices to be integrated. A team of four former Brown & Wood partners left to join French firm Gide Loyrette Nouel and launch its London operation, but beyond that, the departures were kept to a minimum.

Sidley has always had an Anglophile approach to London, and that culture has now been accepted by the merged entity, which in 2005 moved into new space in Basinghall Street that got everyone finally together under one roof. The management is all English over here, with two of the partners on the firm's global executive board, with a say in every crucial decision.

Organic expansion

The training contracts have been a feature of the office here for a long time, and there is a well-established programme that the firm is really committed to —a large part of the success here has actually been attributed to that commitment to organic as well as lateral growth.

The hours are not easy, and the example set by rainmaker Graham Penn, the securitisation star who frequently bills more than 3,000 hours in a year, is one to be aware of. But that said, the work is really as good as you are going to get outside the Magic Circle, so the hours are inevitable. Perhaps because of a lack of headline-grabbing M&A deals, Sidley is often wrongly overlooked on the list of U.S. firms that are successful in London. In fact, the opposite is true: the firm has shown that playing to your strengths is the way to stamp your authority on this market.

Simmons & Simmons

...ropemaker Street
London EC2Y 9SS
www.simmons-simmons.com

OTHER LOCATIONS

Abu Dhabi • Brussels • Düsseldorf • Dubai • Frankfurt • Hong Kong • Lisbon • Madeira • Madrid • Milan • New York • Oporto • Padua • Paris • Qatar • Rome • Rotterdam • Shanghai • Tokyo

MAJOR DEPARTMENTS & PRACTICES

Administrative Law & Judicial Review • Asset Finance• Asset Management & Investment Funds • Banking • Brands & Trademarks • Capital Markets • Corporate Finance • Corporate Recovery • Derivatives • Employment • Employment Law Training • Environment • EU & Competition • Finance Litigation • Financial Litigation • Financial Services & Market Regulation • Fraud & Corporate Criminal Defence Insurance • Insurance • Intellectual Property • International Arbitration • IT & E-Business • M&A Disputes • Mergers & Acquisitions • Outsourcing • Pensions • Private Capital • Private Equity • Product Liability • Professional Liability • Projects • PFI/PPP • Real Estate • Share Incentives • Tax • Telecoms

THE STATS

No. of lawyers: 1,000
No. of lawyers in London: 450
No. of offices: 20
Trainee intake: 50 (2005)
Trainees retained: 81% (2005)
London managing partner: Mark Dawkins

BASE SALARY

Trainee: £31,000
Newly Qualified: £55,000

GRADUATE RECRUITMENT AND TRAINING MANAGER

Vickie Chamberlain
Graduate Recruitment Manager
Phone: +44 (0)20 7628 2020
E-mail: recruitment@simmons-simmons.com

THE BUZZ
WHAT EMPLOYEES AT OTHER FIRMS ARE SAYING

- "Great firm to work for"
- "Slightly off the pace"

THE SCOOP

Simmons & Simmons is the original all-singing, all-dancing City of London law firm that, just like many of its rivals, spent a huge amount on global expansion and going full service in the 1990s, and then began to wonder what to do with it in 2000. Ever since the mid-1990s, when a whole slew of partners started quitting the firm, often for the more profitable American law firms that were opening in London, there have been questions about the firm's long-term sustainability. These questions have turned out to be premature, to say the least.

Comeback kid

But Simmons has an uncanny knack of making comebacks, and at the moment suggesting that Simmons would not be here in five years time would be nothing short of insulting. In 2001 came the first resurgence, when Simmons restructured its partnership compensation model so that the top performers would be convinced to stay, and profits bounced right up to a level that competed with other major City players.

Alas, there was another wave of partner departures and bum figures, and then in 2004 the firm elected a new managing partner in the form of financial services partner Mark Dawkins, who is an affable chap loved by the banks, and he promised to get Simmons back up to its rightful place at the top of the market. And so he did: the numbers announced for the year-end April 2005 were much better, and Simmons once again was a happy place to be. In 2006 the firm boosted newly qualified pay to match the £55,000 announced by Linklaters and raised first-year trainees' salaries from £29,000 to £31,000. Simmons also promoted its largest partnership group in four years, with 15 lawyers making the grade.

Finding its place

The problem for Simmons has been the one that has plagued so many of its contemporaries: it is not as big or as profitable as the Magic Circle, but neither is it a nimble specialist boutique that can attract clients simply with its service levels. It needs major deals to feed its hordes of assistants across the globe, but it doesn't have the brand of the top six to win the very biggest deals.

In 2001, when Janet Gaymer, the firm's high-profile head of employment, became senior partner, the firm underwent a change in management. She is a genuine leader in the legal market in terms of thinking on people management, and spent much of her time working out how to keep the partners motivated and the best assistants on board. Unlike her predecessors, she recognised the firm had to change to keep its people, and stop taking the departures as personal affronts.

Happy young lawyers

In 2005-2006, Simmons placed in *The Sunday Times* Top 100 Graduate Employers survey and, in 2004, the firm made the list for the *The Sunday Times* 100 Best Places to Work. Simmons certainly appears to have some of London's happiest young lawyers. In 2004, Gaymer even pioneered a new system for assistants whereby those that want to work more flexible hours and slow their progress on partnership track can do so without losing benefits or responsibilities.

But at the start of 2006 Gaymer announced she would stand down in April at the end of her five-year term. She has been given a government appointment as the new Commissioner for Public Appointments in England and Wales. David Dickinson, head of the firm's international banking practice, assumed the position of senior partner in July 2006. Dickinson had previously served as Simmons' managing partner from 1999 to 2005.

Work hard, play hard

But while Simmons may have the cosy reputation as a "nice" place to work, it is still not afraid to put in the hours, and partners do bring in whopper deals. The highlight for 2005 was undoubtedly the bumper appointment by Telefonica to advise it on its £17.7 billion bid for O2, the mobile phone operator. The work was won through Simmons' strong Iberian practice.

Other major clients include Shell, Barclays, HMV, JPMorgan, Bacardi and GlaxoSmithKline. Indeed, the Simmons corporate practice can sometimes appear a selection of disparate but first-rate niches: the firm is the leader in London for hedge funds, is one of the top advisers to the life sciences industry, has a phenomenal financial institutions regulatory practice, and is one of the best for employment, to name but four.

On the mainstream corporate finance, which is after all the mainstay of any serious London firm, Simmons holds its own—there is a strong equity capital markets team under partner Tim Field, which pioneered the new Accelerated

Initial Public Offering in 2004, for Center Parcs and Northumbrian Water, and won a whole raft of awards for its efforts.

All the mod cons

Simmons moved into glam new offices at the turn of the 21st century, too, and there is no doubt that that move gave the firm a shot in the arm in the confidence stakes. The firm's fantastic building at CityPoint—almost the closest London gets to a skyscraper—has all mod-cons and is loaded with amenities for employees, including a flashy restaurant and first-rate conference facilities.

What's more, Simmons has an art collection that is the envy of most of the City, and not just because it looks so good. One of the firm's partners has been supporting young British artists for decades, and the firm was one of the first to purchase Damien Hirst and Tracy Emin work, which is now worth a lot of money. The corridors are thus full of great works of modern art, often with an international feel to reflect the firm's overseas footprint.

Beyond London

Simmons now has 19 offices outside of London, with its practices in Asia, the Middle East and Southern Europe being genuine market leaders. Those outposts have cost money, but with Mark Dawkins' renewed focus on cross-selling and business development, they do appear to be starting to bear fruit, especially if Telefonica is any sign of things to come.

Simpson Thacher & Bartlett LLP

Citypoint
One Ropemaker Street
London EC2Y 9HU
Phone: +44 (0)20 7275 6500
www.stblaw.com

OTHER LOCATIONS
Hong Kong
Los Angeles
New York
Palo Alto
Tokyo
Washington, DC

THE STATS
No. of lawyers: 741
No. of lawyers in London: 46
No. of offices: 7
London managing partner: Walt Looney

MAJOR DEPARTMENTS & PRACTICES

Antitrust • Asia • Banking & Credit • Regulatory Advice • Bankruptcy • Capital Markets & Securities • Convertible Debt • Corporate • Corporate Governance • Europe • Executive Compensation & Employee Benefits • Exempt Organisations • Financial Products • Government Investigations/Business Crimes • High-Yield Debt Offerings • Initial Public Offerings • Intellectual Property • International • International Arbitration • International Capital Markets • Investment Funds • Investment Management • Investment Management M&A •Insurance/Reinsurance • IP Litigation • IP Transactions • Labour • Latin America • Lease & Transportation Financing • Litigation • Mergers & Acquisitions • Offerings • Personal • Private Funds • Product Liability • Pro Bono • Project & Infrastructure Finance • Real Estate • Registered Funds • Securitisation & Derivative Products • Securities/Shareholder Litigation • Structured Finance • Syndicated Lending • Tax

THE BUZZ
WHAT EMPLOYEES AT OTHER FIRMS ARE SAYING

- "Top-notch, excellent"
- "Not as good as they think they are"

PLUSES
- High compensation
- Early responsibility

MINUSES
- "Long hours culture"
- Lack of support staff

NOTABLE PERKS
- "Generous" relocation bonus
- Free dinners and car rides

GRADUATE RECRUITMENT AND TRAINING MANAGER

Dee Pifer
E-mail: dpifer@stblaw.com

THE SCOOP

Simpson Thacher & Bartlett is one of the most profitable and esteemed law firms in the world, and its London office opened way back in 1978, largely with a mandate to support the existing American clients when they made their first forays across the Atlantic. Today, the firm's London mergers and acquisitions practice is as highly rated as the firm's as a whole. The 46-lawyer office is also right up there on the most complicated cross-border leveraged finance transactions, as well as boasting the capability to handle litigation, tax, competition or real estate matters.

Branching out

Until 2002, the London office of Simpson Thacher was an American-only affair—the practice was staffed by U.S. lawyers on secondment from the mother ship in New York. Then the firm shook the market with the hire of Euan Gorrie, a banking partner from Allen & Overy. He has since been joined by two other English lawyers, partners Stephen Short from Ashurst and, in 2005, Tony Keal, also from Allen & Overy. All three are on the finance side, with a brief to advise both lenders and U.S. private equity houses on the banking issues of European acquisitions.

So far the firm has shied away from hiring English corporate capability, not least because the addition of such partners would require significant support teams, with English law associates then being required across tax, competition, and so on. Still, with one of the top brands for private equity in the world, and acting for some of the most acquisitive clients around, it seems just a matter of time before the firm ditches its policy of referring corporate work to English law firms, and decides to start playing the U.K. law game itself. For now, Simpson Thacher offers great opportunities for junior English lawyers on the banking side, or working alongside Americans in other disciplines.

Wonder work in private equity ...

Simpson Thacher was the law firm that advised Kohlberg Kravis Roberts & Co (KKR) in the record-breaking acquisition of RJR Nabisco back in the 1980s, a deal so enormous it was the subject of a book, *Barbarians at the Gate*, which is still a must-read for anyone swatting up on just what private equity, and leveraged buy-outs are all about. KKR remains one of the firm's most loyal clients, alongside rival private equity house Blackstone. On the banking side, the roster of investment banking contacts is second to none.

Though often working on the U.S. aspects, Simpson Thacher gets its hands on nearly all of the biggest deals going on in Europe, and regularly tops global M&A tables. In 2005, the London office worked for Blackstone on the sale of its €1 billion European office portfolio, and advised a consortium of buyers including Apax Partners, KKR, Blackstone, Permira and Providence Equity Partners on their $12 billion bid to buy TDC, Denmark's largest phone company. That deal, when it closed, was the largest private equity takeover ever done in Europe, and second only to RJR Nabisco worldwide.

... and beyond

Although the private equity client base is the envy of so many competitors, there is much more to this office. For example, lawyers from Simpson's London office represented Deutsche Bank in connection with the $4.9 billion refinancing of Invensys; Goldman, JPMorgan and Deutsche Bank in $1.7 billion of high-yield financing for Cablecom GmbH; JPMorgan, Deutsche Bank and others in $3.11 billion of financing to support the ntl/Telewest merger, and assisted adidas in its acquisition of Reebok.

On the contentious side, London worked alongside U.S.-based colleagues to advise clients General Electric and the Bechtel Group in a settlement with the government of India over claims relating to the Dabhol power project in that country. Both clients owned 10 per cent stakes in the project, which was the largest foreign investment in India to date, and the pair had claims in arbitration against the government, while litigation had been brought against them in India. Simpson Thacher had been working on the mammoth case for four years, and settled days before the start of a three-week hearing in London in 2005.

Global powerhouse

There is a lot more to Simpson Thacher than just London, and the fact that this small office is its only representation in Europe suggests a reticence to splash cash outside the home country. That said, Simpson Thacher has ventured outside New York with some determination in the last decade, and is now a real player in Silicon Valley, to which it was a newcomer in 1999, and in Hong Kong and Tokyo.

The Tokyo office, for example, is one of the leading practices of any U.S. law firm in Japan, with a focus on capital markets and M&A that again mirrors the rest of the firm. The firm acts for clients like Shinsei Bank, Elpida Memory and Seiko Epson Corporation, and worked on all five of the largest initial public offerings in Japan in 2004. In 2005, the Tokyo office advised Slimco Corporation in its $1.4 billion IPO, Japan's largest IPO of the year. The firm also advised the underwriters in the $3.3 billion IPO of China Shenhua Energy, one of China's largest IPOs of the year.

What will they do next?

Just as the market is anxiously anticipating Simpson Thacher's move into English corporate work, so, too, it awaits with trepidation the firm's expansion into continental Europe. While the firm may not need to invest in expensive offices elsewhere, the market seems to be there for its taking. Clients that use Simpson Thacher in America treat it as a go-to adviser for everything they do in the U.K. Though such clients may hire Herbert Smith or Slaughter and May for English law advice, it is the Simpson Thacher partners who will call the shots on strategic issues even if they're not doing the documentation.

GETTING HIRED

Premier league

Simpson Thacher & Bartlett is one of the premier names in law and the firm's hiring practices reflect its high-end status. Here's what the firm is looking for, according to one young American-trained associate in the London office. "Grades are more important than the prestige of the applicant's school", he reports. "But it is still highly competitive and most new hires are from the Ivy League." The firm considers its summer program the primary focus of its recruiting efforts and some U.S. summer associates may also be assigned to Simpson Thacher's London office with rotations ranging from two to six weeks. The London office is staffed with both U.S.- and European-trained attorneys, and, unsurprisingly, gives preference to lawyers also able to speak any of the other major, non-English European languages.

OUR SURVEY SAYS

Early responsibility and talented colleagues

Simpson Thacher's young attorneys have plenty of praise for their "great and talented" colleagues and their "very interesting" assignments. A junior corporate finance solicitor enjoys "working on some of the most prestigious deals in the world and a team attitude where everyone's input, including junior associates", is welcome. He also praises the firm for being "a small office, which provides a lot of responsibility early on."

However, the relatively small number of highly-coveted positions at this firm do have their downsides, according to insiders. "The work is interesting and high profile and the atmosphere is good (no yelling and lots of camaraderie), but satisfaction goes down when there is little praise and respect or appreciation for the amount of sacrifices made and for the lack of respect for personal obligations", complains one corporate solicitor.

Mixed reports about the culture

While a number of solicitors praise Simpson Thacher's "friendly" vibe, other gripe about the "very poor team spirit and low morale." Mostly, though, the firm's attorneys seem to be in good spirits and "tend to get along." Reports one second-year attorney, "People try to help each other out."

However, several insiders are critical of the state of partner-solicitor relations at the firm. One third-year complains about partner attitudes that underscore the fact that "associates are employees." (They're not?) A mergers and acquisitions solicitor adds, "Associates socialize with associates and partners socialize with partners."

Sink or swim

Simpson's approach to training will not appeal to those who require a lot of handholding. There is "virtually zero concern for my professional development", whines one junior solicitor. Another junior attorney adds, "It is very much a sink or swim environment with very little formal training. There is very little mentoring done by partners."

As for office space, one banking solicitor reports that while senior attorneys may have spacious digs, the offerings have become "bad for new joiners." A corporate attorney adds that the "London offices are large, but the designer had never heard of ergonomics." (It must be noted that the firm increased its office space by 50 per cent in March 2005.)

With great pay comes tough hours

Whatever other concerns they may have, almost nobody at Simpson Thacher complains about the pay. Solicitors are "very well paid," reports one attorney, though he notes that "Americans get a much better package." The firm's compensation, he adds, is much more generous than "U.K. firms and other U.S. firms in London."

Simpson solicitors report billing anywhere from 175 hours per month to upwards of 250 hours. And though long hours can be expected at most any major firm, the requirements at Simpson Thacher are especially tough, solicitors report. In one banking solicitor's opinion, the "long-hours culture" is "totally self-defeating and inefficient." A junior corporate associate says, "The hours do go up and down a lot. Part of the dissatisfaction is that you will have lots of down time followed by insane hours—there is no middle ground and no balance." However, a corporate finance and capital markets attorney suggests that long hours are just the nature of the beast. "Corporate law is what it is," he shrugs. "Long hours are standard. But there is a boom-bust type of work load where you are either full out or have nothing to do."

SJ Berwin LLP

10 Queen Street Place
London EC4R 1BE
Phone: +44 (0)20 7111 2222
www.sjberwin.com

OTHER LOCATIONS

Berlin • Brussels • Frankfurt • Madrid • Milan • Munich • Paris • Turin

MAJOR DEPARTMENTS & PRACTICES

Banking • Commerce & Technology • Commercial Litigation • Corporate Finance and M&A • E-Commerce • Employment • EU & Competition • Financial Services • Intellectual Property • Investment Funds • IT • Media & Communications • Outsourcing • Pensions • Pharmaceuticals & Biotechnology • Private Equity • Public Law • Real Estate • Reconstruction & Insolvency • Sport • Structured Finance • Securitisation • Tax • Telecommunications • Trade Marks

THE STATS

No. of lawyers: 500
No. of lawyers in London: 400
No. of offices: 9
Trainee intake: 37 (2005)
Trainees retained: 76% (2005)
London managing partner: Ralph Cohen

BASE SALARY

Trainee: £30,000
Newly Qualified: £55,000

GRADUATE RECRUITMENT AND TRAINING MANAGER

E-mail: graduate.recruitment@sjberwin.com

THE BUZZ
WHAT EMPLOYEES AT OTHER FIRMS ARE SAYING

- "Very good at what they focus on"
- "Mercenary"

THE SCOOP

SJ Berwin was only founded in 1982, by a group of four partners with a vision to do something slightly different. It is the younger brother of Berwin Leighton Paisner, and the two remain arch-rivals. But within 20 years SJ Berwin had made it to the top 20 of U.K. law firms, and the expansion that defined the firm in the early days has continued unabated.

Punching above their weight

SJ Berwin today is one of a small group of elite mid-tier English firms that, though boutique in size, nevertheless punch above their weight and compete with much larger rivals for mandates. Outside the Magic Circle, it is this group that is really setting the pace for the London market, alongside others such as Macfarlanes and Travers Smith.

Like these two, SJ Berwin has cut itself a place in the mid-market corporate arena largely on the back of a private equity practice, which remains one of the best around. The firm, through senior partner elect Jonathan Blake, has a reputation for establishing funds that is second to none. It has been doing it since the 1980s, when private equity was called venture capital, and things like hedge funds were nowhere to be seen.

Fun with funds

But the funds practice has gotten more sophisticated, as the clients have, and now extends into real estate funds as well as corporate finance vehicles. On the corporate side, the firm is notoriously criticised for its inability to convert this work setting up funds into corporate deals—private equity houses may ask SJ Berwin to set them up, but they often go deeper into the Square Mile when they start spending the money on acquisitions.

Still, that just means SJ Berwin has a ready-made client base to continue to market to. The firm is a leader in a whole raft of other areas—it is amongst the best for property work, for financial services, for litigation and arbitration, and for EU and competition work. The defining thing about the firm is its American atmosphere though—unlike traditional English law firms where partners are remunerated according to how long they have been practising, SJ Berwin was set up with a more U.S.-style meritocratic partner pay structure, where partners are compensated according to the work they generate and deliver (aka "eat what you kill"). This can mean that partners focus on their own businesses rather than on cross-selling, and rivals criticise SJ Berwin for operating more like a barristers' chambers than a law firm, where partners plough their own furrows.

Wheeler dealers

SJ Berwin's largest clients include buy-out funds Apax and Bridgepoint Capital, while on the finance side it works for Royal Bank of Scotland, and in real estate it acts for Brixton plc and British Land. What's more, the firm continues to win lucrative new instructions—last year it won its first work for Goldman Sachs Private Equity, and scooped the work to advise Lion Capital, which used to be the European arm of America's Hicks Muse Tate & Furst before splitting off and going alone.

The corporate practice does well, despite constant knocking that it is not reaching the incredible potential it could. In 2005, the firm worked on some 120 private equity transactions, covering the whole range from fund formations to management buy-outs and billion-pound acquisitions. The practice won Law Firm of the Year from the European Venture Capital Association for 2005, with highlights including work for the U.K. government on its Enterprise Capital Fund initiative, and other lobbying work on behalf of the industry at both the national and international level.

Mid-size, but full service

On the property side, the firm started 2006 by advising British Land on sales of £137 million worth of retail property, and worked for the Crown Estate on further lettings in Regent Street. It also advised Redevco on the letting of a major Oxford Street property to low-cost retailer Primark. On the public corporate work, the team acted for British Film Entrepreneurs selling Capital Films, and advised Pipex Communications on its share issue on the London Stock Exchange.

With a top-tier competition practice, strong tax and an arbitration team that is amongst the best in the U.K.'s mid-tier, SJ Berwin is one of only a few firms of its size that can genuinely claim to be full service. What's more, there is an international network that is increasingly setting itself apart from the rivals, with the end of 2005 seeing the opening of an Italian practice with an impressive private equity team from White & Case's local office.

Award winners

All of which means it's no surprise that SJ Berwin keeps bagging gongs for its efforts. The firm won *Legal Week*'s U.K. law firm of the year award in 2005, won Real Estate Team of the Year at the 2005 *Legal Business* Awards, and scooped the Best Achievement in Copyright Practice award at the World Leaders European IP Awards.

2006 will be a transformative year for the firm, though, with established senior partner David Harrel, who was a founding partner and has been at the helm almost since day one, giving up the leadership to Blake, the private equity funds guru. How this will affect the firm's direction, cohesiveness and corporate practice is all the subject of much debate across the City.

Leading the way in pay

In 2000, it was SJ Berwin that sparked the City's salary hikes for assistants when it followed the footsteps of American law firms and increased wages across the board, rather than risk the best lawyers heading elsewhere. More recently, the firm announced it would match the City's new benchmark of £55,000 for newly qualified lawyers. But it's not just SJ Berwin's eager young recruits who are making more money: the firm's average profit per equity partner for 2005-2006 reportedly jumped by more than 23 per cent to £710,000. Rumours persist that SJ Berwin, the most American of the U.K. law firms, will soon succumb to advances of U.S. law firms seeking merger. It would certainly make someone a very attractive bride, but with deals and clients like it's got just now, you've got to ask why it would need it.

Skadden, Arps, Slate, Meagher & Flom LLP and Affiliates

40 Bank Street
Canary Wharf
London E14 5DS
Phone: +44 (0)20 7519 7000
www.skadden.com

OTHER LOCATIONS

Beijing • Boston • Brussels • Chicago • Frankfurt • Hong Kong • Houston • Los Angeles • Moscow • Munich • New York • Palo Alto • Paris • San Francisco • Singapore • Sydney • Tokyo • Toronto • Vienna • Washington, DC • Wilmington

MAJOR DEPARTMENTS & PRACTICES

Banking & Leveraged Finance • Capital Markets • Corporate Restructuring • EU & Competition Law • Energy/Projects • International Arbitration/Litigation • Mergers & Acquisitions • Private Equity • Tax

THE STATS

No. of lawyers: 1,750
No. of lawyers in London: 89
No. of offices: 22
Trainee intake: 4 (2006)
Managing partner: Bruce Buck

PLUSES

- High pay and quality work
- "Informal work environment"

MINUSES

- Long hours
- Poor IT system

NOTABLE PERKS

- Staff restaurant
- Technology allowance
- Taxis and dinner when working late

BASE SALARY

Trainee: £35,000
Newly Qualified: £82,200

GRADUATE RECRUITMENT AND TRAINING MANAGER

Lisa Head
Legal Hiring Manager
E-mail: lhead@skadden.com

THE BUZZ
WHAT EMPLOYEES AT OTHER FIRMS ARE SAYING

- "Exceptional"
- "Hard-nosed and hard work"

THE SCOOP

Skadden Arps opened its doors in London back in 1989 at a time when its New York practice was thriving. Of the countless American law firms doing business in Europe today, Skadden has been handling the largest deals on the most regular basis. Joining and excelling at the firm requires hard work—the New York ethos has certainly crossed the pond—but the rewards are high and the transactions are of the highest calibre.

Bucking convention

Today, Skadden is regarded as one of the old-school elite of Manhattan, favoured by investment banks and involved in most major deals. But this wasn't always the case. During the 1980s, the firm was something of an outsider in the legal community. Led by name partner Joe Flom, Skadden had begun to play an active role in hostile M&A, counselling companies bent on absorbing, buying out or simply taking over their rivals. It was a practice that was shunned by much of the Wall Street elite, who considered it altogether unbecoming to partake in corporate hostility. Thus, Skadden had much of the lucrative market practically to itself.

Awash with cash and grand ambitions, the firm arrived in Europe in hopes of orchestrating similar deals here. It launched with the hire of Bruce Buck, an American who, at the time, was running New York rival White & Case's London operation, and set to work building a practice. The move made Skadden unusual amongst its competitors for two reasons—first, Skadden did not come to Europe because its clients beckoned it to do so, rather, because it spotted an opportunity: namely, to work on the same mega-M&A transactions here that it had so successfully coordinated in New York. Secondly, from day one, Skadden staffed its London office with true-blooded Brits, rather than New Yorkers on overseas postings. The move afforded the young London office a regional familiarity with the market that offices staffed with American expats often struggle to achieve.

Going native

Buck has now been in London for more than 20 years. His impeccable relationship to the firm's U.S. leadership has allowed him to oversee the growth of the London office into one of the largest owned by a New York firm. From day one, Buck was convinced that the key to a successful London practice would be the hire of—yes, English lawyers. When the rules changed to allow American firms to do so back in 1995, he was one of the first to take the plunge.

In 1996, Skadden hired Michael Hatchard, an English M&A partner who was at the time, with mid-tier U.K. law firm Theodore Goddard. Hatchard offered extensive experience in mergers, strategic investments and, tugging on Skadden's heartstrings, transactions governed by the U.K. Takeover Code. When Skadden came upon Hatchard through an investment banking contact, management decided he'd make an excellent fit in the London office and made him an offer he obviously couldn't refuse. While other U.S. law firms transacting in London chose, mostly as a matter of practice, only to hire from the English Magic Circle firms, Skadden once again chose to break ranks—and once again, it paid off.

Growing gains

At the turn of this century, Buck really got the hiring bug, and began a dramatic expansion of the firm's London operation. Joining Hatchard was James Healy, a young lawyer who joined from Freshfields and was promoted through the Skadden ranks to partnership. Then came Lovells' private equity star Allan Murray-Jones, Tim Sanders who was the head of tax at the local office of McDermott Will & Emery, and then banking partner Mark Darley, also from Lovells. Next came the addition of a contentious practice as well as international arbitration, with the hire of Paul Mitchard and Karyl Nairn from Simmons & Simmons so that the office can now offer the core capabilities under English law to support a high calibre mergers and acquisitions and securities practice. This hardly marked an end to Skadden's expansion campaign—in 2005 alone, it recruited three new lateral partners: Adrain Knight from Shearman & Sterling, Clive Wells from Allen & Overy, and James Anderson from Clifford Chance.

That said, the firm has no designs on the so-called "low-yield" legal practice areas—employment law, real estate counsel and the like—such areas will continue to be referred to associate English law firms if and when implicated by Skadden's broader practice. The firm's strategy has been to focus on the work at the high end of the market, where it can add value by bringing to bear its experience on complex, high premium deals. It will not, the firm says, attempt to compete with local law firms in the U.K.

Assorted triumphs and one powerful friend

The work successes practically speak for themselves. The firm transferred U.S. M&A star partner Scott Simpson into London in the 1980s, and his work alongside the U.K. law team attracts super mandates. The firm acted for Access Industries on a €4.4 billion buyout of Netherlands-based Basell, represented Gold Fields in successfully fighting off a $7.8 billion hostile takeover bid from Harmony Gold Mining Corporation, and acted for private equity firm Doughty Hanson on its €1.1 billion acquisition of the Moeller Group, one of Europe's largest suppliers of electrical distribution and automation components. Simpson also led the team advising Arcelor in its €26 billion acquisition by Mittal Steel, one of the biggest deals of the first half of 2006.

One especially fruitful relationship for the firm is that of Bruce Buck with Roman Abramovich, the Russian billionaire whose relocation to London has made him the U.K.'s richest man. Buck, who has a well-established Russian practice, advised the billionaire when his oil company Sibneft announced a merger with Yukos in 2002. That deal would have created a $36 billion combined company and the fourth-largest oil producer in the world. Alas, the deal didn't happen, as Yukos' Russian owner was arrested in Russia over alleged tax evasion. Instead, Abramovich subsequently sold Sibneft for a bumper payout, in the meantime having invested £135 million to buy London's Chelsea Football Club. Buck, a long-time Chelsea football fan, thus advised Abramovich on the acquisition and on a number of subsequent player transfers. He is now chairman of the club, whilst still running Skadden's European operations.

Europe wise

Skadden's European investment extends well beyond London. The firm's outposts in Moscow, Paris, Vienna and Brussels are at the top of their game, while operations have significantly expanded into Germany over the last couple of years with an existing office in Frankfurt, joined by one in Munich in 2004. The Munich office boasts a team of private equity partners from Baker & McKenzie. Over in Italy, while the firm does not have its own office, it has a strategic business alliance with local firm Chiomenti Studio Legale, with referrals heading in both directions. While the accordo italiano is the firm's only such agreement worldwide, it has so far proved successful.

Beyond these European establishments, there are no immediate plans for additional offices this side of the Atlantic, rather, the plan is to develop and grow the practices already launched. This is unsurprising given Skadden's European expansion has been marked by a steady, deliberate manner. However, don't let that lead you to believe the firm is as stuffy as some of its rivals. Play your cards right, and Chelsea tickets might be part of the package.

GETTING HIRED

The importance of being earnest

When asked about the firm's hiring policies, Skadden insiders sound almost as if they're quoting the firm's own literature: "Looking to hire driven, committed, bright, fun people [who] would like working in a dynamic environment," reports one eighth-year solicitor. His compeers are equally earnest, invoking the need for "genuine self-starters with lots of energy" who have attained "high educational achievement" and offer Magic Circle training. ("This will no doubt change as the system adapts to include trainees," we're told.) Adaptable "'can do' attitude[s]" are also a plus, as is an Oxbridge degree—"but having said that at least half of the hires in the last year are from other universities and the English group has a lot of internationals." For Americans, it is "VERY helpful to demonstrate some commitment to a career in Europe"; expounds an M&A source, "While no one expects you to say you're never moving back to the U.S., the firm wants to know you are willing to live in London, not just spend a summer vacation here."

OUR SURVEY SAYS

Contrary to popular belief ...

One might think Skadden's solicitors must be among the most embittered in the industry: The tough partners, the long hours, the RSI. Not so fast—our sources belie the firm's sweatshop rep. "Very enjoyable place to work, the work itself is very high quality—not just in terms of size and client base, but also complexity," raves a senior solicitor. "It is both demanding and rewarding. You also get to work with some first-class individuals." Add to the mix "simulating and challenging" cases and "a working environment in which excellence is recognised and rewarded" and a different picture emerges. As one American expat puts it: "I'm young, well paid and living in London. What's not to like?" The "great cases [and] great partners", "substantial client contact" and "ample travel opportunities" certainly don't hurt either.

This is (h)our youth

The Skadden "workload is overwhelming" and the schedule "extreme." "Haphazard" and "unpredictable" hours "make it difficult to make long-term plans" to go on holiday and the like, and those who believe they'll find respite on the weekend might wish to consider this litigator's caveat: "Weekends are treated as though they are weekdays." Thankfully "work hours vary in accordance with the cyclical nature of corporate deals", which means that there are some peaks and valleys time-wise—the valleys, however, are few and far between, making it the "wrong job for balancing family and work." In any event, Skadden insiders are hardly despairing over their hours. Some feel that "the work is stimulating and cutting-edge, which makes up for it in part." Others tell us that the hours are only excessive when "compared to average working hours in Europe, not bad given salary and hours expected in the U.S."

Quid pro quo

What exactly does Skadden give its lawyers to compensate for their blood, sweat, and time? According to U.S. lawyers, a generous "expat package that alleviates the higher cost of living (and higher foreign taxes) for [American] attorneys." For everyone else: not enough. (Is it ever?) Salary is "pretty darned good on arriving. But [we] will wait to see what excuses they have for the amount of any pay increases at time of salary review and bonus in an attempt to keep the profit share amongst the partners", remarks a seventh-year cynic. An eighth-year goes so far as to hyperbolically grumble, "my secretary is better paid (per hour) than me."

R-E-S-P-E-C-T

With most firm decisions coming out of New York, Skadden's London partners have a warmer relationship with their solicitors. The consensus is that the partners are "approachable", "nonhierarchical", and "friendly", and unlike many others at the top of their game, they're willing to join their minions in the trenches. "Partners are much more hands on than at a U.K. firm and they therefore expect associates to take responsibility/put in similar hours when necessary", a lawyer explains, adding that it can be a double-edged sword: "Whilst this is very positive in the sense that it sends a clear message that partners do not expect associates to do anything that they are not prepared to do themselves, it can also lead to pressure on associates, particularly in core practice areas, in terms of hours/ability expectations." "[T]here is a great deal of reciprocal respect between the ranks, which translates into a good deal of trust and positive working relationships" and it is not unheard of "for partners to drop by associates' offices to ask how they are doing or for partners to eat lunch with associates."

"Learning by burning"

The one matter on which most everyone seems to agree is the excellence of partners' informal training and mentoring. A "learning by burning" environment, Skadden's partners "always make themselves available if associates express an interest in mentoring." In particular, "the tax department provides an excellent combination of partner support/input on the one hand and encouragement to work independently on the other." Says one solicitor: "As the quality of both partners and senior associates is very high, the quality of 'on the job' training is also high."

Slaughter and May

One Bunhill Row
London EC1Y 8YY
Phone: +44 (0)20 7600 1200
www.slaughterandmay.com

OTHER LOCATIONS
Brussels
Hong Kong
Paris

MAJOR DEPARTMENTS & PRACTICES
Commercial Real Estate • Competition • Corporate & Commercial • Dispute Resolution • Employment & Pensions • Environment • Financial Regulation • Financing • Intellectual Property & Information Technology • Media & Mergers & Acquisitions • Tax • Technology • Telecoms

THE BUZZ
WHAT EMPLOYEES AT OTHER FIRMS ARE SAYING

- "The ultimate law firm"
- "Lives up to its name"

THE STATS
No. of lawyers: 709 (2006)
No. of offices: 4
Trainees intake: 90 (2005)
Trainees retained: 98% (2005)
Senior partner: Tim Clark

PLUSES
- Great partners and high-quality work
- "No billable hours targets"

MINUSES
- Long hours and little socialising
- Slim chance of becoming a partner

NOTABLE PERKS
- Subsidised canteen
- Discounted membership to gym next door
- Private health care
- Free dinner after 7 p.m., taxis after 9 p.m.

BASE SALARY
Trainee: £31,000
Newly Qualified: £54,000

GRADUATE RECRUITMENT AND TRAINING MANAGER
Charlotte Houghton
Personnel Manager
E-mail: grad.recruit@slaughterandmay.com

THE SCOOP

Slaughter and May stands out from the rest of the pack in London, and two things set it apart: first its phenomenal profitability, and second its unique approach to international expansion. The firm has been part of the City's furniture since 1889, when William May and William Slaughter left what was then Ashurst Morris Crisp & Co (now Ashurst) to start their own firm doing largely railway and mining business. The practice boomed, and with financial institutions like Schroders, Rothschilds, Barings and Morgan Grenfell, all clients of more than fifty years standing, it's little wonder the Slaughters of today walks off with some of the U.K.'s hottest corporate mandates. Though it was the first British firm into Hong Kong back in 1974, Slaughters has found little need for a global footprint to service its premier client base, and the partners have reaped the rewards of shrewd financial management.

Clients to die for

Slaughter and May consistently ranks as the lead adviser to major corporations in Britain, according to Chambers' FTSE Survey: Who acts for corporate Britain? At the end of 2004 a survey of the FTSE 100 found 36 instructed Slaughters, eight more than nearest rival Linklaters.

The firm is most renowned for its corporate practice, largely built in the 1980s when Slaughters cleaned up on privatisation work initiated by the Conservative government of the day. The firm advised on the sell-offs of British Aerospace, Amersham International, Associated British Ports, British Airways, Enterprise Oil, Jaguar and British Telecom, the last of which was the first of the really massive privatisations and occupied more people for a longer period than anything the firm had done before. The BT work placed the firm in pole position to advise the government on the later privatisations of British Aerospace, Britoil, BP, British Gas, British Steel and the electricity industry.

These days the firm continues to lead on some of the U.K.'s most iconic deals: in early 2004 it successfully defended high street champion Marks & Spencer against a hostile bid from billionaire Philip Green, and the firm also advised a consortium of private equity bidders on the massive £1.56 billion bid for London's Canary Wharf development.

What's more, despite its stuffy image, some of Slaughter's most senior partners are serious football fans, and have mixed work and pleasure to advise the Arsenal Football Club on its new stadium, its player transfer dealings and sponsorship deals with Emirates and Nike.

Global work from the Square Mile

Despite unrivalled penetration of U.K. boardrooms, Slaughter and May has not gone the route of many of its rivals by largely shunning international expansion. In 2003 offices in Singapore and New York were closed, and only Paris, Brussels and Hong Kong remain. But that doesn't mean the firm only does U.K. work—it services international deals through a network of so-called "best friends", relationship firms that are independent and pre-eminent in other jurisdictions. Slaughters seconds some of its best lawyers to these other firms, does joint training programmes and pools know-how, with a view to offering a client the best service that money can buy. The best friends list reads like a Who's Who of the world's top law firms: Bredin Prat in France, Hengeler Mueller in Germany, Davis Polk & Wardwell in New York, and many more of the same.

The strategy seems to bear fruit, with the most recent big deal being work alongside America's Cravath, Swaine & Moore and Dutch firm De Brauw Blackstone Westbroek on the unification of Royal Dutch Shell and a new corporate governance structure.

Life beyond corporate

Though lauded by London's *Legal Business* magazine as "the firm of choice for U.K. M&A", there is more to Slaughters than just doing deals. Indeed, lawyers here get a different approach to life from the outset, with what the firm calls its "multi-specialist approach." Instead of becoming an M&A lawyer, for example, young associates are encouraged to learn about all areas of the practice, so that they can deliver specialisms alongside broader commercial nous. You only have to look at the firm's eminently approachable senior partner Tim Clark to see it in action: he does M&A and general corporate finance, covering equity capital markets, demutualisation and joint ventures as needs must. As a smoker, he was one of the partners called in to pitch and win new client Gallaher, the tobacco firm, in 2004. The firm's highest profile M&A partner, Nigel Boardman, also advises football clubs on transfer deals.

Slaughter and May has a crack team of litigators, plus finance, tax, IP, real estate and employment lawyers, all on hand when a client needs them. It advises GlaxoSmithKline on intellectual property, and in July 2005 advised

Bank of Scotland when it won a dispute with the French tax authorities over the entitlements under the Franco-U.K. tax treaty.

Money matters

If you want Slaughter and May to represent you on your deal, you have got to be prepared to hand over some serious money. With some of the largest charge-out rates in the City, partners at Slaughters are amongst the richest in the world, with the average partner taking home £1.12 million for the financial year that ended in April 2006—an increase of 6.5 per cent over last year's PEP. With Freshfields' recent introduction of salaried partners, Slaughters remains the only Magic Circle firm with a pure equity partnership.

And the good news is, the partners aren't afraid to give something back. The firm's charitable fund just paid out to refurbish the playground of St Luke's, the primary school near the firm's office where lawyers also help with literacy schemes and lunchtime sporting activities. Further afield, Slaughters is a member of the pro bono organisations London Panel of Solicitors and LawWorks for Community Groups, and a number of the partners and senior management have signed up to Partners in Leadership, where they pair up with head teachers to help with leadership and management within schools.

With brand spanking new offices on Bunhill Row, just north of Moorgate, Slaughters was one of the first law firms to invest in modern purpose-built City office space. It may have been on the block for a long time, but the firm is not one to stand still.

GETTING HIRED

Making Magic

As one would suppose, gaining admission to Slaughter and May is remarkably demanding and stringent, requiring stellar academic qualifications ("first-class degrees are common") as well as "intellectual flexibility and adaptability." Insiders contend that "academic results are more important than at some other Magic Circle firms", although "an eclectic CV" won't hurt.

Traditionally, Slaughter and May has been a haven for the Oxbridge set, but a number of lawyers report the stereotype is obsolete, dismissing "the perceived Oxbridge bias [as] incorrect." Well, perhaps, although this contention is belied by other reports that contend that "the majority of trainees" are products of Oxford or Cambridge. Then again, others point to the firm's geographic diversity, as there are "lots of people here [from] all over the U.K. and the world." In any event, assuming one's education is up to snuff, the hiring process for trainees involves a single interview with two partners; according to the firm, these are meant to be "relaxed and not a test of technical knowledge."

Surprisingly, laterals reportedly have at least as tough a time getting through the door as do undergraduates. One successful lateral confides, "I had the impression at my main interview that that the firm had already carried out an extensive pre-selection process and had already decided on a very small number of likely candidates."

OUR SURVEY SAYS

Fire in the belly

For many Slaughter insiders, the opportunity to apply one's talents to "fantastic quality work with some of the brightest legal minds on the planet" at one of the most prestigious firms in the world outweighs the sacrifices required. The work is alternatively described as "top class", "exceptional", "intellectually stimulating" and "broad", the latter especially being a quality highly valued by solicitors. "In the year that I have been here I have done a rights issue, a bond issue, private equity work, public M&A and a bank deal," lists a second-year. "Associates are given responsibility as soon as they qualify. A 1 PQE could easily be the pen holder for a prospectus."

The hours. Oh, the hours.

"The work is very good" admits an NQ, "but the hours are long." It is a relief that there are no billable hours at S&M and "no culture of face time", but that does not point to a decline in time spent at the office. "You only work where necessary," explains a solicitor, and that often means "long hours and weekends." On rare nights "walking the corridor at 11 p.m. can be just as busy as 4 p.m.," says an insider, but the "average" day runs more along the lines of 9:30 a.m. to 8 p.m. The same informant reports that partners work equally hard at S&M, but expresses scepticism of the firm's claim "that partners on average bill more hours than associates." Whether or not partners are getting their hands that dirty is may be dubious but a source confirms that, yes, "hours are overwhelmingly the biggest minus. If there were two of me to share the work both of us could have busy and fulfilling careers there." But, a fellow lawyer warns, "If you are worried about the number of hours you are going to be working, a career in a Magic Circle firm is probably not for you."

Socialising is for wimps

The thought of S&M lawyers playing as hard as they work is virtually nonexistent—few firm-sponsored social events, no impromptu drinks night, no making it to the pub for even half of the weekly quiz. Work may be of the highest quality, but social life not so much: "Lawyers tend not to socialise—they are working too hard", an eighth-year states bluntly. That's not to suggest that S&M solicitors are a nasty sort; they are "friendly", "collegiate", "helpful", "supportive" and "much more laid-back than the public perception." "There is very little of the starched collar formal approach that the firm is renowned for," says a contact. "I'm not sure how they will ever shake that reputation but it simply is not true." And some feel that they have been brought closer by the lack of false socialising: "you decide to socialise", a corporate lawyers says, "rather than being forced into fake smiling …" But even with the slim social scene and the hefty workload, competition is not the default setting at S&M. Reports a seventh-year, "People work hard but there is never any sense that they are competing against each other—we are all on the same side."

Keeping it civil, asking no questions

The sense of being team players extends all the way to the top, where—with the exception of "one or two nightmares"—partners are "helpful and respectful" and "civil." "Partners treat assistants with the utmost respect and courtesy", a solicitor tells us. A property attorney describes the upper echelon as having "A very light managerial style leaving fee-earners to get on with work", and another notes the "refreshing" absence of politics among partners. Though the "excellent" formal training is far better than informal training and mentoring at S&M, the "open-door policy" allows solicitors to seek assistance when necessary in the "sink or swim" atmosphere. Once source finds it "encouraging" that partners are "quite diverse in terms of personality and style", instead of a bunch of cookie-cutter drones. Unfortunately, he continues "the only common factors are that every partner is intimidatingly bright and was prepared to put absolutely everything on the altar for their careers. Don't even think about it unless you're prepared to unquestioningly work an all-nighter on Christmas Day, or skip your grandmother's funeral to complete a deal."

Money changes everything

"Compensation is the only thing that would make me want to leave Slaughters", a solicitor remarks darkly. "The work is great, the people are great (by and large), the structures are great, as is the atmosphere", he continues. "The issue is I get paid about 40K less than my colleagues at the N.Y. rate paying firms. And those firms are baying for associates from Slaughters and waving their chequebooks." But there are some who believe their peers' complaints are perhaps unwarranted. "Pay is top-end U.K. market but not commensurate to U.S. salaries", qualifies one lawyer. Someone who declined to specify his yearly earnings was even more practical, describing it as "An amount overly sufficient for my needs."

Speechly Bircham

6 St. Andrew Street
London EC4A 3LX
Phone: +44 (0)20 7427 6400
www.speechlys.com

MAJOR DEPARTMENTS & PRACTICES

Charities
Commercial Dispute Resolution
Construction & Engineering
Corporate
Corporate Tax
Employment & Pensions
Financial Services
International
Private Client
Private Equity
Property & Property Litigation
Technology & Commerce

THE STATS

No. of lawyers: 140
No. of lawyers in London: 140
No. of offices: 1
Trainee intake: 5 (2005)
Managing partner: Michael Lingens

GRADUATE RECRUITMENT AND TRAINING MANAGER

E-mail: trainingcontracts@speechlys.com

THE BUZZ
WHAT EMPLOYEES AT OTHER FIRMS ARE SAYING

- "Good private client"
- "Chip on shoulder"

THE SCOOP

Speechly Bircham is a nimble firm, known for an entrepreneurial spirit that isn't always on show at the big U.K. firms. It is probably best known for its efforts in technology and private equity, but it also has a private client and charities practice that puts it firmly on that map. There is also financial services, real estate and dispute resolution—essentially this is a full-service, slimline firm that is quick on its feet.

Quick on its feet

Speechlys is one of those mid-tier London corporate firms that finds itself perfectly positioned for either greatness, or disappearance. The mid-tier is where all the action is in the City legal market at the moment, with some firms of Speechly Bircham's size hiring like crazy and expanding to pose a real threat to the larger players, and others being taken over by bigger, hungrier practices. Speechlys obviously lacks the resources to take on the top players on the mega deals, but has the one-to-one service approach that clients so often connect with.

By the numbers

The firm's numbers show something is working. Turnover was up 16 per cent last year to a modest £29.1 million, but more impressive was the 38 per cent hike in profits, which meant the average partner now takes home £365,000 a year—well and truly on a par with the respectable firms in the London market, and Speechlys' best ever performance. Roughly 30 per cent of that revenue comes from corporate, the same from litigation, 20 per cent from property, and the rest from private client.

Assistants are generally expected to bill 1,600 hours a year, which is pretty standard by City levels, and there is a steady stream of tasty work coming through. The firm's top clients include Cable & Wireless, Credit Suisse Asset Management, P&O Group, Royal Bank of Scotland, Sainsbury's, Thomas Cook and General Motors' financial services subsidiary GMAC. Though this well-rounded firm is under pressure from just about every angle, it so far is managing to keep on servicing an impressive clientele.

Expanding brief

Speechlys has been growing its partnership of late, kickstarting an expansion drive back in 2002 with two private equity partners from Osborne Clarke. Next up was a real estate partner from Maxwell Batley, an employment partner from Landwell, and then banking and finance partner Andrew Knight from Hammonds.

Knight took over the running of the finance practice, and was able to lure his former colleague and head of Hammonds' Birmingham finance team, Chris Harlowe, to London, where he has since set to work building a restructuring and insolvency team for Speechlys.

More recently, the firm has been bolstered with the addition of a construction partner from Mayer, Brown, Rowe & Maw, and the head of contentious trusts and probate from Boodle Hatfield. What's clear is that the expansion pretty much continues unabated and across the board. But there was bad news this summer when American law firm Brown Rudnick managed to lure the two partners that started it all, the private equity team. They left to launch that firm's U.K. operations in private equity, leaving Speechlys down but not out, and determined to rebuild its practice through a combination of hires and organic growth.

Financiers & fundraisers

The firm's finance practice, though, has gone from strength to strength. In 2006, the team advised Wharton Asset Management on its third securitisation that year, delivering an aggregate portfolio of $10.5 billion in the high-grade asset-backed securities market.

The firm works for Landsbanki Commercial Finance on its U.K. fundraisings, most recently raising money for the backing of a pharmaceutical marketing business called Medical Marketing Research International.

That fundraising work ties in nicely with the firm's practice in venture capital, which is basically what drives the corporate practice. The work is for start-ups and early-stage companies in high tech fields—the firm advised King's College on a recent spin-off company called Cerogenix, which is in drug discovery and diagnostics. The firm has also worked for Imperial College and University College London when their academics have set up corporations.

AIM large

But there is work for larger companies too, albeit often in the telecoms, media and technology fields. Speechlys acted for one of Russia's biggest media businesses, the Video International Group, when it set up a marketing and communications joint venture with global advertising powerhouse WPP Group.

There is also a steady flow of work on the Alternative Investment Market, London's junior stock market, where the firm often advises corporate finance houses bringing young companies to flotation. Through building relationships with the companies at this stage, it hopes to grow with the client and get ever larger work.

Let it flow

At Speechlys, there's good steady flow of smaller deals, working with some of the more interesting companies around. The amounts of money changing hands in these acquisitions and fundraising may well be some way south of £100 million, but they can make all the difference to the management, and thus give real hands-on business experience.

The corporate team worked for a U.K.-listed telecoms group on a two-year programme to draft and roll out global share incentive schemes for over 50 countries, and worked as English legal counsel for a U.S.-headquartered chemicals company in a £320 million sale of its speciality resins and adhesives business, which had more than 1,700 employees in 10 production sites worldwide.

Speechlys is, by all accounts, a nice place to work, untroubled by the international office networks of its competitors. Still, as the examples above show, there is no shortage of international work. The firm puts serious effort into marketing in the United States, and also has referral relationships with other independent firms worldwide.

Stephenson Harwood

One St Paul's Churchyard
London EC4M 8SH
Phone: +44 (0)20 7329 4422
www.shlegal.com

OTHER LOCATIONS
Hong Kong
Guangzhou
Paris
Piraeus
Singapore
Shanghai

MAJOR DEPARTMENTS & PRACTICES
Aviation • Banking & Asset Finance • Commercial • Construction • Corporate Finance • Corporate Tax • Employment, Pensions & Benefits • Funds & Financial Services • Insurance & Reinsurance • Litigation • Outsourcing • Real Estate • Shipping • Technology & Intellectual Property

THE STATS
No. of lawyers: 260
No. of lawyers in London: 200
No. of offices: 7
Trainee intake: 20 (2005)
Trainees retained: 85% (2005)
Managing partner: Sunil Gadhia

PLUSES
- "Nice people"
- "Great location"

MINUSES
- Red tape
- Occasional "pessimism"

BASE SALARY
Trainee: £28,000
Newly Qualified: £52,000

GRADUATE RECRUITMENT AND TRAINING MANAGER
Sharon Green
Training and Development Manager
E-mail: Sharon.green@shlegal.com

THE BUZZ
WHAT EMPLOYEES AT OTHER FIRMS ARE SAYING

- "Fading"
- "Friendly"

THE SCOOP

Stephenson Harwood was once one of the U.K.'s so-called Magic Circle law firms, right up there in the top echelons of legal practices, genuinely battling with Allen & Overy for the best finance mandates. Alas, its descent from such lofty heights over the last 20 years has become the stuff of legal legend, and though the practice remains a serious player in the mid-market, the firm is too often cited as a lesson in how yesterday's heroes can quickly become today's also-rans.

Maritime roots

Stephenson Harwood was once a shipping firm, and that background in maritime and transport law took it into some of the most lucrative asset finance work there was in the 1980s. Its litigation practice was also a strong pillar, but once corporate finance and M&A became the rage, Stephenson Harwood lost the plot a little. Profits began to slide, and with them went the firm's top partners. This firm was hit harder than most by the arrival of American legal competitors on the U.K.'s shores, and suddenly the talent pool was plundered with the lure of bigger and better pay packages, and firms that seemed to be going in the right direction.

A bad marriage?

At the end of the 1990s, Stephenson Harwood seemed to decide that an American merger was its best bet, and there were reasonably public talks with a number of larger potential partners. But alas it was not to be, and instead the firm pulled off a somewhat second-rate merger with fellow shipping and litigation firm Sinclair Roche & Termperley, another struggler in the London mid-market. That link-up added some strong partners, but also brought with it a number of embarrassing liabilities. The Sinclair Roche partnership was sued for negligence on a big shipping case by client Somatra, and was also on the wrong end of a sex discrimination case bought by former partners. Though Stephenson Harwood was aware of both pending cases, and the Stephenson Harwood partners were protected from the potential claims from the outset, the merger nevertheless did nothing to improve the firm's reputation in the City's legal community.

That said, there is a lot of good work going on at Stephenson Harwood, and were it not for the recent trip-ups, the firm would be judged as a good solid mid-market player. It may not be a star—the likes of Clyde & Co and Barlow

Lyde & Gilbert have shown serious profits can be made on the back of similar practice profiles—but it holds its own with decent clients. And the latest financial news is promising: *The Lawyer* reports that in 2006 the firm posted a 45 per cent rise in average profit per equity partner.

On the plus side

Stephenson Harwood's work is largely international. It has seven offices of its own, plus alliances in Greece, South Africa, France, Kuwait and Bucharest. With its three biggest markets being financial services, real estate and maritime law, two thirds of its income is generated in three pretty global sectors. In London, almost 40 per cent of revenue is generated from work for clients based overseas.

The clients are a pretty impressive roll call of international institutions—the largest include HSBC, the Royal Bank of Scotland, Lloyds TSB and KPMG. One undoubted highlight last year was the firm's high-profile work for Westminster City Council, by whom it was instructed to pursue Dame Shirley Porter after the "homes for votes" scandal. The firm's civil fraud group successfully recovered assets worth millions from all over the world, making the partners pretty popular in certain parts of London. In corporate, energy continues to be a big driver. A big client is EDF Energy, which it advised on both a major wind farm project in Portugal, and on its £20 million London Borough of Ealing PFI street lighting project.

The property group continues to perform well too, working for the London Development Agency on the £1.5 billion regeneration of the south side of the Royal Docks, and on the £115 million sale of the Mayfair Intercontinental Hotel. Again, it's not all domestic—the firm worked for London & Regional Properties on the €700 million financing for its acquisition of 273 properties in Germany.

Growing pains

Stephenson Harwood remains committed to getting back to greatness, and certainly the client loyalty seems to indicate that all is far from lost. The problem is keeping the partners on board as profits roller coaster: a drive to slim down the partnership ranks in a bid to raise the take-home pay for those that remained was successful in 2005, but such a strategy is by necessity short-term, and the firm has to deliver again to keep those that stayed on board.

Now the focus is on bulking up with the right people. Autumn 2005 saw the arrival of a new tax partner from Deloitte & Touche, while asset finance partner Christopher St. John Smith also moved over from CMS Cameron McKenna to build out what is now a key area of focus for the firm.

New blood

Commercial litigation got a much-needed boost in the summer as well, with the hire of Paul Phillips from Olswang, where he had acted for American Airlines in deep vein thrombosis cases and jointly led the team that secured the acquittal of the second accused in the Lockerbie trial.

Certainly Stephenson Harwood is now sticking to a strategy it outlined in 2004, which is to focus on adding strength to its key areas. The firm may have lost its way, but a new chief executive in the form of the very young and enthusiastic Sunil Gadhia has inspired hopes in many that, with a clarified vision, the firm is on its way back at least some way towards its former greatness.

GETTING HIRED

No particular schools

For many firms the single most important factor in one's eligibility is education, or rather, where one was educated. Oxford, Cambridge, Durham—it had better be prestigious. Truth be told, Stephenson Harwood seems not to give a toss about academic pedigree. "I do not think that the firm concentrates on particular schools," muses a solicitor who "was raised and studied abroad" (read: doesn't have the Oxbridge credentials). No doubt the firm appreciates a good mind, but apparently its hiring powers don't believe that legal acumen is limited to those from universities that, while having matriculated plenty of geniuses, also have penchants for wooden spoons. Once an applicant's academic bona fides are established, the firm is looking for that elusive combination of "interesting personalities and business awareness." "[W]e are expected to participate in marketing events from a very early stage," reports a source, "and we get involved with clients both at work and socially." In that case we presume that those who can't hold their liquor need not apply.

OUR SURVEY SAYS

Friendly and hardworking

Perhaps they're just good people, but we'd rather believe that it's Stephenson Harwood's "excellent location" a stone's throw from mighty, looming St Paul's Cathedral that reminds the firm's lawyers to respect their fellow humans. How else to explain a corporate firm's reputation for being ever so well-mannered? "Friendly and hardworking," according to a first-year (shouldn't the young ones be more intimidated?), Stephenson's atmosphere is "non-stuffy" but blessed with people who are both lovely and driven. This means that though they are extroverted sorts who "do tend to socialise together", such activity must happen "within the remits that their personal arrangements would allow," says a source. In other words, it can be difficult to pop round to the pub when hours at the firm can "vary considerably", though "this is due to the nature" of certain practices "rather than the firm" as a whole.

The trade-off for practising law in a genial environment may be a general lack of perks, unless you—quite sadly—count "going to nice restaurants as part of our marketing strategy" a privilege instead of a responsibility. Other bummers? Solicitors "do not participate in the decision-making process, but are informed about the serious decisions that may affect [them]." Well, we would hope as much. "Red-tape" can also slow things down. And from what we hear, those sweet Stephenson lawyers have their days; reveals one insider, "sometimes there is a bit of pessimism as to what can be achieved."

Sullivan & Cromwell LLP

1 New Fetter Lane
London EC4A 1AN
Phone: +44 (0) 20 7959 8900
www.sullcrom.com

OTHER LOCATIONS

Beijing • Brussels (Conference Center) • Frankfurt • Hong Kong • Los Angeles • Melbourne • New York • Palo Alto • Paris • Sydney • Tokyo • Washington, DC

MAJOR DEPARTMENTS & PRACTICES

Antitrust • Arbitration • Banking • Bankruptcy & Creditors' Rights • Broker-Dealer Regulation • Commodities, Futures & Derivatives • Corporate & Securities Litigation • Corporate Governance • Criminal Defense & Investigation • EC Competition • Environmental • Estates & Personal • Executive Compensation /ERISA • Financial Institutions • Insurance • Intellectual Property & Technology • International Trade & Investment • Investment Management • Labour & Employment Litigation • Litigation • Mergers & Acquisitions • Private Equity • Privatisations • Products Liability • Project Finance • Real Estate • Securities • Structured, Acquisition and Leveraged Finance • Tax

THE BUZZ
WHAT EMPLOYEES AT OTHER FIRMS ARE SAYING

- "A glittering name on the CV"
- "Overworked"

THE STATS

No. of lawyers: 610
No. of lawyers in London: 58
No. of offices: 12
London managing partner: William A. Plapinger

PLUSES

- Talented and respectful partners
- "Top deals"

MINUSES

- Unpredictable workload
- "Brutal" hours

NOTABLE PERKS

- Subsidised gym
- Cost of living allowance (US expatriates only)
- Discretionary foreign exchange adjustment
- Adoption assistance

BASE SALARY

Newly Qualified: $145,000 (paid in Sterling)

GRADUATE RECRUITMENT AND TRAINING MANAGER

Jamie Logie
UK Recruitment Partner
Phone: +44 (0)20 7959 8900

THE SCOOP

Sullivan & Cromwell was founded way back in 1879 on Wall Street, and immediately set to work on some of the biggest deals of the day, both in the United States and abroad. The firm advised on the formation of the Edison General Electric Company in 1889 (now General Electric) as well as the U.S. Steel Corporation in 1901. S&C has been at the heart of industrial and financial America ever since.

A less-than-full commitment?

On the face of it, the firm's London office would suggest a less than full-throttle commitment to life beyond the United States: more than two-thirds of the lawyers are U.S.-qualified, although more than one-third are not American. The London office has two English partners, Jamie Logie and Craig Jones, who joined from Norton Rose in the late 1990s, and 10 other lawyers who are U.K.-qualified. Logie was a project finance partner at Norton Rose, but, like all other partners joining from other firms through that time, sacrificed that for an of counsel position at Sullivan, only to be made up to partner after arriving and proving himself. Jones joined the firm as a junior U.K. associate in 1999 and was elected a partner at the end of 2004.

S&C is actually one of the more global of the Wall Street elite. The firm opened in Paris in 1928 with a full-service operation acting for financial institutions on both sides of the Atlantic. While the office was forced to close during the war, it reopened in 1962, and was closely followed by a London office in 1972, Melbourne in 1983, Tokyo in 1987, Hong Kong in 1992, Frankfurt in 1995, Beijing in 1999 and, most recently, Sydney in 2001. Today roughly half of Sullivan & Cromwell's elite client base is headquartered outside of America.

A growing presence in London

The London office of S&C has grown to some 58 lawyers, with almost 25 per cent of them qualified to practice U.K. or EU. The thrust of the work is capital markets, M&A (including private equity), project finance, litigation and competition law, real estate and tax—the office saw its resources significantly boosted in 2000 when two New York M&A partners and one New York litigation partner were jetted in to deal with a predicted upturn in deals on this side of the Atlantic. Although, one of the M&A partners stayed for only a couple of years, while the other returned to New York in 2005, the number of partners in the London office grew from eight in 2000 to 17 currently, including four associates elected to partner in London since 2000.

The S&C London office has a threefold mission: to help European corporations when they have U.S. law issues, as well as, increasingly, to advise European clients on European, African, Middle Eastern and Asian deals, and to a much lesser extent, to advise U.S. clients doing deals in Europe. It is certainly a strategy that appears to be working. London-based partner Garth Bray topped the tables for advising on the most European M&A deals for the 12 months ending July 2005, and recently advised financial advisor Goldman Sachs on the massive HVB merger with Unicredito Italiano. In 2004, the firm had a role advising either the purchaser or target on nine of the 10 largest deals, including having acted for France's Aventis when it was bought by Sanofi-Synthelabo, which was the world's largest M&A deal that year. The firm acted in six of the 10 largest deals announced worldwide in 2005, and is currently advising Spain's Endesa in its defense of bids from Gas Natural and E.ON. It also represented the financial advisor to Spain's Telefonica in its acquisition of O2 in the U.K.

When it comes to capital markets, the firm worked for companies on more than 50 per cent of all the U.S.-registered offerings by European corporations between 2001 and 2005, with a value of $195.9 billion compared to $81.6 billion for second-place Simpson Thacher & Bartlett.

S&C has had a rock-solid relationship with Goldman Sachs for decades, and that link has been a huge driver for European expansion. But corporate relationships with the likes of BP, Barclays, Diageo, France Telecom, Philips Electronics, Rio Tinto and Total, all further contribute to a deal flow that is almost second to none.

Resource question

With no shortage of work flowing across the Atlantic, the perennial question in the London market continues to revolve around whether the firm will ever make a more significant move into U.K. law capability. While one in five of the London lawyers are English, and local recruitment is well established, the partnership remains U.S.-dominated and the strategy continues to be to focus on advising on U.S. law issues facing clients in Europe.

Still, if you believe the London legal gossips, S&C has been actively seeking to hire local law M&A corporate finance partners for a long time, but is simply incredibly fussy. The firm maintains it will build the office slowly and only in response to client demand.

On the continent, it has been more ambitious. It has had French law capability since 1962 and brought in its first French partner in 1996, further adding senior partners Gerard Mazet and Jean-Pierre Le Gall from Jeantet Associés in 2001, and three additional French partners since that time. The first German partner in that country came in 2001, when it recruited Freshfields Bruckhaus Deringer partner Wolfgang Feuring, and he was joined in 2002 by a partner from Nörr Steifenhofer Lutz, Konsantin Technau.

This just goes to show that the firm is not as averse to bringing in overseas lawyers as some of its stuffier competitors—Cravath has never hired a partner who is not U.S.-qualified, while Davis Polk & Wardwell hired its first non-U.S. partner only in 2005, in Paris.

For two years S&C ranked in *The American Lawyer*'s A-list, the roll call of the top 20 law firms in the United States based on revenue, pro bono commitment, associate satisfaction and diversity. S&C slipped out in 2005, with its pro bono hours falling 26 per cent on the previous year. The firm blamed some big death penalty cases for distorting the numbers in years gone by, and is still pretty heavily committed to working for free for those less fortunate.

On average, its lawyers devote more than 30,000 hours a year to pro bono and public service matters—in 2005 the firm spent time working with small businesses and individuals after September 11, represented the Legal Aid Society in a suit aimed at getting redress for injuries caused by wrongful conduct on the part of the City of New York, and aimed at improving services for indigent litigants.

There's no doubt that working at S&C is just about as demanding as you will find anywhere, and its lawyers are probably amongst the most stretched in the City. But it is topflight work. Nothing scares an English law firm more than the thought that S&C might become a competitor at some point. This is the firm to watch.

GETTING HIRED

The usual

S&C's official recruiting literature blandly states the firm is "always looking for individuals with the intellect, character and motivation to become outstanding members of the legal profession." According to insiders, the firm's hiring "process is unsurprisingly competitive", as one corporate solicitor puts it. Others at Sullivan & Cromwell are a touch more modest: "Like everywhere else," reports a colleague, "[Sullivan & Cromwell] is looking for smart, competent people." And that does not necessarily mean that "smart" and "competent" are synonymous with "prestigious smarty-pants university." In fact, says the same lawyer, "I don't think school is [the] be all and end all" in terms of winning a stint at the firm. Interest and acumen in a certain area is; a fifth-year reading from the *Book of the Obvious* is quick to point out to potential corporate folks that "Being business-minded helps in the corporate department." Shocker, that.

OUR SURVEY SAYS

Career fulfilment

True, the legal world is not known for offering spiritually satisfying careers (though one might argue that spiritual satisfaction comes from within, but we digress) but Sullivan & Cromwell solicitors, excepting our friend above, are well aware that they're not preserving the Amazon or saving one of those mammals that is frequently befriended by lonely children of divorce in Hollywood films. That said, they feel that "as long as one wants to have the firm life, there is probably no better place to be." The kind of work they do is reportedly "high quality", "generally amazing", "challenging and interesting", and moreover, "the breadth and richness of experience gained in one year here is probably the equivalent of one-and-a-half to two years of experience at another firm," raves a solicitor. "It is a great platform to develop your legal career." Concurs a co-worker "You are immediately expected to take on a good amount of responsibility even as a junior associate, which can be an intimidating (but still interesting) proposition at times."

The human touch

Self-description of their working personae by S&C lawyers tends toward the dry—"highly professional", "committed to excellence and achieving the best results for our clients" … that sort of thing. Away from their desks, however, things warm up. "Colleagues are dedicated and talented lawyers, but, unusually for the City, all have a human side", a novice tells us. "The firm is casual and people are all very professional", with diverse political affiliations. As far as the occasional party or pub crawl is concerned, "Lawyers do socialise together outside of the firm, but it's not the type of place where people are going for drinks every Friday", an insider explains. Partners do join the fray from time to time, hosting occasional events at their homes and at the office. Summarises a source, "It is definitely not a hyper-social place … but at the same time, there are few, if any, people that I would categorise as extremely difficult to work with."

Open relationships

When Sullivan & Cromwell attorneys speak favourably of others at the firm, they also include their partners, with whom most reportedly have "good" relationships. "Partners are very approachable and 'muck-in' with associates", which is more than can be said for a number of partners at rival firms. They "are very professional and truly respect the opinions of associates in the office," raves a solicitor. "They are fully aware that the associates are the engines driving much of the work of the firm and do have an appreciation for this." Yes, agrees a colleague, "On a day-to-day basis, the partners are great. They generally treat associates with respect and are sensitive to personal needs and issues. However, the rating falls down because the partnership does not inform associates or allow them to participate in decision-making." Sounds about right. But you can count on an open-door policy by partners at a firm where formal training "is a bit of an afterthought" though "improving." "Partners doors are usually open and it's really an issue of whether the associate wants to walk through them," we're told. "You can always ask someone for feedback", as "partners are generally willing to help and answer questions."

Don't plan for anything

"The hours can be abysmal", admits an eighth-year, telling solicitors everywhere what they in all likelihood already know about firms in the vein of Sullivan & Cromwell. "Ideally the norm … would be for people to have more of a life outside of work", a desire that falls somewhere between "Find a soul mate" and "Broker world peace" on the grand list of Utopian goals. Yes, hours are "probably the biggest drawback of working here," one lawyer tells us, "though I think most associates know this prior to entering the firm so very few are surprised by it. In my opinion, the below average satisfaction with hours is not so much due to the number of hours rather than the unpredictability of when you may have a bad week hours-wise." "There is no predictability to the work schedule," confirms a peer. That does not mean, however, that there's such a thing as face time, we hear: "I don't think anyone cares how many hours you spend doing something as long as you do it and get it right." At least two Sullivan & Cromwell lawyers (notably both men) are quick to point out that working mothers face an uphill battle. "As a man, I see a lot of emphasis and effort placed on trying to attract qualified women and to address workplace issues for women", muses one of them. "However, I'm not blind to the fact that this must be a very hard place to work for women with children because of the time commitment."

Cashing in

British lawyers working on their home turf have little to complain about: the "overall compensation appears to be the same as other top U.S. firms in the City." American expats, however, score big. Not only is "compensation … at or near the top of the market", a "cost of living adjustment" is tacked on. Declares one not-so-quiet American, "It's fantastic at the overseas offices."

Taylor Wessing

Carmelite
50 Victoria Embankment
Blackfriars
London EC4Y 0DX
Phone: +44 (0)20 7300 7000
www.taylorwessing.com

OTHER LOCATIONS

*Alicante • Berlin • Brussels • Cambridge • Düsseldorf • Frankfurt • Hamburg • London • Munich • Neuss • Paris • *Shanghai
*representative offices

MAJOR DEPARTMENTS & PRACTICES

China
Competition, Regulation & Trade
Construction & Engineering
Corporate
Employment & Pensions
Finance
Financial Services
Insurance
Intellectual Property
Inward Investment (UK)
Leisure
Life Sciences & Healthcare
Litigation & Dispute Resolution
Private Client
Projects
Real Estate
Technology

THE STATS

No. of lawyers: 650
No. of lawyers in London: 321
No. of offices: 12
Recruitment intake: approximately 22
Trainees retained: 93% (2005)
Managing partner: Martin Winter
Senior partner: Michael Frawley

NOTABLE PERKS

- Subsidised restaurant
- Web-based concierge service

BASE SALARY

Trainee: £30,000
Newly Qualified: £53,000

GRADUATE RECRUITMENT AND TRAINING MANAGER

Sophie Ferguson
Legal Recruitment Manager
Phone: +44 (0)20 7300 7000
E-mail: graduate@taylorwessing.com

THE BUZZ
WHAT EMPLOYEES AT OTHER FIRMS ARE SAYING

- "Highly regarded"
- "Ruthless"

THE SCOOP

Taylor Wessing is the Anglo-German product of one of the most significant mergers of equals in the London legal community of late. In 2002, the City's Taylor Joynson Garrett linked up with Germany's Wessing, both firms of roughly 250 lawyers. The ambition was to create a pan-European firm devoted to servicing the technology, media and telecoms sectors, in which both firms already had some reputation. TJG had butted horns with the likes of Bird & Bird and Olswang pre-merger, and had made its name in intellectual property and life sciences work.

Household names

The list of household name clients remains something to behold: think Toyota, Pepsi, Kellogg's and Häagen-Dazs for starters. But the merger is yet to truly deliver on its promise on pan-European mega-stardom. Integration has taken longer than predicted, and the nub of any such combination is to get partners not only talking to each other, but also liking each other and referring work to each other. Reportedly, that has yet to be fully realised at Taylor Wessing.

Still, the ambition is admirable, and the sense by all accounts is that the firm will make the deal work; it will just take its time. The track record shows no shortage of dynamic and ambitious decisions. When Arthur Andersen collapsed, for example, it was Taylor Wessing that snapped up the Cambridge office of what was once Andersen Legal, only to immediately ingratiate itself with the technology community in the university town.

Similarly, instead of chasing U.S. merger partners as so many mid-tier corporate players have done, Taylor Wessing realised early on that the key to winning American clients was jetting round the U.S. meeting partners at American law firms who might refer clients its way. On the far side of the Atlantic, Taylor Wessing now has a pretty established reputation for pressing the flesh, and it gets the deals to make all those air trips count.

Doing deals

The firm's corporate group's recent deals have included advising carbon emissions group ICECAP on its first transaction, whereby it sources and manages the worldwide portfolio carbon credits for a group of participants including ENEL and Marubeni Corporation. Then there was advice to Fujitsu Siemens Computers on a major cross-border TMT acquisition, and work for

Huawei Technologies, the U.K. subsidiary of a large Chinese company, on its agreement for network infrastructure with Vodafone.

The firm's specially formed inward investment team got a fillip in 2005 when corporate partner Daniel Rosenberg, who regularly rubs shoulders with the great and the good of New York, was appointed chairman of Think London's North American taskforce, focusing on inward investment for the capital. That success came after a double-act of M&A works for technology clients GSC Partners and Sybase, both doing chunky deals in the U.K.

Nice skill set

On the intellectual property side, the team advised Principal Investment Holdings on the acquisition and rebranding of Grant Thornton Asset Management, and then in the more general media practice, the firm won a groundbreaking ruling capping costs in an order against a claimant in a libel action, when representing Associated Newspapers.

Finally, there is a real estate practice, which is not to be forgotten, a chunk of which again came from the disintegrating Andersen Legal in London. The firm represents London & Regional Properties, one of the biggest market participants, and recently acted for it securing a large pre-let for its flagship redevelopment of the former Marks & Spencer headquarters in London's Baker Street, in the West End.

All of which means this is a full-service firm, that can more or less turn its hand to anything, and does all of it with some panache. The technology market is where it feels most at home, and where it finds its competitive advantage, but the skill sets of the corporate, finance, real estate and litigation teams are more than capable of taking on others in the City.

New leadership

The firm elected a new managing partner at the end of 2004, Michael Frawley, with a brief to kick-start the integration of the newly global firm. Perhaps as a measure of the task ahead of him, early 2005 saw the introduction, three years post-merger, of the first firmwide body to assess partner remuneration. Immediately after the link-up, the two firms had continued to run two separate financial partnerships, but the committee set to work aligning the systems of pay to get everyone on the same wavelength.

Whilst bedding down will be a long hard road, it hasn't stopped Taylor Wessing expanding, and its progress has not stopped high-quality laterals signing up. The start of 2006 saw the hire of LeBoeuf Lamb Greene & MacRae's former managing partner for Paris, Alain de Foucaud, as the 16th partner in the French office. He will focus on venture capital and local capital markets, while again adding much-needed U.S. contacts and expertise.

Glittery laterals

Frawley's arrival coincided with the election of Paris litigation partner Paul-Albert Iweins to the post of chairman of the French Bar Council, securing the firm one of the most high-profile jobs in the French legal market.

What's more, the London office kicked off the year with the hire of the head of environmental and planning law from Norton Rose, Brian Greenwood, and in Brussels, the end of 2005 saw the launch of a Belgian law practice with a new team of partners from Lawfort. Attracting lateral hires like those is a measure of the faith that the market as a whole has in the ability of Taylor Wessing to make its audacious merger work.

Travers Smith

10 Snow Hill
London EC1A 2AL
Phone: +44 (0)20 7295 3000
www.traverssmith.com

OTHER LOCATIONS

Berlin
Paris

MAJOR DEPARTMENTS & PRACTICES

Banking
Commercial
Corporate
Corporate Recovery
Dispute Resolution
Employment
Financial Services
International
Pensions
Property
Tax

THE BUZZ
WHAT EMPLOYEES AT OTHER FIRMS ARE SAYING

- "Exciting"
- "Mid-tier"

THE STATS

No. of lawyers: 225
No. of lawyers in London: 215
No. of offices: 3
Recruitment intake: up to 25
Trainees retained: 75% (2004)
Managing Partner: Chris Carroll

PLUSES

- No billing requirements
- Responsive and pleasant partners

MINUSES

- "A bit of a goldfish bowl"
- Unpredictable hours

NOTABLE PERKS

- Subsidised Costa coffee (60p a cup)
- Subsidised gym membership
- Free conveyancing

BASE SALARY

Trainee: £31,000
Newly Qualified: £55,000

GRADUATE RECRUITMENT AND TRAINING MANAGER

Germaine VanGeyzel
Graduate Recruitment Co-ordinator
Phone: +44 (0)20 7295 3546
E-mail: graduate.recruitment@traverssmith.com

THE SCOOP

Travers Smith is one of the darlings of the mid-market U.K. legal scene—a small corporate boutique that manages to punch above its weight. The practice has resisted the temptation to grow too fast, but has instead stayed at little over 200 lawyers, focusing its attention on getting the very best deals that a firm of its size can handle.

Private equity at heart

Remarkably, Travers Smith has been in the City of London for more than two centuries, and has grown without acquisition or merger over that time. There are very few law firms worldwide that can boast such an uneventful history.

The practice nowadays has private equity at its heart, with Travers Smith one of the first to identify that market as one that would become huge. The firm built its brand here by advising the management of small companies that were interested in buying out their businesses with the backing of venture capitalists. In so doing, Travers Smith partners found themselves regularly across the table from said venture capitalists, and capable of introducing good companies to them as buy-out opportunities. Hence, the reputation has now expanded so much that the firm is hired by those institutions as well, and it is increasingly growing its business into the mid-market stockbrokers and corporate finance houses as well.

Best friends

Unlike so many of its competitors, Travers Smith has studiously resisted international expansion of late, though small outposts that are little more than one-man shows are now in place in Germany and France. Instead, though, the focus is on best friend relationships with other local law firms. The offices are there to foster those relationships, and to add French or German law capability on deals when it is just a small contributor.

The best friend network is fastidiously maintained, with lawyers seconded back and forth at regular intervals, and partners racking up the air miles visiting potential colleagues. It seems to bear fruit—in all some 45 per cent of Travers Smith's deal flow involves cross-border advice of some description.

Deal perfect

Things haven't always been easy for Travers Smith, and it's fair to say that when the corporate world was slow at the start of this century, the bigger firms made a fine job of fishing in the Travers pool. But, as the markets have bounced back, so have the firm's fortunes (and things were never dire—no one was laid off, just the pay packets took a hit).

On the M&A front, the firm does some big deals: it advised 3i buying National Car Parks for £555 million, and worked for Peel on its £771 million acquisition of The Mersey Docks and Harbour Company. Travers became synonymous with ntl, the telephone and cable group, in the late 1990s, and advised it on its U.S.$6 billion deal to merge with Telewest Global, an astonishing deal for a firm of Travers Smith's size. It had previously worked for the group on the £1.27 billion sale of its broadcast division.

In capital markets, too, the firm does well, particularly as it strengthens its profile with the City's stockbrokers. The firm worked for Numis on the flotation of Empire Online, which listed on the Alternative Investment Market for £512 million, one of the largest initial public offerings (IPO) on that market. The team also advised Numis on the accelerated IPO of Centaur Holdings, which was a landmark deal.

Sweet spot

Private equity is Travers Smith's "sweet spot" though—the market in which it feels most comfortable. The team is one of the strongest for mid-market U.K. deals, particularly as the larger law firms chase the increasingly international segment of the industry. Travers Smith worked for management on the £1.35 billion management buy-out of Saga, the service provider for the over-50s, and for management on the £2.2 billion sale of Coral Eurobet, the gambling group. Then there was work for purchasers buying Pets at Home, for €330 million, and for the sellers on the £245 million disposal of Earls Court & Olympia, the concerts-to-conferences venue in central London.

Rivals have at times carped that Travers Smith lacks the requisite support areas to deal with such large transactions, and while there have been few partner departures in recent years, those that have left have fuelled speculation of a weakness on the finance side. Still, the firm is building its banking capability, and also has leading capabilities in pensions, tax, fund formation and real estate, to name but a few. In the autumn of 2005 the firm's real estate team advised Golfrate, the property company, on its purchase of

The Criterion and The London Trocadero, both centres in the heart of London's Piccadilly Circus.

Pro bono publico

The stability of the team at Travers Smith, a firm fairly devoid of both partner-level arrivals and departures—suggests a tight-knit culture. Those at this firm believe in its vision, and work hard to prove that, as they put it, you don't need to work in a "factory" to deliver big deals for high-profile clients on the London legal scene. In July 2006, Alasdair Douglas, former managing partner and current head of the tax department, took over as senior partner, replacing Christopher Bell who retired after 35 years with the firm.

Travers Smith makes a good contribution to its community and has a healthy commitment to pro bono work. The firm has acted on a number of death row cases for the Caribbean Capital Cases Committee, and has taken on cases from the Bar Pro Bono Unit. Trainees in the litigation department are encouraged to take on their own pro bono cases through the Free Representation Unit. Beyond that, there is the LawWorks Initiative, which the firm has been involved in for several years, in partnership with the Paddington Law Centre. The firm co-founded the Inns of Court School of Law Evening Advice Clinic in 2002, where solicitors join with law students to advise Holborn residents on their legal problems. There's charity work too—the firm gives free employment and property law advice to North London's Open Door charity, which gives counselling and psychotherapy to young people.

GETTING HIRED

Modestly immodest

It is a top priority of Travers to bring on board "quality" candidates who can easily slip into the firm's environment of assured, "commercial, down-to-earth and easy to get on with" lawyers. This translates into "type[s] who have strong but not over the top personalities" with "understated confidence." Part of this stems simply from preference, but it is also due to the fact that being a smaller firm, "it's important [a solicitor's] temperament and character fits the firm" in addition to the expected "Oxbridge/red brick unis and 2:1 degrees." None of this means that Travers wants a humourless group of drones; those hiring crave people who are "extremely conscientious but good fun" with a strong work ethic. "People who take their work and clients' needs, but not themselves, seriously is the classic phrase," we're told. The hiring could be less stressful, but seems to fare far better than most. According to an insider, graduate recruits have "to submit a CV and cover letter", a departure that is "always more attractive than application forms." Once a prospective Travers lawyer has been vetted, two interviews will determine his or her fate, with the first "an assessment of personality" and the second a tag-team situation with a partner duo. It can be fairly tough, says a lawyer who lived to tell about it: "They asked me strange questions, challenging my responses in an effort (it seemed) to get a 'rise' out of me to see how I would react. I left the interview feeling that the partners were having a joke at my expense to some degree. I later found out they were very impressed with my responses and wanted to hire me." Phew, what a relief.

OUR SURVEY SAYS

Perfect harmony

According to its solicitors, "very harmonious" Travers Smith is a hotbed of legal brilliance, mutual respect and affability. A "conservative, friendly, open, understated" culture, Travers is filled with "hardworking, professional people ... for whom work is not the be all and end all." Though "at the senior levels it is almost entirely male, white and public school educated", the firm remains steadfastly flat, with "good mixing of all staff" at formal firm activities or "impromptu drinks" at locals like the Bishop's Finger. But Travers lawyers are the first to say that despite the social, collegiate atmosphere, there is "no pressure/need for it to become the focus of one's social life." Still, it is a benefit when one is the new kid on the block, a second-year recounts: "I was not left to fend for myself at lunchtimes when I first joined." Even better, with "few major egos" at Travers "colleagues feel fully able to bounce ideas off of others, and equally to help when approached." "Mostly very like-minded people who you feel glad to work with," raves a third-year. "They are a decent bunch," concludes a younger (though wary) attorney: "Most of them are loved up with each other, which is a little weird."

Great expectations

It's easier to keep spirits up not only when people are genuinely nice, but also when billing targets are nonexistent and partners are supportive of lawyers having a life. "Firm is realistic about work expectations—it is up to you to get done what needs to be done," a contact tells us. "We are not expected to stay late for the sake of it but if there is work to be done, then the (obvious?!) expectation is that you get it done in time!" It's such a simple philosophy that it makes rival firms appear rather ridiculous by comparison. This doesn't mean it's always easy working at Travers; however, it does mean appreciation of time spent at the office instead of at home. "You have to work hard of course, but there is an understanding when you have worked an exceptionally tough patch that it's good to have a lighter week or two," offers a member of the tax group. Overall, things work pretty well at the firm: "With no billing targets, the firm has a unique culture of work, and information sharing and the support within and between departments is very good."

In good company

Good will at the firm is further generated as partners turn the archetypal open-door policy on its head by working in the trenches alongside their minions. "Partners share rooms with both assistants and trainees and as a result they are very approachable," shares a solicitor. "Everyone is on first-name terms and some partners develop genuine close friendships with assistants", comments another. There have been incidents of partners "treating assistants shabbily", but even in those cases it's "a million miles away from some of the shocking treatment previously witnessed at [my] former firm", a contact tells us. One person does accuse partners of behaviour that "depends on whether they think you make the grade", overall the "fairly young (in attitude if not in age) partners" are respectful, helpful and accessible.

The learning curve

Such an arrangement is also ideal for informal training and mentoring, helping solicitors "learn more effectively 'on the job.'" Though it "is somewhat dependent on the partner you sit with/work with most", most of the time office sharing is conducive to the exchange of information: "Ideas are swapped and problems discussed." Says a fan of the firm's informality and learn-as-you-go culture: "Informal training is the key feature of Travers Smith for an assistant solicitor ... Supervision is therefore constant but not invasive or unnecessarily formal. More important, there is opportunity to learn through seeing and hearing, as well as to learn through doing."

Though it "takes a back seat to the more informal experience and training", there is also "extensive and good" formal training. "We have regular seminars given by both internal and external speakers on a range of subjects", describes a source. "The firm also has a good know-how database and three corporate PSLs who are able to help with fee-earner queries or, at least, point you in the right direction." Training groups are small and more intimate—"usually 10 to 15 assistants attend"—and the training itself "is based heavily on cross- and inter-departmental meetings." Still, "the emphasis is on learning at the coalface under close supervision by partners and more senior solicitors," comments a lawyer. Those who feel that the Magic Circle has it over Travers in the training, think again; the latter's programme is thought of as "more relevant and practical than Magic Circle training schemes." And anyway, ponders a solicitor, it's not worth much in the long run: "Magic Circle firms invest more money, have external education providers and probably spoon feed more. They also treat most trainees as slave labour. I'd rather train at Travers."

The bonus question

Lack of regular bonuses irks a number of Travers solicitors, as does the rule that participation in the pension scheme begins at the four-year mark. "The lack of any formal bonus scheme for assistants is frustrating given the number of hours worked and the variance between departments," an annoyed (and overworked?) lawyer complains. Most of his compeers, however, are content as things are: "If the firm has been exceptionally successful, it has paid one off bonuses across the firm, as it did in the summer of 2005." Base "salary is slightly below Magic Circle rates, but when you consider the atmosphere in the office and the more friendly environment, it's worth taking the drop in salary," we hear. One ambitious lawyer tell us, "Salary isn't really the point for me at this stage of my career-the prospect of partnership is." And anyway, pipes up another, "if we were paid anymore I would fear having to work harder."

Nice guys don't have to finish last

Travers folks concede they have little to moan about. There may be "smaller deals than at Slaughter and May", but the superior co-workers, partners and schedules as well as the openness of the firm make it all worthwhile. "I have only been at Travers six months but have so far found it everything I'd hoped," notes an experienced lawyer. "In particular, it is now clear that they were refreshingly honest throughout the interview process and so there haven't been any unpleasant surprises." A younger lawyer is thrilled that he "received first-class training, get[s] plenty of exposure to good quality work (working closely with a partner) and work[s] in a supportive and friendly environment." And with "good work and people [who] really pull together when times are busy", "no one ever feels out of their depth or unsupported", making it "one of the nicest places to be a corporate lawyer in the City." Discloses an enthusiastic lawyer with two years PQE: "I would not wish to work at any other city law firm."

Trowers & Hamlins

Sceptre Court
40 Tower Hill
London EC3N 4DX
Phone: +44 (0)20 7423 8000
www.trowers.com

OTHER LOCATIONS
Abu Dhabi
Bahrain
Cairo
Dubai
Exeter
Manchester
Oman

MAJOR DEPARTMENTS & PRACTICES
Corporate
Dispute Resolution
Employment
Private Client
Projects & Construction
Property

THE STATS
No. of lawyers: 240
No. of lawyers in London: 163
No. of offices: 8
Recruitment intake: 16-18 (2005)
Trainees retained: 10 of 13 (2005)
Senior partner: Jonathan Adlington

BASE SALARY
Newly Qualified: £43,000
Vacation scheme: £225/week

GRADUATE RECRUITMENT AND TRAINING MANAGER
Matt Bryan
Graduate Recruitment Officer
Phone: +44 (0)20 7423 8312

THE BUZZ
WHAT EMPLOYEES AT OTHER FIRMS ARE SAYING

- "Good local practices in Middle East"
- "Quiet"

THE SCOOP

Trowers & Hamlins can trace its history back nearly 230 years to 1777, when the practice was first established in London. It's been through various incarnations since then, but has gradually grown to become an integrated practice since a merger in 1987 of two equally-sized firms, the Trowers and the Hamlins.

Middle East pre-eminence

Ask the average City lawyer, and they will know Trowers as the firm with the phenomenal practice in the Middle East. The firm has expanded considerably in the last 30 years, first into Manchester in 1973, then to Oman in 1980, Exeter in 1984, Dubai in 1991, Abu Dhabi in 1993, Bahrain in 1998 and Cairo in 1999.

Today, many of the bigger law firms are rushing to open Dubai offices, as the wealthy individuals there, rich on oil, begin investing overseas. Trowers has long been one of the strongest firms on the ground there, and has in that sense stolen quite a march on the competition.

Prestige projects

Trowers has a projects practice internationally that is something to behold, and the likes of which is rarely found in a firm of this size. Recent Omani projects, for example, include prestigious instructions like advice on the Salalah Port, the Manah, Barka, Al Kamil and Salalah Independent Power Projects, the Seeb and Salalah Airport privatisations, and advice to the private sector on the development of the banking and commercial legal statutes.

In Cairo, the newest office, the firm has an alliance with the 100 per cent-owned subsidiary, headed by dual British and Egyptian national Sara Hinton. The firm gives Egyptian law advice through Nour Law Office, which is a local partnership run by Mohamed Nour—something again that is rarely on offer at your average City-based international firm.

And in 2005, in Saudi Arabia, Trowers signed an alliance with the Law Office of Hassan Mahassni, a firm that had previously had a 16-year relationship with New York's White & Case.

Taking AIM in the UK

But to suggest that Trowers & Hamlins is nothing but its Middle East practice would be unfair. Though the London practice is all-too-often overlooked by competitors, it does some good mid-market deals, and has made its mark on the Alternative Investment Market (AIM), London's junior stock market. The firm acted for Asia Energy on its U.S.$52 million placing of new shares on AIM at the end of 2004, having worked on the initial public offering by the company in 2004. The fundraising was undertaken by JP Morgan Cazenove —a rare example of a bulge-bracket investment bank working on AIM, and a great deal for a firm like Trowers to scoop.

In November of 2005, Trowers delivered on three AIM transactions—bringing the firm's total for the year to 14. The team worked for Coal International on its £30 million reverse takeover of King-Coal Corporation and Maple Coal Co. It advised WH Ireland as the stockbroker behind Mediterranean Oil & Gas' £33 million flotation, and worked for Advent Air, the owner of Australian airline Skywest, on its AIM listing. This is a firm with an energy, trade and international flavour that runs right through its lifeblood, and sure delivers the work to go with it. It was the first to roadshow with AIM in the Gulf, trying to attract more businesses from the region to the London stock markets.

School days

In London, the practice does not just act for inbound money, it also has a sturdy projects feel to it domestically. In the second half of 2005 the team advised transatlantic private equity firm GI Partners on the acquisition of six schools and a college for young people from The Hesley Group. It also boosted its public sector commercial team with the hire of a partner from Nabarro Nathanson, Alan Cook, who is a specialist in compulsory purchase orders.

Trowers can attract the lateral hires when it needs them. The arrival in 2005 of Nigel Truscott, the former head of arbitration in Dubai with Denton Wilde Sapte, was a case in point, showing that the firm competes with the very best in the region for talent, if not for headlines.

On the projects and development side, the firm recently won a place on the panel of the London Development Agency, the body that will oversee the capital's Olympic regeneration work, and also regularly advises house builder The Berkeley Group on construction issues.

Community service

Like so many firms of its size in the City, Trowers is committed to its local community. Based near the Tower of London, the firm's location almost physically straddles the haves and the have-nots, nestled as it is between the City and the deprived East End. The firm encourages all its lawyers, including partners, to get involved in both legal and non-legal community projects, including working with St Paul's Primary School in Whitechapel, where lawyers have helped pupils with their reading on a weekly basis since 2000.

The firm is also central to a project called East Potential, an organisation linked to the East Thames Housing Association, which provides accommodation in halls of residence-style property, together with training and education, for young people aged between 16 and 25. The firm offers 10 to 12 work placements to the young Londoners in two tranches each year, giving them a chance at both fee-earning and support department work.

Finally, the firm recently won the Young Solicitors Pro Bono Award for its involvement in Toynbee Hall, a charity set up in the East End to help combat poverty. Every week, a number of solicitors and trainees help out in the evenings giving free legal advice to those in need.

In many ways, Trowers & Hamlins is a dichotomy: the practice of advising housing associations in Exeter would seem the polar opposite of advising on oil pipelines in the Middle East. In fact, the common thread is development in public projects, through offices located where they can be most accessible to the client.

Watson, Farley & Williams LLP

15 Appold Street
London EC2A 2HB
Phone: +44 (0)20 7814 8000
www.wfw.com

OTHER LOCATIONS

Bangkok
Hamburg
New York
Paris
Piraeus
Rome
Singapore

MAJOR DEPARTMENTS & PRACTICES

Competition & EU
Corporate
Employment & Immigration
Finance
Intellectual Property
Litigation
Real Estate
Taxation

THE STATS

No. of lawyers: 200+
No. of lawyers in London: 120+
No. of offices: 8
Recruitment intake: 12 (2006)
Trainees retained: 80% (2005)
Chairman: Frank Dunne
Managing partner: Michael Greville

BASE SALARY

Trainee: £28,500
Newly Qualified: £50,000

GRADUATE RECRUITMENT AND TRAINING MANAGER

Danielle Black
Graduate Recruitment Officer
Phone: +44 (0)20 7814 8000
Fax: +44 (0)20 7814 8141
E-mail: graduates@wfw.com

THE BUZZ
WHAT EMPLOYEES AT OTHER FIRMS ARE SAYING

- "Good in asset finance"
- "Doesn't know what it wants to be"

THE SCOOP

Watson Farley & Williams was only founded in the City in 1982, and is thus one of the comparatively new kids on the block of the London legal scene. It made quite an impact when it first got going, and in a little over two decades has expanded to more than 120 lawyers and offices in New York, Paris, Rome, Piraeus, Hamburg, Singapore and Bangkok.

So special

The firm is a specialist, with a real niche in asset finance, transport and commodities trading. Its clarity of vision has appeared to wobble a bit in the last few years, with a whole raft of unsuccessful merger talks that seemed to throw the future wide open. After trying to do a deal with American firms Squire Sanders & Dempsey and Hunton & Williams, and then with U.K. rival Simmons & Simmons, the firm went back to the drawing board and decided that actually it could do perfectly well on its own. Now it's getting to work doing just that.

There have been departures during this period of navel-gazing, with both the Paris office and the New York practice being plundered by aggressive rivals for partners. Both have been rebuilt and are now, according to the firm, back to full strength. Thus 2005 saw Watson Farley record good growth in both profits and revenue, both increasing by close to 10 per cent, keeping the firm in the top echelons of the U.K. marketplace. At one point Watson Farley was amongst the most profitable law firms in London. It isn't now, but despite its relatively low profile, it still boasts a fantastic practice in its chosen markets, and is one of those niche firms that larger rivals look down on with a large dose of envy.

Shipping out

Though known as a leading shipping firm, there is a lot more to Watson Farley than meets the eye. Major clients include Citibank, The Royal Bank of Scotland, the Government of India and Talisma Malaysia, and the workload has expanded significantly beyond the traditional domain of transport and trade finance. The year 2006 kicked off with the hire of a private equity partner in Paris, Bertrand Dumon, from the French practice of LeBoeuf Lamb Greene & MacRae. He will be the fifth partner in that office, and a welcome addition to the expanding corporate capability.

The French expansion followed significant growth in Hamburg at the end of 2005, when Watson Farley took over Wegener Bechtel Schmidt, a corporate and tax firm that added four partners to the firm's operation in the city, taking it to six partners in all. All of which marked a major fillip to the firm's corporate business, which has been growing well of late. The practice had a record year for work on the Alternative Investment Market, London's junior stock exchange, in 2005, when it worked on 20 transactions, particularly in the mining, minerals and energy sector. Highlights included work for Elixir Petroleum, the Australian resource company with assets in the North Sea, which was admitted to AIM and raised £6.5 million in May 2005.

International boutique

Deals like that play to Watson Farley's strengths—it is at its heart an international law firm with the size and atmosphere of a City boutique. The work is just about as global as it comes, though: one big deal last year was advising Africa Export-Import Bank and Ericsson as lenders to Vmobile Nigeria, in the largest ever financing of a mobile phone project in Nigeria. A consortium of 16 leading Nigerian financial institutions, and six other lenders, provided some $1 billion for the project.

In Singapore, the firm advised a group of ship operators and offshore oil and gas operators on a restructuring and establishment of the Approved International Shipping Enterprise in Singapore, a scheme which allows them to take advantage of the increased profile and activity of the industry in Asia.

Finally, one of the instructions of the year was work for Shanghai LNG (liquefied natural gas) Company. Watson Farley was asked to act on the Shanghai LNG import terminal and sub-sea trunkline project. The win followed the firm's instruction to work for Guangdong Dapeng LNG, which is China's first LNG import terminal, and shows the practice increasingly making a name for itself in the sector.

Small is beautiful

Though it may not be large or high profile, and lacks the resources of so many of its rivals, Watson Farley is able to boast a great culture, and a genuine expertise in its chosen areas. What's more, the partners are hungry to grow the firm, and there is none of the complacency on show at larger practices. In 2005, Watson Farley's Paris office won an award at Les Trophées du Droit in the category of public law, for the impressive development of its team in the year. Furthermore, the firm has a fantastic reputation as a nice place to work, regularly topping tables in surveys of assistants.

Watson Farley offers six four-month training seats, instead of the usual four six-month stints, which means by the time a young trainee is done, she'll have a good overview of the firm, and a relationship with a whole bunch of individuals. The firm has a great reputation as a friendly place with a good atmosphere, and as a niche practice with a clear vision, it's a pretty solid bet. While the finance practice is 40 per cent of the firm's turnover, corporate and litigation are both neck and neck at about 20 per cent each, giving it a nice even spread. And with almost 30 per cent of fees coming from outside London, this is not a firm that's so enormous that even the partners don't know where they have offices.

Weil, Gotshal & Manges LLP

One South Place
London EC2M 2WG
Phone: +44 (0)20 7903 1000
www.weil.com

OTHER LOCATIONS

Austin • Boston • Brussels • Budapest • Dallas • Frankfurt • Houston • Miami • Munich • New York • Paris • Prague • Providence • Shanghai • Silicon Valley • Singapore • Warsaw • Washington, DC • Wilmington

MAJOR DEPARTMENTS & PRACTICES

Antitrust/Competition
Banking & Acquisition Finance
Business Finance & Restructuring
Capital Markets
Corporate/Commercial
Global Dispute Resolution
IP/IT
Litigation/Regulatory
Mergers & Acquisitions
Pensions
Private Equity
Real Estate/Environmental
Securitisation/CDOs
Tax

THE BUZZ
WHAT EMPLOYEES AT OTHER FIRMS ARE SAYING

- "Excellent"
- "Nasty"

THE STATS

No. of lawyers: 1,130
No. of lawyers in London: 116
No. of offices: 20
Trainees retained: 9 out of 12
Chairman: Stephen J. Dannhauser
Managing partner (London): Michael Francies

PLUSES

- "Encouraging environment"
- "High prestige and good work"

MINUSES

- "Hours"
- "Not enough support at junior level"

NOTABLE PERKS

- In-house Starbucks
- M&S store downstairs
- Gym membership
- Homemade chocolate chip cookies and sausage rolls

BASE SALARY

Trainee: £35,000
Newly Qualified: £75,000

GRADUATE RECRUITMENT AND TRAINING MANAGER

Jillian Singh
Graduate Recruitment Manager
Phone: +44 (0)20 7903 1074
Fax: +44 (0)20 7903 0990
E-mail: graduate.recruitment@weil.com

THE SCOOP

Compared with many of its compatriots staking out turf in old Blighty, and certainly with the U.K. firms it hopes to overtake, Weil, Gotshal & Manges is but a mere sprog in City terms. The firm has endured some rocky patches since the London office was set up in 1996, but it now appears to be on a more even keel, allowing it to flaunt its considerable strengths in corporate and restructuring work. In early 2006, the firm launched a stunning assault on the U.K. private equity market with the trophy hire of Lovells partner Marco Compagnoni.

From rocky start to private equity triumphs

Established in New York in 1931, Weil Gotshal concentrated its early expansion on the domestic front, waiting until the 1990s to venture abroad. Unusually for a novice traveller, its very first forays were in the former Eastern Bloc, followed by the opening of a Brussels outpost in 1992 and the London branch four years later. The firm had a presence in London before then, but only through the good offices of Nabarro Nathanson, its partner until Weil struck out for a solo career. Weil Gotshal invested heavily in their London venture, ploughing somewhere between £5 million and £10 million into the office and employing a growth strategy of aggressive lateral hiring of U.K.-qualified lawyers. Despite these efforts, the office experienced a rocky start and, in 2000, saw the head of the firm's London operations decamp to White & Case, bringing a slew of Weil Gotshal lawyers with him.

Along with the aforementioned Compagnoni, Weil also elected to partnership rising private equity star Jonathan Wood, who had been a senior assistant at Lovells. The two-partner haul will take Weil Gotshal's private equity capability in London to five partners. The firm's push to widen its band of European private equity clients scored a boost as Weil's London arm picked up its first major instruction for Bridgepoint Capital. It is understood that a conflict at Bridgepoint-regular Travers Smith handed Weil Gotshal the deal, a $535 million (£302 million) bid for environmental consultancy Environmental Resources Management (ERM) from 3i.

Francies brings home the bacon

Corporate head Mike Francies has concentrated on the firm's niche strengths rather than broadening its scope and this turned out to be a wise move. Francies has presided over an impressive turnaround, and even the number-crunchers in New York must be pleased with London's growth. U.K. turnover rose 4 per cent in the 2004-2005 year, to £52 million, or about 10.5 per cent of Weil Gotshal's total turnover worldwide, although profits per London equity partner lag behind PEP on a global basis. Still, management rewarded the office's efforts by boosting associate pay in July 2005, giving the young bloods some of the highest pay packets in the City; the firm maintained tradition this year by establishing £75,000 as the new benchmark for newly qualified attorneys at U.S. firms. New York has even conceded that devolving some of its power might be a good thing; to that end, Weil Gotshal is expanding its global management committee in order to give non-U.S. lawyers a greater say. (Francies has been the lone international member for some time.)

Nobody has a bad word? Nobody?

With London now going full steam ahead, the awards have come rolling in. In 2004, Weil Gotshal won the U.S. Law Firm of the Year award from *The Lawyer,* which noted: "It has truly been a triumphant 12 months for Weil Gotshal." Francies, meanwhile, copped a nice little prize of his own: Partner of the Year. "Francies has personally made Weil Gotshal's London office a recognised force in the U.K. and on the European domestic scene," said the publication, adding that, even more astonishingly, "nobody in the City has a bad word to say about the man."

Among the Weil London office's juiciest corporate deals was advising Songbird, the consortium with the £1.7 billion winning bid, on the hotly contested 2004 Canary Wharf auction. That transaction also impressed *The Lawyer* enough to shortlist the firm for its Corporate Team of the Year 2005 award; other major instructions in 2004 included advising on the £1.6 billion auction for pharmaceuticals group Warner Chilcott.

January 2005 saw the defection of corporate heavyweights James Gubbins and Paul Claydon to Morrison & Foerster. Rumour has it that Claydon and Gubbins generously postponed their departures until Weil Gotshal could complete its arduous search for a senior partner uncowed by Francies' long shadow, and in September 2004 the firm managed to lure ex-Travers Smith partner Mark Soundy to its private equity practice. His arrival no doubt spurred private equity house Apax Partners, a longtime Soundy client, to name Weil to its three-firm panel in early 2005.

Custard pie

Hopefully such deals signify that the firm has diversified beyond formerly faithful trophy client Hicks, Muse, Tate & Furst, which Weil Gotshal advised on a number of major acquisitions, including its £93 million buyout of Weetabix in 2003 and the £100 million purchase of Ambrosia by portfolio company Premier Foods that same year. When subsidiary Yell launched its IPO in 2003 and Premier followed suit in 2004, Weil was the natural choice to advise on the offers. But while Premier has stuck with the firm, tapping it for advice on its £70 million acquisition of such iconic brands as Bird's Custard and Angel Delight from Kraft Foods and its £172 million buyout of Marlow Foods (not to mention a contentious instruction on the recall of its Sudan 1-contaminated Worcester sauce), Hicks Muse has proved a trifle more flighty. With the U.S. and European arms of the private equity house splitting in January 2005, SJ Berwin has muscled in on Weil's former monopoly of the European business, nabbing away an instruction to advise the newly renamed Lion Capital on its acquisitions of posh shoe brand Jimmy Choo and noodle bar chain Wagamama.

Bankruptcy bonanza

Life is rosy in the restructuring group, if not for its insolvent clients such as Enron, Parmalat, Eurotunnel and Telewest. Bankruptcy has long filled the coffers at Weil, and the firm has recently helped pick up the pieces of the Enron debacle in both the U.S. and the U.K.; advised the administrator of Parmalat (billing a cool €200,000 to €300,000 a month for such work, according to *The Lawyer*); plucked a prime role advising Channel Tunnel operator Eurotunnel on extricating itself from its £6.4 billion pile of debt (thereby relegating Eurotunnel adviser Herbert Smith to the corporate trenches); and worked on the financial restructuring of Telewest Communications. Lest one think that life at Weil Gotshal is all corporate and bankruptcy, well, that's not far off the mark, but the firm does also boast significant practices in capital markets (clients include Barclays Capital, Bear Stearns, Deutsche Bank, Lehman Brothers International and UBS Warburg).

Manning the ManU ramparts

Weil Gotshal has imported its Yankee do-gooding intact, setting up pro bono and diversity initiatives that put its City competitors to shame. Weil doesn't just "run up the pro bono banner and then leave it to young lawyers to run down to the CAB on a wet Thursday", as London pro bono chair Michael

Jones put it in *The Lawyer*. To be sure, junior lawyers do put in time at the Citizens Advice Bureau—thereby gaining valuable experience—but senior fee-earners do their bit as well, helping Oxfam set up the Progreso chain of fair-trade coffee shops, for example, and working with disabled children's charity KIDS. Such efforts helped win the firm the title of Pro Bono Initiative of the Year at the 2005 *Legal Business* Awards. And even pro bono can provide a bit of sport, as when two football-mad partners gave free legal advice to a shareholders' group that sought unsuccessfully to keep Manchester United FC out of the clutches of Malcolm Glazer. Weil Gotshal is also involved with Diversity Works and is trying to boost its ranks of female and ethnic minority partners via a substantial diversity mentoring and training program in the London office.

GETTING HIRED

Ever more stringent

Weil Gotshal's London office hires about 10 trainees per year. The firm's solicitors seem to think that the hiring standards at this growing, international firm have become much more stringent in recent years. "It is increasingly difficult to be recruited here", reports a senior banking solicitor from Weil Gotshal's London office. "I don't think that I would get an interview!" Although London's 130 attorneys make it the firm's second-largest branch (after New York), the office's trainees frequently work on cross-border matters, often requiring travel to the firm's overseas locales.

OUR SURVEY SAYS

Highly satisfactory socially

Solicitors at Weil Gotshal report that they enjoy their jobs. As one senior solicitor reports, "The quality of the work and clients is top-notch." One of the most significant reasons for solicitors' happiness is the firm's easy-going culture. A senior corporate solicitor calls Weil Gotshal "fairly supportive and professional with high standards, but reasonably informal." He adds that although the firm is "becoming more demanding of associates", the solicitors are still "quite sociable with each other." A senior banking solicitor adds, "There is a good social scene at the firm and lawyers regularly socialize together." And a midlevel litigation solicitor characterizes Weil Gotshal as a firm where "people know one another and are approachable at all levels."

Great partners and formal training

Two common causes for complaint, solicitor/partner relations and formal training, get high marks from Weil Gotshal insiders. Summarising the generally kind words the firm's solicitors have for their bosses, one happy senior solicitor gushes, "The partners treat me with a lot of respect and I think that the information flow is excellent." Moreover, the firm is reportedly rare among its peers in that it provides substantial and satisfactory training for its young attorneys, the firm sources report. The firm's training programme is described as not only "comprehensive", according a banking solicitor, but also "taken quite seriously." Or as a colleague puts it, "The commitment to training is very strong."

Though informal training could improve

Somewhat incongruously, while Weil Gotshal gets high scores for its partners and formal training efforts, the firm gets low marks for its informal training. "Some partners take a greater interest than others", reports a senior corporate solicitor (although he adds that "mentoring is encouraged"). On the other hand, as a senior banking solicitor adds, "There is a very good mentoring programme which works well and training on an informal basis is also very good."

Compensation rocks, and so do the offices

Insiders have literally no complaints, it seems, regarding Weil Gotshal's compensation scheme. "I think that we are paid extremely well", reports one senior solicitor, "although the gap between us and the Magic Circle has gotten smaller."

Weil Gotshal's London solicitors are particularly effusive about their office space. One corporate attorney says that the London office features "very nice, open, bright offices", which are "fitted out to a high standard." A junior banking lawyer enthuses about the firm's "nice coffee shop." Her peers point out a number of other Weil Gotshal pluses: The firm encourages pro bono work and provides "trainee secondments abroad."

The hours, however ...

Big firms always have big hours and, this firm's solicitors report, Weil Gotshal is no exception. The firm, however, is fairly sympathetic regarding flex-time scheduling, solicitors say. "The firm seems supportive of part-time workers, although there is a need to be flexible and, realistically, available at all times," reports one midlevel attorney. "This is taken advantage of with some more than others. Some full-timers are more understanding than others." But on the whole, Weil Gotshal insiders appear willing to trade the demanding hours for the firm's "prestige" and the "quality of work."

White & Case LLP

5 Old Broad Street
London EC2N 1DW
Phone: +44 (0)20 7532 1000
www.whitecase.com

OTHER LOCATIONS

Almaty • Ankara • Bangkok • Beijing • Berlin • Bratislava • Brussels • Budapest • Dresden • Düsseldorf • Frankfurt • Hamburg • Helsinki • Ho Chi Minh City • Istanbul • Johannesburg • Los Angeles • Mexico City • Mexico City (Monterrey) • Miami • Milan • Moscow • Mumbai • Munich • New York • Palo Alto • Paris • Prague • Riyadh • São Paulo • Shanghai • Singapore • Stockholm • Tokyo • Warsaw • Washington, DC

MAJOR DEPARTMENTS & PRACTICES

Banking & Structured Finance • Capital Markets • Construction & Engineering • Corporate (incl. M&A and Private Equity) • Dispute Resolution (incl. Litigation, Arbitration & Mediation) • Employment • Energy, Infrastructure, Project & Asset Finance • IP • PPP/PFI • Real Estate • Telecommunications

THE STATS

No. of lawyers: 2,000
No. of lawyers in London: 278
No. of offices: 37
No of trainees: 51 (2006)
Trainees retained: 93% (Annualised average to date)
Managing Partner: Duane D. Wall
Senior partner (London): Peter Finlay

THE BUZZ
WHAT EMPLOYEES AT OTHER FIRMS ARE SAYING

- "Pukka US firm"
- "Overworked associates"

PLUSES
- Quality work and social atmosphere
- International travel opportunities

MINUSES
- Lack of partner support
- Complaints about bonus structure

NOTABLE PERKS
- Sign-on bonus of at least £1,500
- CPE/LPC fees and maintenance grants
- Gym membership contribution
- On-site restaurant bakes own cookies

BASE SALARY
1st-year: £36,000
2nd-year: £38,000
Vacation scheme: £300/week
Newly Qualified: £63,000

GRADUATE RECRUITMENT AND TRAINING MANAGER
Emma Fernandes
Graduate Resourcing Manager
Phone: +44 (0)20 7532 1000
Fax: +44 (0)20 7532 1001
E-mail: londoninformation@whitecase.com
www.whitecase.com/trainee

THE SCOOP

No ugly American, the U.S.-based White & Case LLP has fine-tuned its practices to local sensibilities in the 25 countries into which it has forayed. That's not to say it doesn't pack an international wallop, only that its muscle is cloaked in native garb. And thanks to heavy-hitting cases and high-profile lawyers—"Philip of Arabia", anyone?—White & Case's London business is fast becoming the jewel in the firm's crown, with turnover soaring as a result of its booming business.

A friend indeed

White & Case was founded in 1901 by (surprise, surprise) White and Case. Kicking in $250 each to fund the firm's launch, J. DuPratt White (who never even attended law school—take heart, all you English, Classics and PPE students) and George B. Case leveraged their very useful friendship with J.P. Morgan & Co. financier Henry P. Davison into a legal practice with particular prowess in banking. Among other work he steered their way, Davison tapped the duo to organise Bankers Trust Company, which the firm still represents today in the form of its successor entity, Deutsche Bank.

Foreign legions

The firm had foreign leanings early on, handling the legal end of the massive purchases of war matériel that J.P. Morgan & Co. made on behalf of the British and French governments in the Great War, and it opened a Paris office as early as 1926. White & Case prides itself on having U.S.-, British- and domestically trained lawyers throughout the world who are "either native to or fully integrated in the regions where they are based."

In keeping with that ethos, White & Case jumped eagerly when the Law Society decided in 1993 to permit English and registered foreign lawyers to practice in partnership, and it was one of the first foreign firms in London to qualify under the new rules. The firm has poured money and effort into the office over the past several years, swelling its ranks in the Big Smoke by some 400 per cent in a cheeky bid to, as banking and structured finance partner Mike Goetz put it in *The American Lawyer*, "challenge the Magic Circle head on."

All shook up

Of course, no gung-ho expansion campaign can be complete without a smattering of internal turmoil, and White & Case's London office has proved no exception. The firm first revamped its London management in June 2003, establishing an executive committee to replace its executive partner. A scant 16 months later, the powers that be decided to replace the executive committee with a strategy committee and to install Neil Upton as chief operating partner, leading *The Lawyer* to comment that, compared with White & Case's London partners jockeying for power, "Blair and Brown have got nothing on these bruisers." Insiders whispered of tensions between London and New York, and in May of 2005, Upton stepped down. Since then, the firm has revamped its management structure. The firm's COO, Jim Latchford, relocated from New York to London to serve as chair of the London office's reconstituted executive committee and oversees day-to-day operations. Meanwhile, Peter Finlay was appointed to the newly-created position of "senior partner" in London and serves as the "key point of contact for relations with external parties."

Nice office (cough, cough)

In the midst of the management muddle, White & Case decided to uproot its very foundations, moving to spacious new offices in the City, right next to the Bank of England. Following endless delays—builders on the Old Broad Street site reportedly turned up artefacts dating from around A.D. 120, halting construction for a time—the October 2004 move came not a moment too soon: asbestos had been discovered in the firm's old offices the previous May.

I'd like to thank my lawyers, my trainees, my vac scheme participants ...

In the White & Case London office profit per equity partner skyrocketed 73.9 per cent in 2004, rising to £530,000 from £305,200 the year before. Turnover posted a fat increase as well, surging by 42.3 per cent, to £54.1 million. The smashing performance helped White & Case win *The Lawyer*'s 2005 U.S. Law Firm of the Year award, and Upton attributed the splendid results to the firm's heavy investment in its London operations in 2002 and 2003. The *Legal Business* 100 rankings, meanwhile, called the firm "the star of the London market," adding that "London is proving itself to be a driver for the firm to reach its ambitions."

Fat Qat

The engines driving the office's fevered profit pace, however, are White & Case's banking and project finance practices. As a matter of fact, the project finance group won its very own award—Infrastructure Team of the Year—from *The Lawyer*, which was mightily impressed by the Qatargas II deal, a £7.6 billion liquid natural gas project financing that the group put together for sponsors Qatar Petroleum and ExxonMobil. Completed in December 2004, the deal was monumental in both scope and significance; not only was it the largest energy project financing in history and the third-largest project financing ever (behind the Chunnel and a Taiwanese rail project), but it brought together the entire chain of LNG production, from extraction in Qatar to ship and rail transportation to the U.K. to construction of a re-gasification terminal. Qatargas II thus forms a key component of the U.K.'s new strategy of importing gas to offset the dwindling of its own North Sea gas reserves. What's more, the project marked the largest Islamic-law-compliant financing in Qatar, and as if that weren't enough, White & Case put the whole kit and caboodle together in a mere 20 months. Justifiably, then, did *The American Lawyer* dub team point man Philip Stopford "Philip of Arabia." Moreover, the sequel, Qatargas 3, closed in late 2005. This and a host of other deals across the world earned the firm the Global Law Firm of the Year prize at the 2005 *Project Finance International* Awards.

That's a lorra lorra ships

The banking and structured finance practice is also going at full throttle, advising on mega-deals such as the financing for the $6 billion merger of ntl and Telewest. The previous £2.45 billion refinancing of ntl and the £1.8 billion refinancing of Telewest, had helped the team garner the Banking and Finance Team of the Year 2005 award from *Legal Business*. The team chalked up another win when *Jane's Transport Finance* bestowed upon it the 2004 Shipping Finance Law Award for advising Nordea Bank Norge and Citigroup Global Markets on a $1.06 billion credit facility for the acquisition of 47 vessels—the largest ship financing transaction ever completed—raising suspicions that the real reason White & Case moved to larger quarters was because it ran out of space to stash its trophies. Meanwhile, on the structured finance side the team has been busy cementing its position as one of the leading outfits around. In 2005, the 44-strong team advised on more than 75 transactions with an aggregate value in excess of U.S. $16.5 billion.

The firm's capital markets group has been involved with debt and equity securities issues from Kazakhstan to Israel, advising such high-profile clients as Nomura International, Merrill Lynch and Deutsche Bank often on some of the most cutting-edge deals in the market. Joshua Kiernan, head of the firm's London capital markets team and its Israel practice, has also been hard at work advising Israeli flavour and fragrance company Frutarom Industries on its €30 million acquisition of International Flavors and Fragrances, Inc. and its February 2005 IPO on the Tel Aviv and London stock exchanges. Israel's venture capital scene is heating up again, and Kiernan represents a number of technology clients in the country, including Given Imaging, which came up with a wee video camera inside a capsule that can be swallowed like a pill.

Meanwhile the firm's corporate and dispute resolution practices are also setting a fierce pace. The 45-strong corporate team's revenue shot up 50 per cent in 2004 and more than 30 per cent in 2005, as it acted on some very chunky deals indeed, such as a £3.6 billion steel production deal that guaranteed 1,700 jobs at Corus and the $2.19 billion acquisition of Swiss cable company Cablecom Holding AG by global broadband communications giant Liberty Global. More recently, the firm boosted its U.K. corporate practice with the addition of M&A and corporate finance specialist (and former Ashurst partner) Philip Broke.

The dispute resolution team continues to advise on its regular swathe of multi-million pound commercial arbitrations, which by nature can't be named. However, amongst other matters that can be spoken about, the practice is currently defending Ian Norris from a precedent-setting extradition attempt by the United States Department of Justice, which has provoked uproar in the British business community, outraged by way in that the DoJ is using a new extradition treaty between the two countries that was intended to speed up the fight against terrorism. Norris, the former CEO of Morgan Crucible, is wanted in the U.S. for alleged price-fixing. It's a case that's gaining attention all across the country—watch this space.

GETTING HIRED

Writing your ticket

White & Case is growing rapidly, leading a solicitor to comment that "They are expanding so much that the quality is variable, dependent upon the department." Still, White & Case prides itself on taking some of the best, those who would rather eschew the conservatism of the Magic Circle for something—dare we say?—edgier. "Intelligent team players" are esteemed; "shrinking violets" need not apply. And the firm must do quite well matching up personalities with its own culture: it claims that since 1988, "93 per cent of all trainees have continued their career with us after qualification." Not at all a shabby figure and not at all surprising. Unlike most other firms, White & Case places its trainees in four six-month seats in different departments, with a stint in one of the following overseas other locations: Brussels, Frankfurt, Hong Kong, Johannesburg, Moscow, Paris, Prague, Singapore, Stockholm, Tokyo or Warsaw.

For those looking to lateral in as an associate, writing ability and technical knowledge is crucial; one such source tells us that his "First interview was a written legal test."

OUR SURVEY SAYS

We'll have the usual

It may have a roster of strong cases and offices galore, but White & Case is so very ... typical. With "in the dark" solicitors, less-than-desirable hours and prickly partners who "have absolutely no respect whatsoever for associates and behave appallingly", White & Case might seem difficult to distinguish from its peers. But as with such firms, thank goodness for the people; it's always about the people. "Friendly, approachable, [and] collegiate", they make it a "nice place to work" with a relatively "good social culture." "People tend to make an effort to attend functions", according to a source, and the occasional department-sponsored ski outing is always an option, "but generally those who go do so on the basis that it is expected, not because they want to", which certainly makes it less pleasurable. On the whole, unfortunately, there is "little socialising, [as it is] not fostered by practice group partners."

There's a reason it's called "work"

The reason for so little interaction with such wonderful people? Work. That's right, there are those pesky "high professional demands [and] client attention" and "often exceptionally busy" hours that make the whole work/life balance thing just plain "terrible." PSLs have the advantage of "set hours", but all others beware: there "can be some short notice late nights and weekends" and one is "expected to be on call 24/7 if needed." And recovering at the weekend is not always an option, as "work-related travel" often occupies that time slot. In summary, a solicitor tells us: "The work hours are intense and often unnecessary. Partners have no respect whatsoever for associates" time and often keep you "waiting" for them to look at work until very late in the evening, and often into the small hours of the morning."

Compensatory matters

"White & Case will never be a salary leader," reports a contact, "but for the most part they are happy to follow the pack." It must be noted that White & Case's NQ salary of £63,000 is actually higher than the Magic Circle and certainly competitive with the U.S. firms in London. In any event, solicitors agree that their pay "is good", though at least one reminds us that it's 'still cheap per hour!" "The bonus system", however, is "unfair", gripes a source. Alas, perhaps no one is ever truly satisfied with compensation, but for at least one White & Case lawyer, the money isn't really the issue: "Pay unarguably high but cannot compensate for lack of structure or career support."

Ill communication

Though a "good rapport" reportedly exists between solicitors and partners, good rapport does not good lawyers (or relations) make. In the opinion of one insider, "[Partners] are pleasant but lazy. Too many training sessions are cancelled and meetings go by with procrastinations and failure to deal properly with issues." Adds a colleague, "Good general information, much less good on the individual level. There are still no clear directions on the pre-partner path even at the five-year level despite the direct question having been asked via an executive (partner) committee." Even more annoying for White & Case lawyers is the propensity of partners to share "little to no information." "We only learn of things in *Legal Week* like everyone else," grouses an attorney. "If we ask to be involved in anything we are given more work to do." Only one solicitor attempted to be diplomatic, with mixed results: "Varies partner to partner. Can be both fine and occasionally horrific."

Supervise me

Though "most training is 'on the job,'" according to a source, there is actually "very little input or exposure" at the firm to make it so. "Most associates are left to do tasks on large deals and are not told anything of the big picture," reports a solicitor. "This makes development very difficult ... In some departments associates are given large amounts of work and responsibility, without adequate supervision. This puts them under enormous stress."

There is no consensus regarding the firm's formal training program. While some solicitors complain that "Training for associates is pretty much nonexistent in most departments," others report the training is "getting better." In fact, according to the firm, White & Case put on more than 200 training events in its London office in 2005, in addition to a European Academy. Moreover, the firm had an off-site meeting with all London associates late in 2005 to discuss issues of the associates' choosing. Finally, the firm has an open line of communication to the top of the office with an "Ask Jim" facility on its intranet that permits anonymous questions to be asked/points to be made ("Jim" is Jim Latchford, the firm's global COO).

Wilmer Cutler Pickering Hale and Dorr LLP

Alder Castle
10 Noble Street
London EC2V 7QJ
Phone: +44 (0)20 7645 2400

4 Carlton Gardens
London SW1Y 5AA
Phone: +44 (0)20 7872 1000
www.wilmerhale.com

OTHER LOCATIONS

Boston (HQ)
Washington, DC (HQ)
Baltimore • Beijing • Berlin • Brussels • Munich • New York • Northern Virginia • Oxford • Palo Alto • Waltham

MAJOR DEPARTMENTS & PRACTICES

Antitrust and Competition
Aviation
Communications and E-commerce
Corporate
Intellectual Property
International Arbitration
International Trade, Investment and Market Access
Labour and Employment
Litigation
Securities
Tax

THE STATS

No. of lawyers: 1,082
No. of lawyers in London: 59
No. of offices: 12
Trainee intake: 2 (2005)
Co-Managing Partners: William F. Lee, William J. Perlstein

BASE SALARY

1st-year: £71,000 (2005)
2nd-year: £82,000 (2005)

GRADUATE RECRUITMENT AND TRAINING MANAGER

David Gent
UK Recruiting Partner
Phone: +44 (0)20 7645 2519

THE BUZZ
WHAT EMPLOYEES AT OTHER FIRMS ARE SAYING

- "Cutting-edge, vibrant, modern"
- "Lacking local talent"

THE SCOOP

The marriage of American firms Wilmer Cutler Pickering and Hale and Dorr was not just one of the biggest legal stories of 2004, it was also produced a mouthful of a moniker—"Wilmer Cutler Pickering Hale and Dorr LLP"—which the firm ditched when it rebranded as WilmerHale in January 2006. Whilst the combined firm continues to iron out post-merger kinks, it appears to have retained and even built on many of its strengths.

CP and QCs

Established in Washington in 1962, Wilmer Cutler Pickering was the brainchild of consummate D.C. power broker Lloyd Cutler and his chum John Pickering, an ardent defender of civil rights. In a 2003 interview for an oral history project, Cutler claimed that the firm's London office grew somewhat fortuitously out of the Penn Central railroad bankruptcy. One of the marketers of the company's commercial paper in Europe tapped Wilmer Cutler Pickering as counsel—apparently a friend of Cutler's recommended him after all the law firms with corporate and banking experience turned down the instruction because of conflicts of interest—and thus was the London branch born in 1972 "out of just this one little recommendation for one lawsuit." (Not to call the legal superstar disingenuous, mind you, but 1972 just happened to also mark Parliament's vote to join the European Common Market.) Despite such a seemingly accidental inception, the firm built up a formidable U.K. practice with particular prowess in arbitration; in fact, in 1997 arbitration partner Arthur Marriott was one of the first two solicitors ever appointed Queen's Counsel. His newfound right to wear a wig did not increase his fees, however; "I think lawyers charge enough anyway—probably too much," Marriott told *The Times*. (Speaking of disingenuous, Marriott decamped to Debevoise & Plimpton LLP four months later).

Hale storms London

While perhaps the more venerable firm, Hale and Dorr, which traced its roots back to early 20th-century Boston, waited until 1990 to set up a London beachhead. Originally established in partnership with California's Brobeck, Phleger & Harrison LLP, the London office, along with outposts in Oxford and Munich, was subsumed entirely into Hale and Dorr following Brobeck's dissolution in 2003. Hale and Dorr's London operation reflected the firm's strength in corporate, technology and intellectual property, most specifically in the areas of information technology, software and life sciences; the firm also worked with the investment banks, venture capitalists and the other moneybags that serve such companies.

Honeymoon? What honeymoon?

It's fair to wonder, then, just what the two stood to gain from joining forces. The stock line is that Wilmer needed Hale and Dorr's depth in corporate and IP work while Hale would benefit from Wilmer's securities and litigation expertise, but some have whispered that one or the other got the best of the deal, given Wilmer's bigger numbers in Europe—101 lawyers, versus Hale and Dorr's 40. Rumours of power struggles have been dismissed by the firm, which points out that, from the outset, two partners, one from each side of the merger, have served on the firm's management committee.

One might assume that the sheer expense of maintaining two London offices must be a drag on the bottom line, and in fact *The Lawyer* reported that the firm was "understood" to be looking for new office space that presumably would house its entire London staff. Quite to the contrary: since the merger, the firm refurbished its Alder Castle premises and, as of March 2006, was in the process of doing the same at Carlton Gardens, home of the firm's rapidly-expanding international arbitration group.

More than the sum of its parts

So far, however, the financial part of the merger equation seems to be panning out very nicely indeed. In its first year following the tie-up, the firm shot from 58th to 12th place in the *Am Law* 100 rankings on the back of £415 million ($750.5 million) in turnover, up 14 per cent on the previous year's combined total of £350.8 million ($659 million) for both firms—strong evidence that the merger has increased business rather than merely aggregating it. Revenue growth was even stronger in the U.K., where turnover swelled 33.3 per cent, to £20.9 million ($38 million). "The costs of merger are considerable, but I'm very pleased," Pillman told *The Lawyer* in June 2005. "We've seen a modest recovery in the corporate technology market in 2004, and our arbitration practice goes from strength to strength."

To the LCIA Born

The international arbitration practice is spearheaded by London-based superstar partner Gary Born, widely considered one of the world's top lawyers in the field (and *Chambers*, *Euromoney*, *Global Counsel* and *The*

Legal 500 can't all be wrong), with able assistance form partners Steve Finizio and Wendy Miles (both widely-recognised as leaders in international arbitration in their own right) and John Trenor, whom Wilmer relocated from its Washington office in March 2004. The team takes instructions from companies in institutional and ad hoc arbitrations as well as from states involved in international law disputes; Born represented Eritrea in an arbitration against Yemen, for example, and *The Legal 500* reports that the firm has handled disputes under the laws of a whopping 30-plus different legal systems in recent years.

High flyers

Competition partner Suyong Kim has won kudos for her expertise, with The Legal 500 recommending her as "a practitioner of exceptional calibre", and the IP group bequeathed by Hale and Dorr is unparalleled (a number of the techie lawyers work out of Oxford, the better to pounce on promising university spin-offs). Every burgeoning tech company needs a raft of eager funders, and partner Chris Grew is WCPHD's VC guru (*Business XL*, for one, named him one of the "50 People to Transform Your Business", the only lawyer cited on the list). Aviation, too, is one of the firm's strong suits; its lawyers helped found the 15-airline Star Alliance and in 2003 advised the group's members on issues related to the Iraq war. The name of the aviation game is now airport berths, and Wilmer Cutler Pickering Hale and Dorr's aviation business is soaring thanks to slot swots such as Michael Holter.

David Byrne—the former EU Commissioner for health and consumer protection, not the big-suited Talking Heads front man-joined the firm as special counsel in March 2005. He will work out of Brussels and London, advising the firm and its clients on international regulatory and enforcement issues, particularly those relating to science and technology. In a possible swipe at Little Englanders, Byrne noted in *The Lawyer* that "it's no accident I'm with a U.S. firm. They have clients that want to engage with the EU."

Withers LLP

16 Old Bailey
London EC4M 7EG
Phone: +44 (0)20 7597 6000
www.withersworldwide.com

OTHER LOCATIONS
Geneva
Greenwich
Milan
New Haven
New York

MAJOR DEPARTMENTS & PRACTICES
Agricultural property
Banking
Charities
Company & Commercial
Employment & Employee Benefits
Family
Fraud & Asset Tracing
Insolvency
International Trust Litigation
IP & IT
Private Client
Professional Negligence
Property

THE BUZZ
WHAT EMPLOYEES AT OTHER FIRMS ARE SAYING

- "Solid all rounder"
- "Mindlessly aggressive"

THE STATS
No. of lawyers: 338
No. of lawyers in London: 193
No. of offices: 6
No. of trainees: 26 (2006)
Trainees retained: 70% (2005)
Chairman: Diana Parker
Joint managing directors: Margaret Robertson, Bill Swift

PLUSES
- No face time required
- High marks for training

MINUSES
- Hierarchical
- "Old-fashioned" partnership

NOTABLE PERKS
- Subsidised café
- CPE/LPC fees and maintenance grants
- Conveyancing assistance

BASE SALARY
Trainee: £28,000
Newly-qualified: £45,000

GRADUATE RECRUITMENT AND TRAINING MANAGER
Julie Walling
Human Resources Manager
E-mail: julie.walling@withersworldwide.com
www.withersrecruitment.com

THE SCOOP

Founded in London in 1831, Withers LLP has long been the firm of choice for the filthy rich. The firm's original bread-and-butter private clients were the landed gentry, but as wealth increasingly transcends borders, Withers has become as jet-set as some of its flashier clientele.

Toffs only, please

Withers makes clear right from the start that its lawyers don't take instructions from hoi polloi. Joe Bloggses need not apply; the firm's own literature spouts on about "the globally wealthy", and Withers describes itself as "the first international law firm dedicated to the business, personal and philanthropic interests of successful people, their families and advisers." With a client roster consisting of over 15 per cent of the *Sunday Times* Rich List, 10 per cent of the 50 wealthiest European-based families with U.S. connections and a significant number of the Forbes 400 list of the richest Americans, it's not a stretch for joint managing director Bill Swift to gloat that "many of our clients have personal wealth exceeding the value of some NYSE- and LSE-listed companies." Withers derives around half its turnover from this glittery bunch and thus can't afford to be snooty about those who inherit their lucre vs. the self-made wealthy: "We protect all of them from the effects of tax, political instability, bad investment, extravagant children and divorce," states the firm. Ah, the problems of the rich …

Perhaps it's not surprising, then, that a firm that counts the Duke of Marlborough, Madonna and the family of Sheikh Fahad Al-Sabah among its clients has engineered some interesting juxtapositions itself in recent years. In 1999, for instance, Diana Parker became senior partner of the venerable Withers, the first woman to hold such a position at a top City law firm, and in 2001 the firm moved to swanky new digs just opposite the Old Bailey. (Appropriately enough for Withers' somewhat schizophrenic, Wellies-meets-new-money image, the office's traditional, listed façade masks a sleek, state-of-the-art glass structure within.)

If this is Tuesday, it must be Gstaad

Then in January 2002 the firm pulled a real shocker: a merger with U.S. private client firm Bergman, Horowitz & Reynolds. As transatlantic unions go, the merger has been smooth sailing for all sides, and the firm now boasts three U.S. outposts—in New York, New Haven and Greenwich, all of which practice under the Withers Bergman LLP banner. In addition to the firm's office in Milan, it opened an office in Geneva in autumn 2005. Rumour has it that an additional U.S. office on the West Coast, most likely in Los Angeles, is on the cards as well. Why Geneva? Because that's where the money is: "One-third of the world's privately owned wealth comes from or is managed in Switzerland," joint managing partner Margaret Robertson said in *Legal Week*. Withers' increasingly international flavour reflects the needs of its jet-setting clients, who think nothing of hopping from Saudi to St. Trop (yawn) and expect their law firm to keep up. Not only does Withers employ more Italian speakers than any other City firm—molto grazie!—but it also offers the largest team of specialist U.S. private client lawyers in Europe and has seconded a sizable contingent of U.K. lawyers to the States.

LL Cool P

As if a major merger weren't enough on its plate, Withers converted itself to a limited liability partnership shortly thereafter, once again breaking ground by becoming the first sizable U.K. law firm to do so under the Limited Liability Partnerships Act 2000. The firm's status as a pioneer has meant having to sort out numerous kinks in the process, but at least Withers' corporate group can now wield its expertise in putting together LLPs as a unique selling point. Moreover, Diana Parker, who became the firm's chairman upon the merger, mentioned in an interview with *The Lawyer* that she had "always thought that LLP status would benefit not only partners in the firm, but also clients, because one is not so reluctant to take on risk."

Not withering, but steadily ripening

As you might expect, the financial road wasn't entirely paved with gold following the merger but since then, Withers has generated strong growth in global revenue. While Withers' heavy dependence on fat-cat private clients cushioned the firm nicely during the recent economic slump (Robertson told *The Lawyer* that such business tends to be countercyclical, explaining that "in times of economic and political instability, people think more about getting their assets in order"), its profits in the 2001-2002 year were flat due to legal costs associated with the merger. Turnover the following year swelled 20 per cent, sending profits up 17 per cent, but in the year ended June 2004, Withers booked a one-time cost related to an "onerous" property lease, reducing its profit margin by around 2.5 per cent and holding profit growth to a negligible .7 per cent. Since then global turnover has been steadily on the increase rising by 6 per cent in the 2003-2004 year, to £52.4 million and to £60.3 million in the 2004-2005 year.

Messy divorces and mad hatters

Withers is now widely considered to have the world's largest private-client practice, but that's not to say it has neglected other areas in favour of *Hello!*-worthy cases such as helping Madonna and Guy Ritchie keep ramblers off their estate or persuading Baroness Thyssen-Bornemisza to pay the legal bill she racked up with her high-powered silk. Headline clients also mean headline relationship cock-ups, and Chambers has ranked the firm's family practice as No. 1 in London, with particular expertise in cohabitation, prenups, divorce and issues involving children. In May 2006 the firm won a landmark ruling when the House of Lords upheld a £5 million divorce settlement in favour of Withers' client Melissa Miller against her ex-husband Alan. The key factor was apparently not the length of the marriage—the Millers had been married less than three years—but Mrs Miller's "reasonable expectation" of maintaining the couple's high standard of living.

The firm's corporate clients, meanwhile, range from Barclays Private Bank, Benetton, Renault Formula 1 and Henkel, which it advised on its purchase of the Sellotape business from Verdoso Holdings, to luxury fashion brands Lulu Guinness, Stella McCartney, Moschino and milliner Philip Treacy (in a glorious stroke of synergy, Ascot Racecourse is also a client). In addition, Withers has litigated on behalf of the Elite Model Group in defamation proceedings against the BBC; the firm also offers specialist litigation expertise in trusts and probate as well as fraud, employment, insolvency, professional negligence and art.

Arty-farty

The firm's art and cultural assets group received a major boost from the 2003 hire of Pierre Valentin from his previous post as legal counsel for Sotheby's Europe, and Withers now offers artists, dealers, collectors, museums and other arts organisations advice on everything from droit de suite to Holocaust claims to authenticity and tax issues. In one recent World War II-era case, Withers acted for the Cathedral of Benevento, located in southern Italy, in bringing a claim against the British Library, which in 1947 had acquired a 12th-century missal written in the rare Beneventan script from a British army captain. Whilst the good soldier had apparently purchased the book in good faith during his tour of duty in Italy, in March 2005 the panel deemed that the missal had previously been looted and that the Cathedral retained a moral claim to the work.

Codicil Rock

In keeping with its stated aim of servicing the philanthropic interests of its clients, Withers also has a respected legal team dealing with charities and not-for-profits. In fact, it ranks No. 2 in among U.K. law firms in terms of its number of charity clients, counting 153 do-gooding organisations as of 2005. Clients in the sector include Cancer Research UK, the RSPCA, the Salvation Army and the UK Film Council. And—*Hello!* again—Withers lawyers acted for nine of the 11 charitable residuary beneficiaries of the estate of a record producer responsible for most of Elton John's early works.

GETTING HIRED

In the round

Though Withers finds a number of universities appealing (Oxford, Cambridge, Durham, Bristol) and a certain level of academic achievement attractive (2:1), it does not treat these preferences as carved in stone. In fact, it appears that the paramount requirement at Withers is being a "well-rounded individual" who has skills the firm can use. No doubt the firm is "competitive," one solicitor informs us, "[but] I would say no particular class/category/school/background you have to comply with ... [you] just have to be very able." It also helps to have more dimension than a pub placard, as the firm "tends to recruit interesting individuals" who have "a genuine interest in the type of work." That said, the latter contact adds "that the HR department do genuinely try to ensure the best selection is made for both the candidate and the firm." That's where the interviews come in: be prepared for two of them, plus a series of written exercises and a presentation.

OUR SURVEY SAYS

The joy of work

Perhaps we're jaded, but Withers attorneys are so happy and pleased that it strikes Vault as suspicious. "I love my job", enthuses an super chipper third-year. "The work is challenging, exciting and fast-paced. Yes—it can be stressful, but the pressure adds to the enjoyment." If that were the sole confession of legal career satisfaction—no, delight—we'd, quite frankly, write it off; but lawyer after Withers lawyer expresses such fulfilment. A second-year explains, "We do interesting work for interesting clients who have diverse needs, this means that there is never a dull moment and gives good job satisfaction." Others report a "great diversity of work, good colleagues and a life outside of work", with "recognition ... often given for" a job well done. Plenty of responsibility, even for less seasoned solicitors, is also a contributing factor, along with the overall level headedness of those who call Withers their home away from home. Shares a first-year, "very happy with my job, more money would be nice but no complaints, good firm, nice people, much better than my previous firm."

(Big) Brotherly

Culturally Withers—described as "dynamic and expanding, but still small enough for everyone to know each other—in recent years, shed its 'stuffy' image" as a bastion of "the great British Reserve" becoming "by City standards ... a fairly relaxed and friendly firm." The "inclusive, enterprising, liberal and driven" firm is also benignly social, with individual departments tending to break off into their own activities, "but there are a number of department and firm-wide socials events during the year," a third-year shares excitedly. "We have a pub quiz tonight with fish and chips wrapped in paper served mid-way through the quiz!" Despite the fact that "at times [Withers] can be quite competitive", solicitors are known to build friendships outside of work. Some, however, feel that the growing firm, while not as political as some, "has slightly lost [its] sense of camaraderie. Though the smaller teams are friendly, the firm sometimes suffers from its increasing size and an increasing corporate feel. There is a faint hint of 'big brother' about the place," observes a first-year.

Just managing

Withers partners also manage to maintain cordial ties with their underlings, and the two groups "act well as a team." "Partners have good relationships with solicitors and are willing to work alongside them, and provide guidance and support when needed." details an attorney. "Partners are often willing to show a human face, and appreciate good work." "Younger partners in particular' are "approachable and "highly value the help of assistants", and at large partners "treat assistants as equals and respect their opinions." But like any other firm there are always a few at the top who "get stressed," as a solicitor generously phrases it. Lawyers do complain that, with the exception of those who head the litigation group, "there is still a cloak of secrecy regarding partnership decisions." "Very good relationships, but not always the best communication of decisions/management," summarises a source. "Administratively the firm could be run better as the partners are good lawyers not necessarily good managers!" declares a first-year.

Not-so-basic training

Partners extend their approachability and overall niceness to informal training, providing "plenty of support-especially for trainees." They offer "feedback and useful advice" and "are always willing to listen and coach." The "excellent knowledge sharing" is also available among senior assistants. "There are obviously partners in the department who are more approachable than others," concedes a Withers contact, "but there is definitely a 'door leaning' culture, and assistants are encouraged to ask questions and discuss cases." Thankfully, that does not mean that formal training is given the heave-ho. It is 'brilliant and extensive" and "superb ... both internally and externally." Partners "encourage" solicitors to take part in all of the firmwide offerings as well as those within departments. (Corporate in particular is "very good.") "Training is frequent and whilst up-to-date does not neglect the basics," comments an approving solicitor.

Having a life and loving it

Perhaps the key to Withers solicitors' eerie contentment is their schedule. The firm's hours are "generally very reasonable ... and flexible" and have only got "better as more fee earners were taken on", with part-time opportunities for men and women alike and a "good attitude to working mothers." The family and real estate practices go through periods of difficult hours, but, says one family lawyer, "We are encouraged to leave on time ... when it is quieter-there is no culture of staying until late to 'save face'." "The firm encourages a work/life balance," confirms a peer, "and this is achievable."

Bonus woes

There is a "great balance between what we are paid and the hours we have to do," a pleased attorney tells us. The compensation at Withers is "excellent" and "healthy", though bonuses—"awarded to solicitors billing 1,400 chargeable hours with a realisation ratio of 80 per cent"—are one bone of contention among solicitors, with some calling the system "very generous" and others saying it "could be better." Substantiates a source, "The bonus scheme is much criticised and very hard to achieve with the effort involved not matching the reward at the end."

Wragge & Co LLP

3 Waterhouse Square
142 Holborn
London EC1N 2SW
Phone: +44 (0)87 0903 1000
www.wragge.com

OTHER LOCATIONS
Birmingham (HQ)
Brussels

MAJOR DEPARTMENTS & PRACTICES
Corporate
Dispute Resolution & Litigation
Finance
Human Resources
Real Estate
Tax
Technology & Commerce

THE STATS
No. of lawyers: 457
No. of lawyers in London: 70+
No. of offices: 3
Trainees retained: 100% (2004)
Managing partner: Richard Haywood
Senior partner: Quentin Poole

NOTABLE PERKS
- Christmas gift
- LPC/GDL fees and maintenance grant
- Child care vouchers

BASE SALARY
London
1st-year Trainee: £28,000
2nd-year Trainee: £31,000

GRADUATE RECRUITMENT AND TRAINING MANAGER
Julie Caudle
Phone: +44 (0)80 0096 9610
Fax: +44 (0)87 0904 1099
E-mail: gradmail@wragge.com

THE BUZZ
WHAT EMPLOYEES AT OTHER FIRMS ARE SAYING

- "Good reputation across the board"
- "Too big in one region"

THE SCOOP

Perhaps they're simply a modest bunch, or maybe it's just sheer Brummyness, but the lawyers at Wragge & Co LLP seem remarkably down-to-earth for a firm that has transcended its regional roots to carve out a competitive niche for itself in London and abroad. Indeed, the firm boasts a 100 per cent trainee retention rate and has been ranked among the best companies to work for in the U.K. (24th on the *Sunday Times*' list and 46th in *FT*'s ranking)—evidence that its impressive profit growth has not come at the expense of its Midlands charm.

Brummy character, London cachet

Established in Birmingham in 1834, Wragge was content to stay close to home until 2000, when a merger with intellectual property firm Needham & Grant necessitated the opening of the Waterhouse Square office to provide a base for its now top-flight IP team. Although Wragge & Co is the largest U.K. firm not headquartered in London, its office there has nevertheless expanded prodigiously (the IP lawyers have since been joined by property, private equity, employment and pensions, and e-business teams). True, the economic slump of a few years back did result in the firmwide loss of about 100 staff members—through attrition, thankfully, not layoffs—but Wragge's staff roster is now 90 per cent longer than it was in 1998. London was even granted its very own managing partner, Paul Howard, in February 2004, and Senior Partner Quentin Poole has said he envisions a total headcount of 250 in the office by the end of 2008.

Wragges to riches

Profits are increasing along with the payroll. Turnover in the fiscal year ended April 2004 was flat; Poole called the results "very respectable" given the tough economic climate, but the partnership generously opted to take a hit to their own pay packets (profits per partner dropped 17 per cent) in the interest of longer-term investment in the firm's future. That strategy has evidently paid off in spades: The firm's income for the 2004-2005 year surged 11.6 per cent, to £88.5 million, and those martyr-like partners are chortling all the way to the bank thanks to a 44 per cent increase in profits per partner, which reached £300,000 for the first time ever. (In keeping with its family spirit, Wragge & Co is a proper partnership, with all 105 partners receiving an equity stake in the practice. Come to think of it, that's a sight more egalitarian than most families we know.)

Following the spectacular financial showing, Poole crowed to *The Birmingham Post* about Wragge's standing as the "Rolls-Royce of professional services", noting in particular the advantages of having offices in both Birmingham and London. "Our unique business model, delivering a full-service Birmingham office plus expert capability in London, means we can maximise our cost advantage and deliver top-quality commercial advice to all clients, irrespective of geography," he said. In other words, a posh London storefront that can pass work back to Birmingham—undercutting its City competitors by charging Birmingham prices, naturally—means lorry loads of money. Of course, the firm is no longer Blighty-bound either; Wragge has a satellite office in Brussels as well as a formal association with German firm Graf von Westphalen Bappert & Modest and a network of foreign referral partners. Some 25 per cent of Wragge's business is international in nature, and elevating its overseas profile is a firm priority.

M&S & MoD

The firm's clients range from Marks & Spencer, which Wragge's real estate team advised on its April 2005 sale of Michael House, the retail giant's former headquarters, all the way to the Ministry of Defence, which it advised on a £220 million Royal Navy housing project. The Marks & Sparks instruction was a real coup for the firm, which beat out a number of competitors bidding for the plum job. Other real estate work has included advising on the launch of the Islamic Bank of Britain, the first U.K. retail bank to comply with Islamic law, and an instruction from the Arsenal Football Club to advise on the redevelopment of its Highbury stadium. The IP team, meanwhile, has scored some choice instructions of its own, in particular advising Dyson on a landmark case in which the vacuum cleaner manufacturer invoked its design rights against a supplier of spare parts. The High Court ruled in favour of Dyson in December 2004, establishing an important precedent for manufacturers and other design-based sectors. Wragge's IP dynamos also secured a victory for Roxio, owner of the now outlawed file-sharing system Napster, in a domain-name dispute with the Treasury Solicitor's Department.

Coming up roses

Wragge wielded some flower power early on in 2005, advising private equity company 3i on its £20 million investment in Interflora, the largest florist network in the U.K. The private equity team also picked up a new American client, advising the Brian McBride family—founders of Cleveland's Yellow

Cab Company as well as the Cleveland Browns football team—on its £3.5 million investment in London black cab network Radio Taxis. And the pensions team hasn't been resting on its laurels, either; the group followed up its 2004 *Legal Business* award for Employment and Pensions Team of the Year by bringing on as clients the actors' union Equity as well as listed companies Inchcape, Alstom and Jacques Vert. Lawyers in the London office also acted as advisers to the Greater London Authority on its successful bid for the 2012 Olympics, and in the spiciest instruction of all, the London brands team advised HP Foods on its sponsorship deal with Channel 4's Richard & Judy show. The company's Worcestershire Sauce will now be indelibly linked with fellow saucy household staples Richard & Judy.

Princess Di(versity)

One would think Wragge might take a breather after its string of successes, but rather than flopping on the sofa and watching mindless, er, mind-expanding television all day, the firm is hard at work promoting equality and diversity both within and without its ranks. In June 2005 the Law Society and the Commission for Racial Equality named Wragge & Co Best Service Provider in recognition of its work with local communities to open up opportunities for ethnic minorities, and the following month Race for Opportunity ranked the firm as one of the U.K.'s Best Newcomers in the effort to improve racial attitudes in the business sector. Wragge was the only law firm listed, and in response to the accolade, HR Director Linda Bellis stated, "We must take every step we can to get the message out to ethnic minority communities that law is not the preserve of the white male." The firm is also active in its support of the disabled, sponsoring top-ranked U.K. women's wheelchair tennis player Kay Forshaw in her quest for gold at the 2004 Paralympic Games. Forshaw lost in the quarterfinals, but Wragge couldn't have asked for a more fitting symbol than the scrappy underdog making a go of it in the big league.

GO FOR THE GOLD!

GET VAULT GOLD MEMBERSHIP AND GET ACCESS TO ALL OF VAULT'S AWARD-WINNING LAW CAREER INFORMATION

- Access to **500+ extended insider law firm profiles**

- Access to **regional snapshots** for major non-HQ offices of major firms

- Complete access to **Vault's exclusive law firm rankings**, including quality of life rankings, and practice area rankings

- Access to **Vault's Law Salary Central**, with salary information for 100s of top firms

- Receive **Vault's Law Job Alerts** of top law jobs posted on the Vault Law Job Board

- Access to complete **Vault message board archives**

- **15% off** all Vault Guide and Vault Career Services purchases

more information go to
www.vault.co.uk/law

VAULT
> the most trusted name in career information™

About the Author

Brian Dalton is Vault's senior law editor. He holds a JD from Fordham and a BA in History from Middlebury.